T0301187

SAS
DAGGERS DRAWN

Damien Lewis

SAS

DAGGERS DRAWN

IN FOR THE KILL:
THE MAVERICKS WHO MADE THE SAS

QUERCUS

First published in Great Britain in 2024 by

QUERCUS

Quercus Editions Limited
Carmelite House
50 Victoria Embankment
London EC4Y 0DZ

An Hachette UK company

The authorized representative in the EEA is Hachette Ireland,
8 Castlecourt Centre, Dublin 15, D15 XTP3, Ireland (email: info@hbgi.ie)

A CIP catalogue record for this book is available
from the British Library

HB ISBN 978 1 52941 388 5
TPB ISBN 978 1 52941 389 2
Ebook ISBN 978 1 52941 390 8

3

Maps by Bill Donohoe
Typeset by CC Book Production
Printed and bound in Great Britain by Clays Ltd, Elcograf S.p.A.

MIX
Paper | Supporting
responsible forestry
FSC   FSC® C104740
www.fsc.org

Papers used by Quercus Editions Ltd are from well-managed forests and other responsible sources.

For:

Lieutenant Colonel R. B. Mayne, DSO & Three Bars,
Légion d'honneur, Croix de Guerre.

The Pilgrim

Picture Credits

Cut off from the land that bore us,
Betrayed by the land that we find,
When the brightest have gone before us,
And the dullest are most behind –
Stand, stand to your glasses, steady!
'Tis all we have left to prize:
One cup to the dead already –
Hurrah for the next that dies!

The Revel, Bartholomew Dowling

'Their activities are extremely dangerous'

2nd Panzer Division report on the SAS, October 1944

Contents

Maps   xii

Author's Note   xv

Preface   xvii

Chapter One: War With Hate   1

Chapter Two: Making Like the Enemy   20

Chapter Three: The Wild Geese   38

Chapter Four: Fallen Among Spartans   55

Chapter Five: Ambushing the Ambushers   76

Chapter Six: Chitty Chitty Bang Bang   95

Chapter Seven: Paddy's Men   113

Chapter Eight: Get Rommel   130

Chapter Nine: Hans the Good German   148

Chapter Ten: If You Go Down in the Woods Today   169

Chapter Eleven: Leave No Man Behind   186

Chapter Twelve: Get Pétain   205

Chapter Thirteen: To the Last Man   229

Chapter Fourteen: Into the Fatherland   252

Chapter Fifteen: Murder Run   272

Chapter Sixteen: Mechanised Mess Tins   288

Chapter Seventeen: First into Hell   305

Chapter Eighteen: Get Hitler   316

Chapter Nineteen: Borstal Boys   330

Afterword   345

After the War   350

Acknowledgements   364

Acknowledgements on Sources   373

Reference to Sources   376

Selected Bibliography   383

Index   386

Key Locations in France

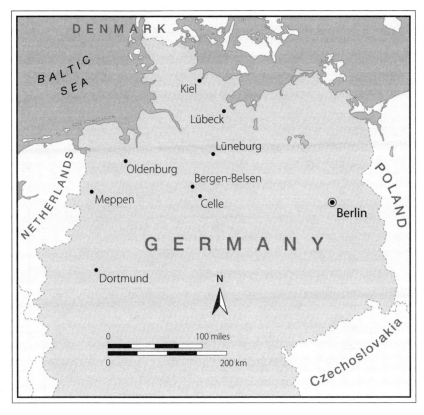

Key Locations in Germany

Author's Note

There are sadly just a handful of survivors from the Second World War operations told in these pages, or at least there were at the time of researching and writing this book. I have been in contact with as many as possible, plus surviving family members of those who have passed away. For all those contributions and input, I am immensely grateful. If there are further witnesses to the stories told here who are inclined to come forward, please do get in contact with me, as I will endeavour to include further recollections of the operations portrayed in future editions.

The time spent by Allied servicemen and women as Special Service volunteers was often traumatic and wreathed in layers of secrecy, and many chose to take their stories to their graves. Memories tend to differ and apparently none more so than those concerning operations deep behind enemy lines. The written accounts that do exist tend to differ in their detail and timescale, and locations and chronologies are sometimes contradictory. Nevertheless, I have endeavoured to provide an accurate sense of place, timescale and narrative to the story as depicted in these pages.

Where various accounts of a mission appear to be particularly contradictory, the methodology I have used to reconstruct where, when and how events took place is the 'most likely' scenario. If two or more testimonies or sources point to a particular time or place or sequence of events, I have opted to use that account as most likely, while also taking into account the relative verisimilitude of each of those accounts.

The above notwithstanding, any mistakes herein are entirely of my own making, and I would be happy to correct any in future editions. Likewise, while I have attempted to locate the copyright holders of the photos, sketches and other images and the written material used in this book, this has not always been straightforward or easy. Again, I would be happy to correct any mistakes in future editions.

As it was originally conceived of as an airborne unit – using parachutes to drop behind enemy lines – the unit was named the Special *Air* Service (my emphasis). In due course many other forms of insertion to target were adopted – on foot, by vehicle, and by submarine and landing craft.

This is a true story. Any sections of speech are taken from contemporary accounts of reported dialogue, diary entries, letters or memoirs written by those involved. Any number of those documents – war diaries, scribbled notes, signals logs, letters home – were written under the most difficult circumstances and often in some haste. Doubtless, they were never intended for publication. Accordingly, I have standardised spelling, corrected grammar and simplified acronym use, to make the book easier to read (e.g., 'Amm' is rendered as ammunition; 'Ack' becomes acknowledge). References to the source documents can be found in the notes provided at the end of this book.

Preface

THE WAR CHEST

Ten years ago I was invited to visit the home of Fiona Ferguson (née Mayne), one of Lieutenant-Colonel Blair 'Paddy' Mayne's nieces. Upon her uncle's death it fell to Fiona to be the keeper of the flame, safeguarding the Mayne family archive, and especially what became known as the 'Paddy Mayne War Diary' and her uncle's war chest. In the loft of the family's Mount Pleasant home, in Newtownards, a trove of wartime memorabilia had been secreted away. This included Mayne's uniform, carefully wrapped in brown paper, plus a large wooden chest, with the words 'Lt. Col. R. B. Mayne DSO, Mount Pleasant, Newtownards, C. Down, N. Ireland. 39247. HOLD. C.O. 1st SAS' stamped on the lid.

Visiting Fiona and her husband Norman's home, I was able to study the contents of that war chest at first hand. It proved to be brim-full of SAS reports, diaries, letters, photographs and film, plus various eclectic wartime memorabilia. I was also able to study the gutted skeleton of the original *Chronik* of Schneeren, a massive leather-bound tome that Mayne and his raiders had purloined from the town of Schneeren, in north-west Germany in spring 1945. This they had transformed into a diary-cum-scrapbook embodying the SAS's wartime history (what became known as the *SAS War Diary*). Needless to say, all of this constituted a treasure trove of SAS wartime history.

As I sifted through the contents of the war chest, the war diary and the related materials, I encountered a feast of untold behind-enemy-lines Second World War history. The first book I wrote based upon that rich store of materials is *SAS Brothers in Arms*, which tells the story of the first eighteen months of the SAS at war. The sequel to that, *SAS Forged in Hell*, tells of the SAS's war in Italy, in 1943. This book follows on from those two, picking up where they left off, though it is equally readable as a standalone story.

Fiona and the wider Mayne family offered me access to Col. Mayne's wartime memorabilia generously and freely, in the spirit that this story might be written.

To tell it has been a privilege and an honour.

Damien Lewis
Dorset, March 2024

Chapter One

WAR WITH HATE

The pair of dust-enshrouded vehicles rumbled through the patchy sunlight, the perilous track snaking through thick, undulating forest. As the foliage overhead thickened, the light turned to a blanket of shadow, then all was a blast of blinding brightness again, as the cover thinned once more. Tough conditions to master. Difficult on the eye. Demanding maximum concentration for the man at the wheel. But to these battle-hardened warriors there could be no better vehicle in which to navigate such terrain, for they'd learned to cherish their nimble Willys jeeps, and come to see them as one of the greatest inventions of the war.

At least the terrain beneath the jeep's wheels was relatively dry, as the chunky, off-road tyres fought for grip. It was the summer of 1944, and in this part of Nazi-occupied France their patrol was operating hundreds of miles behind enemy lines. Everything they needed to sustain human life and to wage war had been dropped in here, including men and machines, each jeep being released from the belly of a Halifax or similar heavy bomber, with a giant parachute lashed to each of its four corners. Not a small number had 'roman candled', the 'chutes failing to open, the one-thousand-kilogram vehicle plummeting to earth, to smash itself to pieces close by the waiting men.

These two jeeps were among five here that had weathered the

drop, and were now the chief means by which this patrol of the Special Air Service was spreading havoc and chaos where the enemy least expected it. The lead vehicle, bristling with rapid-firing twin Vickers-K machineguns, reached the point where the track emerged onto a narrow sun-washed highway. Though the forces of the enemy rarely ventured far into the forbidding wood-land and thickets – chiefly the domain of the French Resistance, and those Allied troops who had dropped in to arm them – any open road was a different matter. No matter its size, it posed a potential hazard.

Captain Derrick 'Happy' Harrison, riding in the lead vehicle, slowed at the exit to their forest redoubt. By rights, today's was not a combat mission. No enemy convoys had been reported by their French contacts, for Harrison's men to go haring after in hot pursuit. Today, they were engaged upon nothing more exacting than a vehicle-maintenance trip, for one of the gun-mountings on the rear jeep had failed. At the nearby town of Aillant-sur-Tholon there was a workshop run by friendly locals who should be able to weld it up, never mind that such repairs would be exe-cuted under the noses of the enemy. That was today's somewhat workaday mission, but still experience had proven that constant alertness and caution paid dividends.

As Harrison paused at the edge of the woodland, his finely tuned battle sense was nagging at him. Something was amiss. Back at their training base in Britain, Lieutenant-Colonel Blair 'Paddy' Mayne, the commander of 1 SAS Regiment, had taken Harrison aside for a private word before deploying. A champion boxer and an acclaimed rugby international before the war, by the spring of 1944 Mayne had earned a legendary reputation as the special forces raider and commander par excellence. For much of that time Harrison had served as one of his deputies, and they were kindred spirits.

Mayne had glanced at Harrison, tapped a finger against the side of his head, and began speaking in that soft Irish brogue that so typified the man. He had a 'blueprint' of the perfect SAS recruit. While no one might meet it exactly, when Mayne studied a man and listened to him, he had to 'come close'. He went on to outline the key criteria: stamina was critical, both mental and physical; a keen intellect was vital; so too was a natural affinity to bond as part of a team, as were versatility and a certain confidence, without brashness. The intelligence Mayne sought wasn't the classic sort forged by a formal education. It was more the innate, animal cunning and intuition that gave a man a sharp battle instinct, plus a certain ability to think outside the box – to imagine and to do the unexpected, and so confound the enemy.

That Mayne had sought to share such insights with Harrison reflected the high regard he had for the SAS captain. Those were also the chief characteristics that defined the SAS commander himself, as if Mayne were modelling his recruits upon his own, very particular persona. Harrison had been dropped into this area of France, the Yonne, in the north-central part of the country, on Mayne's personal instructions. The SAS commander knew that he could trust Harrison to operate more or less without guidance, and to make the tough decisions needed on the ground. Now, as he was poised to turn onto the road leading towards Aillant-sur-Tholon, that burden of responsibility rested heavily on 'Happy' Harrison's shoulders.

Harrison had earned his peculiar nickname while waging war across Italy in the summer and autumn of 1943, the SAS forming the tip of the spear as the Allies thrusted deep into the 'soft underbelly of Europe'. There the fighting had proven terrible and fierce. By the time they had withdrawn, Mayne's force had lost almost a third of their number – killed, wounded, taken prisoner or with their nerves frayed beyond measure. During one mission alone, the ferocious siege of the Italian port town of Termoli, the SAS had suffered their heaviest casualties from a single attack, losing twenty-one men when the enemy had shelled their trucks. But at all points Harrison had remained 'cool under extreme conditions', showing fine leadership qualities, hence the nickname – 'Happy Harrison.'

'See that?' Harrison remarked. 'What d'you make of it?'

He was eyeing the horizon to the east of their Forêt de Merry-Vaux base. Above the distant trees a swirl of dark smoke writhed into the air.

A figure came forward from the rear jeep. 'Looks as though it's over towards Les Ormes,' he observed. 'Something big on fire.'

Harrison concurred. He'd first met Lieutenant Stewart Richardson back at their training base in Darvel, Scotland, a few months earlier. A relatively new recruit to the SAS, Harrison had come to know his deputy as being 'keen as mustard' while on training and exercises, and as irresponsible as a schoolboy when not. By now, they were good friends. Their present deployment was Richardson's first chance of seeing action with the SAS, and he naturally deferred to Harrison's rank and experience. What were they to do next, he wondered. The smoke lay bang in the direction that they needed to travel, if they were to reach that workshop in Aillant-sur-Tholon.

'Carry on,' Harrison declared. 'Keep our eyes open. It may be further than we think.'

In this rolling, densely wooded countryside, judging distance could prove tricky. That conflagration, and whatever was causing it, might lie well beyond their destination. Or it might not. There was another thought foremost in Harrison's mind. Such billowing clouds of smoke normally spelt trouble, and trouble had to signify the presence of the enemy, which meant that battle might need to be joined. Whatever the case, it was towards the site of that mystery burning that they had to head.

The jeeps swung east, turning onto the open highway. Harrison got his driver, Lance Corporal Jimmy 'Curly' Hall, to put his foot down. Hall, who hailed from Newcastle-upon-Tyne, was a relative youngster among the SAS, though most tended to be in their early twenties. Signing up to the Army in 1939, he had lied about his age, for he was only sixteen at the time. After serving with a series of anti-aircraft batteries, he'd volunteered for the SAS while still in his teens. He'd gone on to take part in some of the unit's most iconic missions, including the daring July 1942 raid on Sidi Haneish airfield, in the North African desert, in which eighteen jeeps had thundered onto that remote airstrip and cruised up and down the runways shooting up scores of enemy warplanes.

Hall, with his typical Geordie humour and his shock of sandy hair – hence 'Curly' – was a long-standing and popular member of the unit. He also had a year's more experience at the sharp end of operations than Harrison. In the summer of 1943, he'd been part of Mayne's force that had formed the vanguard of Operation Husky, the Allied landings on Sicily. As the SAS had been sent in to seize the all-important enemy naval base of Augusta, Hall had suffered a gunshot wound to the thigh, spending four months in hospital. Battle-scarred, jocular, always smiling, he had only just turned twenty-two years of age when they'd parachuted into this part of France.

In short order the jeeps were thundering along the uneven roadway, throwing up a cloud of dust as they went. In this deeply rural part of north-central France, farmers tended to be busy with their oxen-and-carts all summer long, and the roads ended up coated with dirt from the fields. Hence the jeeps leaving a pall of dust in their wake, just as they were doing now. Up ahead the billow of smoke kept growing both in size and in density. It appeared ominously angry and dark, the underside lit by roiling flames.

As Hall powered the leading jeep over the crest of a ridge, Harrison signalled him to an abrupt stop. Both vehicles skidded to a halt. They'd come to a fork in the road, beyond which lay the village of Les Ormes. From the left-hand branch there came the distinctive crack-crack of gunfire, while ahead a number of buildings could be seen burning fiercely. The village was barely five hundred yards from end to end, but as far as Harrison could tell the bulk of the gunshots and smoke and flames seemed to be coming from the far side.

Moments later an elderly woman appeared on a bicycle, pedalling fiercely in their direction. Harrison could see that her grey hair was in disarray and streaming in the wind. Head down, it was only as she neared the jeeps that she realised Harrison and his men were there. She glanced up, her heavily lined face slick with tears. Recognising the 'parachutistes anglais', she jumped off her bicycle as she came level with them.

'Quick, gentlemen,' she cried, 'save yourselves ... The Boches ... there!' She pointed towards the burning buildings. 'Now I go to fetch the Maquis.'

A second figure riding in the rear jeep, a Frenchman known as Marcel Fauchois, was there to act as Harrison's translator. Invaluable, in a situation such as this, and especially since Harrison's own French was decidedly ropey. Fauchois' real name was Marcel Friedmann. He had every reason to adopt a fake identity. Even younger than Hall, Friedmann had fled Paris while still in his teens, had survived incarceration in a concentration camp, before finally making it to Britain in the summer of 1943. He longed to fight, for his entire family had disappeared without trace, and with Jewish heritage he feared the worst. Having volunteered for 4 (French) SAS Regiment, he carried a fake Canadian passport under that assumed name, 'Fauchois'.

Friedmann had parachuted into France alongside Harrison et al. on his twenty-first birthday. The 'Maquis' that the old lady referred to were bands of guerrilla fighters, most of whom had fled to the woods to avoid being pressganged into the *Service du travail obligatoire* (STO) – Compulsory Work Service – which supplied forced labour for Nazi Germany. Hundreds of thousands of French men and women had been shipped eastwards under the STO, to work in the Reich's armaments factories and other key industries. Increasingly, the Maquis had armed themselves and become a bastion of the Resistance, and it was one of the SAS's roles here to equip them for war.

Harrison bade Friedmann keep the old lady with them for a moment, as he tried to process all that she had said. She seemed determined to hurry onwards, in an effort to bring the Maquis to the aid of the people of Les Ormes. But perhaps there was a better way.

'Quickly,' Harrison demanded, 'how many Boches are there?'

'Two hundred . . . three hundred,' she ventured. 'Who knows? A lot . . . Too many for you . . .'

Again, she tried to pedal away, but again Harrison stopped her. *They* would go fetch the Maquis, he declared. With their jeeps they would be far quicker than one elderly lady on her bicycle. 'Leave it to us,' he reassured her.

The old woman's look of astonishment turned to one of overarching gratitude, mixed with relief. Repeatedly she thanked Harrison and his men, before remounting her bicycle and hurrying back towards the burning village. No doubt she had family there that she needed to protect from whatever horrors were unfolding.

Harrison turned to his comrades. 'Well,' he prompted, 'what do you think? Go for the Maquis or attack the village ourselves?'

They were five men riding in two jeeps, boasting eight Vickers-K machineguns, one of which was attached by a dodgy mounting. Up ahead, there were several hundred enemy, if the lady were to be believed. Harrison had no doubt in his mind what they should do, but still he sought the views of the others.

'I say attack,' Friedmann ventured, as ever keen to have a crack at *les sales Boches*.

Hall spoke next. If they went to fetch the Maquis, they would be too late to save the village, he reasoned, and that wasn't on.

'Brearton?' Harrison queried. Trooper Tony Brearton was Richardson's driver, a fellow 'tankie', hailing from the Royal Tank Regiment originally.

'Let's have a crack at them,' Brearton declared, simply.

Last, Harrison turned to his deputy. Lieutenant Richardson was of the same mind as Hall. If they went to fetch the Maquis, the village was done-for.

It was unanimous.

Hurriedly, Harrison explained his plan of attack. Rather than heading down the main drag, the Route du Couvent, they'd make a right turn, after which they'd hang left and left again, so coming into the village from one of the side-roads. That way, they'd have the element of surprise, Harrison reasoned, and could blast their way through, guns blazing. They should be in and out before the enemy even realised what had hit them.

'The odds are fifty-to-one against,' Harrison concluded, in his quiet, soft-spoken way, 'but I hope they'll get such a shock that we'll pull it off.'

Typically, the two jeeps were flying Union Jack flags, for the men of the SAS were serving in France as the bona fide troops of a bona fide military nation, and they made little effort to hide. Likewise, they were dressed in full SAS uniform, complete with their distinctive beret and 'winged dagger' cap badge.

The original inspiration for the design was either the flaming sword of Damocles, or King Arthur's Excalibur, but even by then, summer 1944, its origins had been subsumed under a growing body of legend. As the jeeps got under way again, turning south onto Route de Raloy, they gathered pace, tyres humming on the tarmac and flags fluttering in the slipstream.

They headed into the gathering storm, Harrison and the other gunners making their weapons ready, the distinctive clatch-clatch of a round ratcheting into the breech echoing through the narrow streets. Originally a weapon designed as an aircraft gun, the Vickers-K's high rate of fire made it ideal for airborne combat, wherein engagements might last for just a few seconds. With its hundred-round drum magazine armed with a mixture of tracer, ball, incendiary and armour-piercing bullets, the Vickers-K could churn out a devastating rate of fire. Bolted to their jeeps in pairs, it had proven the perfect weapon for SAS raids.

For Harrison, there had been only one decision to make, back at the crossroads. To have turned away from Les Ormes would have been unthinkable. It was in his blood to stand up for the underdog, and these villagers were just that. In a sense, Harrison had always believed himself to be different, and something of an outsider. In his early years he'd been abandoned by his mother, an opera singer, who'd sought fame and fortune in the USA. With a mostly absent father, he'd been brought up by his 'Auntie Kathleen' as best she was able. Life had been far from easy, and the lack of parental love had forced Harrison to adopt a fiercely independent mindset.

He was noted for his sympathy for the underdog, his sensitivity and humility, plus his open-minded outlook. And his principles. Harrison stood by his principles. His unorthodox upbringing had also left him with a maverick, leftfield kind of mindset.

While such characteristics might not have suited much of the wider military, in Paddy Mayne's SAS they were highly prized.

The quaint houses of Les Ormes, with their cream-coloured façades, white-painted shutters and high-pitched, gracefully curved roofs were familiar to the SAS men, but the choking, acrid stench of burning and the staccato crackle of gunfire were alien to this otherwise sleepy village. Thick smoke wafted down the narrow side-streets, the hot fumes being channelled between the tall buildings as if in a wind tunnel. Turning north once more, onto Rue de l'École, the lead jeep thundered towards the town square, with Harrison hunched ever closer over the twin Vickers bolted to the passenger-side dash.

They'd barely come into view of the square itself before he spied his first enemy. A figure dressed in the distinctive uniform of the reviled *Schutzstaffel* turned toward the jeep, pistol clutched in one hand, and began to stroll toward them. Only an SS officer would carry such a weapon. Even as he glanced at the on-rushing jeep, a growing sense of surprise in his gaze, the SS officer died. Standing in his seat, Harrison had unleashed a first lethal burst, cutting the man down in his steps.

In an instant the SAS captain took in the wider scene, as the jeep roared further into the square. The ancient church, l'église Notre-Dame-de-la-Nativité, lay at the centre of the square, with its high red-tiled roof above gently rounded, whitewashed walls. Parked to one side of that were the distinctive forms of a large German truck and two staff cars. Ranged in front of them was a rank of grey-uniformed SS and, ominously, some two-dozen villagers lined up as if for some macabre kind of parade.

Harrison didn't pause. His finger hard on the trigger, he poured in the fire, the twin muzzles belching smoke, the weapon thumping out the deep percussive beats as each round fired, spent brass shell casings glittering through the afternoon sunlight.

Within seconds he had punched a line of rents through all three enemy vehicles. First one then the others burst into flames. As terrified SS men dived for cover, Harrison followed them in his sights, pouring rounds into them. Screams and agonised cries rang out across the square, figures fleeing in all directions.

'Many died in those first few seconds in front of the church,' Harrison would write of the moment, 'lit by the flickering flames of the burning vehicles.'

But even as he unleashed fire, he felt the jeep judder to a halt. It came to a stop no more than thirty yards from the church, within a stone's throw of the nearest enemy. Bullets hammered in from all sides now, as those SS who had escaped the initial onslaught began to recover from the shock. Glancing at Hall to see why they'd halted, Harrison spied his form slumped over the steering wheel. By the horrific amount of blood that had soaked through his uniform, Harrison knew that Hall had to be dead, which meant that their jeep was going nowhere. So much for blazing through Les Ormes in a burst of fire and glory.

Keeping one finger on the trigger and blasting out the fire, Harrison tried hitting the jeep's starter. The engine was stone cold dead. It must have been struck in the same burst of fire that had killed Hall. Nothing Harrison could do about that now. Then, as if to make matters worse, his gun jammed. He wasn't about to try to clear a stoppage in the midst of such a firefight, for to do so was inviting death. Instead, he dived for the Vickers bolted to the jeep's rear and opened up with that. But after one long burst it too seized up. In a desperate effort to keep the enemy at bay, Harrison lurched across Hall's body and grabbed the single Vickers bolted to the driver's side, letting rip with that. But two long bursts, and it too had locked solid.

A dead man at the wheel, a dud jeep and no guns working. How could it get any worse? For a moment Harrison feared he was done for, but then he heard the cacophony of fire erupting from his rear, as the second jeep blazed into action. Brearton must have seen the dire straits that Harrison had got into, for he'd brought their vehicle to a halt against one wall of the side-street, so enjoying a modicum of cover. While Harrison was grateful for the supporting fire, it did little to relieve his own predicament. He was pinned down in the middle of the town square and horribly exposed.

Bullets ricocheted and sparked off road and walls, as the enemy fire intensified. Desperate for some means to fight back, Harrison grabbed his M1 carbine, firing off the first fifteen-round magazine in short order. As had always been the case, SAS soldiers were largely free to carry whatever weapons they chose. In the early years of the war, American 'Tommy guns' – Thompson submachine guns – and German 'Schmeissers' – MP40 submachine guns – had been favourites. But more recently, the US-manufactured M1 carbine had become their go-to weapon. With its folding butt, single shot or semi-automatic mode and light weight, it was a superb weapon, as Harrison well appreciated. In short order he burned through another and yet another magazine, trying to beat back the enemy from the stricken vehicle and from Hall's bloodied form.

Upon parachuting into France, Harrison had injured his left hand. It had been his thirteenth parachute drop on the thirteenth of the month, and sure enough it had been plagued by bad luck. Over time, the SAS had developed a means to ensure the crushing weight in their rucksack wasn't strapped to their person when they jumped. Otherwise, leg and back injuries were bound to ensue. Instead, they'd devised a rope and pulley system, one that allowed the heavy pack to be lowered until it hung from the jumper's parachute harness, suspended some thirty feet below. That way, the pack was the first to touch down, taking the impact of its own fall.

But on Harrison's 13/13 jump, the rope had decided to jam. As he'd fought to release it, suddenly it had sprung free, while at the same time wrapping itself 'like a maddened snake' around the fingers of his left hand. As the heavy load reached the end of its drop the rope jerked tight, and his hand had been riven with pain. He'd managed to drag it free, but the middle finger at least was broken. With the injured hand crudely splinted and bandaged, it hadn't caused him a great deal of trouble . . . until now.

As he hammered out the rounds, and grasped for fresh magazines, the ungainly splint kept getting in the way. Blast and confound it. A German soldier made a dash forward. Harrison unleashed a shot from the hip, dropping him. Figures leaned from the upper windows of the buildings that ringed the square, taking potshots. Harrison fired whenever he spied movement, acting on instinct, but he feared it was only a matter of time before he got hit. Stay where he was and he was dead, that was for certain.

Reaching for Hall's bloodied form, he hoisted the dead man onto his shoulders. But as he went to make his move, so the enemy's fire redoubled. Grabbing his carbine once more, Harrison found himself assailed by streams of tracer, the blazing arcs cutting across the air in a terrifying, scorching fireworks display. Dancing this way and that, 'like a boxer as if to dodge the flying bullets', Harrison fought for his very life.

A shout echoed from behind him. 'Look out! The orchard on your left.'

Glancing that way, Harrison spied a low wall, with beyond it a grove of apple trees. Braving the fire, he sprinted for the wall. He reached it, popped his head and his carbine above the parapet, only to spy two-dozen enemy troops advancing towards him 'at the double'. Firing as fast as he could pull the trigger, he unleashed a barrage of aimed shots, driving them back.

Eventually, the sheer weight of enemy numbers forced him to fall back to the stricken jeep once more. While it provided a degree of cover, he knew it was a death trap. Suddenly, unexpectedly, another figure appeared beside him. It was Friedmann. The young Frenchman had dashed forward to retrieve Hall's body, aiming to drag it across to their one surviving vehicle.

'Get back, you fool!' Harrison yelled. 'Get back.' There was zero sense in getting another good man killed.

Ignoring his commander's warnings, Friedmann hoisted Hall's body and prepared to run. Thirty yards separated him from the one good jeep, but as he readied himself to move the Frenchman became the focus of the enemy's fire. Sensing that he was not to be deterred, Harrison took up a position in the cover of the wrecked vehicle and hammered out blast after blast of covering fire. Moments later, Friedmann broke cover and made a dash for it, and Harrison was left alone once more in defiance of the enemy.

How many magazines did he have left, he wondered. All of a sudden, he remembered that it was his wedding anniversary. What a crazy thought to be having at a time like this. Then, even more bizarrely, he wondered just how furious his wife would be if he got himself killed on this day, of all days.

He felt a kick to his right hand, and a sudden numbness. He glanced down, only to realise it was sheeted in blood. Amazingly it still seemed to be usable, and with his fingertips he managed to fish out another magazine from his parachutist's smock-top. After a good deal of fumbling, he got it clipped onto his carbine and ready to fire. By now both his left and his right hands were injured – one from the parachuting accident, the other from enemy fire. Unsurprisingly, his aim was growing unsteady.

The enemy had seen him jump with shock when he had been hit. Sensing he was injured they intensified their onslaught. A figure stepped from behind a tree to take more careful aim. Harrison raised his weapon, which was now slick with blood, and pulled the trigger. All he felt was a hollow click. Damn! Another stoppage. As he lowered the carbine to investigate, he felt his hand whip back for a second time, the enemy gunman's shot tearing across his knuckles.

Two rounds were jammed in the M1's breech. As bullets ripped through the air all around him, Harrison struggled to wrench the dud magazine free and to deal with the stoppage. But his hands were slippery with blood and numb with pain. Finally, he managed to clear the weapon and to get a fresh magazine slotted into place, and somehow, miraculously, he was still alive. He raised the M1 once more, only to hear a cry from behind him.

'Run for it!'

As if to underscore the sentiments, Harrison heard the wild revving of the jeep's engine. He stole a glance in that direction. The vehicle had been turned around, and Stewart, Brearton and Friedmann were aboard and good to go. They yelled out again. Firing as he broke cover, Harrison made a dash for it. By the time he reached the jeep, it was already under way, and he made a crazed leap for the rear, hands dragging him aboard. As Brearton put his foot on the gas, so Friedmann blasted out a parting barrage from the vehicle's rear Vickers, pouring a sustained burst of fire into the square.

In a cloud of smoke and dust, the lone jeep thundered back down the route by which it had come. Having exited the village, Brearton made for the cover of the nearest woodland. From there, along narrow, almost untraceable tracks, they made their way back to their Forêt de Merry-Vaux base camp. Once they'd reached it, Harrison had his wounded hands cleaned and bandaged, before breaking the news to all that Curly Hall had been killed. It was a hard thing to reveal. Hall, 'always bright, cheery and philosophical', had been with Harrison ever since he had volunteered for the SAS. As he was painfully aware, had he not stood up to operate the twin Vickers, the burst of fire that had killed Hall very likely would have nailed him instead.

That evening, Lieutenant Richardson took a patrol back into Les Ormes. The SS had cleared out. No one knew for sure why they had swooped on the village. Some believed they were an advance guard for a German convoy that intended to pass that way. Others said it was a 'reprisal' raid for the SAS presence in the region. As Harrison and his men were learning, such brutalities were not uncommon across Nazi-occupied France. As well as torching the houses, the SS had seized twenty villagers for execution. They had just got started, murdering the first two, when the SAS jeeps had blazed their way into the square. In the ensuing carnage, and as the enemy casualties had mounted, the rest of the condemned men had managed to break away.

As Harrison would report on the day's action: 'Enemy losses 50–60 killed and wounded, two staff cars destroyed, and one truck knocked out. Hostages awaiting execution made their escape.'

Shortly, the villagers of Les Ormes held a funeral to bury their dead. They only had the one coffin, but they offered it to the SAS. Hall was placed therein, and laid to rest in the village cemetery, which lay adjacent to the road leading to Aillant-sur-Tholon, which had been the patrol's intended destination that fateful day. He was buried with the two dead villagers murdered in the SS reprisals, lying to either side of him. It was powerful symbolism to demonstrate that the young SAS trooper had not died in vain.

In due course, Harrison would be awarded the Military Cross for his daring actions at Les Ormes, and Friedmann the *Medaille militaire* (Military Medal), a French high valour decoration. Sadly, Freidmann's would be posthumous, for he would die that

November even as the SAS pushed the enemy back towards the borders of Nazi Germany. His citation would read: 'Completely disregarding the danger Friedmann rushed through enemy fire . . . to his friend, pulled his body from the jeep, and carried it to cover. Not wanting to abandon it, he disregarded the patrol commander's orders.'

One of those who attended Hall's burial was Sergeant James 'Jock' McDiarmid, an SAS veteran who'd earned a reputation for being practically indestructible. Like Harrison, McDiarmid, a wild Scottish warrior and veteran of the Black Watch (Royal Highlanders), had long served under Mayne. As the SAS had spearheaded the first Allied landings onto mainland Italy, he'd undertaken a martial feat that typified the man. While fighting a murderous battle uphill across exposed ground, he'd been shot by a sniper. Regardless, McDiarmid had continued to lead his section, until 'pain and loss of blood forced him to stop'.

Later, during the siege of Termoli, as the SAS had tried to evacuate their wounded they'd come under fire from an upstairs window. Slipping into the building, McDiarmid had silenced the enemy gunman with his bare hands. He'd emerged, growling: 'He'll fire that Beretta no more. I wrapped it around his fucking head.' Likewise, here in the Yonne it was McDiarmid who had scored first blood. Leading a jeep patrol, he and his men had stumbled upon a German bicycle party. Opening fire with their Vickers, they'd forced the enemy to pile off their bikes and flee into the nearby woods. McDiarmid had led the charge after them. Following a short and savage exchange of fire, the enemy had given themselves up.

Eight very frightened German soldiers had emerged, hands in the air. McDiarmid then had a problem. Harrison's force were in no position to take prisoners. Even if they could establish some kind of POW cage in the forest, it would have taken half their force to guard it. That wasn't why they were here. With little other option, McDiarmid had handed the POWs to the commander of the local Resistance, warning him to take good care of them. That man had vowed that he would indeed take very good care of the eight Germans. But even as McDiarmid's patrol had departed, there was the harsh crackle of gunfire, leaving him in little doubt what had transpired. Clearly, they'd misunderstood what McDiarmid had meant by 'take care of them'.

As he gazed into Hall's coffin, the loss of his comrade hit McDiarmid especially hard. In North Africa, where the SAS had evolved into the ferocious, hit-and-run raiding force that had proved so effective, German General Erwin Rommel had promised a 'war without hate'. In many ways it had been just that. Across the wide open expanse of the desert, the Axis and Allied armies had clashed in a theatre mostly devoid of civilians, where gentlemen soldiers could wage a 'pure' war. The rules of combat were to be respected. Prisoners would be taken and safeguarded, as the Geneva Convention demanded. Brute savagery would be eschewed.

In many ways the SAS's desert operations had embodied that spirit, combining a piratical, freewheeling means of waging war with a certain quixotic, chivalrous intent. From the autumn of 1941 to the spring of 1943 they had roved across the open desert in a series of daring raids, and there had been a definite romanticism and dash about their missions that had thrilled the blood.

But here in Nazi-occupied France, as McDiarmid and others were beginning to realise, the war was being fought with unbridled hate, and often against those who could least defend themselves. Likewise, for the SAS the distinction between right and wrong was at risk of starting to blur. Hall had been killed while trying to prevent an act of mass murder. The SAS had killed the executioners in mid-execution, so barely in the nick of time. In light of the savage behaviour of the SS and their brethren, men like McDiarmid were starting to appreciate why the French gave no quarter.

Before deploying to France, Mayne had given strict orders regarding the clemency to be extended to German soldiers. 'Before they surrender, the Germans must be subjected to every known trick, stratagem and explosive which will kill, threaten, frighten and unsettle them,' he had declared, 'but they must know that they will be safe and unharmed if they surrender.' It was vital that the enemy realise there were 'British soldiers behind their lines and if they surrender . . . they will be taken to a safe place and unharmed.' But how could such strictures be adhered to in such a hate-filled environment? In such a war as this, were Mayne's orders realistic? Feasible? Achievable? Certainly, in the hearts of some of Harrison's men a dark anger and rage was starting to take hold.

This war was turning dirty and murderous. In France, as the SAS was learning to its deep regret, the local villagers were being forced to pay a terrible price, as a dangerous and vengeful enemy had its back forced relentlessly against the wall. With the armies of Nazi Germany desperate to keep their iron grip on Western Europe, and to prevent the Allies from advancing into the Fatherland, so the hatred and the bloodshed would only worsen. Increasingly, the men of the SAS, fighting deep behind enemy lines, would find themselves the target of the enemy's savage intent. In short, this was no war without hate. Quite the reverse.

And in truth, the worst of the terror was still to come.

Chapter Two

MAKING LIKE THE ENEMY

Harrison's task within Operation Kipling, as his mission was codenamed, had been quite different at the outset. Initially, he and his men had been charged to keep the lowest possible profile and to avoid all contact with the enemy. Instead, they were to scope out landing zones (LZs) for a glider-borne force, so that an entire SAS squadron could be airlifted into France, together with their forty-odd jeeps and all necessary supplies. Once there, they were to rove across the length and breadth of the Yonne, ambushing German forces as they were driven back from the Normandy beaches.

On 6 June 1944, 'D-Day', Operation Overlord had been launched, the assault on the Normandy coast, in which 1,200 aircraft had led the way, followed by 5,000 surface vessels, in an amphibious landing that had put 160,000 men-at-arms ashore on the first day. Some two million Allied troops would be landed in France by the end of August. But once Harrison and his small band of SAS had been parachuted into the Yonne, and had selected the LZs for the incoming gliders, the airborne landings had been cancelled. Deprived of their key purpose, Mayne had given them new orders: they were to break cover and to let slip the dogs of war.

But now, with his left hand splinted and his right wrapped

in bandages, after Les Ormes, Harrison was left feeling next to useless. Yet there would be little time to pause for reflection or self-pity. A villager came dashing into their forest hideout with an urgent warning. A massive convoy of enemy motor vehicles was heading in their direction. Imagining they had hit the jackpot, Harrison dispatched his jeeps to ambush the approaching force. Feeling somewhat sorry for himself – what a time to be injured! – he sat in camp, gazing at his hands and straining his ears to catch the first sounds of gunfire.

Instead, the next thing he knew was his own jeeps roaring back into their forest base, after which came another jeep, and then a long line of similar vehicles. A familiar figure jumped out of one of them and came bounding over. He thrust out a hand.

'Hello, Harry. Hear you've been getting yourself into a mess.'

'Where on earth have you sprung from?' Harrison countered, in consternation. Harry – short for Harrison – was his other nickname.

The man before him – beaming ear to ear – was none other than Major Tony Marsh. The last Harrison had seen or heard of him, he was supposed to lead the force that would fly in by glider. So how on earth had Marsh ended up here, and with what looked like twenty-odd jeeps to his name? The answer epitomised the SAS do-or-die spirit. As Allied forces had broken out of the Normandy beachheads, so a series of aerodromes had been seized. Into one of those had flown Marsh's entire force, riding in a fleet Douglas C-47 Skytrain transport aircraft, known as the 'Dakota' when in British service.

John 'Tony' Marsh, 'young, bouncing, blond and extremely good looking', was actually so damned handsome that he was forever getting ragged about it by his comrades. Always seeming to be up to one prank or another, at one point in his career he'd all but burned down the officer's mess of the Duke of Cornwall's

Light Infantry, his parent regiment. Marsh loved playing the high-spirited, eccentric Englishman, but mostly as a foil to his fearless soldiering. In truth, there was little he didn't know about how to train and handle men, as he'd proven during the SAS's North African and Italian operations.

Marsh was a veteran of Mayne's Great Sand Sea raids, in which an entire SAS squadron had based itself deep in the Sahara desert, amid a supposedly unnavigable mass of giant sand dunes, so as to hit Rommel's supply lines from the least expected direction. And Marsh, like Harrison, had also weathered the hell of Termoli, being awarded a Distinguished Service Order (DSO) for his actions there. In short, he had proved himself time and again in the heat of battle. And now, he'd done it again, leading a massed convoy of jeeps through enemy lines and deep into Nazi-occupied France.

That story itself was mind-boggling. The operational instructions issued by Mayne had been precise: 'Radio silence between jeeps; guns cocked and safety catches off but no firing unless under attack.' They were to push ahead wearing full uniform, but having removed their all-too-distinctive SAS berets. This was all about slipping through unnoticed and unmolested, and masquerading as the enemy. In addition to their Vickers-K guns, each jeep was fitted with a Bren light machinegun bolted to the driver's wing, and carried a US-made bazooka stuffed in the rear. Each was also equipped with two self-sealing fuel tanks to greatly boost range.

After their North African and Italian operations, the war-weary SAS had been shipped home to Britain, to rearm, refit and recuperate, and to prepare for their role in the D-Day landings. Charged to massively boost their numbers, they'd expanded from a unit that was just a few hundred strong to some 2,500 men-at-arms. Accordingly, there were scores of newbies within

Marsh's squadron, men who had volunteered for the SAS that spring, and for whom France was to prove their baptism of fire. Wisely, Mayne's policy had been to couple the old hands with fresh recruits, so that experience might guide and temper raw enthusiasm. It was also designed to ensure that there would be little sense of 'us and them' between grizzled veterans and fresh recruits.

Like many of the newbies riding with Marsh's squadron, Lieutenant Roy Close hungered to fight. A veteran of the British Expeditionary Force, and of the abject defeat in France in June 1940, Close had been plucked from the Dunkirk beaches by a minesweeper, even as enemy warplanes had strafed and bombed remorselessly. During the retreat across Belgium and France, he'd learned to hate and despise those Luftwaffe aircrew, as they had shot up roads clogged with refugees. Coming across the bloodied forms of women and children time and again, Close had dug deep to find a core of steely calm, pledging to fight the Nazi onslaught to his dying breath.

Of modest birth, he'd been brought up in a cramped north London home, one heated by a feeble coal fire, and with a home-made wireless for the family's entertainment of an evening. He'd grown used to his parents being hunched together at the kitchen table, trying to plan the week's budget on limited means. After service in the Royal Navy, Close's father had started a small company supplying typewriter parts, but his business partner had absconded taking most of the funds. With his father driven into unemployment, a trip by bus to the West End to see the bright lights of Oxford Street was a real treat.

Educated at local state schools, Close had excelled at sport – first-eleven cricket, football and swimming – but had floundered academically. He'd left school at sixteen, with the headmaster advising him to take a job as a clerk in the Post Office. But soon war was declared and Close signed up to the Royal Army Services Corps. In due course he'd found himself facing the Nazi onslaught in France and fleeing from the hell of Dunkirk.

Haunted by those terrible experiences, Close was absolutely certain that Nazism had to be defeated. It was a case of fight or see Britain and the world ruled by a 'brutal foreign dictatorship'. He was utterly convinced that the 'future of free, democratic society' depended on winning the war. In that spirit, and 'believing we must destroy a great evil', Close had gone on to volunteer for the SAS. In the interim, he'd been persuaded to go for officer's training, turning men like him into 'temporary officers and gentlemen'. Or rather, more commonly men somewhat different to him. Close wasn't of the privileged officer class, and class was still something that tended to define the upper ranks of the British military. Regardless, he had made the best of it he could.

What had riled him a great deal more was the fact that, try as he might, he seemed unable to get into the fight. 'Since the Blitzkrieg had devastated the Low Countries and France, destroyed the British Expeditionary Force . . . and sent us to the beaches of Dunkirk, I had not faced the enemy,' Close lamented. He vowed to do something to change all that, but what? The answer came with his volunteering for airborne forces. Then, in early 1944, he'd heard a recruitment speech and jumped at the chance of volunteering for SAS selection.

With two fellow airborne pals, Ed Mycock and Tom Bryce, Close went for the interview. The prospect of serving in such a unit, one that had proved 'guerrilla warfare' could pay such high dividends, was hugely exciting. It seemed like a God-given opportunity to satisfy his hunger to fight. Still, he, Mycock and Bryce decided that, like the Three Musketeers, either all of them would be chosen, or none would go. That was all well and good, yet it had fallen to Close to be the one to deliver their ultimatum to the Commander of 1 SAS, Lieutenant-Colonel Blair 'Paddy' Mayne.

Close was the last of the three to be ushered before him. Behind a desk sat this huge figure, seeming awkward in such a formal setting. Close gave a crisp salute, as befitted a qualified paratroop officer.

'Good morning. Sit down, Mr. Close,' Mayne greeted him, in his soft Ulster brogue.

There had followed a series of questions, mostly about Close's time serving in France, and how he felt about his experiences 'on the road to Dunkirk and on the beaches'. There then came the obvious query: why the SAS? Close parroted his carefully prepared speech about the power of guerrilla warfare and the potency of small-scale SAS-style raids, before delivering his somewhat awkward ultimatum. They hoped all three would be selected, him, Mycock and Bryce, or it would be none at all.

With just the hint of a smile, Mayne responded: 'So, it's giving the Commanding Officer an ultimatum already, is it?'

Close muttered something about not intending it to sound that way, just that they were friends and they would like to serve together.

'Very well,' Mayne concluded, 'I'll bear that in mind.'

Cringing with embarrassment, Close was dismissed. Outside, he gave the bad news to his fellows. His ultimatum – if that's what it was – had gone down like a lead balloon. They figured they'd screwed up. Close was persuaded to go back in to speak to Mayne, and to make it clear that they'd overstepped the mark. Moments later, he once more found himself standing before the inscrutable figure seated behind his desk.

'Another ultimatum, is it?' Mayne asked.

Garbling his words, Close did his best to explain that they'd changed their minds. In fact, they'd each happily take their chances.

'Thank you. I'll bear that in mind also.' After such shenani-
gans, Close and his pals were utterly amazed when they learned
that Mayne had accepted all three of them into his fellowship.
A few days later, Close arrived in Darvel, a small village in the
Irvine Valley, in Ayrshire, engirdled in the Scottish hills. Finding
his way to the 1 SAS regimental headquarters, he was guided
towards the officer's mess. The convivial buzz of men chatting
and drinking drew him to it. As he stepped into the dimly lit bar
room a row of faces turned to scrutinise the newcomer.

A figure broke away, and steered Close towards a giant individual who was leaning with one elbow on the bar. Wearing
smart battledress and tie, Close's gaze was drawn to the man's
distinctive medal ribbons, which revealed that he'd been awarded
the DSO and Bar. Typically, the DSO was for acts of a high degree
of gallantry, just short of deserving the Victoria Cross. Mayne
had won his first in North Africa and his second in Italy, and
there were few who could boast two such decorations. In short,
Close was in awe of the man.

'Paddy, this is lieutenant . . . er . . .' The man who was trying
to introduce him had forgotten Close's name. He volunteered it,
after which Mayne gazed at Close intently, searching his memory.

'Ah yes, the sassenach who gave the CO an ultimatum about
who he should recruit. Welcome to the Regiment.'

'Thank you, sir. I'm sorry that—'

Mayne waved away the apology. 'Have a drink.'

'A beer please, sir.'

'A sassenach drink,' Mayne muttered, before ordering up a
pint of beer.

'Sassenach' is a word of Gaelic origin, often used by the Scots
and Irish as a disparaging name for the English.

An Ulsterman, hailing from County Down, Mayne was proud
to be Irish. A gifted rugby player, he'd been capped six times for

the Irish rugby team before the war. One of his teammates had described him as being 'a very quiet chap. At first glance you would think he wouldn't hurt a fly, but we soon discovered that when steamed up he would do anything.' Mayne had prided himself on the fighting calibre of the Irishmen he'd recruited into the SAS – north or south of the border, it didn't matter. 'Paddy was Irish all right,' Captain Malcolm Pleydell, the SAS's first medical officer, had remarked at the time, 'Irish from top to toe; from the lazy eyes that could light into anger so quickly, to the quiet voice and its intonation.' Close took a sip of his beer and set the tankard down on the counter.

'Come on, man, knock it back,' Mayne urged, and with that he downed his whisky – very much *not* a sassenach drink, it seemed.

Knowing he was being tested, Close – a novice drinker, at best – opened his throat and forced the pint down.

'Another pint, Corporal,' Mayne ordered. Close was aware that the chatter had died down. All eyes were upon the two of them. Scrutinising his initiation. He took the fresh pint, as Mayne grabbed a whisky, and forced it down, banging the empty tankard on the counter even as his guts revolted at the sudden onslaught.

Mayne smiled. 'Good man. You drink well. Are you a strong man?'

Somewhat nonplussed, Close replied that he imagined that he was.

'Good. Try this.' Mayne picked up a bottle top from the counter and squashed it flat between the thumb and finger of his right hand. Close tried to reciprocate, but to no avail. No matter how many fingers, and then hands, he brought to bear, he could hardly put a dent in the thing. He glanced 'shamefully' at Mayne, to see a kindly humour shining in his eyes.

'No matter. I expect your fighting is better than your strength. Come and join me at dinner.'

Close did just that, and they proceeded to have a delightfully unrestrained chat. He was struck by how soft Mayne's voice was, as he asked him all about parachute training, and about defeat in 1940 and Dunkirk.

'Outgunned, disastrous,' was how Close characterised it.

'It will be different this time,' Mayne assured him, portentously.

Such had been Close's induction into the ranks of 1 SAS. In rapid order he would come to realise that, 'in a curious way, we were like a self-disciplined family, of which he [Mayne] was the head. My lasting respect for Paddy Mayne began at that moment.'

Ironically, Roy Close's first brush with the forces of Nazi Germany wouldn't be as he'd imagined it, with machinegun, dagger and grenade. Instead, it would be to make like the enemy, and to bluff their way through their lines. Mayne wasn't with their party, as those twenty jeeps crawled through no-man's-land. Instead, it was Major Marsh leading the charge. No one had tried this before – a mass penetration by jeep through the German positions. But if anyone other than Mayne could pull it off, it was Marsh. With his 'relaxed, friendly manner of command, which was much respected by all', he was the perfect frontman for all that was to follow.

The first sign that the long convoy of jeeps had left Allied territory was the marked absence of any American forces, either tanks or trucks or troops. The terrain seemed uncannily deserted, the houses bereft of the slightest sign of life. They'd entered into the ghost land between the lines, and the very realisation of it sharpened their battle sense, putting nerves on edge. Roy Close found himself gripping the twin handles of his Vickers machineguns, as their jeep nosed towards the unknown.

His driver was one Alec 'Boy' Borrie, a man with a not dissimilar background. A fellow Londoner, Borrie had earned his nickname due to his remarkably fresh-faced countenance. Even in his SAS uniform, Borrie looked like a boy scout. Like Curly Hall, he'd lied about his age in order to sign up. He'd joined the Gordon Highlanders, claiming to be eighteen, but in truth was barely sixteen. The son of a railwayman father and a shop-assistant mother, he'd attended the local school, at which his worst and best memories were being forced to drink a beaker of boiling hot milk every winter's morning, and 'putting the school bully in hospital after a fight on the way home'.

School had done little for Borrie's education, but had certainly hardened him for life. Whenever a fight broke out at his Barnehurst, south-east London school, the headmaster would arrange the boys in a square, with the pugilists dead centre. The two would proceed to batter it out, until one or other got hurt and the fight would be stopped. 'After that,' Borrie concluded, 'I was not afraid of taking on anyone or anything.' At age fourteen he'd left school and taken an apprenticeship in a local joiners, Barber & Blanchards. One of the senior employees turned out to have a habit of beating the apprentices with a heavy wooden rod. But when he reached across to strike Borrie, he got walloped on the head with a large wooden mallet instead.

Threatened with the sack, Borrie decided the army was a better option, and especially since Britain was at war. But months of guard duty with the Gordon Highlanders had left him frustrated and bored. When the opportunity had arisen to volunteer for the SAS, he'd jumped at the chance. Some three hundred had been interviewed by Mayne. Just thirty had made it through. Mayne had asked the strikingly youthful Borrie how he would feel about killing. Borrie had answered in his typical plain-spoken way: 'I haven't done any yet, so I don't know. I think it'll be okay.' Maybe it was due to his guileless attitude – his up-front honesty – that Borrie was one of the few selected.

Parachuting courses had followed, at the end of which there were twenty-five remaining. After that, the remorseless training with the SAS had begun, as they prepared to operate in small units for extended periods behind the lines. At the end of that, their number had been whittled down to fifteen. By that time, Borrie had got the measure of Mayne. 'He was a gentleman . . . He'd put his arm on you shoulder and ask you nicely – "Would you ever mind going and doing so and so" – and you couldn't refuse. He was an officer men would follow one hundred per cent. No doubt about that.'

As the jeeps probed no-man's-land, a village loomed in the distance. Close studied it, hearing a voice murmur something from the driver's side. Borrie was practically whispering, as if a few words overheard in English could give them away.

'Look ahead, sir,' he muttered.

Close glanced where Borrie indicated. Far in front lay a café, and beside it was a stationary column of vehicles. In the lead was the distinctive form of a German halftrack – a *Sonderkraftfahrzeug* 251 armoured personnel carrier – with beyond that a line of military trucks. The enemy had clearly been heading north towards the front, but had halted for some refreshments. German troops were stood around the vehicles smoking, and drinking what Close presumed had to be coffee. Whether the halftrack was manned or not he couldn't tell, for the vehicle had shadowed slits for windows.

Marsh kept the convoy motoring forward, as if they had every right to be there. As the noise of their approach became audible, faces cast curious glances towards the approaching vehicles. 'Clearly they were puzzled,' Close noted of the enemy. Someone riding in the lead jeep had an inspired idea. From their earliest operations, the SAS had tended to ensure that a German speaker was embedded within their units. Often, they were German or

Austrian Jews, men who had escaped from the Reich and volunteered for special forces, and who had every reason to fight like the devil incarnate.

One of those yelled out a greeting: 'Hallo, Kamerade!' And then he waved.

All along the line of jeeps figures followed suit, waving for all they were worth. After a brief pause, the figures at the café seemed to relax noticeably and they returned the greeting. Smiling as if they were the best of comrades, the men in the jeeps roared past the stationary German convoy, until those in the rear vehicle gave a last smile and a wave. As Close's rear gunner told him later, the German troops had kept an eye on them all the way down the road, until a welcome bend had spirited them out of view.

More enemy traffic appeared on the road, as vehicles and men streamed towards the frontline. At each encounter the same tactic was employed, until it became 'a bit of a game', as Close described it, 'waving to them as we went past'. A good way into their journey, the convoy pulled beyond the French city of Orléans, some 350 kilometres south of the Normandy beaches. Up ahead Close spied a long line of military trucks, each with a figure standing on the passenger seat, his weapon at the ready. At the head of the column rode an armoured car, and there was a decidedly business-like and martial attitude to the entire set-up.

In a sense, the saving grace for Marsh's convoy was the fact that they were so deep inside enemy territory. To the German forces riding in that column, it would have seemed inconceivable that the approaching vehicles could be anything other than friendly. At anything other than very close scrutiny, the camouflage smocks of the SAS could pass as German paratrooper uniform. Though aware of some very curious stares as the two columns thundered past each other, again the smile-and-wave ruse seemed to do the trick.

A little later there was another, utterly bizarre moment. A voice was heard breaking radio silence, as someone at the rear of the column made a call to Marsh.

The SAS major's response was to hiss a reminder: 'Radio silence! Radio silence!'

But the voice at the rear was not to be quieted. 'We have four more vehicles in convoy!' he announced.

Unbelievably, a small group of German vehicles had tagged themselves onto the end of the much larger British force. Thankfully, in short order the SAS turned off south-east, heading into the Yonne. The enemy vehicles continued straight on, and as they parted company both sides bade their farewells with a last wave.

'I think it was on that journey that I felt most friendly towards the enemy,' Close would remark of their incredible foray through hostile territory, 'probably for the one and only time during the war.' By the time Marsh had led the convoy safely to Harrison's redoubt in the Yonne, he'd proved how sheer audacity and breath-taking bluff could win the day. But now that Marsh had spirited in such a potent fighting force, the time for the smile-and-wave act was over.

Right away, he and Harrison dispatched patrols to all corners of their area of operations, charged to 'seek targets and destroy'. Close and his eight-man troop set out in four jeeps, establishing a temporary camp near the town of Châtillon-en-Bazois, over an hour's drive south of Harrison's Forêt de Merry-Vaux base. Ensconced in thick woodland, once the jeeps had been driven up the dirt track it was easy enough to use cut tree branches to brush their tracks away.

With the vehicles thus concealed, the men dug shallow trenches beneath the bushes, which provided basic cover and would double as their sleeping quarters, and then established a sentry watch. The jeeps were heavily loaded with rations, and while open fires were a total no-no, with mess tins balanced over the small, smokeless paraffin blocks they carried in their kit – almost akin to fire-lighters – they got busy brewing up hot meals and the all-important mugs of tea.

While the tea was a straightforward affair, meals were not. For 'security reasons', all the labels had been removed from the tins, and nearly all of their food was tinned. The idea was that a discarded tin sans label could not betray the presence of the British troops. 'But it also meant we did not know what was in the tins,' Borrie remarked. 'You might open two, to find you had stewed steak and rubber-like processed cheese for dinner, or some other unlikely combination.' One of Close's troopers, Chris Tilling, didn't seem to mind much. They took it in turns to cook, and Tilling's solution was simply to 'dap it all in'. That became his nickname – 'Dap-it-in-Tilling.'

With their camp set, Close and his men studied their maps, working out exactly where they would concentrate their efforts to try to ambush the enemy. Forty eight hours later they hit solid gold, or so it would seem. A tradesman in Châtillon-en-Bazois had passed them some hot information: a German convoy was due through their region in the next hour or so. It was mid-morning, and they would have to move fast if they were to catch it. Hurriedly, Close and his men made one final check on their Vickers guns and grenades, before all four jeeps trundled down the track, and turned west onto the road leading towards Châtillon-en-Bazois. Ahead lay several sharp bends with good cover to either side. They selected an open stretch between two curves, and began to disperse the jeeps along the straight, with each hidden in the thick trees.

Close's plan was pretty straightforward. His jeep, the last in line, would open fire on the lead vehicles, so halting the convoy.

That would be the trigger for the others to unleash hell, raking a long stretch of what should then be a stationary line of vehicles with a torrent of rounds. The aim was to cause 'maximum damage when the convoy stopped.' To their rear lay a track heading north into the depths of the forest. When massively outnumbered, as they were bound to be, it was essential to be able to hit hard and to run just as effectively. Ambush sprung, that track would be their route of escape.

As Borrie backed their jeep into cover, he was thankful that he'd only recently serviced their Vickers guns. Each hundred-round magazine had been emptied, oiled and then rearmed with that magical mixture of bullets – 'one ordinary, one tracer, one armour-piercing, one explosive in that order all the way through, then rewind the springs to the correct tension.' Despite such preparations, Close's patrol were almost caught unprepared. They were still shunting their jeeps into position, when the grunt of engines sounded from the far side of the bend, and a first vehicle came into view.

In pole position was a motorcycle outrider, with a MP40 sub-machine gun slung across his chest. Behind came a far juicier target – a German staff car, painted in its signature mottled-grey camouflage. Beyond that was a truck crammed with heavily armed troops, and then behind it again was another covered truck, and then another and another. After a while Close stopped counting. All his concentration was focused on the lead vehicles, as he tried to judge just how close he could allow them to get before opening fire, thus ensuring the maximum number would be caught in the ambush.

When he judged the time was right, he got his driver to ease forward a fraction, and then his twin Vickers spat flame. The first burst cut down the outrider, his motorbike sliding across the road in a hail of sparks and crashing into a nearby ditch.

Swinging his guns onto the staff car, Close saw its windows shatter in a shower of glass, as a line of jagged bullet holes were torn in the bodywork, the figures inside slumping forward as they died. The vehicle's lone gunner managed to squirt off a few rounds from his machinegun, before he too fell.

All along Close's line of jeeps, muzzles sparked, as a good dozen or more Vickers pounded in the fire. Those troops riding in the first truck leapt free and tried to find cover beneath the wreckage of the staff car, or behind the engine block of their own vehicle. As Close and his comrades ripped into the convoy, more figures were cut down, but those who survived began to fight back, darting out from cover to unleash the odd burst. Close swept his gun right, the storm of bullets from the twin muzzles punching through the second and third trucks, even as desperate figures made for the cover of the ditch on the far side of the road. From one of the jeeps someone lobbed a grenade. It sailed over a truck, exploding on the far side in a flash of orange and gout of thick black smoke.

The fire from the dismounted troops was becoming worrisome, and Close ordered one of his men to concentrate on keeping their heads down. But there was worse to come. One of the trucks, about midway along the stranded column, had come to a halt broadside on to the jeeps. In an instant, the canvas side had dropped away, to reveal a pair of machineguns mounted on tripods to either end of the truck bed. The moment the canvass fell, they opened fire, but thankfully that first burst went high. Moments later, they'd adjusted their aim, and a storm of rounds went hammering perilously low over the jeeps.

Figuring they had to be 'Spandaus' – the belt-fed MG34 machinegun – those enemy guns could more than match the Vickers-K's rate of fire, as Close well appreciated. Nicknamed 'Hitler's buzzsaw' by Allied troops, it could hammer out 1,200 rounds per minute, and right now they were engaging at very close quarters. The next bursts were too close for comfort, but in this duel to the death the SAS proved quicker. Having swung his twin Vickers around, Close opened up on the nearest MG34, saturating its gun team with deadly fire. To his right, another of the jeeps took on the second Spandau, and again the duel proved an unequal one, for that gun also fell silent.

It was a very large convoy, and Close couldn't see the tail end of it. By now, some five trucks had been reduced to burning wrecks, and others were damaged, plus the staff car was finished. Scattered across the road and under the vehicles were many dead. The terrible cries of the injured rent the air, even as the cacophony of fire pulsed back and forth. But above the hellish din, Close detected another noise now, one that he had least expected. From the opposite direction he could hear the grunt of powerful engines. It could only be a second enemy patrol, drawn here by the smoke, the firing and the explosions.

An instant later Close gave the signal to break contact. They'd wreaked havoc, but were in grave danger of getting trapped between two powerful enemy forces. He paused as the two furthest jeeps swung around and took to the track leading deep into the woodland. But as the third went to depart, so a burst of fire struck the driver in the hand, and he lost control of the vehicle, which careered into the roadside ditch. In a flash, Borrie had seized the initiative. Reversing his jeep alongside the trapped vehicle, they dragged the first of the stranded men onto their jeep, and then Borrie, cool as a cucumber, got hold of the wounded man and manhandled him aboard.

There was zero time to inspect his wounds. Enemy troops were swarming aboard their machinegun truck, preparing to get the Spandaus working once more. As the SAS raiders hared off into the forest, they heard 'bullets zipping past and smacking into the trees all around', but the enemy gunners couldn't seem to get a clear shot. Moments later the firing ceased, and all that could be heard was the grunt of the jeeps' 'Go Devil' straight-four petrol engines, and the yells of alarm and agony echoing through the woods from behind.

Once they were a good distance away, Close called a halt. The eight men gathered for a heads-up. The adrenaline and the 'taut feeling of excitement' was draining away, to be replaced by the caution of the hunted. They decided against returning to their camp directly, for to do so they'd need to travel on open highways. Instead, they identified a remote patch of woodland to hole up for the night. It was isolated from any human settlements, which should help guard against enemy reprisals. Not having thought to bring much food, 'dinner' was steaming tea and 'biscuits', over which they exchanged stories of the battle. As an SAS section, it was their first time in action, and for four of their number – Borrie included – it was the first time they had ever faced the enemy in combat. On balance, they felt they had done pretty well.

In fact, the impression those eight men had left must have been utterly fearsome. After the departure of the SAS jeeps, the war-ravaged enemy convoy had reversed course, and headed back to Nevers, the city from which it had set out earlier that morning. In its wake it left a trail of burned-out trucks and overturned cars. That evening, a heavy force of German troops did return to the ambush spot, to comb the woodlands thereabouts, but of course they found no one. By then, Close and his men were long gone.

They had struck from the forest like ghosts, and faded away just as quickly.

Chapter Three

THE WILD GEESE

With no medic to hand, the treatment given to Lance Corporal Joe Craig, the injured member of their patrol, was basic in the extreme. They soaked a 'piece of fairly clean cloth' in antiseptic and proceeded to stuff it right through the wound, 'in one side and out the other,' after which they bound it up with a fresh bandage. Amazingly, within a week or so it had 'healed up beautifully'.

Long before then, they had a surprise intruder at their forest camp. The first sign was a decidedly plummy voice crying out: 'Are you there? I think you are somewhere there!'

The next moment a figure appeared riding through the forest on a bicycle, dressed for all the world like an English country squire. Bedecked in tweeds from head to toe, he even had the unmistakable form of a deerstalker hat perched atop his head. Here in the depths of Nazi-occupied France it was quite incredible. Close let the mystery figure cycle on by, for he just didn't know what to make of it all. He wondered if the man was some kind of bizarre Gestapo plant. Or was the seemingly inconceivable true – was this parody of an English country gentleman somehow genuine, and possibly trying to proffer some kind of help?

Fortunately, Close had a French SAS man embedded within his

patrol – Corporal Johnny Barongelle. Once the lone cyclist had given up calling and searching, Close asked Barongelle to pull on the set of civvie clothing that he'd brought with him – blue trousers, shirt, beret and the all-important shoes; British army boots were a dead giveaway – and sally forth to seek answers. A while later Barongelle was back, grinning broadly. Their odd visitor was well-known thereabouts. He was the Marquis de Pracontol, and he lived in a nearby chateau with his Scottish wife. He was also a well-known Anglophile, not to mention a bastion of the Resistance.

Close remained sceptical. He decided to arrange a meeting in neutral territory, so as not to betray the location of their camp. Using Barongelle's good offices, a message was got to the Marquis de Pracontol, setting the time and place for the rendezvous, which lay just off a stretch of nondescript highway. Only Close and Barongelle went forward to meet him. The rest remained in the camp, on high alert. The appointed time came and there was no sign of the marquis. But just as Close was about to leave, a figure appeared.

Turning off the road he strode into the trees, and Close was able to get a proper look: 'trilby hat, tweed jacket, collar and tie, with breeches stuck into gaiters.' There was a moment of tension as Close stepped into view, his carbine tucked under one arm, before the stranger darted forward and thrust out a hand in greeting.

'Good afternoon, Lieutenant. I'm sorry to be late. I was busy when the baker telephoned me. I am happy to meet you. My name is Pracontol.' The 'baker' was Johnny Barongelle's chief contact in the nearby town.

Close was finding it hard to credit that he was really here, deep in hostile territory, meeting with a 'French aristocrat dressed like an English gentleman and speaking impeccable English'.

The marquis went on to explain that he was a great friend of the British, and appreciated how much they were assisting the French Resistance, as was he, as best he could. With much relish he described how very frightened the German forces had been, after Close's patrol had ambushed their convoy, and as they brought their dead and wounded into Châtillon-en-Bazois.

Then the marquis turned to the reason for his visit. He and his wife would like to host Close and his men for dinner at their chateau. It would be an honour, he explained, and he felt sure they would all appreciate a good solid meal. Close was dumfounded. On the one hand, it was all so polite and courteous, but on the other, if they were to be trapped by the enemy, where better than at the marquis' castle? Close demurred. They were on duty, and they had to safeguard their men and machines at all times.

The marquis was not to be so easily denied. His chateau was quite secure, he explained. In close to a thousand years it had never been taken. There was only the one way in, the gates were kept firmly locked, and the long driveway was overlooked by stout, crenellated walls. There was even a secret tunnel that led from the cellar under the nearby road and out towards the river, plus his friends in Châtillon-en-Bazois, the baker first and foremost, were in the habit of telephoning him a warning if ever the enemy were heading his way.

To Close it seemed almost impolite to decline a dinner invitation so graciously offered. He told the marquis that he would have to consult with his men. The decision was not his alone. The Frenchman understood completely. If they could make it, they should send a message via the baker, he suggested. In the hope that they would come, he would prepare a dinner and be ready to meet them at the chateau gates at 6.30 that evening.

They parted company, Close and Barongelle returning to their camp. All were keen to hear what had transpired. Was their base blown? Did they have to up sticks and move right away? They 'held a council not of "war" but of "trust"', as Close described it. After an animated discussion, it seemed clear to everyone that the marquis didn't have to invite them to dinner at his castle if he were an agent of the enemy. He knew the rough whereabouts of their base. He could have reported their presence long ago. Close decided they could go, but three men would remain with the jeeps in the chateau's courtyard, to be relieved halfway through the meal.

Plan set, the message was sent via the baker. At 6.30 on the dot, the convoy of jeeps rolled up to the chateau's grand entrance. Still fearing this was 'the most unwise decision' that he would ever make, Close explained to the marquis the precautions he wished to take. The Frenchman agreed wholeheartedly. In fact, he would go one better. The men guarding the jeeps would be served food and drink at their posts. Once inside the imposing chateau, they spied the massive kitchen, with 'the largest table I have ever seen', as Borrie described it. Some six feet wide, it would have seated 'at least 30 people,' and 'all the food was piled up along the centre, for you to help yourself, which of course we did!'

Moving to the grand dining room, Close found himself seated below a crystal chandelier, while above stretched a stone-vaulted ceiling, over walls heavy with aged paintings of the marquis' forebears. Close and his men were unwashed, badly shaven, and wearing clothes that they had been living in for days on end, but neither the marquis nor his feisty Scottish wife seemed to mind. Over innumerable courses at dinner, and as the wine flowed, the marquis waxed lyrical about how the French had weathered the brutal Nazi occupation, and about the stirrings of the Resistance.

In both city, town and shire, he recounted, the people's anger and shame at the defeat of France and the nation's subjugation were palpable. But in the countryside especially, from the earliest moment resistance had seemed possible. While the larger settlements were garrisoned by enemy troops, few villages and hamlets could be. That meant that intelligence could be gathered, as the rural folk went about their day-to-day business, tending their crops and livestock. Enemy troop movements; vital installations; locations of key commanders – all of that could be passed to the Resistance, as its forces gathered potency and form.

But of course, the Nazi occupation had fatefully divided France. Defeat and subjugation had spawned both collaborators and resisters, plus the far larger body of French men and women who had no choice but to keep their heads down and acquiesce. Pitting Frenchmen and Frenchwomen against each other, he feared that the deep enmities and the scars so caused would take generations to heal. For Close, the conversation provided a stunning insight into the realities of the war in France. In short, he suspected the insight and understanding so gained would prove invaluable.

The marquis used this building as his summer residence, he explained. His main place of abode was his principal chateau, near Champlatreux, just outside of Paris. He invited Close to visit when the war was over. But for now, at least, neither the SAS commander nor any of his men were going anywhere. 'With all the wine we had drunk we had to stay overnight to recover,' as Borrie explained it. The following day, the marquis' wife briefed Close and his men about enemy strengths all through the area, before introducing them to the Mayor of Châtillon-en-Bazois as the 'Englishmen who have killed sixty of the enemy . . . and have come to liberate the town.'

Having bade farewell to the marquis and his wife, Close and his men decided to act upon some of the intelligence they had garnered from their hosts – the location of the nearest German military headquarters, in a large country house set in its own grounds. Taking a roundabout route to avoid enemy patrols, they reached a building that just had to be their target. Yet the scene appeared so peaceful, it seemed impossible that this could really be the place. Pulling their jeeps off the road, they settled down to watch, just in case it was 'the residence of a harmless French family'.

With the evening light fading, their patience was rewarded. At the rear of the house figures appeared, shadowy, but clearly identifiable by their uniforms. Minute by minute it was growing darker, and the raiders had a long way to fare to make it back to their base. Close decided to attack right away, executing a '"blind" shoot-up'. In that spirit they roared up the driveway. With Close's jeep taking pole position, and with the others flanking him, they gave the grand residence one hell of a wakeup call – a Vickers-K broadside. Wherever they spied movement, the .303 inch rounds tore through doors and windows, showers of shattered glass and wood tumbling down onto the grounds outside.

Having raked the entire façade from end to end, and spying no further movement, they inched the jeeps closer, searching for the slightest sign of life. Not a living thing showed behind shot-out windows and shattered doors. With darkness gathering, Close signalled that they should pull out. It was well into the night hours before they made it back to their base. It was hard to tell what damage that shoot-'em-up had done, but as they were soon to learn, half-a-dozen casualties had been caused in the melee, plus the building had been evacuated and was never occupied again by the enemy.

On withdrawing from that action, the jeeps had been motoring along a narrow lane and had knocked over a goose in the twilight. One of the vehicles had screeched to a halt, and those riding in it had grabbed the carcass and thrown it in the rear. It was too good a chance to miss; fresh meat for the evening's pot.

But a few miles later there was an explosion of yelling, for the goose had come back to life with a vengeance and was not best pleased. In an instant the jeep had come to a stop, and those riding in it had bailed out, as the rest of the patrol dissolved into laughter. 'With five machineguns and two pistols between them, they were being chased by an irate bird,' as Borrie recalled.

Having survived the wild goose attack, a message was received by radio from London. By a roundabout route, and checking out some local Maquis along the way, Close was ordered to rendezvous with Derrick Harrison and Tony Marsh. The bulk of C Squadron – their unit – was poised to move out, heading south towards the Morvan, a craggy region forming the northernmost extension of the Massif Central, one of France's chief mountain chains. Though the peaks in the Morvan were relatively low – the highest, Haut-Folin, was just shy of 3,000 feet – it was rugged, heavily forested country, interspersed with wild rivers and lakes, and far less bucolic than the Yonne.

There, one of the first SAS squadrons had parachuted into war in France. Indeed, the vanguard had dropped in even as Allied forces had hit the Normandy beaches. They'd been on the ground for weeks now, suffering from the horrendous weather that tended to dog the Morvan, plus a number of bruising and bloody confrontations with the enemy. In short, Mayne feared that many of those men in the Morvan were suffering from 'battle fatigue' and that they were in urgent need of being relieved. So, C Squadron was to head south, to take over where A Squadron would leave off in the Morvan.

One, much-reduced force was to remain in the Yonne, and it was not to be commanded by Close, Harrison or Marsh. Instead, one of Mayne's youngest officers, but a stalwart of operations, was to take over. In due course, a local French newspaper, *La Nièvre Libre*, a clandestine publication founded during the Nazi occupation, would recount his and Paddy Mayne's story, being among the first publication to reveal the presence of the SAS deep behind the lines in France. The article captured the essence of the man taking over in the Yonne, and of the SAS commander who accompanied him.

Headlined 'The first British Parachutists to land in France', the article opened by describing the appearance of a mysterious jeep-borne force, one that the reporter first mistook to be American. These soldiers, 'with the build of rugby players, surely belonged to American units'. But not a bit of it, the reporter continued. 'From the first jeep leaps to the ground a tall blond man with the epaulettes of an English colonel,' the article continued. 'He is followed by a captain with the eyes of a child.' Paddy Mayne and Captain Peter Davis had just arrived at a local hotel, on war-fighting business. Leaving a force on guard outside, they'd headed inside and the reporter had followed.

Sensing a story, he'd asked Mayne for an interview. But as Davis spoke impeccable French, it made sense for him to do the talking. In any case, Mayne would prefer his deputy to take the limelight. A student of modern languages at Cambridge University before the war, Davis's early military career had been dogged by ill-fortune. Born in India in 1921, he'd signed up to the army in 1940, still a teenager, but with high hopes of 'daring and glory'. Yet at officer training he'd found himself mired in the 'snobbery and ignorance' of the officer's mess. Deeply disillusioned, he'd volunteered for the SAS, finding 'a small body of men under young and intelligent officers who abhorred routine and spit and polish' and who coexisted in 'harmony and mutual respect'.

The youngest officer then serving with the SAS, by the summer of '44 Davis was still only twenty-three years old. With his 'baby-faced' look, it was little wonder that the French reporter had characterised him as having 'the eyes of a child'. But as events were to prove, Davis had the heart of a lion.

'Where did you earn your stripes?' the reporter asked Davis, for openers.

'I did the Libyan campaign . . .' Davis explained, 'and Rommel's damn Panzer Divisions gave us a lot of trouble . . . Then came Tunisia, the landings in Sicily and finally the war in Italy . . . where we engaged the enemy in violent combat.'

'How did you come to France?' was the next question.

'I arrived back in England . . . My superiors granted me permission – a short time to embrace my family – then, with my men, I underwent intense training in preparation for the Normandy landings . . . We English were ready to chase the Germans from French soil . . . We were determined to expel the Teutonic threat from these borders and to drive out this race of pretentious conquerors.'

At that juncture, the interview had to stop, for Mayne had called Davis away. The reporter wandered outside and chatted to one of the men on the jeeps instead. 'With the phlegm that so characterises the British,' he wrote, 'that man told me: "We are the first English to be parachuted into France. A few hours before the D-Day landings we were dropped into the very centre of your country."'

Before the reporter from La Nièvre Libre could dig any deeper into the story, Mayne signalled the convoy to get under way. There was work to be done.

The first overt sign that Captain Davis and his men were in the thick of the action was when a short radio message was received at SAS headquarters in London. It was 31 August 1944, and it read simply: 'From Capt. DAVIS. Action with strong enemy convoy on the LACHARITE–CLAMECY–AVALLON road. It is imperative that the bridge at LACHARITE be bombed and strafed. Action summary following.'

What had transpired was as follows. Harrison, Marsh, Close and all were preparing to leave for the Morvan, with Paddy Mayne in the vanguard, so that A Squadron could be relieved. Quartering enemy-occupied France by land and by air, Mayne had somehow managed to be in all places at once, or at least to appear wherever and whenever he was most needed, while at the same time miraculously avoiding the predations of the enemy.

As their convoy of jeeps had readied itself to depart, so Davis had set out on a mission of his own. With nine jeeps and two-dozen men, he commanded the Operation Kipling rump party. Crawling along the track leading away from their Fôret de Merry-Vaux base, a jeep overturned on the treacherous surface. Both men riding in it were injured, and Davis's deputy, Lieutenant Bryce, was forced to remain behind, to tend their wounds.

Reduced to seven jeeps and nineteen men even before battle was joined, Davis was determined to get in among it, for enemy convoys were rumoured to be moving along the N151, a major highway that passed through the region. But due to the delay with the overturned jeep and the wounded, it was well after nightfall by the time the raiders reached their intended ambush spot, a stretch of road adjacent to the village of Nannay, which lies some fifteen kilometres east of the town of La Charité-sur-Loire.

Overnighting in a patch of woodland, by nine o'clock the following morning there was still not a sniff of any movement on the highway. Impatient for action, Davis signalled the off, for they would seek out the enemy wherever they might find them. Even as the seven jeeps were manoeuvring onto the road, so the 'head of a German Convoy appeared about 300 yards away'. Seizing the initiative, two of Davis's men, Troopers Grierson and Pagan, swung their jeeps towards the enemy and the Vickers blazed fire. In the van of the enemy column were a saloon car and a truck packed with infantry. Within seconds Grierson and Pagan had found their targets, and .303-inch rounds were tearing into the lead vehicles.

But the German troops were quick to react, and it was no more than sixty seconds before a pair of enemy machineguns began to return fire, supported by ground troops with rifles and sub-machine guns. Sensing quick and decisive action was called for, Davis led one group of six men on foot to hit the enemy from the left flank, while one of his sergeants did the same on the right, as the pair of jeeps continued to hammer in fire. The survivors of the Vickers onslaught were hunkered down in a roadside ditch, and Davis managed to lead his patrol to within thirty yards of their position.

A 'lively small arms and grenade battle ensued.' For a good five minutes SAS and German troops traded blows, 'tossing grenades at each other like toffee apples', as Davis described it. As the battle reached its climax, Davis signalled Pagan's jeep forward, and directed it to spray the roadside ditches with Vickers fire. So effective was this combined foot and jeep assault, that Davis was able to fight his way through to the lead enemy vehicle. Dead and injured lay scattered around the saloon car. As Davis and his men gathered up the enemy's weaponry, he managed to seize a prisoner. He looked to be no more than eighteen years old, and seemed 'extremely scared'.

Facing the firepower and sheer aggression of the ambushers, the remainder of the enemy column turned tail, heading back the way it had come. 'Beyond occasional sniping it was again quiet,' Davis reported. In the wreckage of the saloon car he discovered an officer's map case. Turning to the prisoner, he demanded that he talk. Claiming to be a Pole press-ganged into service with the German military, he seemed 'only too willing' to tell all. The convoy hailed from the 338 (*Stamm-Kompanie*), a unit tasked with training German infantry. Some 350 strong, from what the prisoner, plus the documents in the map case, revealed, it was made up of 'two infantry companies, supported by a machinegun section, plus an anti-tank and anti-aircraft section'.

Having learned all he could, Davis ordered a withdrawal. Before pulling out, he made sure to tell the wounded enemy troops that he and his men were British, in an effort to guard against any reprisals. He added that they were the 'advance guard of a large force', just to put the fear of God into the enemy. Even as they pulled out, he could hear grenade blasts and mortars being fired, as the German column opened fire on imaginary targets and spent their ammunition upon ghosts. Davis had a feeling that the enemy would be back, and this time he was determined to be ready and waiting.

Having driven some three kilometres back towards Nannay village, he spied the perfect ambush spot. Three hundred yards from the road was a convenient hillock, with a thick hedge fringing the summit. To the rear lay the ideal escape route: a dirt track heading into the Forêt de Donzy, a dense woodland criss-crossed with a maze of further such pathways. Having eased the jeeps behind the cover of the hilltop hedge, the Vickers commanded a fabulous field of fire. Davis's patrol was also carrying some Ordnance ML 3-inch (81mm) mortars, and he got his gunners to site them so they menaced a long stretch of the roadway.

Ambush set.

That afternoon the hours clicked past slowly, the tension mounting. At one stage, a pair of villagers cycled up to Davis's position, to reveal that they had just been fired upon by the enemy. That would explain the machinegun and rifle shots that they'd heard a short while before. All sensed that their adversaries hadn't gone far. They were biding their time, before attempting another go at running the gauntlet of the La Charité-sur-Loire to Clamecy road. The evening shadows were lengthening by the time Davis and his men detected their first concrete signs of the enemy – and what a sight it was.

Nosing out from the same direction as before, they spied the vanguard of a massive force. At least thirty vehicles strong, at the head rode a phalanx of scout cars – light armoured vehicles, but still far more robust than the SAS's thin-skinned, open-topped jeeps. Behind them came some three-dozen military trucks, and several were towing Flak 30 20mm wheeled cannons, chiefly an anti-aircraft weapon, but equally devastating in a ground-fire role. As was glaringly obvious, the enemy had more than enough firepower to make mincemeat out of Davis's patrol. Yet in truth, the ambushers didn't know the half of what they were facing.

As luck – or sod's law – would have it, the convoy ground to a halt directly below their hilltop position. The only possible reason for doing so had to be to clear the nearby village of Nannay, that was unless someone had betrayed Davis and his men to the enemy. Working on the adage that it was best to strike first and strike hard, the young SAS captain gave the signal and the combined firepower of some fourteen Vickers-K guns let rip. 'We knocked hell out of them for five minutes, firing about four thousand rounds of tracer and incendiary,' Davis would remark of the battle that ensued.

The enemy's response was immediate and blistering. Within seconds they had started returning deadly accurate fire. More to the point, three of the trucks dropped their canvas sides, revealing a Flak 30 cannon, a mortar and a machinegun mounted within. Immediately, those weapons opened up, 20mm cannon rounds and mortar bombs blasting into Davis's position, and exploding on all sides. The very air seemed alive with tracer. The battle was murderously intense, yet first blood fell to the SAS as one truck, then another, and finally a staff car burst into flames. By now, Davis had spied German troops streaming up the slope, aiming to surround his position, plus he feared the scout cars were racing around to his rear.

It was high time to bug out. Breaking fire and roaring down the rear slope of the hill, Davis's jeep made a beeline for the forest, the other vehicles doing likewise. Going like the clappers, it was now a case of every jeep crew for itself. Davis had set a rendezvous point (RV) in the depths of the Forêt de Donzy. While his jeep reached it relatively unscathed, at least one round had torn through its windscreen, and when a second vehicle turned up, it proved to have a bullet lodged in the spare tyre bolted to its rear. The last jeep to reach the RV had been chased by a German scout car most of the way, but worst of all two jeeps and five men were found to be missing.

Davis lingered at the RV for a good sixty minutes, by which time it was nightfall. He was reluctant to tarry any longer, for 'fear of being surrounded'. Instead, they would pull back to Donzy village itself, which lay some nineteen kilometres north of the ambush point. Even as they withdrew, they could hear wild firing, as 'the enemy continued to give battle hotly for one-and-a-half hours.' Spooked once more, the enemy were loosing-off at mirages and at ghosts. 'They must have got through a devil of a lot of ammunition firing at nothing at all,' Davis would remark.

After overnighting near Donzy, Davis and his men ventured into the village the following morning to make contact with the Resistance. There, they discovered four of their missing men. They had been guided to the village by sympathetic locals, their jeeps having been riddled with fire and put out of action. Davis's final missing man, a Corporal Connor, turned up soon after. Amid the melee of the battle, Connor had been captured by the enemy. But not for long. As German troops had continued to fire upon each other, a mortar bomb had landed near by, sending Connor's captors diving for cover. Giving the nearest one 'a hefty kick in the stomach', Connor had made a break for it and got clean away. So it was that after two such audacious ambushes on the same stretch of road, Davis's force was minus two jeeps but had suffered not a single casualty.

Local villagers reported in the fullest detail what had transpired. After Davis's first attack, the enemy had returned in force, placing seven anti-tank guns along the roadway while they combed the woods for the British ambushers. Finding no one but their own wounded, they had seized and executed two locals. That evening, their convoy had set out once more, only to run into Davis and his men for a second time. Late into the night ambulances were seen beating back and forth from the ambush site evacuating casualties, and there were reports of forty to fifty dead, with twice as many wounded.

Once again, the enemy convoy had retraced its steps to La Charité-sur-Loire, only this time there were some fifteen wrecked vehicles in tow. At one stage during the battle, a German officer had decided to shoot two of his own men, in an effort to force the others to fight. Knowing their attackers were British, the enemy commanders feared a much more concerted assault was coming. Once back in La Charité, they had barricaded the entrances to the town, sited antitank guns and mortars, and put a heavy force on watch. So, in addition to the death, injury and material damage caused, the blow to the enemy's morale must have been devastating.

This was something the SAS had learned from the earliest days of its operations. If hidden forces were able to strike seemingly at will deep behind enemy lines, it drove a coach and horses through any sense that enemy troops could be safe, no matter where they might be. Increasingly, the SAS had learned to target their senior commanders, for all the obvious reasons. With no one left in charge, no orders could be given, and all fell into chaos and ruin. And equally, if no man was safe, no matter his rank, that fuelled a further collapse in the enemy's morale. Increasingly, the SAS would concentrate on doing just that, or 'cutting the head off the Nazi snake', as they termed it.

Here on the road running east from La Charité-sur-Loire, Davis and his men had certainly achieved all of that and more. But the SAS captain was far from done. His final action in the Yonne would be the most audacious yet. A report came in of over 18,000 German troops seeking to surrender to the Allies. Their position lay an hour south of Davis's base, at the town of Nevers, but that didn't much deter him, and neither did his comparatively lowly rank. In his own report on the incident, Davis described how he promoted himself in the field to 'the rank of Colonel, with a view to making it more easy for the Germans to surrender . . . Left camp at 1800 hrs with twelve jeeps.'

Making it up as he went along, Davis composed a letter addressed to the German commander, arguing that he had been 'detailed by General PATTON to take charge of his surrender and disarm his men'. Having crossed the Loire – the river runs through Nevers – Davis learned of a massive German column up ahead. He went forward to investigate, having first attached a 'very large white flag' to his jeep and seeking to parlay. The senior German officer he encountered was an *oberstleutnant* – a lieutenant colonel. That man confirmed that yes, in excess of 18,000 German troops under General Botho Elster had been poised to surrender. But in fact they had already done so . . . to Generals Robert C. Macon and Otto P. Weyland of the American military.

Beaten to it by a whisker, 'Colonel' Davis removed the white flag from his jeep, executed an about-turn and motored back north. Another member of C Squadron, Lieutenant Mike Mycock, had just recently accepted the surrender of 3,000 demoralised German troops, so the theory behind Davis's actions had been sound. For his actions in the Yonne, Davis would be awarded the Military Cross. His citation lauded the ambushes around Nannay village, facing a force 'vastly superior in numbers of men and much more heavily armed', during which Davis behaved with 'coolness and calculated determination' ensuring that 'not one of his men suffered the slightest injury'.

By the time Davis and his crew had made it back to their Fôret de Merry-Vaux base camp, the entire place was more or less deserted. The remainder of C Squadron had slipped south, making towards their new area of operations.

They were headed to the Morvan, a place where Hitler's war with hate would truly come of age.

Chapter Four

FALLEN AMONG SPARTANS

Two months before 'Colonel' Davis had attempted to take the surrender of General Elster's corps, a large body of SAS had prepared to board a flight of waiting warplanes. It was June 1944, and Allied forces had landed in Normandy and were fighting to hold the beachheads. The mission of the SAS was a simple, yet vital one. They were to drop deep into France, seeking to 'sabotage the enemy's lines of communication and sources of supply'. The aim was to stop the forces of Nazi Germany from reinforcing their positions along the coast, and from driving the Allies back into the sea.

Targets were of a twofold nature. The first were those pre-identified in Britain as being vital to destroy – rail lines, and other key infrastructure. Second were those that the SAS would discover for themselves on the ground, such as trains loaded with fuel and ammo. At times, targets might be transmitted by radio to London, for the RAF to launch airstrikes, plus crucial intelligence on enemy strengths and movements was also to be sent through. Presuming the Normandy landings were successful, the secondary mission of the SAS was then to hound and harass enemy forces as they attempted to retreat east, towards Germany itself. All told, the SAS would execute more than forty separate missions across France over the summer and autumn of 1944, involving the men of two British regiments, plus two French regiments and a Belgian squadron.

The fifty-odd souls gathered for tonight's flight were some of the earliest to attempt to drop into France. But nothing was ever for certain when climbing the steps of a giant Short Stirling four-engine 'heavy', an aircraft originally designed as a bomber, but converted into a makeshift jump-platform by having a large slot, affectionately known as 'the bathtub', sunk into the belly of its fuselage. Through that the SAS parachutists would plummet, arms and legs tight together, and as quickly as possible, for drop zones (DZs) in rural France were never overly large.

But that was only if they got the green light to go. Often, aircraft were forced to turn back. The weather could prove impossible, and over the Morvan, tonight's intended destination, it tended to be famously dank, mist-shrouded and drear. Often, the reception party that was supposed to be waiting on the ground – signal fires and torches marking out the DZ – was nowhere to be seen. Sometimes, the pilots and navigator failed to find the right spot. Sometimes, the warplane would get pounced on by an enemy fighter or get pounded by flak, and only barely manage to limp back to British shores. Just occasionally, an entire aircraft – and the men she carried – would be lost without trace.

Among those SAS mustering at RAF Fairford – their place of departure – a tall, strapping fellow somehow caught the eye. Almost the odd-one-out, there were few outward signs to suggest that he was different, but decidedly different he was. At around six feet two in height, and with a broad, rugby player's physique, beneath the shock of unruly dark hair he had the calm, level gaze and the classic good looks of a Greek god. He had the air of a man who could handle himself on the sports field, in the boxing ring, or at the height of battle. But in truth, when the story of his exploits in France hit the newspapers in the winter of 1944, the headlines would read: 'PADRE . . . DROPPED WITH THE PARATROOPS. SAS men attended church in German-held fields.'

Uniquely among the men milling around that airbase, he was heading into war unarmed. Instead, he carried with him a few bibles, an oaken cross, plus a silk altar cloth died maroon, and – somewhat incongruously, perhaps – emblazoned with the SAS's winged dagger emblem and motto, *Who dares wins*. As far as he knew, no padre had ever parachuted in with the SAS deep behind the lines, but he was determined to blaze the trail. And knowing 1 SAS to be a singing regiment – the men were forever breaking into song – he had packed as many hymn books as he could carry.

Typically, a few notes of song rang out through the dusk air, drifting across RAF Fairford via the Tannoy system. It was the unmistakable tones of the Regimental Sergeant Major singing the SAS's de facto anthem, one that they had borrowed from their arch-rivals, the Afrika Korps. When waging war across North Africa, they had grown accustomed to camping out of an evening, waiting to raid an enemy base, only to hear the garrison raising their voice in song, to the poignant, soul-searching tune of 'Lili Marlene', a German love song that had become popular among their forces during the war.

Over time, the SAS had stolen that tune, bastardised the words and made it their own. So much so, that when Paddy Mayne's forces had sailed from North Africa back to Britain to begin training for the D-Day operations, the German POWs who were likewise packed aboard that ship had been utterly flummoxed. When first they'd heard Sergeant Bob Bennett, a tough-as-old-boots cockney and veteran raider, belting out what they saw as *their* anthem, they were 'mightily puzzled'. As Bennet's 'rich baritone voice' gave a daily rendering of what sounded for all the world like 'Lili Marlene', they'd gradually come to accept it, and finally to be entertained, but of course, it was doubtful if they could actually understand the words.

The first two verses that floated across Fairford aerodrome that June evening – every word and cadence known to all by heart – calmed the nerves and stiffened the blood of those poised to drop into the unknown.

There was a song we always used to hear,
Out in the desert, romantic, soft and clear,
Over the ether, came the strain,
That soft refrain, each night again,
To you, Lili Marlene, to you Lili Marlene.

Check you're in position; see your guns are right,
Wait until the convoy comes creeping through the night,
Now you can pull the trigger, son,
And blow the Hun to Kingdom come,
And Lili Marlene's boyfriend will never see Marlene . . .

The final verse of the SAS's composition – which, incidentally, had been penned by Paddy Mayne himself – was a pointer to the future; to where all the Allied efforts were focused now, as the fortunes of the war truly turned.

Afrika Korps has sunk into the dust,
Gone are the Stukas, its Panzers lie in rust,
No more we'll hear that haunting strain,
That soft refrain, each night again,
For Lili Marlene's boyfriend will never see Marlene.

Oddly, perhaps, for a man of God, the padre had caught the Lili Marlene bug just as strongly as anyone. Mayne had issued his men with a set of song sheets, which included their version of 'Lili Marlene', with a note typed beneath the title reading: 'With apologies to Africa Corps.' Along the bottom of each sheet ran the invocation 'If you can't sing, hum or whistle!!!!' There was never any excuse not to raise a voice in Mayne's SAS, and during training at Darvel the padre had proved the perfect candidate to provide accompaniment on the piano.

Having volunteered for a singing regiment, the padre had learned to belt out the words to 'Lili Marlene' along with the best of them. They'd be singing in the officer's mess far into the night, and the same with the sergeant's mess too. No one who served in the SAS ever heard that haunting melody without a 'quickening of the pulse and a stab of recollection'. For the padre, as for every man in that elite force, Lili Marlene was the song they cherished most of all. It was the symbol of their regimental esprit de corps and their 'common bond'.

As the final lines drifted over Fairford airbase, Padre the Rev. J. Fraser McLuskey, chaplain to 1 SAS, joined the other men boarding the three waiting planes. With all the religious paraphernalia he was carrying, he had almost forgotten to pack his little folding pocket knife. In retrospect, it would prove to be a lifesaver. As McLuskey went to scramble up into the 'gloom of the fuselage', he paused to shake hands with those seeing him off, and was all-but blown off the ladder by the backwash of the four Bristol Hercules engines, which were spooling up to speed.

Major Tommy Langton, who commanded the Headquarters section, was there, full of bonhomie and a few last words of encouragement for those about to depart. So too was Major Phil Gunn, the SAS's superlative medical officer (MO). McLuskey and Gunn had studied at Edinburgh University together, and the SAS padre was pleased to shake the SAS medic's hand as they parted, especially since Gunn was so revered by the men. With the last aboard – they were sixteen in this aircraft – the door slammed shut, and the padre felt the giant warplane swing around as the tyres gripped the runway and the aircrew readied for take-off.

A short pause, and then, with the roar of the engines thundering in his ears, the Stirling gathered speed and took to the darkening skies. A three-and-a-half-hour flight lay ahead, to speed them to the Morvan, if all went to plan. A familiar figure, Captain Laurence Roy Bradford, was seated nearest to the bathtub, for he would lead the jump. The morning after the padre's somewhat shock posting to the SAS – he had had no idea what kind of unit he was joining – it was with Bradford that he'd sat down to breakfast. In fact, the padre had been sandwiched between Bradford, a Devon man, on the one side, and Lieutenant Les Cairns, like McLuskey a Scot, on the other.

For whatever reason, the padre had barely taken his seat before he'd realised that he felt 'completely at home'. Chatting with Bradford and Cairns, he'd decided that 'if this particular unit would have me, this was where I would stay.' What had struck him most, apart from the friendliness of all, was their extreme youth. He'd noticed an officer across the table – 'fair hair and strikingly handsome features' – who looked no more than twenty-three or twenty-four years old. Yet he commanded an entire squadron and wore the ribbon of the DSO. That, of course, was Major Tony Marsh.

The padre had just come from an informal and entirely unexpected kind of interview with Lieutenant-Colonel Mayne. He noted, just as quickly, that everyone in the mess referred to their commander simply as 'Paddy'. Only a very few old hands could do so to his face, yet 'never, either by officers or men, did I hear him called anything else.' Paddy, then, was the padre's new chief;

little did McLuskey know that this would be the start of a wonderful partnership, SAS commander to SAS man of God.

McLuskey was slated to go as the ninth jumper, so leading the second stick of eight men. As he gazed around the Stirling's darkened hold, he noted the silhouette of the tail-gunner far aft, and the 'occasional glimpse of sky' through the slit-like portholes. The aircraft's dispatcher had the unenviable job of ushering all sixteen men out through the jump-hatch; 'of yelling "GO!" in such a way that one just "Goes!"' With no fighters flying escort, and heading deep into hostile airspace, these flights truly ran the gauntlet. Yet the RAF dispatchers were obliged to undertake fifteen such sorties, before they might be transferred to less risk-laden duties. To a man the SAS saw these unsung heroes of the RAF as 'smashing blokes'.

It was too dark to read, but as they passed over the French coast the aircrew reported that the fires raging in Cherbourg were clearly visible. Below the lumbering aircraft – 'steady as a London bus, if not a good bit steadier', as the padre described her – the extent of the Allied invasion forces was laid out before them; warships, landing craft, makeshift harbours, armour and men stretching across the Normandy beaches from horizon to horizon. And on the far side, the enemy positions. But as McLuskey well appreciated, they were on their way to wage their 'own private war' behind these frontlines.

The padre's had been no privileged upbringing. Scotland born and bred, the family had fallen upon hard times, moving to the tall, dreary tenements found in the less salubrious parts of Edinburgh's South Side. His father had lost the family laundry business, uprooting the entire McLuskey clan. From troubled beginnings, the self-effacing young McLuskey had pulled himself up by his bootstraps, and by war's outbreak he'd been a padre at

Glasgow University with a thriving parish. He was also happily married to Irene Calaminus, a German pastor's daughter.

McLuskey had met Irene in 1938, when touring Nazi Germany as a young divinity graduate. There he'd witnessed at first-hand how the Nazi state had stamped its iron control over all forms life in Germany, including the church. Any power – any system – even belief in God, was viewed as a threat to the all-controlling grip of the Reich. In short, belief in anything but National Socialism was dangerous. Senior Nazis promoted so-called *Positives Christentum* – 'Positive Christianity' – a credo that denied the Jewish roots of the faith and sought to replace the Bible and the cross with *Mein Kampf* and the swastika.

With war's outbreak McLuskey and his wife had agreed that the scourge of Nazism had to be fought, and the padre would have to do his bit. At first he'd agonised about whether he should volunteer as a combatant or a man of God. Eventually, he'd gone for a strange kind of a hybrid – he'd be a padre, but in an elite airborne combat unit.

At jump school he'd been thrown in with a mixed bag of typical rough-and-tough paratrooper types. But McLuskey was no fading violet. When it had come to the 'milling' – the obligatory three-minute, nose-to-nose test of raw aggression and fighting power – he'd stayed the course and hadn't needed any more 'patching-up' than most of his opponents. In fact, of the four padres on that jump course, one, the ironically named Goode, had delighted all by 'smiting his opponents in the boxing ring in a most un-clerical and unbrotherly fashion'.

A ham-fisted jumper, McLuskey was in the habit of 'landing like a tonne of bricks'; it was the first time in his life that he'd actually seen stars. He was forever getting ribbed, due to his habit of taking out his false teeth before executing the jump, and secreting them in a pocket of his jump smock, 'so placed that it would be hard for them to bite me'. Despite such trials, he'd weathered his eight jumps. 'Well, Padre, you've diced with death eight times!' was how his jump instructor delivered the good news. He'd won his wings and 'there can have been few awards which gave such satisfaction.'

Once jump-qualified, the padre needed to be assigned to a unit. It turned out that all the vacancies in the Parachute Battalion had already been filled. There was but one opening left. A unit calling itself the Special Air Service was in need of a chaplain. What was this outfit, McLuskey had asked? No one seemed to know. It was frightfully secret and all very hush-hush. The one upside for McLuskey was that the mysterious Special Air Service was headquartered in Ayrshire, so not so far from home.

He'd caught the train to Kilmarnock Station, itself a short drive from Darvel. A car took him to the headquarters, which turned out to be a pleasant house set in thickly wooded grounds, lying at the end of a very long and very bumpy driveway. It was early in the morning, possibly too early for breakfast, but the front door stood open and so the padre had wandered in.

He was met by an unusual situation. The dining room seemed busy, if somewhat somnolent, and around the embers of the fireplace slumped several officers in a state of repose. What made it all the odder was that a 'small and exceedingly wheezy gramophone' was blaring out the sounds of 'Mush-Mush-Mush, Tooral-i-addy' – something of an Irish fighting song.

Oh, 'twas there I learned readin' and writin'
At Bill Bracket's where I went to school
And 'twas there I learned howlin' and fightin'
From my schoolmaster Mr O'Toole.
Him and me, we had many-a scrimmage,
And the devil a copy I wrote.

There was ne'er a garsún* in the village,
Dared tread on the tail of me . . .
Mush, Mush, Mush tural-i-addy
Singin' Mush, Mush, Mush tural-i-ay.
There was ne'er a garsún in the village,
Dared tread on the tail of me coat.

The party at the fireplace – some of whom seemed more dead than alive – may well have been up all night, the padre figured. Among their number McLuskey noticed an exceedingly large individual lever himself to his feet and heave himself in his general direction. While he didn't quite demand to know who the devil the newcomer was and what the devil he was doing there, the padre got the impression that was what was being asked of him. Noticing the man's lieutenant colonel insignia – it was Paddy Mayne, of course – McLuskey tried explaining that he was the new unit padre, but it was immediately clear that 1 SAS had not been expecting one.

Still, a padre had come, Mayne declared, and thus the padre must have breakfast. In any other unit as war-hardened as this, such an unexpected newcomer might have felt 'acutely uncomfortable'. McLuskey had no combat experience and no battle honours, and he had 'never seen so many decorated men together before'. Yet he quickly realised that here, the 'most experienced of the operatives were those who took themselves least seriously; and provided you fitted in, you were made one of this distinguished family.' Some didn't fit in, of course, and they simply didn't last. In a unit such as this, there could be no other way. 'Men were individuals, and everyone mattered.'

About 350 strong at the time, everyone seemed to know

---

* In Irish, a 'garsún' is an idiotic boy or a troublemaker.

everyone in 1 SAS. There was little formal discipline, but 'no unit in any army ever possessed a greater degree of loyalty,' as the padre quickly came to appreciate. All were volunteers and each had been hand-picked. The very idea of being '"returned to unit" was a nightmare . . . And so there was a good deal of discipline self-imposed.' Due to their unorthodox training and role, coupled with the long years spent at war behind enemy lines, these men had a somewhat fluid grasp on 'the conventions and even the laws of society. Learning to live dangerously had weakened the sanctions of the normal . . .' But the padre got that. It had to be hard trying to live in two very different worlds by one set of rules.

As McLuskey was soon to learn, while the unit trained hard it partied even harder. Often, too much drink was consumed by too few, but such revelries were born out of a fellowship that was utterly genuine and sincere. That these men extended 'so freely their trust and their friendship' humbled the new arrival. They had offered him a precious, irreplaceable gift. He had never 'lived with such a group of men before . . . It was easy to be brave in their company and difficult to be a coward.'

Realising that the SAS was preparing to parachute deep behind the lines, the padre was determined not to be left behind. He argued for a frontline role, but that meant doing all the same training as the men. Shortly, he was 'out on schemes, splitting up into small parties of five or six . . . living off the land, sleeping by day and moving only by night.' These were no-holds-barred affairs, in which the Home Guard and the police played an enemy hunter-force, and each SAS patrol was set some kind of impossible-seeming challenge, often to travel from A to B by whatever means and without being caught.

In this manner, and as the padre observed, 'at least one fire engine went temporarily astray', electrifying the countryside as it went charging about manned by seemingly 'irresponsible ruf-fians' and with its bell clanging to the rhythm of 'Lili Marlene'. No means of conveyance or concealment was off-limits, and in this way a Royal Naval submarine was 'unaccountably seized and held by a group of madmen who didn't seem to know that armies are supposed to operate on land'. While such unorthodox behaviour was accompanied by a great deal of derring-do and high spirits, as all appreciated, soon the Home Guard would be replaced by the Gestapo and SS, at which point the lessons learned would surely prove invaluable.

After months of training and partying hard, McLuskey found himself the only man aboard that Stirling poised to drop into Nazi-occupied France unarmed, and deeply unsure what might lie in store when he got there. In fact, he'd often wondered whether he should be carrying a weapon. Like this, was he an unfair burden on his friends? But as he was soon to learn, 'they liked to see the padre without the weapons they had to carry. They wished to see in him a man of peace . . .' and equally a 'symbol that the arms they must bear were dedicated to the cause of peace . . .'

As the Stirling droned onwards, McLuskey dropped off to sleep. It was a nudge in the ribs that woke him, as the all-important mug of tea was passed around. For whatever reason – flak, enemy fighters – the pilot threw the giant aircraft into a series of evasive manoeuvres, and for a while 'control of the tea mug' demanded his total attention.

Eventually, the dispatcher gave a cry: 'Half an hour to go!'

Figures lumbered to their feet, grabbing their kitbags and struggling to strap them to their legs, before McLuskey realised that in all the chaos his helmet and gloves had gone missing.

Voices began yelling: 'The padre's helmet! The padre's gloves!'

Eventually, his helmet and one glove were found and returned to him. With his static line – a length of cord that attached at one end to a wire running along the roof of the fuselage, and to his parachute at the other – firmly clipped on, he was good to go. Sixteen figures bunched together, as the dispatcher opened the bathtub and the onrush of icy air hit them hard.

'Ten minutes to go!' he cried.

A quick chat to the pilot, and the dispatcher had an update. The weather was holding good, but enemy fighter aircraft were zipping all about, so they would have to jump as quickly as possible. They shuffled closer together, as voices yelled out good-naturedly.

'No need to push!'

'Who d'you think you're shoving?'

The jump light attached to the roof of the fuselage glowed red. It was the warning signal – prepare to jump. All eyes were glued to it, as Captain Bradford prepared to launch himself through the 'patch of grey that was the exit hole'. Moments later the light switched to green, and he was gone. As if moving as one body, further figures leapt, and the padre suddenly found himself on the brink. Heaving up his kitbag, he forced himself forward and into thin air. Aware of himself falling, 'whipped by the wind and hanging on like grim death', the next moment he found himself seemingly jerked powerfully upwards, 'twisting and turning' as his 'chute caught the air.

He'd made a good jump.

Now to make a good landing.

Playing out the rope that lowered his rucksack, he scrutinised the terrain below, but it showed only as a sea of inky blackness. Slowly, shape and form materialised from the gloom. The padre was descending over what appeared to be a vast expanse of forest. With not a clearing in sight, he prepared himself for the inevitable, wrapping his arms and hands around face and head, to offer some kind of protection. An instant later the kitbag dangling beneath him crashed into the tree-tops, and the padre followed, coming to a crashing halt with a most peculiar sensation ringing in his head and ears.

For a moment he figured he'd made a half-decent landing, before realising the reason for his acute discomfort: he was hanging upside down. How far off the ground he was, he had no idea, for all was pitch darkness. One of his legs was 'hurting like blazes', and it seemed hopelessly tangled in the parachute lines. Wondering what on earth to do, the padre suddenly remembered the penknife he'd slipped into his smock almost as an after-thought. He grabbed it and began to saw at the parachute rigging. A while later all seemed to give way, and he fell, 'crashing head first through innumerable branches', until there was an almighty blow and his entire world went black.

It was daylight by the time the padre regained consciousness. He had a headache the likes of which he'd never known, and was feeling weak and nauseous. A soft whistling drifted through the trees. Fearing it might be a trap, McLuskey eventually decided it sounded like a distinctly 'friendly, British whistle', and so he recip-rocated. Moments later the familiar figure of Trooper Micky Flynn emerged from the surrounding vegetation. Small, wiry, unflap-pable, he took one glance at the sickly padre and his parachute tangled in the branches, and understood instantly all that had happened. With few words, he grabbed the padre's heavy kitbag and hauled the sickly man to his feet, before manhandling him and his belongings across the valley towards their rendezvous.

In cutting himself down, the padre explained, he'd manage to lose his knife during the fall.

'That's okay,' Flynn told him. 'I've got two. Have this one.'

In France with the SAS it was always 'okay', as the padre was to learn. This was his first real insight into the meaning of such camaraderie deep behind enemy lines.

Half-carrying the padre, Flynn steered him to a nearby road. On the track leading to it they stumbled into a 'small, swarthy individual' who was dressed in civvies, but brandished the familiar form of a Tommy gun. It was a member of their Maquis reception party. Together, they made their way along the country lane, before they rounded a bend and a most extraordinary sight met their eyes. Before them on the grass verge was a huge, bulging bus painted bright red, one that the French had captured from the enemy. 'It was their proudest possession,' as the padre observed.

Milling around the bus were dozens of McLuskey's fellow parachutists, those who had been dropped from the three Stirlings. Plus there were the distinctive figures of Major Bill Fraser and Lieutenant Ian Wellsted, the SAS commanders who'd formed the advance party dropped into the Morvan. Both men appeared woefully pale, their faces lined with strain. Apparently, they hadn't slept for several nights running, for they'd been out manning the DZs and awaiting the in-load of men and supplies. With a German armoured car unit patrolling the nearby roads, there was real tension in the air as they herded the new arrivals aboard the bus.

At first glance Bill Fraser, a tall, gangly, boyish-looking figure, with protruding ears and a frame largely of skin and bones, was an unlikely-seeming SAS warrior, but he'd more than proven himself during four years of waging war. Born and bred in Aberdeen, Fraser's forebears had served with the Gordon Highlanders, and he'd follow suit, enlisting in that regiment aged nineteen. The first of his family to be commissioned as an officer, Fraser knew he wasn't from the 'officer class', as he saw it, which had made him somewhat uncomfortable in the officer's mess, until, that is, he'd volunteered for the SAS.

Fraser had earned his spurs the tough way, being one of the most battle-hardened of all. In June 1940, aged just twenty-three, he'd served with the 1st Battalion the Gordon Highlanders in the spirited but doomed defence of France. Retreating to the port of Saint-Valery-en-Caux, they'd been ordered to hold the line so that the mass of British, French and Allied troops could be saved from the beaches. Wounded in action, Fraser was one of the few to be evacuated. Surrounded, and with little ammunition, food or water remaining, the bulk of the Gordon Highlanders had been forced to surrender, along with much of the 51st (Highland) Division. German General Erwin Rommel had taken the division's capitulation, and he would go on to earn the nickname 'The Desert Fox' in North Africa. It was something that Fraser had never forgotten: Rommel's card was marked.

Finding himself back in Britain, Fraser was plagued by his wounds and the crushing sense of defeat. The Scotsman responded in the only way he saw fit: he volunteered for Special Service, and was accepted into No. 11 (Scottish) Commando, joining Paddy Mayne and other future SAS stalwarts. Awkward, quiet, a real deep thinker, Fraser – along with Mayne and others from the commando – went on to volunteer for the SAS, after which he distinguished himself by blowing to pieces thirty-seven enemy warplanes during his first ever mission. Since then he'd proven ferocious in battle, hopelessly injury-prone, yet a true survivor, having brought one patrol 'back from the dead', spending weeks crossing the sunblasted Sahara on foot. In short, he was an iconic figure within the SAS, second only to Mayne in terms of martial prowess and renown.

By contrast, his deputy, Ian Wellsted, was a total unknown as far as the SAS was concerned, and a complete combat virgin. The son of a military family, Wellsted was very much of the officer class. His father had served as a colonel in the First World War, and the young Wellsted had been sent to the famously martial boarding school of Wellington. Diagnosed as chronically asthmatic, his boyhood fascination with all things military had been thwarted. Instead, he'd gone to Cambridge University, where an academic career had beckoned. But with the outbreak of war, Wellsted found that his asthma would be conveniently overlooked, and he signed up with the Royal Tank Regiment. Four years later he'd still not seen any action, so had volunteered for airborne forces.

An imposing figure physically, he was the second biggest recruit at jump school, and was paired with the largest, an 'enormous Canadian', for the milling. Three times the Canadian had knocked Wellsted 'clean out of the ring', but each time he'd come back for more. In short, he'd acquitted himself well, only to break his leg during the final stages of training. A long convalescence had followed, during which Wellsted's father had passed away. It was the spring 1944, and Wellsted had felt the loss deeply. Not only had his father been a good man who had taken him fishing, shooting and riding, but he'd been the surrogate father to Wellsted's wife, Margot, who was an orphan.

Feeling somewhat at a loss, Wellsted had been dining with Margot in a fine London restaurant when he'd spotted a tall figure sporting the ribbon of a DSO and Bar, along with some strange airborne insignia. That chance encounter was to be Wellsted's first experience of the 'legendary Paddy Mayne'. Learning just who and what the SAS was, he hungered for an opportunity to join them. A few months later he'd seized his chance. Mayne had visited RAF Ringway jump school seeking recruits. Wellsted, along with Les Cairns, a Scottish officer, and Lieutenant Puddle

Poole, an airborne instructor, were among the six that Mayne had selected.

Upon arrival at Darvel, one of the first people that Wellsted had encountered was Bill Fraser, whose 'humorous mouth and eyes gave his whole face a puckish, irresistibly jolly expression'. When Fraser had headed off at 5.30 p.m. on the dot, to return with a tankard brimful of ale, Wellsted decided A Squadron, Bill Fraser's command, was the place for him. Intense bouts of training had followed, of a similar type to that which Padre McLuskey had experienced, until one day Wellsted and his men had been sent off to try out some carrier pigeons. They were intended for use when an SAS patrol had landed safely in France, to wing the good tidings back to Britain.

Setting out in a training aircraft, Wellsted and his party had strapped the birds to their chests in specially designed cardboard containers. Sadly, the weather proved intemperate, and many of the hapless birds had been strapped on upside down. After the long and tumultuous flight, a number of the birds had been released, only to 'stagger about drunkenly' before refusing to fly anywhere. Worse still, as some of the human trainees had been airsick, it turned out that they had vomited all over their pigeons, which 'quite understandably, proved unable to fly'.

Far more successful were the squadron parties, in which all ranks would get gloriously drunk on Suki – a 'dreadful concoction of red wine and rum' – while raising the roof to the tune of 'Lili Marlene'. Wellsted found the booze-ups 'remarkably useful'. They were a golden opportunity to engage in quarrels, and to brandish and then bury hatchets, while learning the truth about those he commanded, those who commanded him, and about himself too.

Les Cairns, the Scottish officer who'd been recruited along-side Wellsted, had coined a nickname for him – the Gremlin.

In part it was because there were simply too many 'Ians' in the SAS, so it would avoid any confusion. In part, it was because the Gremlin – a mischievous folkloric creature, always up to one prank or another – so typified Wellsted's persona. Little did he know it, but in France that would become his official title, especially among the Maquis and the Resistance, who would know him as 'Captain Gremlin'.

Nickname aside, Wellsted must have mightily impressed his seniors, Mayne first and foremost. When the SAS commander had needed an advance party to drop in on Operation Houndsworth, as the Morvan mission was codenamed, he'd chosen Wellsted to lead it. On 6 June 1944, in the hours immediately preceding the D-Day landings, Wellsted had led a group of three into the Morvan. Padre McLuskey was among the first to appreciate how much they all owed to that advance reconnaissance team. Wellsted and his men had found and proved the DZs, forged bonds with the Maquis, established base camps and scoped out the strength of enemy forces thereabouts, and all in a region that 'had to hold the world record for drenching downpours'.

Padre McLuskey and the other new arrivals were herded aboard the big red bus, until there were men standing on the running boards and a handful of Maquis fighters perched on the roof, brandishing Bren guns. All looked set for the off when someone remembered the bus had a faulty starter motor. All piled off once more, and with a concerted shove it coughed and kangarooed into life. Bristling with weaponry, the bus set forth, with a Maquis truck and civilian car leading the way. The road twisted and turned, climbing ever higher into densely wooded country. After a final hairpin bend, the convoy ground to a halt amid much horn-tooting. Maquis guards emerged from the forest, and the newcomers were led up a forest path to what turned out to be a reception feast.

Though the cuisine was prepared in the most basic conditions of a forest camp, it did much to confirm the French flair for the preparation of fine food. Some two hundred Maquis inhabited the base, which had all the appearances of being a cross between a scene from 'Robin Hood and a Hollywood film set'. There were the young and the old, some in a mixed bag of uniform, while others were dressed in civvies. There were Maquis veterans of many months, and the newcomers of just a few weeks. In recent days the entire gendarmerie – French paramilitary police – of a nearby town had come to join them. They were dotted about 'looking much too . . . law-abiding, in their neat blue uniforms', as the padre noted.

Part of Bill Fraser's remit here was to arm the Maquis, and air drops of weaponry had helped boost their fighting strength. Despite appearances, there was a real system and order to the camp. The leader of the merry band was a distinguished-looking white-haired colonel, and he had his men gripped under firm control. A regular watch was in place, he had a camp telephone which somehow linked him into the nearest town, while an extensive network of intelligence gatherers provided early warning should the enemy be on the move. As a local force with which to link up, Wellsted and Fraser reckoned they had chosen well in the Maquis Jean, as this band was known.

After much feasting, the newcomers departed to their own SAS camps. The padre went with Fraser and Wellsted, who had borrowed one of the Maquis Jean's civilian cars. Fraser's base, near the village of Chaleaux, lay deep in a dense patch of forest, and it was accessible only by a narrow path. Upon reaching it, the padre discovered a force about thirty-strong, with parachutes rigged as makeshift tents scattered throughout the trees. From somewhere they had begged, borrowed or stolen a large tarpaulin, which was a crucial piece of kit, for the rains were torrential.

These men had an ill-fed, almost famished look about them, which was hardly surprising. For days on end the weather had prevented any airdrops, and they had been running desperately short of food. The three Stirlings had dropped scores of stores containers, and there was a 'celebratory meal' that evening. From the off, the padre was acutely aware of 'the sense of oneness our outlaw state had given us'. Stripped of the worries and concerns of normal life, here the deep basic needs of man came to the fore. All were 'homesick and sometimes afraid', and especially since the period of reconnaissance was over. By now, Fraser and his men knew where the key enemy targets were. It was time to go on the offensive; to strike first and strike hard.

Barely had McLuskey and the newcomers settled in, than it was a Sunday. All took it as given that there would be a service. The padre's drop container had been retrieved, which was crammed full of what he called his 'church'. In a clearing beside the camp the altar cloth and cross were placed on a makeshift table. The forest was still, green and fresh after a night of rain. The smell of pines and of the camp's open fire drifted on the summer air. Men gathered in shirt sleeves and smocks, and the hymn books were handed out. As the padre would come to realise, the volume of the day's singing would come to reflect just how close the enemy were. With no reports of any incursions, the men belted out the hymns – a singing regiment to the core.

But as fate would have it, the enemy would arrive that very Sunday, ushering in a war with hate as never before.

Chapter Five

AMBUSHING THE AMBUSHERS

'This is what comes of having a service, padre!'

The grumbling was good-natured – typical SAS humour – as the men of Fraser's A Squadron digested the news. Building up their forces in the region, the enemy had decided that this Sunday was the day to launch their first strike.

A warning had reached the SAS base. A force of some sixty to seventy Germans mixed with 'Grey Russian' troops – former Russian POWs, who had been press-ganged into service with the Wehrmacht – had been spotted in nearby Montsauche-les-Settons a small town set among rolling hills and dense forest. Worse still, they were reported to be seizing 'hostages' among the local townsfolk – those they accused of working with the Maquis. As all knew well, such hapless captives faced the horrors of interrogation and worse at the hands of their captors.

The force was preparing to set out in convoy, and so a decision was made to ambush them as they left Montsauche in an effort to rescue the prisoners, and before the enemy could muster any form of offensive action. An attack party was hastily pulled together. It consisted of fifteen Maquis fighters, plus seven SAS, under the command of Captain Alex Muirhead, and with Wellsted – Captain Gremlin – serving as his somewhat uncertain deputy. As Wellsted readily admitted, he'd never been in combat, and as the rest were 'old soldiers' he declared that for this action at least he was to be treated as simply one of the men.

Muirhead, commonly known to all as 'Bertie Wooster', after the amiable English gentleman of the Wodehouse novels – was a tall, slender fellow with an unruffled cool. He'd been a medical student before the war, and was also a talented artist, exhibiting at the Royal Drawing Society. During the SAS's 1943 assault on Italy, Muirhead had been charged by Mayne to raise a mortar platoon, to boost their firepower. While he'd never once fired a mortar, he'd set to it with vigour, schooling his men 'entirely along his own lines and in complete defiance of the training manual'. When Mayne had led his force ashore in Sicily to take the all-important Capo Murro di Porco gun emplacements, Muirhead's mortar team had been the first to open fire, round number one scoring a direct hit on the battery's giant magazine, which had gone up in a massive, violent explosion.

Thus Muirhead's modest 3-inch (81mm) mortar had taken out a monster enemy shore gun, which had menaced the entire Allied invasion fleet. There was to be a similar, delicious irony to the coming battle in the Morvan. The inbound enemy force consisted of two large trucks, a fleet of smaller cars, plus a motorcycle outrider. They were there at the orders of the German general who commanded the wider region, the convoy's commander happening to be that general's son. On his father's orders, he was to drill his men in the art and craft of how to mount a proper ambush. In the hills and forests of the Morvan, they sought the perfect terrain in which to launch a textbook ambuscade – only, they were about to ride into the guns of the Maquis and the SAS instead.

In short, if all went well the ambushers were about to get ambushed.

Muirhead's plan, drawn up with the help of the local Maquis

commander, was beautifully simple. The British would hit the head of the convoy, the French the tail. They'd site their forces along a steep stretch of highway, where the trucks would be forced to change through the gears as they crawled up the incline. The hidden ambushers would be ranged along one side of the road, so there would be little danger of them inadvertently hitting each other. The attack would be opened by the hurling of a 'plastic Gammon Bomb' at the lead truck, after which 'everything was to open up until not a German was left'.

The Gammon Bomb – more formally known as the No. 82 grenade – consisted of an elasticised bag with a screw-on fuse. Light and compact when empty, each Gammon Bomb could be stuffed with just the right amount of plastic explosives and DIY shrapnel to suit the intended target. When filled to the max it was even effective against armoured vehicles, hence the elite force's nickname for it: the 'hand artillery'.

At the top of the incline, the road veered hard right, disappearing out of sight. Just around that corner Wellsted and one other, Corporal F. 'Sylvo' Sylvester, would be waiting. They would string steel wires across the highway, stretched from tree to tree at around the height of a motorcyclist's torso. The aim was to let the outrider through the main drag of the ambush, so as to ensure the entire length of the convoy was within range by the time the Gammon Bomb was thrown. If the wires didn't do the trick, Wellsted and Sylvester were to stop the motorcyclist at all costs, to prevent him from racing off to raise the alarm. Corporal Sylvester was one of Muirhead's long-experienced mortar men, who'd been in the thick of it in Italy, so Wellsted knew he was in good company.

Lower down the hill, Sergeant John 'Nobby' Noble and Trooper Desmond Peter Middleton would man one Bren light machinegun, while Lieutenant Johnny Cooper and Sergeant

Zellic would brandish another. Zellic was a Yugoslav who'd joined the French SAS and was attached to the Morvan mission as an interpreter. Noble, a tough Scot, was particularly adept with the Bren, which was accurate up to 1,000 yards. During the July 1943 assault on the Capo Murro di Porco – the Cape of the Pig's Snout – he'd used a Bren to take out eight enemy snipers. For that and similar heroic actions Noble had been awarded the Military Medal (MM). He was partnered with an equally battle-hardened warrior in Middleton, who had first been wounded in action in August 1941, in Greece, when serving with the Royal Artillery, the first of many such injuries suffered in the heat of battle.

Middleton would have an extra-important role to play in the coming action. Today, and for all of their time serving in the Morvan, he would serve as the de facto nursemaid to Wellsted, talking him through battles and easing him into a combat-commander's role. Born and raised in Sheffield, Middleton's father ran a pub – 'family tradition had it that he was the only teetotal landlord in Sheffield at the time.' A son of the 'Steel City', as Sheffield is known, beneath his rough, hard exterior Middleton was a shy, kind and thoughtful soul with an innate love of children. Twenty-two years of age, he'd planned to become a priest before war had darkened the horizon.

Middleton carried in his kit the 'A Squadron Song Sheets Nos 1–7', his favourite being Sheet No. 5, which they'd entitled 'The Green Eyed Yellow Idol', and which he could recite by heart. The first verse reads:

There's a one-eyed yellow idol to the north of Kathmandu,
There's a little marble cross below the town;
There's a broken-hearted woman tends the grave of Mad
   Carew,
And the Yellow God forever gazes down.

Set in Nepal, it tells the story of a wild young British officer, 'Mad Carew', who steals the 'green eye' of a 'yellow god' – an emerald in a gold statue – to impress the woman of his dreams. But he's wounded in doing so, and while weakened is murdered by a devotee of the yellow god, who returns the jewel to its rightful place. Not a lot is revealed about Mad Carew, apart from the fact that he was 'worshipped in the ranks', and perhaps that explained Middleton's devotion to Captain Gremlin – Wellsted – and the fact that it was to be reciprocated most wholeheartedly. As Wellsted would avow, Middleton – known as 'Midd' to all – was the 'most experienced soldier of us all', perfect for nursing him through his '"Baptism of Fire" in the Morvan'.

As for Cooper, a sergeant, he'd been nicknamed 'The Kid' due to his striking youth. Recruited by SAS founder David Stirling personally, Johnny Cooper had been the youngest of all the SAS originals, just nineteen years of age when he'd joined the fledgling unit. Upon winning his sergeant's stripes, Cooper had been inducted into the sergeant's mess, being obliged to drink a pint tankard of cherry brandy in one. Practically a teetotaller, he'd been sick for forty-eight hours, vowing never to touch a drop of the stuff again. Cooper was already the recipient of a Distinguished Conduct Medal (DCM) for the daring SAS raid on the North African port city of Bouerat.

Having played a key role in a string of further SAS raids, Cooper had formed part of David Stirling's February 1943 patrol, in which he had attempted to cross from the eastern to western fringes of the Sahara, to link up with the American-led forces who'd spearheaded the Operation Torch landings. Tracked by an elite force specially raised by Rommel, Stirling and most of his patrol had been captured. But Cooper, together with SAS navigation supremo Lieutenant Mike Sadler, plus one other, had managed to escape, crossing vast tracts of hostile desert on foot to make it back to Allied lines.

In short, barring Wellsted, Muirhead's ambush party was as tough as they came. Small in number, they were as long-experienced in action as it was possible to get. Further down the hill, the Maquis were concealed behind large piles of cut timber heaped beside the road, armed with a British Bren and a captured German Spandau. Though heavily outnumbered, the ambush forces were in position, weapons ready, faced blackened with dirt and soil, and primed to unleash hell.

It was late that Sunday evening by the time the ambush was set. The convoy was expected at any moment. Time dragged. The sun slipped towards the horizon. Men fretted. Maybe the enemy weren't coming? Maybe they'd decided to overnight in Montsauche? Maybe they'd left the town by a different route? An old man driving a bullock cart laden with timber clomped slowly by. As Wellsted swatted at the evening's flies, he wasn't sure that he 'wanted the Germans to come at all'.

But then they heard it – the 'distant clash of gears' as a truck hit the incline. From his position at the head of the ambush, Wellsted could see nothing, but quite suddenly the din of battle cut through the evening stillness. Almost simultaneously there was the 'unmistakable roar' of a Gammon Bomb exploding as it was hurled into the lead truck, and a deafening eruption of Bren fire. Clutching his carbine ever more tightly, Wellsted tensed for the outrider to appear, but as the sound of rifle fire and grenade blasts echoed up from the road below, he figured the lone motor-cyclist must have been caught in the ambush.

Together with Sylvester, he dashed downhill, rounding the bend so the length of the highway opened before them. At the forefront, the leading truck was a blazing inferno, the windscreen a shattered mess, 'the bodies of the men . . . lolling grotesquely in their seats'. Beyond that lay a saloon car, and it too was a shattered wreck. 'A huddled form twitched on the road beside it.' Further on, the nose of a second truck was visible, and presumably that was being subjected to a barrage of French fire. Diving into cover at the roadside, Wellsted and Sylvester linked up with the others. As Muirhead was able to tell him, the outrider had turned back, but hopefully the French had dealt with him.

With the ambush well and truly sprung, Muirhead ordered his men on the offensive. They rose from their cover and dashed forward, Brens at the fore. As they went about clearing the ditches at close quarters, so the firefight intensified, a Spandau sparking into action, ricochets whining through the trees. Middleton and Sylvester were like 'anxious nursemaids' with Wellsted, as they took the fight to the enemy.

'Take a shot at those Germans in the ditch, sir,' one ventured.
'Where?'
'There! Look, that one's just popping his head up, sir.' Bang! 'I think I got the bastard, sir. Look, just beyond him, have a go at that one, sir.'

Bang! Bang! Bang!

'Oh, you missed, sir. Better luck next time.'

Together, they fought their way through to the burning truck. Shots were still ringing out from inside it, but whether it was a last-ditch show of defiance or the results of exploding ammo, no one could tell. On top of the cab a wounded enemy soldier was 'writhing in the flames and groaning'. As the ambushers emptied their weapons into the length of the vehicle, they heard the cries of the dying. Beyond the truck lay a roadside ditch, and the majority of those who'd survived the initial onslaught were hunkered down in there.

From the cover of a pile of timber, Wellsted lobbed a first grenade, under Middleton's directions. It sailed way beyond the ditch, bursting in an open field. But the second detonated on the very lip of the thing, and 'no more heads appeared'. Pushing further down the road, Wellsted and his comrades neared the Maquis' position. Suddenly, a German soldier erupted from cover and dashed across the road. Shooting from the hip, Sylvester 'hit him mid-stride', and he 'tumbled into a heap against the wall'. As Noble joined their advance, he detected a suspicious noise from a roadside thicket. Dropping onto his haunches, he fired a savage burst from the Bren and all movement ceased. Later, a wounded German corporal would be discovered there.

The head of the convoy was now entirely subdued. A Maquis who spoke passable German hurried over and began shouting for any surviving enemy to surrender. There was no response, 'perhaps because all the Germans within earshot were dead, wounded or very badly shaken,' as Wellsted observed. But learning that the motorcycle outrider had slipped the net, Muirhead figured it was time to withdraw, before the enemy could rouse reinforcements. Leaving Wellsted, who spoke decent French, to explain all of that to the Maquis, along with Sylvester as escort, the rest pulled back into the shelter of the trees.

Wellsted had words with the Maquis commander, telling him to make himself scarce, lest the enemy returned in strength. The lone Spandau still seemed to be 'burping away' and there was the odd burst of rifle fire, and the French seemed reluctant to withdraw while there were Germans left to fight. All of a sudden, from one of the burning vehicles appeared a figure who appeared to be miraculously unharmed. Grey-haired, dressed in civvies, he was one of the hostages that the enemy had seized in Montsauche. The Germans had also taken his motorcycle, which they'd loaded onto one of the trucks, and with admirable chutzpah the former hostage began to berate Wellsted for having set the truck ablaze, so destroying his cherished steed.

83

Three more hostages had survived the onslaught, though one was badly injured. The youngest, no more than a lad, embraced Wellsted in a highly emotional state. More pressing was the issue of prisoners. It was simply impossible for the SAS to take many at all, yet scattered around the truck were any number of wounded enemy troops. Back in Britain, they had been told to 'shoot straight' so this problem wouldn't arise. For a moment Wellsted was tempted to shoot them 'in cold blood', but even as he drew his Colt pistol, he knew that he couldn't bring himself to pull the trigger on defenceless men.

Instead, he left them where they lay. On all sides the Maquis were searching the dead, pulling off their boots – much prised – and grabbing ammo and weaponry. Taking one last look at the burned-out truck, Wellsted realised with surprise that an apparently dead man had come back to life. By his blood-stained uniform and insignia, the SAS lieutenant knew him to be an enemy officer. Dragging him to his feet, the man began to plead for his life.

'Je suis anglais,' he cried. 'Ne me tuez pas!' I'm English. Don't kill me!

'So you're English, are you?' Sylvester demanded. 'Let's hear you speak it.'

'No spik English well, Secret Service!' he replied.

At that, Wellsted demanded to see his papers. The captive's eyes shifted about nervously, as he sought some kind of a get-out.

'Secret Service,' he repeated. Then: 'No British, russe!'

Thankfully, the ambushers had a genuine Russian in their number. Squat, powerfully built, blue-eyed, and known only as 'Alexis', he was a former Red Army soldier who'd escaped from the enemy to join the Maquis. He stepped forward, his eyes boring into the hapless officer.

'Vous, russe!' – You, Russian! he cried, in his basic French, before unleashing a torrent of words in his mother tongue.

The officer dressed in bloodied and soiled field grey seemed to wither and shrivel, before replying in a subdued and fearful Russian. He and Alexis were fellow countrymen, only they were fighting on opposite sides of the war. Alexis sprang at him now, dragging a 'vicious little automatic' pistol from an inside pocket and handing it to Wellsted. That done he spat in disgust, grabbed the officer's binoculars from where they were strung around his neck and swung them savagely against the man's head. After that, Alexis spun the captive around, and booted him up the track towards the distant Maquis camp. An enemy officer, he was doubtless privy to useful intelligence, and Alexis was marching him off for a thorough questioning.

Wellsted lingered until the evening deepened into dusk, but still the French would not withdraw. They were busy searching for weapons among the dead. Wellsted gathered an armful of rifles, before he decided it was time to leave. Sylvester had already departed and he made his way back through the woods alone. The path took him via the Maquis camp. There, he found the wounded enemy officer in mid-interrogation. Even as he arrived on the scene, he spied a Maquisard draw off the man's boot, and tip it up draining it of blood, which 'spread slowly across the rough mud floor.'

Wellsted reassured the captive that he was a British officer, and that as long as he didn't try to escape he would not be killed. From his questioning, and other intelligence gleaned, it became clear that for the loss of one man killed – a Maquisard – they had accounted for as many as forty enemy dead, with many more wounded. They'd also rescued four of the hostages and seized a quantity of ammunition and arms. As the icing on the cake, the German general's son who had commanded the ambush party had been cut down by the opening burst of Nobby Noble's Bren.

The following morning, the Operation Houndsworth War

Diary for 25 June 1944 noted there was major 'flap' on, as the enemy returned in force. An SAS trooper, Burgess, had just been brought into camp. Having broken his leg while parachuting into the Morvan, it was crudely splinted and bandaged. Disguised as a French civilian, the plan was to smuggle him into Saulieu, the nearest large settlement, to get an X-ray at the town's hospital. En route Burgess had overnighted in a local village where he had been 'fêted and kissed by all the girls, come to see their first Englishman'. But as fate would have it, Burgess would not reach hospital any time soon.

After breakfast, Wellsted was sent out to recce the surroundings, for trouble was brewing. Reports filtered in of an enemy column some two hundred-strong and supported by armour, descending on Montsauche once more. En route, they had paused at the village of Ouroux-en-Morvan, 'amusing themselves' by tossing grenades into a roadside café, leaving windows shattered and bloodstained dining tables. Pressing on, the enemy had climbed into the high ground to revisit the site of the previous day's ambush, only to blunder into a Maquis patrol. The French, firing from the cover of the woods, had got the drop on the Germans, and a dozen or more had been hit.

The bear had been severely mauled, and yet more enemy were reported to be inbound. Reluctant to venture into the thick forests, the German commanders turned their ire on the locals. As the thud of heavy gunfire and the chatter of machineguns echoed around the hills, so the town of Montsauche was all-but razed to the ground. The Germans had ordered all inhabitants to leave, before shooting those who refused and setting the place ablaze. Only the gendarmerie and the post office seemed to have been spared, even the town's church being put to the torch. After they were done, Montsauche was left a smoking ruin, and 'not a dwelling house remained habitable'.

Horrific though it was, the 'reprisals' had only just started. Next, the village of Planchez suffered a similar fate, as the enemy went on the rampage. As the sounds of such brutality echoed around the hills, much of this was clearly audible to the SAS, and the horrific message it sent hit home. While the enemy might raise 'hatred against themselves to a fever pitch' by such actions, in truth such brutal reprisals against the locals 'did much to discourage future Maquis activities', as all appreciated.

With German forces searching high and low for information on the location of the Maquis and SAS hideouts, it was only a matter of time before concerted attacks materialised. Sure enough, the first enemy counterstrike would hit the SAS – and the Maquis – where they were absolutely at their most vulnerable.

As Johnny Cooper would note, the kind of war-fighting the SAS faced here was the direct opposite of what they had experienced in North Africa. In the desert they could spot the enemy from a vast distance. Here, in the dense forests and mist-enshrouded hills of the Morvan, the SAS could stumble upon the enemy when only yards apart and thus had to be 'constantly on our toes'.

Making the most of the thick tree cover, German troops converged on a local castle, the Château de Vermot. With its solid, high-walled towers and their pointy-hat roofs, the enchanting chateau lay in a heavily forested setting, which enabled the enemy to creep close to its windows and doors. The building's thick bastions shielded a secret: it was the site of the Maquis' – and SAS's – clandestine hospital. Here, wounded fighters were brought to recuperate, amid the basic accoutrements that a makeshift medical centre could muster.

One of those ensconced there was a legendary SAS figure, Sergeant Fred 'Chalky' White, DCM, MM. A professional footballer before the war, playing for a Manchester club, White had won his first decoration in North Africa, where he'd been wounded in the back, and his second during the last-ditch defence of Termoli, in Italy, when defending what had become known as Bren Gun Ridge. Pulling his troop back from a section that was about to be overrun, he'd realised his fatal error, for the enemy would punch through the SAS's thin line of steel. His reaction was to dash back alone to plug the gap, no matter that a 'storm of bullets tore into the area and mortars exploded on all sides'. Parachuting into the Morvan, White had landed on a rooftop and injured his back for a second time, at the same time as Burgess had broken his leg, hence his evacuation to the Château de Vermot hospital.

It was six o'clock in the evening when White awoke to the shocking experience of having 'the head of his bed riddled by a burst of machine-gun fire', and shattered plaster falling all around him, bullets hammering into the walls. As the enemy closed in – 'a mixed German and "Grey Russian" force about 250 strong, with mortars, rifles, grenades and numerous machine-guns' – the medical staff managed to spirit White and other patients out of the chateau's rear entrance. The Maquis guards gave battle, one young fighter taking out the lead enemy truck with a PIAT – an awkward, spring-fired anti-armour weapon. Miraculously, White and the other patients were hurried into the woods, and not a man among them was killed or captured.

A bizarre stand-off ensued, as the vastly superior enemy force poured fire into the thick woodlands to the rear of the chateau but seemed unwilling to press home their attack. Bringing up mortars and grenade launchers, they began to plaster the treeline with murderous fire, driving the Maquis back, the walking wounded and the medical staff carrying the stretcher cases deeper into the trees. Still the enemy seemed reluctant to follow. But as for the chateau, it lay well within their grasp.

It was clearly a makeshift hospital with clean white beds in neat rows, a decent surgery kitted out with racks, cupboards and rows of bottles, plus the unmistakable reek of ether. Château de Vermot was no Maquis or SAS headquarters. It was a place of care for the wounded. Even so, the enemy 'with cool deliberation . . . smashed every bottle. With complete and painstaking thoroughness, they broke every instrument.' Their internal destruction complete, they then 'gave the lovely old chateau over to the flames'.

Even as the chateau burned, so a most unusual individual stepped into the fray. One of the 'Cloak and Dagger Brigade', Colonel Sir James Hutchison, a small, wiry figure with a shock of grey hair, served with the Special Operations Executive (SOE), more commonly known as Churchill's Ministry for Ungentlemanly Warfare. Charged to take the fight to the enemy in all the ways that were forbidden, SOE specialised in raising guerrilla armies, sabotage, bribery, blackmail, corruption, money laundering and more. Hutchison, all of fifty-one years old, was among the first Allied operators dropped into the Morvan, and he was working closely with the Maquis. More to the point, his dedication to the cause knew no bounds.

Earlier in the war, Hutchison – a First World War veteran, who'd served with the 19th Lancers (Fane's Horse) – had fought in France and North Africa, during which time his name and likeness had become known to the Gestapo. With his identity thus blown, he'd offered his services to SOE, but was warned that he would need to disguise himself most convincingly if he were to be of any use as an agent behind the lines. Undeterred, he'd checked himself into a Harley Street clinic and demanded to be given a new face.

The plastic surgeon had eyed him doubtfully. 'It can be managed,' he declared at last, 'but I'm going to give you a good doing.'

'The more thorough the better,' Hutchison had enthused.

The surgeon had proceeded to lop off the prominent bridge of Hutchison's nose, to slice off the tops of his ears, while adding some bone from his pelvis to his chin. Once the scars had healed, Hutchison had paid a visit home. His seven-year-old son had answered the door. 'Hello, Peter, is mummy in?' Hutchison had asked. Gazing up with the 'serious unrecognising look of a child', the boy had dashed off, yelling out 'Mummy, there's a man at the door to see you.' Proof positive that he was unrecognisable as his former self.

In the Morvan, Hutchison was using the cover name of 'Colonel Hastings', and as a Maquis–SAS go-between his services would prove invaluable, not to mention his intelligence-gathering skills. Right then, as the Château de Vermot was consumed by flames, Hutchison spirited an urgent message across to Bill Fraser's SAS camp: he and his men were needed at the chateau as soon as possible. If they could make it there in time, a force of some 250 enemy were present, and the SAS would be perfectly placed to hit them from the rear and give them a right bloody nose.

Fraser wasted no time in mustering his forces. 'At 1900 hours two detachments set out under Major FRASER and Captain WISEMAN in the pouring rain,' an SAS report on the action noted. In fact, Fraser had gone one better, intending a two-pronged attack on the enemy. One patrol, under the superlative command of Lieutenant Johnny Wiseman, and with SAS stalwart Reg Seekings as his deputy, would hit the enemy from the one flank, while Fraser would lead a second party to hit them from the other. Caught in a pincer movement, the enemy were about to pay dearly for their assault on the chateau-hospital.

Wiseman had soldiered alongside Mayne and Fraser from the very start, being a fellow No. 11 Commando veteran, an early

SAS recruit and one of Mayne's Great Sand Sea raiders. Over the years he'd learned both to respect and to fear the formidable commander. While admiring him enormously and being 'very proud to be taken on with him', at times Wiseman perceived Mayne to be 'frightening . . . Not a man to get on the wrong side of.'

A Cambridge arts graduate – small, stocky and fiery of temper – Wiseman had found Mayne 'exceptional . . . in action; the calmest, quietest man,' no matter how fiercely the bullets might fly. But under the influence of drink, he could prove dangerously unpredictable. Once, when hitting the rum and lime in North Africa, Wiseman had suggested that they shave off half the beard of one of their comrades who'd managed to annoy them. Instead, the giant Irishman had pinned Wiseman himself down, and with a cutthroat razor had sliced off half of his beard. 'After that nothing . . . ever frightened me!' Wiseman declared.

As for Wiseman's second-in-command, Sergeant Albert Reginald 'Reg' Seekings – one of the unit's originals and a self-confessed 'rough, tough so-and-so' – was a born fighter. During the unit's assault on the Capo Murro di Porco headland, Seekings had led his men on a furious bayonet charge, twice: once to take the enemy gun battery and a second time to silence a mortar unit. For such actions Seekings had been awarded an MM, to add to his Distinguished Conduct Medal (DCM) – Britain's oldest award for gallantry, ranking one below the Victoria Cross – which he'd earned during desert raiding operations.

Seekings, like so many, held Mayne in high esteem. After David Stirling's capture and Mayne's appointment as commander of 1 SAS, Seekings would remark that only he could have taken over at that juncture. 'Paddy Mayne was the man by now. Paddy was Paddy in no uncertain terms.' A boxing champion before the war, two of Seekings' bouts had been against a fellow future luminary of the SAS – Sergeant Charles George Gibson 'Pat' Riley. Hailing from Redgranite, Wisconsin, Riley was an American by birth, but had somehow blagged his way into the British Army. He and Seekings had gone toe to toe in the ring at the Women's Institute Hall in Wisbech, and while closely matched, Riley had won both bouts on points. The fact that both men had found their way into the SAS reflected the quality of the recruits it attracted, not to mention the calibre of those heading out to ambush the enemy at Château de Vermot.

The rain pelted down. Typical Morvan weather. Creeping through the undergrowth proved a wet and miserable business, but still Fraser's men knew they had to hurry, if they were to catch the enemy before they withdrew. Even so, it was well into the dusk hours by the time Wiseman and Seekings were anywhere near the chateau. Disoriented from the long and soaking march, they had no idea exactly where the Germans had sited their rear-guard. All of a sudden, they emerged from a dense patch of undergrowth to find the road to the chateau right before them.

On Seekings' shoulder was Sergeant Jack Terry, another long-serving desert veteran. A few hundred yards away lay some trucks, guarded by a machinegun. Seekings suggested they crawl ahead to attack that enemy concentration. Worming their way forwards in the gathering darkness and the drenching rain, eventually Seekings popped his head up to check exactly where they were. He emerged from the undergrowth, to find himself staring down the barrel of a machinegun.

'Look! Germans!' Seekings hissed, raising the alarm.

Moments later he tumbled forward, a bullet in his neck. The machine-gunner had opened up, and as Seekings tried to raise his carbine to fire one-handed, the enemy's weapon jammed. Moments later, the wounded Seekings found himself being dragged back through the bushes by Terry. Seeing the state of his battledress 'smothered in blood', Seekings feared that his 'arm had been blown off'. Behind him, a third figure, Lance Corporal 'Pringle' Gibb, executed some magic work with his Bren, blasting the enemy gunner and his weapon to hell.

Under Gibb's covering fire, Seekings dashed back fifty or sixty yards, dropped his precious pipe, ran back for it, then retraced his steps, before collapsing from loss of blood. As Wiseman drew his men back to some high ground, Seekings, swearing at the top of his voice all the time, was hurried towards the SAS camp. There, a Maquis doctor was called to attend to his wounds. As his stand-in medical assistant, he had the six-foot-two figure of Padre McLuskey at his side.

For the first time ever, the padre found himself assisting with 'a surgical examination'. By torchlight they discovered that 'a bullet had entered the back of Seeking's neck and lodged itself near the base of his skull.' But no matter how he might probe about, the doctor could not get a grip on the round, so eventually they decided to leave it where it was. This was to be the start of a remarkably unorthodox friendship between the plain-spoken and avowedly ungodly Seekings and the 1 SAS padre.

But first, Bill Fraser's patrol was to be in fierce action back at the Château de Vermot highway. As Wiseman held firm at his position, soaked to the skin but with his guns covering a long expanse of the road below, so Fraser and his men, after an 'even longer and wetter march', crept closer to the enemy's far flank. Emerging onto a high point overlooking the terrain below, Fraser could see the village of Vermot laid out, and nearer still a group of enemy soldiers gathered at the roadside.

As Fraser studied the scene, instinct told him that the party below had to be waiting for something. Silently he positioned his Bren gunners, then settled down to watch. Shortly, a few more troops gathered, and then, in ones and twos an entire enemy platoon turned up, bearing heavy mortars and machineguns. Finally, a German officer appeared and ordered his men to prepare to move out. But in truth, most of them would be going nowhere.

Fraser gave the word, and the combined firepower of four Brens tore into the figures gathered in the dusk below, as blazing muzzle flashes lit up the darkening hillside. Chaos ensued. Trapped in the narrow streets, the SAS gunners cut down the enemy in their droves, as the intense fire ricocheted off walls and tarmac. The yells of panic intermingled with the cries of the wounded, as for 'several minutes the slaughter continued'.

Finally, Fraser called a ceasefire. As quickly as the Brens had opened up, they fell silent. Surveying the scene below, the SAS major found it hard to believe that more than a handful of the enemy could have avoided the onslaught. 'It was afterwards estimated that no more than ten men escaped uninjured from the fracas,' the SAS War Diary noted. As darkness descended, Fraser led his men in a hurried march back towards their base. Though they were soaked to the skin and exhausted, he had a sense that they would have to move camp right away.

The more they prodded the hornet's nest, the more the enemy would come hunting, scouring the Morvan and hungering for vengeance.

Chapter Six

CHITTY CHITTY BANG BANG

Fraser and his party abandoned their camp. What they couldn't carry they buried, and what they couldn't bury they booby-trapped, so that if the enemy did come they would get a very nasty welcome. It may have seemed premature to be leaving, but Fraser had an acute sixth sense for battle, and right now it was screaming that they had to get moving.

Every time the enemy had ventured into the heart of the Morvan, they had been hit hard. Their one success – apart from their savaging of the local towns and villages, which could hardly be termed as a military victory – was their gutting of the Château de Vermot hospital, but even that had been of limited value. Either they returned to the hunt in greater numbers, or they would be forced to accept that they had lost control of the Morvan to the Maquis and the British parachutists – a region lying towards the very heart of France.

As they couldn't in all conscience admit that a large tract of Nazi-occupied France had fallen to their enemies – and long before there was the sniff of a breakout from the Normandy beaches – they would have to try to stamp out all resistance. And there was a wider strategic point at play here. From their bases in the Morvan, Fraser's men had already struck at vital rail and road links, which the enemy needed to speed their forces, and critical supplies of ammunition and weaponry to the Normandy coast. If the troublemakers of the Morvan were left unchallenged, such sabotage efforts would only worsen, and that was something the Nazi war effort could ill-afford.

No one among Fraser's party was kidding himself that the present circumstances weren't grim. On the run, with no shelter and limited food supplies – they could eat only what they could carry or scavenge – and with torrential rain falling, they faced a dire trial. Laden with their wounded, sticking to remote and isolated hills and valleys, they scoured the seemingly impene-trable forests for a new and more secure camp. As Johnny Cooper would write of this juncture, it was a 'security and vigilance period', during which they feared being surrounded in their camps by the 'irate Germans'.

Wiseman's report on this time admirably captures the tone.

For a week . . . we were very short of food. Having received a tin of stew . . . for feeding 28 men, we decided to toss for it in syndicates of 7. Ian Stewart's syndicate won, and with much relish the stew was cooked and divided, with the rest of us looking on jealously. Poor Ian had just received his portion, when he tripped over the fire and upset it all on the ground. Two days later Ian's syndicate again won the toss for seven eggs. Ian's cook decided to make an omelette, but Ian, who fancies himself as a cook, said he would make his own. His omelette, being nearly finished, was upset into the fire . . . The expression on his face helped considerably to make the incident so amusing.

Fraser and his men were doing their best to keep their spirits up, but conditions were appalling. Understanding that 'the position of our camp was now known to the enemy', there was no option but to hide during the daylight hours and move only at night. Fraser steered them towards a hidden valley that he had reconnoitred shortly after dropping into the Morvan. Carrying their two casualties – Seekings with his neck wound, and Burgess with his splinted leg – the journey 'felt like an eternity' and especially since 'we slipped and slithered a great deal' in the rain-lashed darkness. Tellingly, the padre would write, 'spent the day in great discomfort in the pouring rain.'

Finally, they reached their destination, a cleft in the hills bathed in moonlight. The scent of clover drifted up from open fields, and beyond lay the tiny village of Mazignien. At the head of the valley was a dense belt of trees, which screened a small clearing beyond. It was just as dawn was breaking that the exhausted fugitives reached it. Bedding down wherever they could, Fraser and his men woke sometime later to a new day, and to the sun shining brightly at last.

A small stream ran through the clearing, and in no time they were in it, washing themselves and their uniforms. Fraser's choice of camp was a good one, and in the bright June sunshine spirits lifted considerably.

At the village of Vermot, as elsewhere across the Morvan, the lives of the locals had descended into hell, even as Fraser and his party had been making their way to their fallback camp. Sure enough, the enemy had returned in strength. Having scoured the forests where they believed the SAS and Maquis to be based, and finding little but abandoned camps and the discarded detritus of war, they realised again that they had been duped. Their British and French enemies struck like ghosts from the woodland shadows and disappeared just as swiftly like wraiths. It was infuriating. Deprived of their vengeance, they turned their ire and their firepower on the locals.

An enemy column headed directly to the village of Vermot, the site of their most recent trouncing. The chateau-hospital lay some five hundred yards to the west of the village, which was little more than a hamlet. Terror descended upon the ancient winding streets. A group of village men were rounded up at random, and shot to death or left brutally injured. Every house in the settlement was set aflame, as the enemy ensured that Vermot would be left a smoking ruin. Amid the chaos and the carnage, women were seized and raped, including a fourteen-year-old girl.

Withdrawing from the smouldering ruins, the enemy column reached Dun-les-Places, a larger village. Claiming to have been fired upon by gunmen positioned in the church tower, they halted and the curé – the village priest – was seized. Anyone with a usable weapon was with the Maquis, and the Maquis – like the SAS – were busy shifting camps. There were no gunmen in Dun-les-Places or anywhere thereabouts. Regardless, the priest was frogmarched up to the belfry, from where he was shoved out with a rope around his neck. In full view of the villagers, he was hanged until dead, after which the rope was cut and his corpse 'fell sickeningly'.

Not content with that, the round-ups began. In Dun-les-Places there was a turncoat of a Frenchman – a Gestapo agent. A reviled species, he had compiled a list of those males in the village he claimed sympathised with the Maquis or the British parachutists. Enemy commanders rounded up every man, after which they were herded into the church square. There they were gunned down, their blood spilling across the hallowed ground, the bullets punching holes in the church's stout walls and thick oaken door. Still not satiated, the enemy commanders ordered the bodies be mutilated with grenades and bayonets. In addition to the priest, the dead included the most prominent citizens of Dun-les-Places, including the mayor.

Finally, enemy commanders dispatched men to burn the houses 'of those who had helped us', as one SAS man would put it. A guard was mounted on the heap of bloodied remains at the church, and for forty-eight hours the villagers were denied the decency of a proper burial for their loved ones. As the Operation Houndsworth War Diary would record for 27 June 1944, Duns-les-Places had been 'given over to rape and murder'.

In the midst of such horrors, and even as the village was consumed by flames, the SAS was about to pay a visit. In the Morvan, Fraser's men had wisely maintained discrete camps. While Fraser's party were in one, Muirhead's were in another, plus there were one or two satellite bases. At Muirhead's camp they heard dire reports: Bill Fraser and his men had vanished, as some '1,500 Germans supported by tanks and artillery' assaulted his and the nearest Maquis' positions. Whatever truth there was to the rumour, it raised the alarming issue of radio sets, and losing their all-important link to London.

Every SAS officer and sergeant possessed a small 'listening set' – a radio which could be tuned in to the BBC to hear the news. They would hear reports of 'the battles swaying back and forth on those Normandy beaches 400 miles away . . . upon the fate of which our whole future depended,' as Wellsted would describe it. The BBC were also charged to send coded radio messages to Allied units across France. SAS bulletins were to open with the sing-song French nursery rhyme 'Sur le Pont d'Avignon'. If that was heard, then all ears would be strained to catch a message specific to their own mission.

Each SAS patrol had its own 'SABU' call sign – SABU being an acronym for 'safe-all-business-as-usual'. As the nursery rhyme faded out, so the BBC announcer would declare: 'I have messages for SABU 10, SABU 12, SABU 14 and SABU 19 . . .' Each of those patrols would then know to keep their ears peeled for whatever was about to be spirited across the airwaves. But here in the Morvan, only two W/T sets existed that could transmit and receive messages direct from the SAS's London headquarters, and both of those were at Bill Fraser's camp. Were he to vanish, so too would those sets, and with them the only means of receiving orders or of calling in airdrops.

Wellsted was charged by Muirhead to take to the road and to find out what had happened. With weather conditions having prevented the dropping of jeeps, the only means of conveyance was one of the Maquis' decidedly dodgy cars. With France being sucked dry of petrol to fuel the Nazi war machine, the small vehicle ran on 'wood alcohol' – methanol, a poisonous form of alcohol produced by distillation. The burning of the unorthodox fuel gave off a 'abominable smell' and reduced still further the 'strength and reliability' of the vehicle's ancient motor.

Armed with a Sten submachine gun, a carbine and grenades, Wellsted and the Maquisards set forth. At every village and hamlet they paused to ask the locals 'if there were any Boches about'. At each they got the all-clear, until they entered Bonin, beyond which lay Dun-les-Places. At Bonin they got the warning – the 'enemy had been up to some devilry in Dun'. As Bill Fraser's camp lay beyond Dun-les-Places, they felt they had no option but to continue. Attempting to race through the village, they tore ahead as fast as the car would go. Following the Maquis' lead, Wellsted, seated in the back, got his carbine poked out the window, as all 'hoped for the best'.

They hit the village outskirts, which seemed eerily deserted. At one house a weeping and hysterical woman was discovered. The entire place was held by the enemy, she revealed, plus the womenfolk had been molested, dozens had been murdered and the curé hanged from his own church. Though 'smoke hung low over the roads and the smell of burning was heavy' in the air, they pressed on. At the last moment, Wellsted remembered a stony back lane that cut through the village outskirts. He'd first used it when taking Chalky White to the Château de Vermot hospital after his parachuting accident. Directing the Maquis driver towards the lane, they bumped along its uneven surface as smoke and flames rose on all sides. Shortly, they were out the far side of the village, making for Bill Fraser's camp at 'all possible speed'.

They reached it and parked the car, Wellsted going ahead on foot to investigate. Whistling softly the tune of 'Sur le Pont d'Avignon', he hoped to hear an answering call. Nothing. Not a cry from a sentry nor any other sign of a human presence. All was an eerie stillness and silence. Wellsted reached the camp, only to find a 'scene of desolation'. The ashes of a dead fire still held the odd cooking utensil. Discarded kit and empty parachute containers were scattered all about. Then Wellsted stopped dead. At his feet there was a tin of chocolate, lying in the open in a clearing. It was just too inviting and too obvious to be genuine. It had to be booby-trapped. As all had agreed, if a camp was about to be overrun, nasty surprises would be left for the enemy.

Backing away carefully, Wellsted returned to the car with a 'confused and heavy heart'. With no other option, they decided to return to their own camp. En route, they paused at Le Vieux Dun, a hamlet lying some three kilometres north of the main village. An old lady answered the knock at her door. Her face was a mask of abject terror. The Boches were everywhere, she warned, pleading with Wellsted and his Maquis brethren to go. If she spoke with them she would be shot, she said, as she pleaded with them to leave.

They pushed on towards Dun-les-Place. Forewarned, they approached with maximum caution. At the junction where their route met the l'Huis Gally road, they halted. To their left lay the Mairie – the mayor's office – and to the right the church, though all was shrouded in a thick pall of smoke. Wellsted and two Maquisards got out, weapons at the ready, while the third remained at the wheel. Guns cocked, grenades gripped in hand, they stole ahead, as the car crept forward at their heels.

Smoke cloaked their movements. The crackle of flames and the crash of falling roof beams drowned the noise of their advance, while the flickering light from the fires lit their way. At last they reached the turning that led onto the narrow, stony track they sought – the one they had used before. Whistling up the car, they piled into it and set off. But a few moments later they realised their mistake. Somehow, inexplicably, they had reached a dead end.

They paused at a house, as a Maquisard rapped on the door. A terrified old woman answered. They had taken a wrong turn, she warned. They needed to retrace their steps, then swing east onto that unnamed track, which crossed over the River Cure, and then speed on their way. And quickly, for the place was still crawling with the enemy. Trusting to luck, they executed an about-turn, and with weapons jammed out the windows once more, they sped back through the village. With Wellsted praying as he had rarely prayed before, they roared 'at top speed' around the front of the benighted churchyard, before swinging right onto the route that they needed to take. Amazingly, 'not a shot was fired, not an alarm was raised.'

Surprise must have won them the day, and especially since the bodies of the dead were still piled in front of the church, over which the enemy were standing guard. Speeding out of Dun-les-Places, they turned onto a winding forest route, and were soon lost among the kind of terrain where the enemy would be loath to follow, sticking to narrow tracks hemmed in by walls of tall, dark trees.

*

A couple of days later two figures arrived at Muirhead's camp. Weary, and having weathered a most difficult journey on foot, they were Fraser's men. They were able to brief Muirhead and Wellsted on all that had transpired, and alert them to the location of their new base. Situated above Mazignien village, it lay just a dozen kilometres north-west of Dun-les-Places, but was as isolated as it was possible to get in the Morvan.

Fully a week had passed without any contact between the two SAS parties, and in that time the battle landscape in the Morvan had shifted markedly. Having wreaked their unspeakable horrors, the enemy had mostly departed. The SAS and Maquis had endured, while their oppressors had left empty handed. Their forces had been badly mauled, and they had sought recompense, but now 'the crisis was over'.

As Wellsted would later reflect, 'this was our greatest single success.' Had the Maquis been shattered, and the SAS wiped out or captured, operations in the Morvan would have ground to a halt. Instead, 'we were set to begin our operations against the enemy in earnest.' It was time for Bill Fraser's raiders to get to work with a vengeance.

On that note, Fraser sent a report into SAS headquarters, telling of their victories. The reply that came back was damning with faint praise. 'Well done, but refrain from engaging in Maquis battles, get on with cutting the railways.' Which rather missed the point. Here in the Morvan at least, the Maquis battles *were* the SAS's battles, for without secure bases from which to operate, and into which to call in airdrops of supplies, no strategic sabotage would be possible.

At Bill Fraser's new camp, they were fortunate enough to have the squadron's medical officer, Mike McReady, join them. But it was McLuskey himself whom Reg Seekings credited with nursing him back to full health. 'This is where the padre . . . saved my life, because by this time I'd seized up,' Seekings declared. Throughout their long and perilous trek to their new camp, the padre had carried not only his own kit, but most of Seekings' as well. For some reason, he'd taken the wounded pugilist to his heart. As Seekings appreciated, 'McLuskey really nursed me, really looked after me.'

One morning the padre went about giving the injured SAS sergeant a shave. As the cut-throat sliced through his thick stubble, the two men – superficially so very different – fell to talking about what they most liked to read. Seekings' favourites were lurid detective novels. The padre's, somewhat predictably, was the New Testament. But being a parachuting padre, along with his hymn books he'd brought a pile of popular thrillers to help the men pass the days, for on missions such as this 'you spend your time being either bored or scared.'

In short order, the padre was spied reading some of Seekings' detective stories, and using phrases like 'I'm just gumshoeing around'. As Seekings had told him, he liked his books the bloodier the better. The padre suggested getting some decidedly bloodthirsty thrillers dropped in with the next resupply flight. He also shared his worries with Seekings as to whether he should really be unarmed, or whether he should be prepared to use a gun.

'Have you ever carried a gun?' Seekings asked.

'No.'

'Well don't start now. We'll look after you.'

The padre still seemed troubled. What would happen, he wondered, if he was in a jeep and the driver and gunner got wounded? Would he be justified in taking to the Vickers-K guns to protect his brother SAS? Seekings told him of course he would. McLuskey then posed the obvious question: would the battle-hardened SAS sergeant possibly teach him how to use the Vickers-Ks? Seekings agreed that he would. Once he was fully healed, the padre would get a proper lesson on the Vickers. And so an unlikely-seeming bond was forged.

In truth, these two men were not so very different. Beneath his rough, prize-fighter exterior, Seekings had a soft-hearted side, and a burning desire to do what was right. In the Morvan he would become known as the 'Le Maquis anglais', due to his sympathies for the locals and their long struggle against the Nazi occupiers. And he was not averse to stepping in personally, when he saw a French man or woman being abused. Seekings, a proud working-class man, was also loyal to a fault, having recently refused to take an officer's commission, fearing that it would isolate him from the men.

As for McLuskey, he was starting to realise just how much his experiences in the Morvan were changing him, from the comfortable Glasgow University chaplain of heretofore. As he tended to Seekings' injuries, he asked himself why in the 'peace and security' of his own home he'd never realised how fortunate he was. 'If the privileges of the normal were ever mine again, would I learn to remember their value?' Two weeks serving 'as a guerrilla' had truly sorted out his 'scales of values'.

Unwittingly, the padre was providing an incredible morale boost to his spiritual charges. Wherever possible he held 'services in fields', the men singing 'a few hymns in a very low key! If morale dipped he was always on hand to boost it.'

It was now almost a month since the Operation Houndsworth advance party had dropped in. In the interim, much had happened to plague Bill Fraser's men and to depress their spirits. Chief among them was this: every time they had hit the enemy, so the enemy had in turn wreaked vengeance on the locals. At Dun-les-Place it had reached its terrible apogee, but it was perhaps at Vermot that the cause and effect had seemed so direct.

Bill Fraser and his men had ambushed the enemy platoon from the heights above the village. The next day, it and its people had been reduced to a smoking ruin.

So, it was timely indeed when a buzz of excitement flashed around their new camp. A message had come in via the radio. Their commander, Lieutenant-Colonel Mayne, was going to broadcast a message to them that very evening. Not a single man was absent, as his unmistakable tones drifted from the radio across the forest clearing. He began, as was his wont, by giving permission to smoke. Then, in his 'pleasant Irish voice', and clipping his words as was his custom, he proceeded to give a talk over the microphone that made his speech seem far more audible and accomplished than ever it did when delivered in person.

He sent a message to one and all, embracing every SAS patrol that was spread across France. 'He knew each operation that had been tackled and he seemed pleased with the results,' McLuskey remarked. And somehow, Mayne had 'a message for almost everyone. It would have been difficult to exaggerate the effect on our party of that short talk; nothing could have boosted morale so effectively. It heartened and cheered every man . . .' Before signing off, Mayne shared with them a secret. Shortly, he would himself be dropping in to join them. 'This put the finishing touches to the tonic.'

As all appreciated about Mayne, 'the gift of leadership and the ability to inspire complete devotion and loyalty were his to an exceptional degree.' McLuskey would characterise his special magic thus: 'He was idolised by his men. More than that, he was both loved and trusted by them in a unique degree. You see, his men knew how much he cared for them. Careless for his own safety, he was very jealous for theirs. Risks there had to be, but everyone knew if Paddy authorised a venture, it must be well worthwhile and worth the risks involved. Everyone knew that

Paddy would be in it too – *there with the men he loved, where the going was toughest and the danger greatest.* Paddy did more than send others – he went himself too.'

Throughout June 1944, Mayne had been obliged to sit back in headquarters, planning and overseeing operations and dispatching his men into harm's way. Indeed, there were reports that he had been banned by higher command from deploying into France, for fear that he might get himself killed or captured. Such were the vagaries of command. But now, via this message, Mayne had given his men the nod. He was coming. Sometime soon he would be dropping in to join them, determined to be in the thick of it – there with the men he loved, where the going was toughest and the danger greatest.

As a second great fillip to their morale, they were about to receive an airdrop, and this one would be delivering some very precious, if cumbersome cargo. One of the chief reasons why Fraser had chosen the present camp was due to the ideal terrain it offered for a hidden DZ, secreted in the nearby valley. For 5 July 1944, the Operation Houndsworth War Diary recorded: 'Mazignien DZ manned. Lt. TROWER and 3 jeeps arrive. One lands in the forest and 40 trees have to be cut to get it.' Or as Wellsted would describe it, the night of 5/6 July hosted 'the most momentous *parachutage* since the Squadron had arrived'.

After several nights of no-shows due to bad weather, the signal finally came that the drop was on. Three Halifaxes would be flying in, their holds stuffed full of supplies for the men on the ground, plus each aircraft would have a jeep strapped to what had once been the bomb bay. 'Excitement ran high in the camp' as they set out for the DZ. Word had gone out, and both Maquis and SAS from the sister camps had gathered. By midnight the valley was thick with expectant faces, gazing hopefully to the skies, praying that the night would remain clear. It did, and at 2.00 a.m. on the dot the first giant warplane hove into view.

Shortly, the starlit heavens were filled with the glowing outlines of parachutes. Slung under each was the cigar-shaped form of a drop container. But amid that mass of billowing, rustling silk there was also something quite different – 'a jeep with parachutes attached to each corner, drifting down among the hampers and containers.' As if by magic – Chitty Chitty Bang Bang; the vehicle that could fly – that first vehicle landed directly in the centre of the valley, the steel cradle that held it settling onto the soft grass. The second jeep fell 'not so conveniently among trees.' As for the third, it landed 'most inconveniently', arriving on a riverbank upside down and suspended by the branches into which it had plunged. In fact, the third jeep's descent had much in common with Padre McLukskey's earlier drop, and the priority was to ensure they got it down without quite the same degree of harm as he had suffered.

The first two jeeps were quickly retrieved, and after 'a little persuasion' they were fired up and were soon ferrying supplies from the DZ back to the camp. The third jeep was the issue. They needed to get it down before daybreak, for the vehicle and its four silk appendages would be clearly visible from the road that snaked along the valley floor. After countless trees were cut, somehow they 'righted it' and 'had it on its four wheels'. It seemed miraculously unharmed by its 'rough reception' and shortly it was beetling along under its own power and making haste to Fraser's camp. Generous supplies of petrol had been dropped, along with a proper stocking up of the SAS's larder. Spirits were already high, and that was before someone opened a container to find it stuffed full of a veritable bonanza – mail from home!

Shortly after each man had deployed into France, 1 SAS's

Regimental Sergeant Major Graham 'Johnny' Rose – a former manager of a Woolworths department store, and one of Mayne's trusty deputies – had written a letter to each of their families. In fact, they were proforma letters, with only the recipient's name filled in by hand. Still, the sentiments were genuine and the level of care they embodied was admirable.

'The following information is available regarding your son, 1435568 Trooper A Middleton,' began the letter dispatched to Middleton's parents. 'He was dropped by parachute into France on 21/6 and up to the time of writing was quite safe and well. You may take it for granted that he is safe unless you hear to the contrary from us. He will not be able to write to you for some time, but will be able to receive your letters, so please keep writing. Cheerio, keep smiling, and don't worry.' The result of such missives was the positive shower of letters delivered by pannier to A Squadron.

As the padre concluded, it was a very happy day, with tea, cigarettes and, most importantly, word from home. From previous operations, the SAS had learned the positive morale impact of mail drops: 'The effect on officers and men of receiving letters from home under such conditions cannot be overestimated.' Eventually, a means would be found for each man to send a brief personal message by W/T to home, and again the effect upon morale was immeasurable.

One of those who found a particular enjoyment from his mail was Captain Gremlin – Wellsted. His wife, Margot, had penned a letter, and he was eager to devour its contents.

Darling heart, this is just an odd letter written on the spur of the moment as I feel so very lonely for you – it's to tell you how terribly much I miss you all the time – even though I don't often write it in my letters – it just gets me too depressed.

It's just to say that I love you and am very proud of you, my dearest one, and how terribly glad I am that I married you. I long so much to see you again and be held close to you – so please hurry back, darling, and meantime take care of yourself.

I love you, dear heart.

Your Margot.

Before leaving for the Morvan, Margot had given Wellsted a miniature, carved in ivory and intricately painted – it was a tiny likeness of herself. He folded that precious letter in a piece of soft cloth, and wrapped it around the miniature, for safe keeping. Often, he'd shown that pint-sized statuette to some of the French he'd met here in the Morvan, finding it especially effective in establishing friendly relations when calling at remote farmsteads. It showed that while he might seem a hardened soldier, at heart he was just like them, a family man with a cherished sweetheart back at home.

That evening there was a feast and a party of sorts at Fraser's camp. It was long overdue. Micky Flynn – the man who'd rescued the padre, after he'd cut himself free and fallen on his head – doubled as the camp cook. A warm-hearted Irishman and a veteran SAS operator, Flynn chivvied the officers and men alike to peel potatoes, collect water and firewood, and generally assist. Empty biscuit tins made fine saucepans, and their Fairbairn Sykes fighting knives – a razor-sharp, double-edged dagger – served as DIY tin openers. But Flynn's prised possession was a genuine ladle, which someone had managed to procure from a nearby town.

Now they were properly supplied, barter with the nearest farms restarted. Fresh eggs were a premium, and the accepted rate of exchange was four eggs to a bar of chocolate. Bread was also sought after, but that generally had to be paid for in hard cash, as were fresh vegetables and meat. Tonight's feast was a tinned repast direct from the new ration packs, but augmented by whatever they had bartered. Well fed, the men gathered around the cooking fire for a rare treat, for a flagon of rum had been included in the parachute drop. With jeeps on hand, some bright spark suggested a barrel of wine might be carted up from the nearest Maquis camp, for they were known to have them. It proved 'very raw stuff', but beggars couldn't be choosers.

As the firelight flickered, the flames lighting up the shadowed fringe of trees that surrounded their clearing, Fraser and his men had the undeniable air of a piratical crew. Moving through such densely wooded and punishing terrain had wrought havoc on their appearances. Forcing a way through dense thickets had shredded their trousers, ripped sleeves from shirts and cut to ribbons other items of uniform. While many of the men had opted to wear puttees – tough woollen wraps, running from boot-tops over ankles and shins – as protection from the mud and thorns, they too had ripped and frayed and disintegrated. Once gone, a bootlace lashed tightly around the trouser bottoms was the next best option. Leather boots, constantly wet, were disintegrating.

Berets, collars and ties had become lost when crawling through the bush. Instead, the SAS had adopted the Maquis habit of wrapping strips of colourful parachute silk around head and neck, forming passable scarfs and bandanas. Wellsted had adopted two such silk bandanas. One, white, was for social occasions – like rum parties. The other, black, was for fighting. Even those who'd managed to retain their berets didn't much favour them. The long-lived sandy beret of the SAS founders had been done away with, on orders from on high. In its place, the SAS had been obliged to wear the red beret of all airborne forces. It shone out like a beacon; hardly suitable for operations behind enemy lines.

Bathing facilities were limited. Shaving even more so, the competition for hot water from cooking fires being fierce. Giving in to the seemingly inevitable, Wellsted and Johnny Cooper – 'The Kid' – started a moustache-growing competition. Cooper would be the loser, as Wellsted embraced his inner Groucho Marx with unbridled enthusiasm. He vowed never to shave, not until 'France was free again', and so ended up with a decidedly hirsute look. During the sunshine his monster moustache seemed 'very fine and fierce', but it had a habit of drooping 'dreadfully' in the rain, lending Captain Gremlin 'an air of deep depression'.

With items of uniform falling apart, and with the lack of resupply, local seamstresses were commissioned to sew parachute-silk replacements. 'Very smart they looked too.' As the Maquis were equally short of proper uniforms, they adapted whatever they could find. The odd items of British battledress retrieved from a parachutage were combined with clothing scavenged off German corpses. The enemy's boots were the most prized item of all. The result was that, in time, 'it was almost impossible to tell the SAS in their stained and ragged uniforms, with their gaudy parachute scarves and ill-assorted boots, from the Maquis . . . whose choice of bright scarves was unimpeachable.'

Well fed, well armed, well rested, and with fresh news from home, morale among Fraser's raiders rocketed. And now they had wheels. With the jeeps to hand, they could range far and wide, quartering the Morvan for the enemy, and packing the kind of punch afforded by a rank of Vickers-K guns. Right now, all they needed was a prime objective, against which to unleash the first mobile raid. As luck would have it, just days after the jeeps had dropped in, they would be handed the juiciest of targets.

It was something to put a spanner into the Nazi war engine, striking a powerful blow for the Allies.

Chapter Seven

PADDY'S MEN

It was 6 July 1944, and the Operation Houndsworth War Diary recorded: 'Capt. WISEMAN left for DIJON area with one jeep.' The first figure to speed out of camp at the wheel of one of their precious new vehicles, Johnny Wiseman was heading towards a French city set a hundred kilometres to the east, and well beyond the borders of the Morvan. The area just to the north of Dijon was reported to be a target-rich environment, and Wiseman's aim, and that of his small party of raiders, was to hit the enemy's vital road and rail links. As the one jeep couldn't possibly carry all of his patrol, plus their kit, a motley band of Maquis vehicles tagged along behind.

Wiseman's camp would end up being 'the most dangerous place of all', as he and his small band of raiders proceeded to wreak havoc under the enemy's very noses. The base he sought was in a thick grove of pine trees, but stationed all around it were some 30,000 German troops. One garrison was even positioned in the neighbouring valley. Undeterred, perhaps Wiseman's greatest feat would be calling in a series of RAF airstrikes on prime targets. His force was six-strong, all told, and it included Lieutenant Tony Trower, newly arrived with the jeeps, Sergeant Jack Terry – the man who'd rescued Reg Seekings after his neck injury – plus three others. For such a tiny force, the damage they would inflict on the enemy was out of all proportion.

The same day that Wiseman set off from Fraser's camp, a major attack was being prepared by Muirhead and Wellsted, at theirs. A careful reconnaissance had revealed a synthetic fuel plant, situated near the town of Autun. It lay some sixty kilometres to the south, on the very borders of the Morvan, but the prize made the perilous journey more than worth the risk. Synthetic fuel – or synfuel – is a man-made liquid petroleum substitute most commonly made from coal. As the Nazi war machine was desperately short of fuel for its Panzers and warplanes, from the earliest briefings the SAS had been alerted that fuel tankers and fuel trains were prime targets.

If Hitler's Panzer divisions could be starved of fuel, there was no way in which they were going to join the fight, as the Allies endeavoured to break out from the Normandy beaches. For the whole of June, battle had been more or less deadlocked. A series of attempted breakthroughs by British and US forces had been met by fierce German resistance, as the battle had raged through the *bocage*, dense hedgerow country lying inland. Repeated set-backs had left the Allied commanders flummoxed. There was 'gloom' at Supreme Headquarters Allied Expeditionary Force (SHAEF), as the stalemate set in. But likewise, and unbeknown to the Allies, the enemy situation was desperate. They were fast using up men and machines in the bitter fighting, and only by rushing in replacements might their frontlines hold.

Fuel was the key, so depriving the enemy of it was essential. Shooting up fuel trains was fabulous, but taking out an entire plant would be a whole different level. The mission to attack the Autun facility was led by Muirhead – Bertie Wooster – and incredibly, he had within his number none other than Reg Seekings. It was the end of the first week of July when their lone jeep set forth, so no more than a dozen days since Seekings had been shot. Regardless, he seemed raring to go. As his good friend

114

the padre would note, 'The bullet lodged in Reg's neck hadn't kept him off operations for long.' In fact, that enemy round would remain firmly in place for most of the remainder of the war.

The target was so vital that Fraser had allotted two of his precious jeeps to the mission. In the lead vehicle rode Muirhead, together with a Maquis guide. In the rear was Seekings, manning the Vickers-K guns, with Johnny Cooper at the wheel. Each jeep was loaded down with mortar bombs, Muirhead being a past-master with the 3-inch mortar. The plan of attack had been worked out to the last detail, for the mission was beset by challenges. Chief among them was the coal mine that lay directly beneath the fuel plant, and the French miners who worked there. Attacking at night, and lobbing in a mixture of incendiary and high explosive (HE) bombs, the plant should be rendered into a raging inferno, but that risked 'hundreds of miners' being 'trapped below', only 'to die for lack of oxygen'. But having learned that the night shift stopped at 2.00 a.m., and wasn't restarted until 4.00, that provided the raiders with a narrow window.

The journey south was routed along a series of minor roads, which were unlikely to host enemy patrols. Whenever the pair of jeeps reached a main junction, they would halt, reconnoitre on foot, and only move off once the coast was clear, ensuring there was a break in traffic both ways. By the time they were nearing the plant, the sun had long set, and it was a clear, starry night. Muirhead selected a large field that overlooked the target, which lay around a thousand yards away, outlined in the light of moon and stars. The squat, square towers, the massive cylindrical storage tanks, the riot of pipework and the neighbouring rail terminal stood out in ghostly silhouette against the sky.

Working silently and swiftly, the mortar was set up, its heavy baseplate planted firmly in the ground, the gaping tube pointing skywards. While Muirhead zeroed it in, Seekings, Cooper and the others primed the bombs. They'd fire two smoke first, for the bursts of those would indicate exactly where the shots were falling, and Muirhead would doubtless need to readjust his aim. The force of the backblast tended to drive the baseplate into the earth, so the sighting almost always needed tweaking. Shortly before zero hour, all was ready, and the attack party settled down in a tense silence to wait.

They'd decided to run past the 2.00 a.m. shift-end by a good twenty minutes, to allow time for the miners to leave. Bang on the dot at 0220 hours, the first smoke bomb was dropped down the tube, and with a hollow thump it went winging its way towards the plant. A second followed instantaneously, and as they watched for the fall of those first two projectiles, they were pleased to spy two bursts of white smoke wreathed in the eerie light. A slight adjustment and they began to 'fire for effect', lobbing '40 Mortars HE and incendiary bombs by moonlight', as the Operation Houndsworth War Diary noted. At such a range, there were five bombs in the air at any one time, as they began to slam down among the facility, wreaking mayhem.

Caught by utter surprise, the German guard force presumed an air raid was in progress. The ghostly wail of the air-raid sirens rose above the factory, punctuated by the rhythmic blasts of exploding mortar rounds. Though the skies were empty of warplanes, the staccato crack of anti-aircraft fire rang out from the factory, as the German gunners loosed off at imaginary assailants. Then above the cacophony of noise there arose another sound entirely – a whirlwind-like roar as the giant tanks of synthetic petroleum went up in a tower of smoke and fire. By the time the last bomb was winging its way through the air, the facility was 'ablaze and the sky was lit up by flaming petrol'.

Figuring that 'discretion was the better part of valour', Muirhead and his men freed the baseplate from where it had embedded itself in the ground, stamped out the indentation, cleared away boot and tyre tracks as best they could and got motoring. The aim was to leave not the slightest clue as to the land-borne nature of the assault, just in case they ever needed to return for a sequel. Equally importantly, this way the enemy would never know what had happened – it would be as if the plant had been consumed by some mystery, fire-breathing monster of legend.

As the raiders closed the field gate and pulled away, they marvelled at the success of such a simple yet effective mission; the 'plant superstructure stood out gaunt and grim against the glare'. In due course, they would learn that the Autun fuel plant had burned for four days solid, the enemy struggling to extinguish the flames. As it had produced some 7,500 gallons of fuel per day, the attack had punched a significant hole in the Nazi war effort. A petrol train waiting in a siding had also been hit, and it too had burned for days on end. They had managed to destroy a vital 'source of fuel for the German army', as Cooper would conclude.

Back at their base camps the buzz went around. The jeeps had hit home. The Autun plant had been well and truly put out of action, and that was entirely the kind of mission they had been sent here to achieve. Further patrols were out blowing the railway lines that cut through the region. And while Muirhead had been busy mortaring the fuel plant, Wellsted had spearheaded another, similarly daring escapade. As with Autun, the mobility provided by the jeeps would prove key, plus the intelligence provided by the locals.

Some 130 kilometres due south of their Morvan base, a tantalising target was reported: two airfields, located at Volesvres and St-Yan, along with newly built hangars and other mystery facilities. Already, Fraser had been able to radio in to London precious intelligence – the coordinates of a V-1 flying bomb assembly plant. On 13 June 1944, the first of these rudimentary cruise missiles had been unleashed on Britain, as Hitler sought to use his much-vaunted *Vergeltungswaffen* – Vengeance Weapons – to crush the Allied attempts to liberate Europe. No one knew exactly what the Volesvres and St-Yan facilities harboured, but the fevered construction efforts suggested it was something vital to the Nazi war effort.

Wellsted had set out in a jeep crammed with raiders, and never mind that their route would, of necessity, take them through the centre of a German garrison town. In a sense, this was his true baptism of fire: a mission fully under his command, with everything to play for. He had his trusty minder, Middleton, at the wheel, and crammed in the rear were Corporal 'Swag' Jemson, plus Trooper Grady. Grady was a Yorkshire lad with a French mother, who, handily, spoke decent French and German, plus he was a natural with explosives. As for Swag Jemson, he was a tall, weathered figure hailing from Lancashire, who'd served with the Parachute Regiment in Italy, before volunteering for the SAS. A 'most cheerful character', as Wellsted would describe him, Jemson was a demon on the Bren gun. Their Maquis guide was a former French Army tank commander, known as Jean-Paul to all, and he was bullet-proof reliable. It was a strong team for a mission of real dash and daring – that was if they could pull it off.

In their crowded jeep laden with explosives – it was carrying six people in all – they would have to pass through the town of Toulon-sur-Arroux, which could not be avoided, for it offered one of the few means of crossing the Arroux river. As they crept towards the town's bridge in the dead of night, the noise of loud snoring came from the German barracks block that lay to one side. Somehow, they managed to slip through undetected.

Finally nearing the outskirts of Volesvres aerodrome, Wellsted, Jemson, Grady and Jean-Paul were dropped, for the jeep was needed back in the Morvan. A rendezvous was set several days hence, and from that point onwards the raiders proceeded on foot.

Flitting like wraiths through the night, they approached the giant hangars at Volesvres, only to discover that the place was deserted. It had been abandoned in favour of the satellite airstrip at St-Yan, where construction work had been in full swing. Switching targets, they'd stolen towards St-Yan, as signs in both French and German declared: 'It is absolutely forbidden to trespass onto this aerodrome.' Wellsted led them forwards and shortly they were upon the airfield itself, but another disappointment awaited. Whatever was in the process of being built, the enemy hadn't finished construction yet, and there were no aircraft, or flying bombs or the like to sabotage.

Wisely, Wellsted chose not to waste their charges on an aerodrome which very likely would never be finished in time to aid the Nazi war effort. In any case, they'd already spied a fallback target. Melting away into the darkness, they resolved to blow up the Paray–Digoin railway line, which, as they'd noted, was heavy with enemy rail traffic. Plus they'd endeavour to execute a 'daylight hold-up of the tram' which served the Lyon to Toulon line. Searching for the ideal spot, they found a place where a derailed train should carve up a good length of track, before it tumbled into the canal that lay to one side of the railway embankment.

Holed up in some nearby woodland, Wellsted and his men prepared their charges, while chatting softly in an effort to kill the daylight hours. Having talked about the kind of music each favoured, the conversation turned to the thorny topic of 'the moral justification of blowing a trainload of troops to Kingdom Come'. The chat was awkwardly multilingual, as Jean-Paul tried to practise his English, Grady his French, and Wellsted was forced to break into French whenever Jean-Paul seemed to be having problems. As for Jemson, his habit of peppering his sentences with expletives made it impossible for any Frenchman to follow. Teased unmercifully for his blaspheming, over time Jemson's diction would grow clean as a whistle, while Jean-Paul's English would become fluent, and Wellsted would be 'swearing like a trooper'.

As the night thickened, there was sabotage to pursue. They crept down to the canal and crossed the bridge that forded it. Wellsted left Jemson with his Bren to hold that crossing – the route by which they would withdraw. Jemson was not to open fire, he warned, 'even if Hitler at the head of a Panzer division comes marching over this bridge'. Only if the enemy fired first was Jemson to let rip with the Bren.

That agreed, Wellsted, Grady and Jean-Paul pressed on. Creeping along the railway embankment, they reached their chosen spot. Removing his backpack, Wellsted drew out the 'long string of Cordtex with the Lewes bombs dangling from it like some hideous fruit on a fantastic vine'. Cordtex is detonating cord, while Lewes bombs were the favoured charges of the SAS, having been invented by one of the unit's founders, John Steel 'Jock' Lewes, who had sadly been killed on one of the earliest desert operations.

Jamming the explosives tight beside the rails, Grady, their demolitions expert, busied himself readying the fuses and timers, plus an 'ingenious little contrivance' made up of a string of grenades, which effectively booby-trapped the charges, should anyone try to interfere with them. As Wellsted observed, 'one false move on Grady's part and the whole operation would have ended . . . with one big bang, but Grady knew his job.' Charges set, the three saboteurs scuttled back along the embankment, making for the bridge as the countdown began.

Halfway there, they remembered they'd forgotten a piece of kit, and Grady ran back to fetch it. Moments later his silhouette was visible once again, as he scuttled back along the tracks. But as he stepped down to join Wellsted and Jean-Paul, 'with a vicious rattle, three Schmeissers opened a devastating fire'. From the direction of the bridge shadowy shapes spat flame. There was a gasp from Grady, who came crashing down the embankment, landing between Wellsted and Jean-Paul. The enemy were no more than ten yards away, and Grady had been injured, though no one yet knew how badly.

The instant the German troops opened up, there was the signature bark of a Bren. True to his orders, Jemson was answering the enemy's fire with his own. Instantly the entire scene was lit by scorching bursts of tracer, red and green streams arcing through the sky. Grenade blasts added to the confusion. Jemson was clearly in the thick of it, which meant the enemy must have staked out the bridge. Grabbing his carbine, Wellsted was about to return fire, when he was struck by a terrible thought. The enemy were here in numbers, and if they got to the charges, they very possibly might have an explosives expert in their party. In which case, all the raiders' good work might be undone.

In the 'only really brave thing I have ever done', as he described it, Wellsted jumped to his feet and, crouching low, began to scuttle back to where 'our handiwork was still clearly visible'. Expecting to be met by a hail of bullets, somehow he made it unscathed. From his pocket he drew out an emergency 30-second fuse. Knotting it into the charges on the rails, he 'pulled the pin . . . there was a most satisfying fizzing noise,' and he took to his heels. Down the embankment he thundered, before throwing himself flat on the dirt, cupping his hands over his ears.

The next moment: 'BLAAAM!'

Wellsted had a momentary vision of the entire upper surface of the gravel embankment seeming to rise into the air, as a violent glow flashed through the darkness and blasted chunks of heavy metal flew in all directions. Then, a ringing, deafening silence. Clambering to his feet, sections of shattered sleeper, steel rails and rock began to rain down as gravity regained control, and Wellsted threw himself into cover for a second time. Once the debris storm had abated, he dashed over to rejoin his men, the entire scene thick with smoke. Glancing behind, he spied twisted, buckled rails, while beyond that an entire section of the track had vanished without trace.

Back with Grady and Jean-Paul, he outlined the plan that was even then forming in his mind. Clearly, there was no route back across the bridge, where the firefight raged unabated. Grady and Jean-Paul should take to the canal and swim for it, while he would draw the enemy's fire.

'I can't swim,' Jean-Paul countered, simply.

'I'm hit,' Grady added, meaning his wounds had to be serious.

Clearly, neither man was about to swim the canal. From the direction of the bridge, the Bren still barked defiance. Somehow, miraculously, Jemson still seemed to be alive, and while surrounded by the enemy he was giving them hell. Jean-Paul suggested Wellsted go to Jemson's aid. A plan was set. Via the canal, Wellsted would swim up to Jemson's position, after which the two of them would endeavour to clear the enemy from the bridge. Once that was done, they'd call for Jean-Paul and Grady to join them.

Plan agreed, Wellsted made a beeline for the water. He reached it, only to find the enemy were there ahead of him. Retracing his steps, he returned to the spot where he'd left Grady and Jean-Paul, but they had disappeared. No amount of calling raised the sniff of an answer. Returning to the canal once more, Wellsted finally managed to slip into the water and he began to swim for it.

Grabbing a length of wood for extra buoyancy, by midway he was waterlogged and sinking fast. In desperation, he jettisoned his weapon – a Tommy gun – and just managed to make it to the far side.

Soaked and exhausted, Wellsted stole across to where he'd last seen Jemson. Not a sign of him anywhere. Whistling softly, the only response was a shiver of movement off to one side, which Wellsted felt certain was the enemy. With no other option left to him, he melted into the undergrowth, after which he began the long trek back to their forest hideout, as bursts of fire and yells of alarm rang out in the darkness behind.

In truth, Jemson was still in the heart of the action, one man against a multitude, and fighting with a cool, calculated ferocity that was breathtaking.

For Swag Jemson, the first sign that they had hit trouble was the sudden appearance of a shadowy form flitting through the darkness in front of him. Soon, there were more, and Jemson was struck by how noiselessly and stealthily the enemy moved, as they took up their positions in complete silence. The German platoon settled itself all around him, yet still he remained immobile and utterly silent. And watchful. The German officer sited one Spandau in a ditch opposite Jemson's hidden position, and a further one down by the canal, while the bridge itself was swarming with troops.

All was quiet, until Grady was spotted and the enemy opened fire. The moment the first shots rent the night, Jemson rose from his ditch like some ghostly apparition, and wielding his Bren from the shoulder had cut down the nearest Spandau crew. That gun never fired again, while the one on the canal towpath couldn't be swung around to hit him, so unexpected was the direction of Jemson's attack. Lowering the Bren, and grabbing two fresh magazines, he'd rolled down the slope from which he'd sprung, just as the enemy lobbed two grenades in his direction.

The first slammed into his head, but fortunately failed to explode. The second detonated on the bank above him, and had he not changed position it doubtless would have nailed him. Instead, he found himself lying on the low ground in thick darkness, while the enemy were silhouetted on the higher terrain above. For an hour and a half he fought a lonely battle. Firing in short, aimed bursts and on single shot mode, he kept taking out enemy fighters, while constantly changing position 'to confuse the enemy', who 'never for one moment realised that they were opposed by only one man'.

Eventually, he'd used up all of the ammunition that he carried for the Bren. Unholstering his Colt semi-automatic pistol, he began pumping out single shots from that. So bewildered were the enemy, they had begun to fire at each other. In fact, Jemson 'so frightened and confused Jerry' that for the majority of the time they had been fighting among themselves. More importantly, for Wellsted and the others, it was Jemson's lone actions that had enabled those who had escaped to break away.

Just as dawn was breaking, Wellsted reached their forest hideout. Disturbingly, he found it deserted, for he'd hoped that maybe Jean-Paul, Grady or even Jemson might have made it back there alive. As he drifted into a cold and shattered sleep, he reflected upon how he'd lost all of his patrol on the first ever solo operation that he had commanded. His fitful rest would be plagued by nightmares.

Wellsted woke to full daylight and a sight that brought joy to his heart. Making his way through the trees was a familiar figure – Jean-Paul. 'I could have kissed him,' Wellsted declared. Shortly, the Frenchman revealed all. After Wellsted had left to swim the canal, Jemson's efforts at the bridge had drawn the enemy's attention and their ire. Taking advantage of that, Jean-Paul had helped Grady – who had been hit in the arm, the bullet breaking the bone – over the railway line and into fields on the far side. As the wounded man was in such a desperate condition, Jean-Paul risked approaching an isolated farmstead. The farmer, a true patriot, had promised to shield Grady, leaving Jean-Paul free to head for the rendezvous.

No sooner had Jean-Paul finished telling his story, than there was a crashing in the undergrowth and Swag Jemson emerged. It was time to hear his incredible tale. All out of ammo, and believing his chances of survival were slim, Jemson had buried his escape funds – cash – in a hole in the ground, and dismantled his Bren, scattering the pieces widely, before slipping into the canal. He'd made a break by swimming for it, and remarkably had managed to get away. After a celebratory breakfast, the three survivors took stock. They were desperately short of weaponry. They had two standard-issue Colt .45 pistols and two grenades, plus Wellsted's tiny .22 calibre pistol, the 'vicious little automatic' that the Red Russian, Alexis, had taken off the wounded enemy officer and given to him.

Wellsted and Jemson got busy making some DIY grenades, fashioned from old food tins stuffed with plastic explosives and stones as makeshift shrapnel, and with short fuses attached. Their work was interrupted by the sound of a pony and trap clomping up the narrow track that wound past their hideout. Ominously, it stopped. They heard voices, and then an eerily evocative noise. Someone was whistling 'Sur le Pont d'Avginon' – their signature tune.

They went to investigate, finding a farmer's daughter – 'very pretty, in green jumper and rough peasant's skirt' – holding the reins of the trap, while beside her sat the 'most villainous looking Frenchman' imaginable. This 'sinister individual' had a

125

'drooping black moustache', day's old growth, and was dressed in 'filthy, torn trousers' and a 'loose black blouse'. On his head was perched an 'oily black cap', while his arm was in a rough sling. He dismounted and approached, and as he did so he broke into a broad grin. 'It was Grady.'

His story of escape was the most remarkable of all. Sheltered by the farmer and his family, they'd managed to smuggle Grady to the local curé. The priest had set his arm, bound up the wound and given him the clothes he now wore. The following morning, the farmer's daughter had set off, with Grady riding shotgun. They'd reached the bridge over the canal, where she had dropped him, promising to wait on the far side. Grady had proceeded to walk across, hiding in plain sight. Glancing down the railway lines, he'd spied a work crew busy at repairs, for trains were backed up, including a troop transport crammed with enemy soldiers, and a locomotive hauling fuel wagons. On the far side he'd rejoined his waiting carriage and they'd made their way direct to the rendezvous. Simply incredible.

Shortly, the jeep driven by Middleton arrived to collect them. Before setting out, a figure appeared on a bicycle – one of the locals who'd proved so courageous in assisting the wounded Grady. He'd searched high and low for Jemson's Bren, and with painstaking care had gathered up all the scattered parts. A bundle was strapped to his handlebars. He removed it and handed it, reverentially, to Jemson.

'Christ, it's filthy!' Jemson remarked, as he unwrapped it. Getting out his gun kit, he proceeded to clean it lovingly.

Wellsted and his men were determined to have one last hurrah. They had a few pounds of plastic explosives remaining and it would be a shame not to use it. A short jeep drive away, they set the last of their charges upon a series of massive pylons, which carried high-tension electrical cables to the two nearest industrial towns. Charges set, that night they executed the long drive back to their base.

Halfway through the journey, they halted on a road that wound up into the rocky heights of the Morvan. Pausing for a map-check, the terrain to the south stretched out for miles below. Suddenly, 'a ruddy glow lit up the skyline', and immediately thereafter a 'great blue flash reflected to the very clouds'. Their charges had just blown the electricity pylons.

A few hours later their lone jeep made it back to their Morvan base. From there, Wellsted would make his way to Fraser's camp, to furnish a full report of the operation just concluded. On Fraser's advice, Wellsted would write up Swag Jemson for a high valour medal, and he would duly be awarded the DCM. No doubt about it, Fraser's A Squadron was achieving exactly what they'd been charged to do, here in the Morvan.

While Wellsted had been away, two sharply contrasting air missions had been flown over the SAS bases. After his recent broadcast to the men, Mayne was impatient to get into the field. Fraser had received a warning. The SAS commander was about to fly over their DZ. His aim was to use a newfangled gadget – an S-phone – to speak to Fraser on the ground, even as the warplane orbited overhead. A brainchild of the Special Operations Executive, the S-phone was a 'sort of ground-to-air wireless telephone', as Wellsted would describe it. The inbound plane was there chiefly to drop supplies, but Mayne was also intent on delivering a message to Fraser and his men.

At the appointed hour the first packages had plummeted from the belly of the aircraft, and 'chutes blossomed in the skies. The drop seemed to have gone like clockwork, but try as he might Fraser couldn't raise the hint of any contact with Mayne. Unable to hear the slightest sound, he uncharacteristically lost his temper. Fraser began 'swearing viciously into the machine', unaware all the while that Mayne could hear every word. In fact, the S-phone's speaker was broadcasting Fraser's colourful language through the length and breadth of the orbiting warplane. Regardless, whatever Mayne had wanted to communicate, it was left unsaid.

The following night, there had been a far more serious aerial misadventure, one with fatal consequences. Two aircraft had been inbound, on a mission to drop supplies to the local Maquis. One was a Consolidated B-24 Liberator – an American heavy bomber – with an American crew. The other was an RAF Halifax. Tragically, they had collided just as they arrived over the DZ. At Bill Frazer's camp, the padre had awakened to a comet of fire shooting across the heavens. Moments later, a series of powerful blasts had erupted from near by, as harsh flames lit up the entire area. Hurrying to investigate, it turned out that the one aircraft, loaded with ammunition, had crashed not far away, while the other had ploughed into a field adjacent to the village of Mazignien.

From the smouldering remains, the padre retrieved the dog-tags of the American crew, all of whom had perished 'instantaneously in their positions in the plane'. All morning they worked 'among the smoking wreckage', retrieving the bodies. The terrible smell would haunt McLuskey and the others for years to come. 'Tired, grimy' and smelling 'of death', they stood around the row of graves they'd dug, as the padre read the service. 'We were one family,' he would write. 'These men were our men, and in this last earthly rite I was proud to be their minister.'

The other aircraft posed a far greater problem. The wreckage was clearly visible from the road, and if the mayor of Mazignien failed to alert the enemy, his village would pay the price. He came to check with Fraser, who agreed – it had to be reported in. A force of German troops came to investigate. They gathered up the bodies of the RAF aircrew and took them for burial at the nearest cemetery, at the village of Marigny l'Église.

The Sunday following the twin tragedies, a procession of villagers arrived at the Liberator crash site – the debris was scattered all around the SAS camp – bearing flowers and wreaths. Bill Fraser's battle-worn warriors were struck by 'the sympathy and gratitude' of the locals, which was 'deep and sincere'. As the padre remarked, 'We had our jeeps and our guns. We could fight back and get away. But these men, women and children had to stay and take it.'

And as the SAS fully appreciated, the price they had paid was heavy indeed.

Chapter Eight

GET ROMMEL

While Fraser's SAS had been busy, so too was Sir James Hutchison, whose SOE codename was *Telemetre*. Charged with working closely with the Maquis, he'd become increasingly frustrated by the rivalries that beset the entire French Resistance movement. Any number of times he'd attempted to call in airdrops of arms for one or another Maquis, only to have the London headquarters of the Free French – the French government in exile – bicker, dissemble and prevaricate. For a man who'd gone to the lengths of having his face recrafted by a plastic surgeon so he could serve, it was most galling.

It was made all the more frustrating in that Hutchison carried a letter signed by General Marie-Pierre Koenig himself, the Free French delegate at Allied headquarters, serving under the Supreme Allied Commander, General Dwight D. Eisenhower. That letter stated that Hutchison should be given all possible assistance, but it seemed to cut little ice with the London HQ of the Free French. Increasingly, he'd turned to the SAS, realising that with them a request for a weapons drop was rarely challenged or denied. 'I found a staunch ally in Bill Fraser, and no political niceties cluttered the thinking of the SAS,' he would write. 'They were bent only on driving out the enemy.'

Many among the Maquis had proven equally 'fed up with all

this French intrigue'. One, a Lieutenant Jean 'Johnny' Lebaudy, approached Hutchison offering to work for him and the British direct. Lebaudy was someone with 'no half-formed opinions or irresolution', as Hutchison concluded. Taking Lebaudy at his word, one of their first joint initiatives had been to set up an intelligence-gathering network, staffed by their 'Zoubinettes', as Hutchison and Lebaudy would call them – young French women who could slip by unnoticed where a man would arouse suspicion.

Their first recruit, Claudette, had worked in Paris as a courier for the Resistance, before the Gestapo had got her. Hauled in for interrogation, she'd refused to divulge anything. Then the rough stuff had started. 'They stripped me naked,' she confided to Hutchison 'tied me to a chair, and tipped me backwards into a bath of cold water. They held me there until they saw that I was unconscious. Then they brought me around . . . The next day they repeated the business, and again . . .' Claudette had pretended that such treatment had left her too ill to think or to answer any of their questions. Eventually, they had been forced to let her go and she had fled to the Morvan.

As Claudette had told her story, bravely and matter-of-factly, Hutchison and Lebaudy had been 'lost for words', gazing at her in admiration. The Zoubinettes began to quarter the Morvan, moving on bicycles to hoover up intelligence, and carrying messages hidden in the most ingenious of places. Shortly, they would come up trumps. But before that could happen, Hutchison had a mission of his own to execute.

He received an urgent message from Bill Fraser. They were in need of sorting a landing zone where an Allied warplane could put down. The SOE – Hutchison's outfit – had grown accustomed to flying agents into and out of the field by Westland Lysander, a light aircraft with superb short take-off and landing abilities.

The Lysander could put down on a sixpence. But Fraser had need of a much larger warplane. The plan hatched with London was to fly in a Douglas C-47 Skytrain, to land in the Morvan and evacuate the SAS's growing body of wounded. Since the Château de Vermot hospital had been destroyed, they had been sheltered in a series of makeshift facilities deep in the woods, and were in desperate need of proper medical care.

Back in Britain, during training with the SOE, Hutchison had been instructed in the art and craft of surveying, selecting and operating covert airstrips, and how exactly to call in aircraft to land. Taking Lebaudy, who was a former pilot from the First World War, Hutchison got motoring in the big, black Citroën that he'd acquired locally, complete with its Union Jack mounted on the front, as they searched for a usable airstrip. Behind the wheel he had a trusted Maquis driver, with two more Maquis crammed in the rear, and a bicycle strapped to the back, just in case.

Hutchison had an airstrip in mind, but it lay on the far side of Saulieu, the town at which Trooper Burgess, one of the SAS wounded, had been supposed to get an X-ray of his broken leg. There was no option but to pass through it. They halted at the outskirts, while the Maquis cyclist unstrapped his bicycle and pedalled ahead, seeking intelligence. Assured that the coast was clear, and with Sten guns at the ready, they moved into the heart of town, until, rounding a corner, they spied a German army truck parked outside a café. With no way to turn back, the driver put his foot on the gas, and the 'astonished Germans . . . saw only a fleeting view of a Union Jack fluttering on the bonnet', before the car sped past.

Not far from Saulieu lay a disused pre-war airfield. Along one side ran a busy main road, but the strip itself looked perfect – 800 yards long, and more than wide enough to take a C-47. Checking it out proved somewhat hazardous. Wisely, Hutchison did it after nightfall, and whenever vehicle headlamps appeared, he flattened himself in the long grass that grew on the disused strip. Halfway through quartering the entire expanse, a small reconnaissance aircraft roared overhead, appearing as if it was about to land. Hutchison leapt into one of the hedges that fringed the airfield and waited. The Germans were forever zipping about in such warplanes, trying to spot the smoke from the Maquis cooking fires drifting over the forests. If this one landed, Hutchison wondered if 'there were any way we could capture it', for it was most likely unarmed.

As it was, the aircraft buzzed away and Hutchison declared himself happy that this airfield would suffice. He found the whole prospect intensely invigorating, for the very idea of landing a large aircraft 'by moonlight on an enemy-held field in France' had always fired his imagination, for it was 'pure drama with an attractive tinge of impertinence'. Having codenamed the airfield *Marshmallow*, he reported back to Fraser. Hutchison's news was timely, for the medical evacuation flight was expected in the next forty-eight hours. There was also a dossier of vital documents captured from the enemy that Fraser needed to spirit back into Allied hands.

The wounded were made ready. There was Trooper Burgess, with his broken leg. Corporal Eric Adamson, who'd suffered horrendous internal injuries in a jeep accident. Trooper Grady, with his shattered arm. And more. Aided by the padre, McReady, the SAS's medic, was doing sterling work. Indeed, he and McLuskey had recently 'recruited' a highly unusual medical assistant – 'one of the youngsters enlisted in Hitler's final desperate drive for manpower'. One night an enemy patrol had come to attack the Maquis base, near Mazignien village. Unwittingly, they'd stumbled into Fraser's SAS. In the short but sharp firefight that had ensued, the Germans were forced to withdraw, leaving their dead and wounded.

One of the injured was 'a German boy by the name of Rolph'. Rolph had been shot through the chest, but luckily the bullet had missed all his vital organs. Nursed back to health, he was overjoyed to learn that the padre was married to a German woman and was more or less fluent in German. During their discussions, it became clear that 'Nazi Germany was the only world' that Rolph had ever known. The padre found it amazing how quickly Rolph 'made friends with the men, and how quickly they befriended him'. Employed as a medical assistant, in time he declared his desire was to 'join the Special Air Service!' Yet, had Rolph and his patrol captured any of the SAS, he would 'have taken it as the most natural thing in the world' to torture and shoot them. Brainwashed by Nazi propaganda, youngsters like Rolph hadn't stood a chance.

Even with the assistance of the likes of Rolph, as the wounded were moved from one hut to another, conditions were desperate, especially since they stood little chance if the enemy launched a surprise attack. In fact, all among the SAS appreciated just how the wounded felt, for they too 'slept with one eye open', their escape kits to hand in case they had to make a run for it. Wounded and able bodied alike knew there was 'no future in being captured in this kind of warfare'. The fates of the people of Dun-les-Places, Vermot and countless other villages betrayed what would very likely happen to the SAS, should they be captured.

Though the *Marshmallow* airstrip was ready for the medical evacuation, the C-47 failed to materialise. For several nights it was on-again and off-again, before the pick-up was finally cancelled. The wounded would just have to try to hold on. Even so, Hutchison's daring reconnaissance of that airstrip would not be in vain. Another, quite extraordinary purpose for that disused 'drome was to be proposed. Thanks to the bravery of his Zoubinettes, and Hutchison's own panache, a new target for the proposed airlift was mooted. This time, it was to be a daring and audacious snatch operation, of the kind that had never yet been pulled off during the war.

Hutchison and the SAS had discovered the headquarters of their old nemesis, Field Marshal Erwin Rommel.

Johnny Lebaudy, Hutchison's deputy, actually hailed from fabulously wealthy and high-born French stock. His ancestral home was the exquisite Château de Rosny-sur-Seine, north-west of Paris, which had been requisitioned by the Germans, as had a number of other similar properties in the region. Lebaudy's contacts were able to warn him that one such exquisite building, the Château de La Roche-Guyon, served as the headquarters of Field Marshal Erwin Rommel, who was one of Hitler's key deputies overseeing the Nazi war effort in France.

The Château de La Roche-Guyon sits among verdant woodland, with grounds running down to the banks of the River Seine. A vast edifice built by French nobility, it backs up against limestone cliffs. Since the Middle Ages the castle's ancient keep, perched on a limestone hillock, has kept guard over the river. Many of Lebaudy's staff and groundsmen still worked in the area, and with the help of the Zoubinettes, word had reached Lebaudy that the chateau had been taken over by this foremost German commander. The intelligence even included details of where and when Rommel took his daily exercise. 'Almost always alone, at much the same time every day, he walks in certain woods on the estate,' as Hutchison would note.

Knowing of the SAS's antipathy towards Rommel, Hutchison rushed this priceless intelligence to Fraser at his Mazignien base, sensing that for the SAS, there would be something 'particularly satisfying' in capturing Rommel. On arrival at the camp, Hutchison and Lebaudy got down to business, outlining their plan to kidnap Rommel, and to spirit him out of the *Marshmallow* airstrip to Britain.

'It all sounds like a fairy-tale,' Hutchison concluded, 'but most of these plans do, when you first consider them. Just listen to Johnny.'

As Lebaudy revealed all, a Cheshire cat grin spread across Fraser's boyish, impish features. But as the Frenchman addressed the challenges involved in getting to Rommel and spiriting him away, Fraser's smile faded. When Lebaudy was finished, Hutchison jumped in again.

'Now, Bill, the thing isn't all that easy, but it's not impossible.'

'No,' Bill agreed. 'I believe it's on.'

Fraser had an extra, burning reason to want to nail the German commander, over and above those perceived by the wider body of the SAS. It was Rommel who had masterminded the capture of his former unit, the 1st Battalion the Gordon Highlanders, at the port of Saint-Valery-en-Caux, during the 1940 defeat in France. The majority of those men – those who had survived – were languishing in German POW camps. It rankled. This, now – it offered the perfect chance to even up the score.

They discussed the fine details. Fraser would furnish the vehicles, the firepower and the men. By now he had five jeeps to hand. The Maquis would provide extra gunmen, and an escort back into the Morvan. Along with Lebaudy, Hutchison would provide the intelligence, and the airstrip. Thus they would drive from the Morvan some 350 kilometres north-west – the chateau lay on the far side of Paris – circumnavigate the city, snatch Rommel, and drive back again. As all appreciated, speed would be absolutely essential, for once Rommel was nabbed the entire region 'would be buzzing'.

'God!' declared Fraser, as they contemplated the mission. 'What a coup!' His grin now stretched from ear to ear.

The plan was radioed through to London, but the response was not what all had hoped for. London declared that they were to leave Rommel well alone. Fraser and his men were doing sterling work in the Morvan, and more of the same was called for. In the meantime, having now been alerted to his whereabouts, London had set upon other plans for the German general. Fraser argued vehemently to be given the chance to have a go. After all, he had men with him like Lebaudy who knew the area intimately. But London took the not unreasonable view that it was unlikely that Fraser could safely cross some 700 kilometres of Nazi-occupied France with a German Field Marshal as his captive.

'It's a damned shame,' Fraser exclaimed, as he relayed the news to Hutchison and Lebaudy. 'I believe Paddy wants to keep him for himself.'

In a sense, Fraser had a point, for while Paddy Mayne would not be heading out to kill or capture Rommel, the SAS most certainly would be.

The Operation Houndsworth War Diary of 14 July 1944 recorded the following intel being radioed to London: 'Germans using the bridges over the SEINE which were covered in water in the daytime. Also information about position and defences of Field Marshal ROMMEL's HQ. Details of flying bomb dumps and assemblies near PARIS.' Via the Zoubinettes and other means, Fraser had learned of a submersible pontoon bridge being used by the enemy. Convoys would cross at night, under cover of darkness, after which the bridge would be submerged come daybreak, so frustrating Allied air power. They'd also learned about the site of a subterranean V-1 factory near Paris. But the dynamite intel was the Rommel factor.

By 18 July, four days after Fraser had radioed through his message – and his request to get Rommel – SHAEF had drawn up a briefing concerning 'ROMMEL's Headquarters'. Reports of it being 'at LA ROCHE GUYON seem to be the most reliable because of the convincing factual evidence . . . This location seems perfectly acceptable from a tactical point of view, i.e. for a headquarters that is not only controlling the battle in NOR-MANDY, but also running another Army stretching from the SEINE to the SCHELDT.' The Scheldt is a river in north-east France, which flows through Belgium and the Netherlands, before emptying into the North Sea. In other words, Rommel commanded the Nazi front at the Normandy beaches, and from there right across the entire north of France. No wonder there was such excitement at SHAEF at the proposition of doing away with the German commander.

Days later, the SAS mission to get Rommel was on. Appropriately codenamed Operation Gaff – a gaff being a massive barbed hook, used for snagging big fish – the intent was to 'kill, or kidnap and remove to England, Field Marshal ROMMEL . . .' The trigger for raising a party to drop into that part of France had been the 'signals from HOUNDSWORTH' citing 'reliable information obtained from the estates around ROMMEL's HQ'. The intel sent by Fraser was dynamite, including such details as Rommel's staff being based at the chateau permanently, and that Rommel him-self 'crosses the R. SEINE by motor launch and walks and shoots in the FORET DE MOISSON on the left bank'.

The man tasked with commanding Operation Gaff was the inimitable 'Captain Jack William Raymond Lee'. Lee was in truth one Raymond Couraud. With an American mother and a French father, Couraud had spent half his life in Pennsylvania and half in Paris. A French Foreign Legionnaire before the war, he had deserted from the Legion after the fall of France, becoming a gangster in the Marseille mafia, before meeting with and falling for the American heiress and socialite, Mary Jane Gold. Together, Couraud and Gold had smuggled some two thousand Jews out of France, saving them from the clutches of the Nazis, before their network had been penetrated by the Gestapo.

Forced to go on the run, Gold had fled to the US, while Couraud, her erstwhile lover, had executed a daring escape via Spain to Britain. There, Couraud had signed up for the Special Operations Executive. During his stint with SOE he had deployed on the March 1942 raid on St-Nazaire – Operation Chariot – during which he'd been shot and almost given up for dead. Incredibly, he'd managed yet another miraculous escape, returning once more to Britain, whereupon he'd signed up for the SAS. But during his missions with SOE his cover had been well and truly blown, so he'd changed his name and supposed nationality to that of one 'Jack William Raymond Lee', an American national.

In September 1943, serving with the SAS, Couraud – Lee – had commanded a hijacked train that had steamed into enemy territory, in southern Italy, to rescue the inmates of the Pisticci concentration camp, on a mission commanded by SAS Major Oswald Cary-Elwes. In short, Couraud was daring and fearless and had long experience in unorthodox operations, of which Gaff – a kidnap or assassination mission – was most certainly one. Couraud had under his command five men: two former French Foreign Legionnaires, a German Jew called 'Sergeant Mark', a Russian called Fedossof – all now serving with the SAS – plus a decidedly feisty and spirited Yorkshireman, Lance Corporal Tom Triplett Moore, who doubled as his signals specialist.

'To kill ROMMEL would obviously be easier than to kidnap him,' read Couraud's orders, 'and it is preferable to ensure the former rather than to attempt and fail in the latter.' Kidnapping Rommel would call for excellent 'two-way W/T communication', so an Allied aircraft could be called in, to pluck the German commander out of France. Conversely, an assassination could be 'reported by pigeon'. But kidnapping was by far the favoured option. 'If it should be possible to Kidnap ROMMEL and bring him to this country, the propaganda value would be immense . . . Such a plan would involve finding, and being prepared to hold for a short time if necessary, a suitable landing ground.'

Swiftly, Couraud and his team had got their boots onto French soil: 'Successful landing, good DZ, but three leg bags smashed (string broken).' Equipped with sniper rifles and explosives, barely had they arrived when they received the bad news. Rommel had been driving from his headquarters to the frontline, when his staff car was spotted by a flight of RAF Spitfires. The pilots had swooped onto their target, as the vehicle sped along the road. Bursts of 20mm cannon fire had raked the vehicle, wounding the driver, who'd lost control. The car had stuck a tree and spun off the road. As Rommel was thrown free his face was injured by the windscreen, and he suffered multiple fractures to his skull.

The attack had left the German commander badly wounded and hospitalised . . . and it had also left Couraud deprived of a mission. Sort of. Regardless, he went on the offensive anyway. In 'an extremely fruitful week', he reported that a train was derailed and set on fire, a convoy was ambushed and a high-ranking Gestapo officer shot ('got his papers'), with the *coup de grâce* being their attack on a German staff car, in which a Wehrmacht colonel was killed. At various junctures Sergeant Mark, the German Jewish member of their patrol, had called out to the enemy in German, so 'they thought they had been attacked by Germans, and started shooting each other'.

Couraud and his men managed to make it to Rommel's headquarters, the Château de La Roche-Guyon, without undue trouble. 'I am glad that I do not have to attack this place,' Couraud noted. 'I can see that it is very well protected.' In any case, by the time they'd made it to the injured Field Marshal's HQ, that too had been subjected to RAF bombing raids, meaning that the intelligence furnished by Hutchison and Fraser had well and truly hit home.

In one of the last actions of Operation Gaff, a train was targeted by the Yorkshireman Tom Moore, who stopped it 'single handed' by unleashing '2 mags of Bren gun into the engine'. Moore had scores to settle in France. In February 1942, his younger brother, Jack, had been killed in the Battle of the Java Sea, the naval confrontation in which the Allies had suffered a crushing defeat at the hands of the Japanese. After Jack's death, Moore's service record was peppered with references to him going off the rails – suffering repeated detentions and 'forfeits of pay' for being 'AWOL' (absent without leave), and a host of other misdemeanours, including 'irregular conduct . . . conversing with a man under close arrest'. But once he'd volunteered for the SAS, Moore had seemed to find his natural home.

As Couraud and his men were all out of ammunition and explosives, he disguised himself as a French gendarme and proceeded to cycle across France, passing through enemy lines to link up with the Americans. There, he radioed SAS headquarters, providing the coordinates of a series of enemy targets to be hit by RAF airstrikes. The rest of his patrol – Moore included – were brought out of France in due course, and not a man among them had suffered any injuries.

Rommel's demise – he would later commit suicide, having been implicated in the 20 July plot to assassinate Hitler – came at the same time as German resistance in Normandy began to crumble. As their forces were driven deeper into France, so SAS patrols operating across the country faced both an opportunity and a challenge. On the upside, there were likely to be more enemy forces passing through their regions, offering targets. On the downside, there was more likelihood of stumbling into their convoys inadvertently, as a bloodied and bruised enemy became ever more vengeful and desperate.

With the newspapers shouting out the good news – the Allies had secured their foothold in France – so families across Britain feared for their sons, sent deep behind enemy lines and into harm's way. Far from going after Rommel personally, as Fraser had feared, Paddy Mayne had far less glamorous and thrilling, but equally important, work to do. Letters had to be written to the families of those serving deep in occupied territory, and especially of those who had been injured or killed in combat operations. The value of such letters to the families was incalculable, as their replies to the SAS commander testified.

On 18 July 1944 the parents of 'John', writing from Enfield, in Middlesex, expressed their heartfelt gratitude to Mayne.

Dear Lt Col. Mayne,

My wife and I were very glad to receive your letter . . . telling us of our son John's safe descent into France by parachute, and that you had heard from him since his arrival, and that everything was going well.

We note what you say about his work in France, and we are sure you will find him worthy of the confidence placed in him. We are very glad to know that he can receive our letters, although he cannot reply at present, but we are writing regularly to him . . .

Again, thanking you,

Yours sincerely

[Signature illegible]

In spring 1944 the SAS launched intensive recruitment, plus commando-style and parachute training. In support of the D-Day landings, they were to drop deep into Nazi-occupied France, to stop Hitler's panzer divisions in their tracks. Across Britain they seized trains, trucks, fire engines and even a submarine, honing their means to cause havoc deep behind enemy lines. Training hard, they partied harder, getting 'uproariously drunk' on 'Suki', a 'dreadful concoction of red wine and rum'.

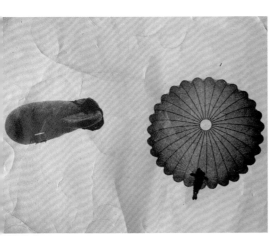

First into action in the Yonne region of France were Captain Derrick Harrison (right of photo), Captain Peter Davis (centre) and Trooper Ron Grierson (left). Harrison would lead his jeeps on a daredevil charge into Les Ormes, saving the villagers from murder at the hands of the SS. As for Davis, having executed a string of daring raids, he'd promote himself in the field to the rank of 'Colonel', in an effort to take the surrender of 18,000 German troops. He was beaten to it by two American major generals (below on the right), who took the surrender of the enemy commanders (below, left of the photo).

Davis (above left) reloading a magazine for their jeep-mounted Vickers K guns, was joined in the field by Colonel Blair 'Paddy' Mayne (below), the legendary SAS commander. While being all but banned from deploying into France, Mayne – a inveterate lover of animals, especially dogs – was determined to lead from the front, at the hard end of operations.

Major Harry Poat (above left), Colonel Paddy Mayne (centre) and Padre J. Fraser McLuskey (right), in the heavily wooded Morvan region of France, where the SAS would carry out a string of breathtaking missions. A 'singing regiment', the men would belt out the padre's hymns at volume, defying the enemy, with Major Bob Melot (below, left) and Sergeant James 'Jock' McDiarmid (right) giving voice with the best of them.

Teaming up with the French resistance (above), Mayne's Morvan raiders would destroy a synthetic fuel factory (right), blow countless railways and derail dozens of trains, while ambushing road convoys at every turn. In response, the enemy launched savage 'reprisals'. They burned down the SAS/Resistance hospital at Château de Vermot (below), and the SS and Gestapo perpetrated terrible atrocities against the locals.

En Morvan
DUN-les-PLACES - Château de Vermot

In the greatest coup of the SAS's Morvan operations, Major Bill Fraser and SOE agent Colonel Sir James Hutchinson would discover the headquarters of General Erwin Rommel (above, on Hitler's left) – their old adversary. Codenamed 'Operation Gaff', the resulting SAS mission to kill or capture Rommel was led by Captain Raymond Couraud, commanding a small team, including Corporal Tom Moore (below), whose daredevil exploits would last long beyond the war.

CHARGE AGAINST COVENTRY
OFFICER DROPPED

Indian Government is not taking any action against Lieutenant Thomas Moore, 26-year-old Briton from Coventry, who as an officer in the Nizam of Hyderabad's State Forces, was reported captured while laying mines before the Indian troops marched on Secunderabad. He is being repatriated to Britain in the first available ship. His trial on charges of treason will not be proceeded with.

Monday Sept. 27 1948.

Lieutenant Moore, British ex-Commando, who was training Hyderabad soldiers near the border, is reported missing.

Wednesday Sept. 15th 1948

Midlanuer to be freed

Lieut.-Gen. Rajendra Singh, G.O.C. Southern Command, asked at a Secunderabad Press conference yesterday what had happened to Lieut. Thomas Moore, of Coventry, who was arrested by Indian troops as they marched into Hyderabad, said that so far as he was concerned he would not detain him, and he would be given facilities to get out of the State.

The future Government of Hyderabad will be decided only after "normal conditions" have been restored, Mr. Patel, Indian Home Minister, said in New Delhi yesterday.

Tuesday 21st Sept 1948.

Mayne's stalwarts in France included Johnny Wiseman (above, right of photo), Bob Lilley (centre, with SAS medic Malcolm Pleydell on his left), and Des Peter Middleton (left). Operating under the noses of the enemy, Wiseman's force blew up a gas-generating plant, tricking German troops and the French Milice (paramilitary Nazi collaborators) to fight each other, while Middleton was on a jeep patrol to blow up a secret German airfield.

Using jeeps parachuted into France (above), the SAS would range far and wide, but would pay a terrible price for their successes. Major Ian Fenwick (left, at the wheel of his jeep, and below, fourth from left), would be but one of many killed in action, while dozens of SAS captives would be murdered under the notorious 'Commando Order'. Issued by Adolf Hitler, it decreed that all such special operators should be 'shot out of hand'.

On 19 July parents from Glasgow wrote:

Many thanks for your kind letter about Jimmy. His mother and I were very pleased to hear that so far he was all right. The Army training made him very fit and we are sure he will do his best all the time. Glad everything is going so well.
Yours sincerely,
G. J. Watson

On 23 July another family wrote from Leicester:

I am extremely grateful for your kind thoughts, as you cannot realise what a relief even the small amount of news means.
Again thank you.
Yours sincerely,
G. H. Parsons

Mayne had also written to the young wife of Lieutenant Cecil 'Jock' Riding, in Glasgow, reassuring her that all was well. In her reply, she expressed how kind it was of the SAS commander to write, and while she longed for news from her husband, she was pleased to know he was fit and well. 'I think all the S.A.S. men are grand,' she added, 'and I hope to meet more of them after the war and to hear of their adventures.' Thanking Mayne for writing, she signed off 'Janie Riding'. Though Mayne wasn't to know it yet, he was poised to have far more to do with her husband, and in the most desperate of circumstances, as the fate of Riding's SAS patrol fell into darkness.

But all of that lay sometime in the future.

*

Even as those letters were winging their way across Britain, so Bill Fraser, writing in the Operation Houndsworth War Diary, noted: 'Sgt. STURMEY's party reports blowing PARIS–NEVERS line . . . Sgt. NOBLE walks back after blowing LUZY–NEVERS line and giving valuable train movement information.' As the battle for France stiffened, he was intent on hitting enemy transport links wherever possible. With more jeeps to hand, Fraser could have achieved even more, but any number of those dropped to the SAS had 'roman candled', as Fraser reported. 'This factor held us up more than anything else, as we suffered from lack of transport until almost the last days . . .' Even so, on foot or by jam-packed vehicle, Fraser was determined to dispatch his patrols far and wide.

Some eighty kilometres due west of their base lay the Fôret des Dames. Remote, isolated, with just a few minor roads passing anywhere thereabouts, it promised a good satellite camp for raiding operations, extending the SAS's reach in the direction of Orléans and Paris beyond. One entire patrol, under the command of Captain Roy Bradford, was to be dispatched there. Bradford it was who'd led the jump from the Stirling in which Padre McLuskey and comrades had dropped into the Morvan. The trouble with the Fôret des Dames mission was that only one jeep was available, and even that was ailing, having taken a real battering during previous sorties.

Dividing his patrol, Bradford and four others would set out as a vanguard, riding in that lone jeep. The remainder, under the sterling leadership of Lieutenant Ooly Ball, plus the redoubtable Sergeant Jeff Du Vivier, would follow riding 'airborne bicycles' – fold-up pushbikes that had also been dropped into the Morvan. Some 60,000 'Airborne Folding Paratrooper Bicycles' had been churned out by the Birmingham Small Arms factory. While the contraption was perfectly usable, its one big problem was the lack of any rack or panniers, or any means with which to carry weaponry, explosives and supplies. While brackets attached to the frame supposedly allowed weapons to be strapped on, in practice, when cycling over the rough terrain of the Morvan, they kept vibrating free and tumbling off. Not great, for SAS patrols operating deep behind the lines.

Bradford and his party intended to establish their base at the Fôret des Dames, while Ball and Du Vivier's bikers would rendezvous with them just as soon as they could make it. Bradford took with him a sterling crew. His front gunner was none other than Sergeant Fred 'Chalky' White, only recently released after his back injury had put him in 'hospital'. His driver was Sergeant Cornelius 'Maggie' McGinn, an old soldier renowned for his upbeat attitude, whose catchphrase was that if he tumbled into water, he'd fail to get wet. A Glaswegian, McGinn was one of the longest serving SAS men among Fraser's party. Another 11 Commando veteran, he'd soldiered in that unit alongside both Fraser and Mayne, and was the man to have with you in a tight corner, as events were to prove.

They also had Trooper William 'Andy' Devine, a fitter – a weapons and vehicles maintenance specialist – riding with them, to keep the jeep moving. And as guide and interpreter, they'd taken Jaques Morvillier, a local Maquisard. Oddly, Chalky White was renowned as having a jinx on the officers with whom he worked: all six of those under whom he'd previously served had been killed on operations. This time, in an effort to defeat the jinx, White was going to have his own team to command at the Fôret des Dames.

They set out at dusk, executing a long night drive, and taking all the usual precautions that now came as second nature to the SAS in the Morvan. At sunrise, the jeep was nosing its cautious way into the tiny village of Lucy-sur-Yonne, some twenty kilometres short of their destination, when it rounded a bend and came 'face-to-face with a German officer and sergeant on foot'. At first, the enemy commander presumed they were friendly and tried to signal them to a stop. White's reply was a 'short burst from the twin Vickers', causing the officer and his sergeant to dive for cover.

The jeep pushed onwards, but almost immediately it came across a German Army truck, parked at the roadside, with another one behind. To either side of the road enemy troops 'were lazing in the fields', causing Bradford and his men to realise what they'd stumbled across – a convoy of German troops enjoying their breakfast. 'It was too late to turn back, so we decided to shoot our way through,' as McGinn noted of the surprise showdown. With Bradford ordering McGinn to step on the gas, 'Chalky sprayed the road ahead with burning lead', and the jeep lurched forwards as enemy troops began 'sprinting for their guns'.

Eyeing the long line of enemy vehicles, McGinn sensed that it was 'a hopeless situation, but we had to carry on'. What made it all the more desperate was the sickly state of the jeep, whose ailing Go Devil engine was capable of little more than thirty miles per hour. Chugging forward, with guns blazing, and with McGinn's 'foot hard down', he counted more than a dozen trucks, each of which had to be carrying some twenty-odd troops. It was five against two-hundred-and-fifty, driving a clapped-out jeep piled high with explosives, yet still they seemed to be making miraculous progress. As the Vickers rounds tore into the stationary vehicles, the 'shock and surprise of the attack' gave them the advantage, and 'they almost got away with it'.

But as they passed another truck, a Spandau spat fire. A round tore into Bradford, wounding his left arm, while Trooper Devine, the 'mechanic sitting behind, had been killed'. He slumped over the rear Vickers, 'his dead hands gripping the triggers'. Still

McGinn nursed the jeep onwards as bullets tore into the roadway on all sides. From the passenger's seat, White fought like 'a devil incarnate', even though he'd been wounded in the left hand. Three times he changed over the twin Vickers drum magazines, burning through eight magazines each of a hundred rounds. All was confusion and chaos, as the SAS poured fire into the 'swarming enemy' at close to point blank range. At one point, the jeep gave a 'sickening lurch' as it careered over a screaming enemy trooper, figures in field grey diving for the ditches to avoid death as it roared by.

But it could not last. They'd reached the very last truck when a heavy barrage of fire swept the jeep from end to end. Bradford 'coughed and fell back', caught by a fatal blast. The same burst wounded Jaques Morvillier, their Maquis guide, who gave a cry of agony as rounds shattered his elbow. Worse still, Chalky White whipped around as he was hit multiple times, with bullets in his leg, and with his shoulder badly torn. Driving a jeep loaded with the wounded and the dead, still McGinn persevered, coaxing the last life out a vehicle that he sensed was about to die. Moments later, it juddered to a halt. Their trusty steed had 'packed in'.

With not a moment to waste, McGinn leapt out, dragged the two wounded men free, and yelled at them to make for a patch of nearby woodland. Quick as a flash, he checked over Bradford and Devine, finding 'without doubt that they were dead'. From behind, McGinn could hear the thump of boots on tarmac, as enemy troops pounded down the road after their jeep-borne assailants. Making a run for it, McGinn dashed for the woods, following the direction that the others had taken.

With little hope of avoiding capture, he dived into the under-growth and froze.

Chapter Nine

HANS THE GOOD GERMAN

From their place of hiding, McGinn, White and Morvillier watched the enemy converge on their bullet-riddled jeep. They saw them search the vehicle, before removing the bodies of their two dead comrades. Next, the German troops approached the woodland – the obvious hiding place for those who had fled – and so began the hunt. For the three fugitives, it was now that luck played into their hands, for while the enemy searched they just didn't happen to look in the right place. Fearing they would bring up a larger force to penetrate deeper into the woodland, McGinn got the wounded men moving.

It wasn't long before White was 'looking very groggy', as McGinn described it, forcing him to call a halt. Back they went into hiding, for McGinn was determined to leave no man behind. He did his best to bandage the worst of White's injuries, and the same for the wounded Frenchman. Sensing they couldn't afford to tarry, McGinn pushed them on, heading deeper into the forest. Eventually, they came to a road. As sod's law would have it, the highway was bristling with enemy patrols, leaving McGinn with no option but to halt once more. Hunkered down in the undergrowth, they waited for nightfall.

Under cover of darkness, McGinn scouted out the road. Signalling the all-clear, he motioned for White and Morvillier to follow. 'All night we walked with periods of rest,' McGinn would report. But the wounded were 'losing blood and getting very weak, and I had to support them'. Past midnight, they entered a cornfield. The crop had been cut and was stacked in sheaves, each of which resembled a mini-haystack. It had started to rain, and as McGinn fully appreciated, the situation of the wounded was desperate. With few other options, he began to build a make-shift shelter out of the bundles of corn, 'where we all rested until dawn'.

At sunrise they pressed on, moving in an easterly direction, so inching their way back towards the Morvan. After an hour or so, McGinn spied a small village lying on the far bank of the River Yonne. Aware of the traditional courageous hospitality of country folk in France, he reckoned they had no choice but to chance making contact. 'We were extremely hungry and I knew that unless we got food and assistance immediately there would be drastic consequences.' The trouble was how to get the injured men across the Yonne, which was some fifty yards from bank to bank.

On the far side McGinn spotted a small boat. Having no other option he slipped into the water, swam across, and made it to the far side. Finding the vessel chained to a tree, after a herculean effort he managed to break the branch to which it was attached, and to prise it free. In that small rowing boat McGinn managed to ferry White and Morvillier, swathed in bandages, across the Yonne. But it was then that they came upon a second obstacle: the Canal du Nivernais ran alongside the Yonne. As luck would have it, a lock-keeper's cottage lay close at hand, the lock providing a route across the canal. With McGinn speaking barely a word of French, he sent Morvillier ahead to ask for help.

The Frenchman seemed to be gone for an age. While they were waiting, McGinn gave White an injection of morphine, 'to ease the extreme pain he was suffering'. Finally, Morvillier returned. The three fugitives were to lie low in a nearby orchard, he explained, for the enemy were still thick on the ground. Eventually, they were helped to an isolated farmstead. The owner, who was in touch with the local Maquis, managed to conjure up a vehicle, and in that the three survivors were driven to the makeshift hospital in the Morvan, which already housed several of the SAS's wounded.

That evening, Padre McLuskey paid the injured Chalky White a visit. While he had only just come around from a dose of powerful painkiller, he was, typically, 'joking away in his imperturbable way'. Three of his fingers had had to be amputated, but the medic hoped to save the rest of his hand. Seeing his injuries, the padre had no idea 'how Chalky had managed to keep firing, with his hand in that condition, but he had, and three lives had been saved as a result', White's own included. Here he was, back in hospital once again, but still 'as cheerful as ever'.

Meanwhile, McGinn, equally undaunted, was giving his verbal account of the mission to Fraser. Unconfirmed reports indicated that they had killed sixty-two enemy soldiers, before their jeep had got raked with fire and those riding in it had been wounded or killed. For his standout heroics, McGinn would be awarded the Military Medal (MM), the citation stressing the way in which he had saved White and Morvillier from death or capture. 'For two days Sgt. McGinn looked after these two, dressing their wounds, administering what aid he could and guiding them back towards the base at MAZIGNIEN.'

Trooper Devine's death was a sad moment, for he was a 'born comedian' not to mention a first-class mechanic, who'd 'worked like a Trojan ... overhauling our much abused jeeps'. As for Captain Roy Bradford's loss, it cast a shadow over the entire Morvan operation. Hailing from the West Country and with a lust for adventure, he was one of the 'finest officers and finest men in the unit', his strength of character being felt wherever he went. McLuskey's last memory of Bradford, who was married with an infant daughter, was at the Sunday service they had shared together, shortly before the ill-fated patrol had set forth for the Fôret des Dames.

Even with Bradford's death, the Fôret des Dames mission was far from over, for Ball and Du Vivier's bicycle patrol was still that way bound. As Bradford's unit had consisted of seventeen originally, there were a dozen men under way, using pedal power. Despite their doubtful means of conveyance – 'our kit had to be tied to the framework of the cycle,' Du Vivier reported, and was 'consistently falling due to the bad road surface' – they had 'no intention of turning back'. With their stop-start progress, they made only eight to ten miles per day, lying up in the woods at night, and swopping chocolate and sweets for 'bread, eggs, bacon etc' with the locals.

After five days they made it to the Fôret des Dames undetected. Finding no one at the rendezvous, they heard an almighty explosion from somewhere thereabouts, just as they parked their bicycles. It sounded as if it had come from the town of Entrains-sur-Nohain, just a few kilometres to the north. As they awaited Captain Bradford's arrival, Du Vivier decided to do a recce to discover the source of the blast, and especially since 'the lads who were with me were extremely anxious to get to work.'

Making contact with a local fisherman, Du Vivier learned that an enemy ammunition train was due through the region, heading towards the front. The local Maquis had got wise to this, and had managed to blow up a section of the line – hence the enormous blast. Even now, rail workers were busy repairing the tracks, for that train – 'two large engines, and about 40 wagons, with 25 personnel as guards' – was preparing to steam on through. As Du Vivier listened, he realised that 'here under our own eyes was a job awaiting us.' If they could blow up that train – never mind that Captain Bradford was way overdue, or that they were equipped only with their dodgy bicycles – that would be a mission to remember.

Du Vivier, with his rounded features, shock of wild sandy hair and eyes that seemed to be forever laughing, was, like Fraser, another Gordon Highlander and No. 11 Commando veteran. Working as a waiter in a Felixstowe hotel before the war, he'd volunteered for the SAS, for he was keen 'to see some action'. Action he certainly had seen, including being on Bill Fraser's patrol that had become marooned in the desert, far behind enemy lines, in December 1941. Missing in action and presumed killed or captured, by the time Fraser, Du Vivier and their handful of fellow desperadoes had made it back to Allied lines, it was as if they were back from the dead. In short, there was little that fazed Du Vivier or would daunt him.

That evening he led a small force from their forest base, west towards their target. Having been put in touch with the local Maquis, two Maquisards were acting as their guides. Taking no half measures, Du Vivier and his men were heavily laden with plastic explosives, Cordtex, and pressure switches. That last item was a pressure-activated detonator device, ensuring the charges would explode at the exact moment that a train arrived. The pair of Maquis guides led the way, for they had 'lights on their cycles', while Du Vivier and his men trailed along in the darkness.

For nine miles they pedalled hard, passing through two towns that were 'occupied by the enemy', but somehow making it through unchallenged. Once they'd reached the chosen spot, they hid their bicycles and set to work. Du Vivier had decided that all of their considerable explosives would be packed under the one rail, which involved the painstaking job of hollowing out space, digging away the gravel using their fighting knives and their bare hands. After two hours' work the explosives could be placed and buried, detonators attached, with the pressure switch wired to the lead charge, the one that the speeding train would first encounter. Finally, two '"Tyrebuster" mines' were added, 'to make a certain job of it'.

The Tyrebuster was a miniature mine, craftily disguised as a lump of mud, a rock or animal droppings. A creation of the boffins working at the SOE's Experimental Station IX, housed in a rambling mansion called The Frythe, in Welwyn Garden City, Hertfordshire, the mines were designed for scattering on roads. But the SAS had developed a spin on the classic use of the things, for they served as a perfect emergency detonator, should a pressure switch fail to work. Once Du Vivier and his men were done, the 'whole job had to be completely camouflaged, as we did not want it to be discovered during the hours of daylight'.

By the time they'd returned to their Fôret des Dames base, a message had been received, relaying the tragic news of Captain Bradford's death and other casualties. In light of that, Bill Fraser had ordered the remainder of the men to return to the Morvan. Even as they had packed up their camp and begun cycling east, so the enemy's ammunition train had got under way, moving in the opposite direction. It had steamed full pelt onto the charges, with no one aboard suspecting a thing. The explosion had occurred just as Du Vivier had intended it to, a massive blast detonating beneath the lead engine's front wheels, ripping up the tracks, as the speeding locomotives thrust ahead on rails that had ceased to exist, for they had been torn into oblivion.

The result, for the enemy, was little short of catastrophic. 'Both engines had been completely wrecked and turned over on their sides,' Du Vivier would report, 'together with a 40 ft wagon loaded with Anti-Aircraft guns. Ten wagons behind were derailed and lying over on the track.' The remaining thirty wagons remained unharmed, and as Du Vivier lamented, 'the truck containing the Germans was at the rear of the train and they were unscathed, but, according to the Maquis, very frightened and demoralised.' With two further ammunition trains following on behind, the entire lot would be held up for days.

By Du Vivier's own reckoning, returning to the Morvan by bicycle proved a 'very ticklish job', especially since every lane, path and farmstead was 'watched by the SS'. But make it they did, heading for Fraser's base camp. Of course, there would be no funeral for Captain Bradford or Trooper Devine. Their bodies had been abandoned where they fell. Retrieved by the enemy, it had actually been left to the local villagers to bury the fallen men. Just to the east of Lucy-sur-Yonne, the village at which they had died, lay the cemetery. They were laid to rest side by side, with simple crosses marking their resting place.

Between Bradford and Devine's graves would be placed a plaque, inscribed: '*Homage affecteux et reconnaissant aux Vaillants, qui loin de leur Patrie, meurent bravements pour reconquérir notre Liberté*' – 'Affectionate and grateful tribute to the Valiant, who far from their Homeland, died bravely to reconquer our Freedom.' As a final twist to the tale, the German commanders at Lucy-sur-Yonne must have recovered a camera from the remains of Bradford's bullet-riddled jeep. They developed the film, and from that produced Wanted posters, complete with SAS mugshots, offering large financial rewards for information leading to the capture of the 'terrorists in the woods'.

No doubt about it, the enemy were shaken. From the Yonne to the Morvan – and further afield – their forces seemed unable to move, without trains being blasted into oblivion, or road convoys being ambushed from the shadows. The constant vigilance that demanded – being always on the lookout for a seemingly invisible enemy – was taking a heavy toll. But so too was it plaguing the SAS. As the padre remarked, while they weren't yet certain what Hitler's specific orders were regarding SAS prisoners, they could hazard a guess. If captured, their Maquis brethren were kept alive only for so long as torture proved effective, after which they were shot.

'None of our men … had been captured so far,' noted the padre, 'but we had no desire to make the experiment.' That fear preyed on the nerves. It meant that every fight was a fight to the death. There could be no surrender. And no matter how watchful Fraser and his men might be, or what precautions were taken when on the move, luck would always prove a factor. Bad luck had plagued Roy Bradford's patrol, with fateful consequences. Lady luck was about to throw another SAS unit into deadly combat, and this time far closer to their Morvan home.

The entry in the Operation Houndsworth War Diary for 21 July 1944 recorded a brush with the Germans in Ouroux-en-Morvan, the village in which the enemy had previously 'amused themselves' by tossing grenades into a roadside café. That had been during the savage 'reprisals', as the villagers of Montsauche-les-Settons, Vermot, Dun-les-Places and elsewhere had paid a terrible price for daring to resist the Nazi occupiers. It was almost a month since then, and in the interim the enemy had got wise to the SAS's presence, pasting those Wanted posters across the region. This clandestine, furtive, guerrilla-warfare-like clash deep behind the lines was coming ever more firmly into focus, as the enemy realised just who they were up against, and the breadth and impact of their activities.

Again, the SAS's lack of proper transport was the catalyst for their 21 July clash. Sergeant John 'Nobby' Noble – the man who'd cut down the commander of the German patrol, when the

SAS had ambushed the ambushers – was taking a local car into Ouroux, seeking repairs. Starved of jeeps, despite the RAF's best efforts to parachute more in, Fraser and his men had resorted to repairing French civilian vehicles – clapped-out Citroëns mostly – to boost mobility. It was late afternoon when Noble set off, with Midd Middleton at the wheel of the jeep, escorting the saloon car for its overhaul. In the rear of the jeep was 'Roger', one of the Maquis mechanics, while the vehicle behind was driven by Lance Corporal Bromfield, with Corporal Bob 'Lofty' Langridge riding shotgun.

As those two vehicles set out for Ouroux, at a large petrol storage depot near Dijon, a German commander had been worrying about an overdue fuel train. So short of petrol were his troops, that when a requisitioned French car was sent out to search for the missing locomotive, the occupants were ordered to steer the most direct route possible, straight through the heart of the Morvan, as opposed to sticking to the generally safer main roads. That German search party had taken to the 'tricky, winding, hill roads' but had got lost, and in that way would end up blundering into Ouroux.

In fact, the Germans had already passed through Ouroux, taken a wrong turn, and been forced to retrace their steps. They entered one side of the village, pretty much as the SAS jeep entered the other. As the Germans drove along the narrow streets, they came face to face with a small military vehicle. At first they presumed it to be a Volkswagen *Schwimmwagen*, literally 'swimming car', a light four-wheel-drive amphibious vehicle used by their own forces. Those riding in the vehicle were dressed in camouflage fatigues, and were wearing some kind of red head-gear, and they presumed they were most likely Grey Russians. As for Noble and his fellows, the sight of a small red saloon car up ahead raised not the slightest concern, for obvious reasons.

It wasn't until the two vehicles were shoulder to shoulder that each side realised their mistake, and instantly 'pandemonium broke loose'. This time, the Germans had the element of surprise, for they were riding in the apparently civilian vehicle. Four jumped out, 'Schmeissers blazing'. For some reason – a stoppage? – the Vickers on the jeep failed to spark up, and for a moment Noble found himself returning fire with his Colt pistol, hopelessly outgunned. Then Langridge and Bromfield dashed forward from their vehicle, and a 'Homeric struggle' ensued in the middle of the road.

A bullet from an MP40 smashed Bromfield's ankle. At the same moment a round from the SAS struck the German driver in the thigh, sending him 'cowering into a ditch'. A long burst of 'Schmeisser fire' stitched a line of holes along the side of the jeep, puncturing a fuel tank, and setting it ablaze, forcing Middleton to fight the flames, rather than engage in the battle. One of the enemy fled across a garden, but was cut down. Big Lofty Langridge, whose Tommy gun had jammed, leapt on the largest of the Germans, a massive bull of a regimental sergeant major (RSM), whose MP40 magazine had just run out of bullets. Locked in close-quarter combat, the battle swayed back and forth across the road, as each giant figure tried to strike the other down 'with the butts of their weapons'.

Langridge was a warrior of long-experience, who'd served in a Guards unit before the war. He was regarded as one of the finest soldiers in Fraser's squadron. But the German RSM seemed to be equally blessed with martial spirit, and neither man looked able to get the upper hand. Eventually, a fourth enemy figure – a man dressed in civvies; very possible Gestapo – stepped forward to shoot Langridge in the back. Noble, who'd been hit once in the brow and again in the shoulder, was quicker, managing to gun the 'Gestapo' figure down before he could open fire.

That left only the RSM, locked in mortal combat with Langridge. Levelling a powerful kick at the German's stomach, Langridge's blow seemed to have as little effect as if he'd booted a barn door. The man seemed indestructible. Noble emptied the last bullets of his Colt into the man's flank, but still 'the fight reeled on'. Finally, Middleton, who'd managed to extinguish the flames using his driver's gloves as protection, unleashed a burst from the Vickers into 'the big German's body'. And so the street brawl in Ouroux was brought to an end.

As the wounded were evacuated and the enemy's car seized, so a massive clean-up operation got under way, to hide all the evidence of what had happened. Driving down to Ouroux, Wellsted oversaw the sanitising of the battle ground, as the last of the glass was swept away. By the time he was done, there was not the slightest sign that there had 'ever been a fight there'. That way, to the German commander in Dijon, it would appear as if his search party had disappeared into thin air.

The wounded were brought into the SAS camp. Bromfield, in great pain, was rushed to the nearest makeshift clinic. The German RSM, who been shot a total of sixteen times, was still miraculously alive. He kept asking for water, and seemed amazed when given a drink, and that he was not being 'ill-treated'. Wellsted explained that he'd been captured by the British, so would not be harmed. He turned out to be an anti-Nazi, but as a dedicated soldier of the Wehrmacht he had 'fought loyally' to the end. 'It was a pity we could not have saved the RSM,' Wellsted reflected. Riddled with fire, he was too far gone. He, and the other badly wounded German – the civilian; Gestapo? – were put out of their misery each with a bullet.

The third enemy captive, Hans, the driver, wasn't seriously hurt. Back in Ouroux, having taken a flesh wound to the thigh, he'd dived into that roadside ditch, before seizing his moment to try to escape. Limping across the street, he'd stolen into a roadside bar.

Clearly petrified, he'd asked the bar-lady, in his execrable French: 'Where is the nearest *route nationale?*'

'Far away,' she'd replied. She'd told him to rest a while, for she would shelter him and help bandage his wounds.

'But the terrorists?' he'd quavered.

'There are no terrorists here,' she'd reassured him.

Somewhat comforted, Hans had allowed himself to be steered into a back parlour, whereupon the good lady had gently locked him in. A few moments later, Hans had been captured.

He turned out to be an 'inoffensive little bank clerk', with zero interest in Nazism, politics or the war. As soon as he realised his British captors were not about to shoot him, Hans was 'the happiest German in all of France', for he'd been on the verge of being posted to the frontline in Normandy. His one big worry was whether his wife would be told he was a deserter, and would suffer accordingly. Wellsted put his mind at rest by promising to radio his name, rank and number to London, so the details could be passed to the Red Cross, who would in turn share them with the German authorities.

His captors had an inkling that Hans could prove useful. Burdened with ever increasing numbers of wounded, the SAS needed hands to tend to their care. In short order, Hans was stomping about camp on his bandaged leg, helping as best he could. He struck up a seemingly unlikely friendship with Micky Flynn, the camp cook, and eventually the two would become joint camp chefs. With Hans speaking barely any English, they managed to communicate in a garbled 'Franglais'. The German's terror of the Maquis, who he knew very well would have shot him, plus his fear of the wild woods, made him an extremely loyal and grateful captive. In fact, he needed no guarding at all.

Hans would turn out to be useful in more ways than any had imagined. Proving himself to be a handy mechanic, he was soon down at the forest workshop, welding up gun-mounts on the jeeps, and carrying out other vehicle maintenance duties. He also proved to have a dry, sardonic sense of humour that tickled the SAS pink. In time, with all of the insignia ripped from his tunic, and draped in a 'gas cape' – a long, waxed cotton coat, originally designed to be impervious to toxic gas – the Maquis presumed that Hans was one of the SAS. But one day a Maquisard spied his German trousers and boots.

'Schleu?' he queried, with a raise of the eyebrows. *You German?* (Schleu was French army slang for Germans.)

Hans had nodded – yes, he was a German.

'Schleu kaput,' the Frenchman had retorted, drawing a finger expressively across his throat.

Hans shook his head.

'Pourquoi Schleu non kaput?' the Maquisard had countered.

'Moi Schleu' – *I'm a German* – Hans had replied, matter of factly. *I'm a German and I'm not kaput.* The Maquisard had practically had a fit.

Having Hans around would also prove massively useful in the gathering of intelligence. A Gestapo car was ambushed, and it turned out to be packed full of documents. As no one could translate written German well enough, the entire cache was handed to Hans. Again, the humour of the moment was inescapable. As he pulled forth a key document covered in 'STRENG GEHEIM' – top secret – stamps, he'd declare, 'Here's a good one for you,' and proceed to bash out a decent sense of its meaning.

Poignantly, the haul of documents included papers concerning the late Captain Roy Bradford, who'd been killed at Lucy-sur-Yonne. They were being sent to Dijon for onwards processing. There were also detailed schedules of train movements and the latest enemy orders, all of which were 'wirelessed to London'. The Gestapo papers reporting on the Lucy-sur-Yonne incident included the names and locations of locals in the area who were alleged to have helped the SAS. The report was destined for the German area commander, no doubt so suitable reprisals could be launched. But of course it never reached him, for it had fallen into the hands of Hans and his SAS brethren.

On 27 July a massive parachute drop took place in the Morvan. Three jeeps were dropped in – one of which sadly roman candled – plus 'two 6-pounders'. The Ordnance Quick Firing 6-pounder was a 57mm gun, mounted on wheels and towable behind a jeep. These guns were the mainstay of Allied anti-tank warfare, and Fraser had requested them for very specific reasons. With all the trouble he and his men were causing, he sensed that the enemy would come hunting, seeking to drive them from their forest fastness. With their significant firepower, the 6-pounders could be the answer he needed, for the time for running was over. They had too many wounded, too much invested in their present operational bases, to give it all up without a major fight.

Back at London headquarters, the stakes for the SAS in France had likewise just altered significantly, and in a way that few could envisage. Before deploying, Mayne had stressed the need to treat German POWs with the respect that their uniform should afford them: *they must know that they will be safe and unharmed if they surrender.* Sadly, the same did not appear to be the case for SAS captives. There were reports and rumours filtering in of SAS patrols going missing across France, and the fate of anyone taken prisoner appeared to be dark.

Working in small, scattered groups, with no media fanfare accompanying their clandestine operations, there was a tendency for the SAS to feel at times like a forgotten army. In a second broadcast to his troops, Mayne assured them that they were not. While their limited numbers might make them feel 'rather insignificant', in truth the enemy feared the SAS 'more than any other unit of the British or American forces'. Mayne reminded his men that he was coming. Regardless of the 'consternation of his superiors', he was determined to drop into France. No one knew quite where he would appear, but he had promised, and he was not a man to break his word.

Strictly speaking, as the commanding officer of a British regiment, Mayne was forbidden from deploying behind the lines. But he had argued vehemently that the ban should not apply to the SAS. After all, they didn't operate anywhere else but behind the lines. That was their forte. He also pointed out that they had the largest clandestine commitment in France of any British military unit, so surely they deserved to have an experienced commander on the ground. His final argument, powerfully made, was that none of the radio reports received by headquarters could give an accurate picture of what conditions were really like for the men in the field. Only the visit of a senior commander could achieve that.

Eventually, he was granted permission to deploy. But he was warned that his scope of operations was to be limited. He should restrict himself to coordinating actions and not to leading any missions, and he should absolutely keep his exposure to risk to a minimum. With a 'disarming Irish smile' and a few quiet words, Mayne apparently consented. Of course, once he had parachuted deep into enemy territory, things might turn out a little differently, but who would there be to witness his actions, or to attempt to upbraid him?

In the Morvan, Fraser's patrols were busy. The Operation Houndsworth War Diary entries for 1 and 2 August included:

'Lieut GRAYSON blew line NEVERS–AUTUN ... blew line NEVERS at CERCY-LA-TOUR ... and blew points in enemy goods yard at SEMELAY.' In a sense, it was hardly surprising when the enemy came in force, targeting their base to the north of Mazignien, and that of the neighbouring Maquis. Forewarned that a large enemy convoy was inbound, Fraser and the Maquis leader worked out a joint plan of defence, the 'trump card' being their newly arrived 6-pounder gun.

A team of oxen hauled it into place, on a highpoint overlooking the approach route that the enemy would have to take. Bren gunner units took up positions all around, some manned by the SAS and others by the Maquis. Just after dawn on 3 August, the enemy convoy was sighted, crawling along the road leading towards their positions. It ground to a halt, and some two hundred enemy troops began to advance on foot. The Maquis and SAS Bren teams, at the vanguard of the defence, opened up, unleashing 'withering fire into the German ranks' and setting the leading trucks aflame.

Enraged, the German commander ordered a nearby farm burned to the ground, as his men tried to press home their attack. A pair of German staff cars were spotted, speeding along the road towards the firefight. One shell from the 6-pounder forced a rapid about-turn, as the vehicles withdrew 'at high speed'. An enemy machinegun, with over a dozen of their troops gathered around it, began to pour in fire. 'Three rounds at 700 yards silenced it' for good. Realising they were faced with some kind of powerful field gun, the enemy withdrew behind a stone wall. Five shells unleashed at five-yard intervals tore down the wall from end to end.

A second machinegun was brought into action by the enemy. Two shells from the 6-pounder flattened it and its crew. It was around midday by now, and the Germans withdrew to lick their wounds. Some two hours later a mortar team set up their tube and lobbed in a first bomb. The 6-pounder replied with three quick shells, the first of which scored a direct hit, the others just to make certain. A second mortar team arrived, and then a third, but this time they sited their tubes behind a hillock, where the 6-pounder couldn't reach them. Instead, an SAS Bren team moved into range and drove them away.

Finally, the enemy commander resorted to an all-out infantry assault, for surely with that many men on the move, the mystery gun could not deal with them all. For a good while the 'whole road resounded to as much thunder as a six-pounder is capable of producing', before the SAS position seemed in danger of being outflanked. At that point they removed the firing pin from the big gun, without which it was useless, camouflaged it, and then withdrew to a second line of defence in the forest. Failing to find the gun in the thick undergrowth, the enemy gave up. As the sun was setting, the German commander called an end to the attack. Laden with their dead and their wounded, the enemy troops stumbled back to their trucks and drove away.

A victory of this magnitude could not be understated. Just as Fraser had intended, some 'two hundred miles behind their own lines, a major German force had been driven off', having suffered heavy casualties. For their part, the Maquis had two dead and one wounded, while not a man among the SAS had suffered so much as a scratch.

Even as that battle had raged around the Mazignien camps, so reports had been received of a similar confrontation at Johnny Wiseman's base, over towards Dijon. There, Wiseman and his men had scored a string of successes, which had compelled the enemy likewise to come hunting.

Wiseman's camp, set adjacent to the tiny hamlet of Rolle, lay some twenty kilometres south-west of Dijon. It was 'the most silent camp', as padre McLuskey would describe it, in terms of Sunday hymn service. So close were they to the enemy, Wiseman and his men could afford little more than a few gentle hums. Their neighbour in the next-door valley was a large German training camp. The farm from which Wiseman and his men bartered eggs and milk was also a favourite haunt of the enemy. Their base was in easy reach of Wiseman's key targets, and he refused to give it up, despite its singularly 'strained atmosphere'. But that called for constant vigilance and maximum concealment.

Wiseman had selected an area that was totally surrounded by bramble thickets. The only way in was to bellycrawl through a winding tunnel that had been 'cut through the briars' for a hundred yards or more. Hidden deep within that seemingly impenetrable mass was a small clearing, which wiseman and his troop had bedecked with tents fashioned from parachute silk. The nearest Maquis group boasted a significant set-up, and somehow they'd established a direct telephone link to the main switchboard in Dijon. The girls manning the facility were all closet Resistance, and they would telephone through a warning whenever an enemy patrol set out on the hunt.

Wiseman and his men were also to develop a back-up warning system. In a strategically positioned village they had a certain house pointed out to them. If there was a pair of blue trousers pegged to the washing line, they would know that German troops, or the hated Milice were on the move. The Milice were the most reviled of all the adversaries of the SAS and the Maquis. They were pro-Fascist Frenchmen who had chosen to serve in the cause of the Nazi occupiers. As one SAS report described them, the Milice were the 'real bastards', being 'injected with Boche frightfulness' and capable of anything.

At Wiseman's camp sentry watches were rigorous. No matter if it was day or night, each man had his allotted position and role should the enemy attack. When the padre dared to pay a visit, driving over from the Morvan, even he had a job to do. He was to drive their jeep along a barely usable track, which Wiseman and his men had hacked out of the undergrowth to create an escape route. The padre was to head for an emergency rendezvous point, at which all who had survived would gather. But Wiseman had with him some of the real old hands of the SAS, and he felt certain they could give a good account of themselves should the enemy come calling.

Captain Johnny Cooper had joined him, fresh from his mortar attack on the synthetic fuel plant. Sergeant Jack Terry was there – Reg Seekings' saviour – and he and Cooper were as thick as thieves. Whenever a night alarm was sounded, they would move with silent, unhurried steps to their vantage-points, fighting knives and Tommy guns at the ready. Reg Seekings was also there – Le Maquis anglais – neck wound seemingly forgotten, though the bullet was still lodged firmly in place, and keen as ever to spread havoc and mayhem.

Trooper Doug Ferguson was there, a former miner from Glasgow. Serving first with the Highland Light Infantry, Ferguson had fought his way across East and North Africa, before volunteering for the SAS. Wounded in action in Italy, at Termoli, he'd been awarded the Military Medal, and had been declared fighting-fit for the SAS's D-Day missions, much to his delight. Trooper John 'Taffy' Glyde was there, a pre-war factory worker from Pontypridd, in South Wales. Married with an infant son, his brother, Emlyn, had been killed while serving with the Parachute Regiment in North Africa, meaning Glyde had scores to settle. With Wiseman, he would get ample chance to do so.

It was no exaggeration to say that Wiseman would become the most famed 'train wrecker in France'. During their first two weeks of operations they had ensured that 'the DIJON–BEAUNE railway was cut three times and the DIJON–PARIS line once, two trains being derailed', as Wiseman would report. Not content with repeatedly blowing the railway lines in his region and scattering Tyrebuster mines to disable enemy convoys, Wiseman's small force had shot up one locomotive crammed full of enemy troops, unleashing a broadside with the Vickers from their speeding jeep. But of course, their standout achievements made them a target, and eventually their base had been discovered.

A young Maquisard was caught by the enemy, and under torture he revealed the location of the SAS camp. A group of Milice, expecting to encounter little serious resistance, had converged on the base, only to be met by Wiseman and his men, wielding Brens. Those few who did escape were sadder and wiser for the experience. Of course, the enemy returned in greater strength. They came in a dawn attack mounted by both Milice and regular German troops. But remaining vigilant as ever, Wiseman and co. had already slipped away.

As the Milice went in to sweep the dense vegetation, the German troops waited to one side, poised to gun down the SAS as they were driven out of cover. Instead, the first figures to emerge from the early dawn mists were the Milice. Mistaking them for their quarry, the Germans opened fire, and so the battle had raged. Twenty-two were gunned down, before either side realised their mistake and declared a ceasefire. In due course Wiseman would be awarded the Croix de Guerre – a high valour French decoration – for his actions around Dijon, the citation praising his immense courage and making special mention of the incident in which German troops and Milice ended up fighting each other.

After the battle Wiseman was tempted to 'lie low for a while', but his martial nature got the better of him. Instead, and inspired by Muirhead's mortar attack on the Autun fuel plant, they pulled off a similar feat at Mâlain, a town to the west of Dijon. There, they sneaked into a gasogene factory – a facility used to generate inflammable 'wood gas' to power vehicles – and blew it to pieces. For good measure, they'd gone on to derail a train 'on the side line at PONT D'OUCHE'. But of course, with their hide-out blown, they were forced to shift camp, one of several such moves they would have to make to keep one step ahead of the hunters.

Such successes – and the associated tension, risk and stress – came at a heavy cost. Paddy Mayne was determined to parachute into France, to get a feel for how men like Wiseman were coping on the ground. It was hard to know, for operations in France were just so different from what had gone before. In North Africa, after a typical SAS hit-and-run attack, the wide-open expanse of the desert offered a beckoning and welcome sanctuary. Even in Italy, once Mayne's forces had run the gauntlet of a mission, they were quickly withdrawn to Allied lines for rest and recuperation. But there was none of that in France. There were just weeks on end of hunting the enemy and of being hunted in return. Relentless. Unremitting. Incessant. Mayne worried what effect this was having.

But before he could parachute in to investigate, the brutal cost to his men on the ground would become all too clear.

Chapter Ten

IF YOU GO DOWN
IN THE WOODS TODAY

On the evening of 6 August the Germans launched Operation
Lüttich, their last major counteroffensive in Normandy. In thick
fog, 145 heavy Tiger tanks rumbled towards Allied lines, seeking
a decisive breakthrough. In London on the sixth, Lieutenant-
Colonel Blair 'Paddy' Mayne was busy dispatching an urgent
message to France. The intended recipient was SAS Captain Cecil
'Jock' Riding – Mayne had written to his wife, Janie, just a few
weeks before; she'd replied, 'I think all the S.A.S. men are grand.'
Riding was the second-in-command of Operation Gain, a force
that had dropped into the area north of Orléans. It was there that
Mayne had chosen to deploy. 'Sgt BUNFIELD (Signal Section)
received a message that Col. MAYNE was dropping that night, if
a DZ [drop zone] be given,' Riding reported.

That same day, 6 August 1944, SAS headquarters had received
first-hand reports of horrific Nazi atrocities; much that the
French civilian populace was taking the brunt of the horror, so
too it seemed was the SAS. In a daring air operation, the survivors of SAS Operation Bulbasket – situated 150 kilometres
to the south of Orléans, around the city of Châteauroux – had
just been lifted out of France, riding in a pair of Lockheed
Hudson bombers that had set down on a remote farmer's field.

The news that the Bulbasket escapees brought back to Britain was chilling.

Both operations – Bulbasket and Gain – had had similar objectives to Bill Fraser's in the Morvan: to sabotage and destroy enemy reinforcements, fuel and ammo destined for the Normandy front. The Operation Bulbasket force was led by the renowned SAS commander, Captain John Elliot Tonkin, a former member of the Long Range Desert Group (LRDG) – the British military's desert reconnaissance and intelligence-gathering specialists. Blessed with a wildly offbeat sense of humour, Tonkin was a Mayne stalwart, having been captured during the 1943 battle of Termoli, after which he'd executed a daring escape, rejoining his unit shortly thereafter.

Now, in early August 1944, Tonkin had pulled off his second great escape, but tragically he had been forced to leave most of his men behind. Having achieved some of the most daring raids of the war, Tonkin's force – some forty strong – had drawn the ire of the enemy. At first light on 3 July their forest base had been surrounded, as an SS Panzergrenadier – armoured infantry – division had closed the trap. Tonkin and one of his long-serving deputies, Lieutenant Peter Weaver, had led the rush to escape, as fierce battle was joined. But in the melee that ensued, thirty-one of Tonkin's men had been captured.

One of those, Lieutenant Tomos Stephens, was grievously injured. Taken prisoner, he was propped against a tree by his Waffen SS captors, and killed with a single shot to the head. That execution set the tone for things to come. A black Citroën car had rolled up. The occupants, Gestapo, got out, strode into the woods, and summarily executed all the Maquisards who'd been seized during that morning's operation. After that, the thirty-one SAS captives were spirited away, seeming to vanish without trace. Tonkin – one of only seven who had escaped – feared the worst.

Reports that filtered out suggested there was little hope for those of his men who had been taken.

As a close friend would declare of Tonkin, 'if a cat has nine lives, John was "the cat of all cats"'. Having escaped the round-up, he'd refused to evacuate, spending over a month in the region on a mission of vengeance, wreaking widespread havoc and mayhem. Reflecting the concern from SAS headquarters, on 30 July they'd sent Tonkin an urgent message by radio: 'Cases are preparing against war criminals. To . . . substantiate mounting mass of evidence you must forward to England by any secured means the names of enemy units, their formation officers and their responsible commanders where atrocities occur.'

By this juncture, the SAS had grown used to French villages suffering Nazi war crimes, but now they were bang in the cross-hairs themselves. Even as he and his fellow survivors were plucked out of France from a makeshift airstrip codenamed Bonbon, so Tonkin feared for those that he'd been forced to leave behind. He'd heard unconfirmed reports that all thirty-one had been shot, and those were the reports that he carried with him back to Britain, to SAS headquarters. As Padre McLuskey would note of the Bulbasket atrocities, they constituted 'a measure of the evil against which they [the SAS] had pledged themselves to fight'.

At the same time as Tonkin's squadron had suffered such a horrific fate, so too had a patrol led by Captain Patrick Garstin – twelve men who had parachuted into a drop zone just to the south of Paris in early July, with sabotage in mind. Supposedly, they were to be met on the ground by a mixed SOE and Resistance reception party. Instead, they had drifted onto the guns of the Gestapo and the Waffen SS, who had lain in a carefully prepared ambush. One man was killed, several injured, but three had managed to slip away in the darkness. Those taken captive – including Captain Garstin, who was grievously injured – were rushed to the Gestapo's Paris headquarters in the Avenue Foch. There, the beatings and interrogations had begun.

Two days after Tonkin and the Bulbasket survivors were plucked out of France, so Garstin and his fellow captives would be driven to a remote patch of woodland, to face a firing squad. They were to be murdered on the orders of Hitler himself, who had taken great personal umbrage at the daring and audacity of Britain's behind-the-lines raiders. Garstin would not survive the executions. Instead, with immense courage, he would tell his men, when facing the executioners, 'I'll distract them . . . On my signal, be ready to make a run for it . . .' In that way two of his fellows had managed to break away. They too would make it back to Britain, bringing eyewitness accounts of the Nazi atrocities.

At SAS headquarters, Mayne was aghast at the news flowing in. He received the reports with 'tight-lipped tension, clenching and unclenching his huge fists' in his rage. To this long-serving SAS commander, who had preached the value of extending clemency to enemy troops wishing to surrender, the 'satanic evil' reflected in these 'hideous murders' was 'utterly loathsome'. The very thought that such close comrades, all of whom he knew personally, and with so many of whom he'd 'shared pleasure, danger and hardship', were no more, killed 'not in fair soldierly combat, but foully murdered', was unconscionable.

If nothing else, it spurred Mayne to get into the field, hence his 6 July radio call to Captain 'Jock' Riding, alerting him to his imminent arrival. Mayne's intended destination, the Operation Gain base, had been carefully chosen. Sandwiched between Garstin's drop zone in the Fôret de Fontainebleau, and that of Tonkin's Bulbasket party, it was the perfect place from which to investigate all that had happened on the ground. To gather evidence and steady the ship. But it was not to be. As Mayne and his small party readied themselves for the flight in and the jump, they received an urgent radio call. Presuming it to be the code-letter for the coming drop – a recognition signal, known only to the reception party on the ground and to the inbound crew – it was nothing of the sort. The drop had been cancelled. At three o'clock that afternoon some six hundred German troops had surrounded Operation Gain's Fôret d'Orléans base, as they sought to capture or exterminate the SAS squadron. At that very moment, the mission's overall commander, Major Ian Fenwick – a renowned book illustrator and cartoonist by trade, who'd earned the admirable reputation of being 'a mad bugger' in the war – was absent from the camp. He was busy readying the DZ for Mayne and his small party to drop into, and Fenwick had left Jock Riding and one other in charge.

'Nobody argued with Fenwick,' one of his comrades would say of him. 'He could get anything done.' His singlemindedness was to be the death of him. Upon learning that their base was surrounded, Fenwick had sent that urgent radio message to Mayne, cancelling the drop, before taking to his jeep and motoring hell-for-leather back towards their camp, to take on whatever enemy he might find there. En route, Fenwick was passed further news from the locals. Their reports were dire. Word was that his squadron had been wiped out pretty much to the last man, and that all of the jeeps had been captured or destroyed. Burning with rage, Fenwick had driven towards the enemy positions, intent on vengeance.

Having lost all contact with Fenwick and Riding, and just as he was poised to join them, Mayne felt poleaxed. That very day he'd been busy in and around RAF Fairford, getting briefed on the coming insertion, readying their jeep which would drop with them and prepping his team. Mayne was accompanied by the superlative Captain Mike Sadler, a man who'd learned his unrivalled navigational skills first with the LRDG, in the North African desert. Becoming the trusted navigator of SAS founder David Stirling, eventually Sadler had transferred to the SAS. Dropping into enemy-occupied France at such a critical juncture as this, Sadler's skills were bound to prove invaluable.

In truth, Sadler was ill – he'd contracted a troubling stomach complaint during the long months that he'd spent behind the lines in North Africa, which had seriously impacted his health. But he remained determined to deploy alongside his commander, for he was 'one of Paddy's closest friends'. So too was Mayne's driver, Corporal Tommy 'Geordie' Corps, a man whom Sadler described as 'disreputable fellow', but in the finest SAS tradition. While Corps loved a drink and could be outrageously uncouth when in his cups, he was a brave and loyal soldier, with a decidedly unconventional mindset.

In Italy, Mayne and Corps had blown up the safe of the central bank of Augusta – the key enemy naval base – emptying it of valuables and a trove of papers. Several other Italian banks had attracted Mayne and Corps' attentions, though they were not always successfully breached. With delicious irony, Mayne would write home about Corps: 'He is a very respectable person, an Englishman. He walks about fifty yards farther than he need do, every time that he enters, so that he may come in by the back door.'

With their stores and weaponry stuffed into leg bags, there was a debate about whether they could afford to take one grenade or two, space was so tight. Even so, Corps insisted on packing a bottle of Jameson Irish whiskey, and Mayne insisted upon taking a tiny little wind-up gramophone, 'like something out of Woolworths', complete with a selection of his favourite records. They were Irish folk songs, with their roguishly rebellious lyrics – 'The Garden Where the Praties Grow', by Johnny Patterson, and

'Come Back Paddy Reilly', by Percy French. To round off the Celtic flavour of his mission, Mayne had an Ulster flag flying from his jeep and shamrocks painted on the bonnet.

But when all was made ready their drop had been cancelled, amid the worrying radio silence that followed from Operation Gain. Mayne remained determined to deploy – even more so, now that the grim fate of so many of his men was becoming clear. Only one place remained where it made sense to drop – that was to Bill Fraser's A Squadron, in the Morvan. Situated some 250 kilometres to the east of Orléans, it was about as close as Mayne could get to the nexus of the horror – the Operations Gain and Bulbasket mission areas – yet was relatively safe and secure.

At 10.00 a.m. on 7 August, Mayne received a message – and a final blessing – from high command: 'Don't delay your travels. Remember your talk with General . . . Good luck.' Flying out of Keevil Aerodrome, in Wiltshire, an RAF base increasingly used for airborne operations, Mayne's insertion at first seemed to be dogged by ill-fortune. Upon trying to take off, the under-carriage of their Stirling had simply imploded, the giant aircraft 'cartwheeling' to a screeching standstill. Miraculously, none of the SAS aboard, though 'bruised and battered', were seriously injured. The only real casualty was the RAF dispatcher, a Flight Lieutenant J. Richards, who was hospitalised.

Undaunted and determined to press on, Mayne, Sadler, Corps and the fourth member of their party, an SAS Lieutenant Winterson, had simply transferred to another aircraft. Deprived of a dispatcher – no replacement for Richards could be found – they'd have to find their own way out of the plane once over the DZ. Without a dispatcher, no details were recorded of the time or the status of the drop. The first news received at SAS headquarters was a short, succinct message from Mayne: 'It was a superb drop.' Throwing their own containers and then themselves out of the aircraft had been a nerve-racking experience, but all had made it safely to the ground.

'The Second World War has thrown up many remarkable men,' Padre McLuskey would write in his wartime memoir, *Parachute Padre*, 'but few more remarkable than Paddy Mayne.' The morning after he'd dropped in, the padre discovered Mayne in Bill Fraser's tent, 'lying lazily on a sleeping bag' beneath the expanse of white parachute silk that formed Fraser's makeshift shelter. Outwardly, there was little sign of the stress that the SAS commander was under, with an entire squadron – the Operation Gain party – having gone missing, and much of a second squadron, the Bulbasket team, missing, presumed murdered. Typically, Mayne was calmly chatting about his plans with Fraser and Sadler, as if the very idea of driving several hundred kilometres through Nazi-occupied France to discover the fate of his missing men was a Sunday stroll in the park.

Well over six foot tall, Mayne looked 'exactly what he was', as the padre noted of him that 8 August morning, 'an amateur boxer and Irish rugby international'. But beneath what was obvious at a glance, Mayne remained something of an enigma. The padre counted himself as blessed that he was one of the few people who had got to know the SAS commander well. It wasn't easy. While he was shy of newcomers and had a 'strong natural reserve', those who were lucky enough to see the other side of Mayne would find him possessed of 'more than his fair share of the wit and charm that come from Ireland'.

While Mayne was not an openly religious man, there was something that drew the padre and the SAS commander together – this man of God and this man of war. Those who got to know him well, and the padre was one, learned to appreciate Mayne's 'deep and simple reverence' for what faith truly stands for. The inherent values of brotherhood – justice, fairness and championing the underdog – were ones that the SAS commander embodied. They were the bedrock of what they were there for; the essence of why they were fighting this war; the heart of the struggle to defeat Nazism.

'Certainly,' the padre would write of Mayne, 'in the bond between him and his men, there was much to speak of that which should unite us all . . .' From the viewpoint of the padre, his faith embodied 'the love that shelters others and will not shield itself. This is the love that men like Paddy will always understand.'

A founder member of the SAS, David Stirling had recruited Mayne as the unit's discipline officer, as well as its physical training supremo. Mayne's concept of maintaining discipline typified the man. Anyone accused of an infraction would have to stand as many rounds as he could in the camp boxing ring, against Mayne, a former Irish Universities boxing champion. But there was one get-out clause. If the accused could offer up some kind of excuse for his misdemeanour, one that would make Mayne laugh, then he would be excused. In truth, there was little need for such enforcement. The discipline of the SAS was self-discipline, for anyone who failed to keep a grip on himself would be returned to unit (RTU'd). And no one wanted to be kicked out of this unique, exalted fraternity.

As the raiding operations had got under way in the autumn of 1941, Mayne had proved himself to be the desert warrior without compare. Within months, he had one hundred enemy warplanes under his belt – bombed, shot up or torn apart by his bare hands – making him a greater 'ace' than any RAF fighter pilot of the war. But more than that, he'd proved himself to be a superlative leader of men. In those freewheeling, piratical, maverick-spirited North African days, Mayne had truly come of age. As David Lloyd

Owen, one of the LRDG's foremost commanders, and a man who had come to know Mayne well, would write: 'As a fighter he was unsurpassed for his very presence in the full flood of his wrath was enough to unnerve the strongest . . . He had all the colour, dash and attraction of a great buccaneer.'

But more than his prowess and his courage, what drew men to him was the extraordinary care and concern he exhibited for those under his command. 'He was determined that he would never lose a single life if that could be avoided,' McLuskey would remark. Raids with the SAS were always risky. It went with the territory. But all knew with Mayne that 'no risk was ever taken without a very much worthwhile end in view.' While all knew that 'the chances of coming home again were barely even,' they also knew that Mayne would not have sanctioned the mission unless the prize justified the risks.

Indeed, in the months running up to D-Day, several plans had been put forward outlining how to use the SAS, which were fought against with great tenacity. 'A good many were rejected out of hand, because Paddy simply refused to allow any men of his to be mixed up with them.' In the most egregious of examples, a scheme was espoused to drop the entire SAS Brigade, about two thousand men-at-arms, just beyond the Normandy beaches, to serve as a 'blocking group' to dissuade enemy counter-attacks. Parachuted in some thirty-six hours before the D-Day landings, how the lightly armed SAS was supposed to stop Hitler's Panzers wasn't entirely clear.

As the SAS War Diary noted, 'the initial role for S.A.S. involvement in D-Day broke all the rules . . . as set out by David Stirling . . . that S.A.S. should be used strategically, deep behind enemy lines . . . For D-Day, the planners decided to drop the S.A.S. just behind the beach-heads.' Viewed as a suicide mission by most, it reflected, not for the first time, the inability of many on high to 'get' what the SAS was all about. Even then, by the spring of 1944, the very idea of behind-the-lines operations – of de facto guerrilla warfare – was anathema to so many in the higher echelons of the British military. To so many, it still wasn't the done thing. It wasn't how the British Army waged war.

That plan was defeated, but at a high cost. At the time, Lieutenant-Colonel Bill Stirling, David Stirling's brother, commanded 2 SAS. Livid at what was being proposed, and at the forefront of the battle to defeat the suicide plan, he was obliged to resign his command, for his criticism had been so glaringly accurate and incisive, and plainly put. With David Stirling having been captured by the enemy in 1943, and now Bill Stirling having fallen on his sword, both of the Stirling brothers were out of the SAS. But in Bill's case, he was right to fall on his sword. The plans were duly changed, and the SAS was deployed deep into Nazi-occupied France to do what it did best.

Even so, the naysayers and the detractors weren't quite done. As the SAS was now formally a part of the Army Air Corps – the aviation wing of the British military – their iconic sandy berets were to be done away with. Instead, they were ordered to come into line with airborne troops generally, and to wear the red beret which all sported. The diktat proved deeply unpopular. Some – Mayne, first and foremost – would stubbornly refuse to obey. He would retain his beige beret right until the end of hostilities. Others would wear the red version until they deployed into the field, whereupon the first thing they would do was whip it off and replace it with a worn and cherished sandy one.

This wasn't just about regimental pride and tradition. For obvious reasons, sporting a bright red beret behind enemy lines wasn't particularly sensible. It was a bullet-magnet. Later diktats were even more absurd. In due course King George VI himself would get involved, somehow objecting to the SAS's tradition of wearing their parachute wings on their left breast. Normally, a jump-qualified British soldier would wear them on his right shoulder. But for the SAS, this unique mark of distinction 'was a privilege which is highly valued by the men', as Brigadier Roderick McLeod, SAS Brigade commander, would write in the unit's defence.

McLeod was right. The wings could only be worn on the left breast once an operator had executed three missions behind enemy lines. It was the mark of the brotherhood. A long-standing practice, 'it had come to mean a great deal in the Regiment,' McLeod argued. 'The men realise that everybody cannot get a decoration, but they regard this privilege, which is visible for all their friends to see, as the next best thing . . . Its removal would be most unpopular . . . It is suggested that if His Majesty was aware of the importance which all ranks attach to this matter, he might be disposed to relent.' Facing such petty – yet powerful – interference and wrangling, it was little wonder that Mayne was relieved to get into the field in France.

Oddly – or perhaps typically – Mayne seemed quite at home in that forest base deep in the Morvan. 'I think Paddy could only live to the full in the open air,' McLuskey would remark. Somewhat 'awkward' in the confines of indoors, civilised living, 'outside, all his awkwardness fell away.' For the first time since the SAS's D-Day operations had commenced, Mayne seemed genuinely happy. Trapped in SAS headquarters, banned from deploying with his men, he had been desperate to slip the net and join his forces at the coal face of waging war. 'This was his life – comradeship, adventure, the open sky above you day and night. In such conditions he could fully be himself.'

While the SAS – at least, the Operations Gain and Bulbasket parties – seemed beset by dangers and calamity, here in the Morvan Mayne was back where he felt most at home. 'The thrill of danger, the challenge to match your wits against the enemy, this highly individualistic way of fighting, the freedom that was ours to live as we liked, to roam and to fight where we chose – this was the life for Paddy,' as the padre would remark. Such a life suited Mayne's temperament absolutely, but the long years of living it made him less attuned to the 'normal and peaceful and conventional' existence that others tended to lead.

The day of Mayne's arrival, Fraser and his party had to prepare for a parachutage. There was much to be done, for a new drop zone was to be tried out. Their regular DZ, in the open valley that ran at right angles to their Mazignian base, was too well known by now. Instead, Fraser had called in the drop to the far narrower valley in which the SAS was camped. With its precipitous sides and thickly wooded flanks, dropping containers to this DZ was going to be a gamble. On the upside, far less work would be involved in hauling the supplies to their camp. On the downside, the heavy loads could fall just about anywhere, including 'crashing down on our small home-made tents'.

Fortunately, the pilot for that night's drop proved 'remarkably accurate' in his delivery. All but one of the containers floated down into the heart of the valley, a few landing in the SAS's 'washroom' – the gurgling stream. One container was spied drifting astray, and frustratingly it was believed to hold the mail. The rest – packed with fresh uniforms, ammo, explosives, rations, cigarettes and petrol – were within easy reach. The camp positively 'hummed with activity', as local farmers brought their bullock carts to augment the one jeep, which went dashing to and fro, ferrying all into its rightful place.

By the time the clear-up was done, the night was still young and the fire burned bright in the camp. With the strains of the Percy French song 'The Mountains of Mourne' drifting through the woods, there was a bit of a party. In terms of a boost to the spirits, that gramophone was equal to 'at least ten hand grenades', as Mayne would argue. The key figures from the SAS's Morvan operations were there, Muirhead and Wellsted included. In view of Captain Roy Bradford's sad death, Mayne promoted Wellsted to the rank of captain on the spot, which in itself was good for morale. 'The whisky was produced and passed around,' as Wellsted remarked, and they 'sat up drinking half the night'.

In some magical way Mayne's 'very presence seemed to throw a protective screen' around his comrades and 'caused their morale to soar'. But as the dawn light filtered through the trees, those in the camp got a rude alarm call. 'The crashing of bombs awoke us,' Wellsted recalled, with the deafening roar of aircraft engines cutting through the forest. A flight of enemy warplanes were wheeling overhead. In an instant, the entire camp was a buzz of activity, figures diving for shelter. As the enemy aircraft couldn't be seen clearly through the thick tree cover, there was no way to hit back at them, and in any case to open fire would only serve to reveal their position.

The enemy pilots were actually after the Maquis' garage – the vehicle repair workshop situated not so far away. A couple of cars were hit, but there were no casualties. Once the German warplanes were gone, Mayne got down to business. He called a meeting with the key SAS commanders, plus the Maquis chiefs, to assess just what was what in the Morvan. Back in the field at last, he was determined to use 'all of his gifts . . . to the full'. Watching Fraser and Mayne talk, it was clear that both men had that indefinable, but instinctive know-how – that innate 'battle sense' which guided their every decision. While both were seemingly 'careless at times . . . each had the flair for the essential'. Both could reach the necessary decisions in the blink of an eye, when tough calls had to be made – just as they did now.

As the padre observed Mayne and Fraser in full flow, he was

struck by how 'Paddy had the keenest eye of any man I have ever met.' He was a sterling shot, of course, but more to the point, 'he noticed everything.' Had he not been known to all as Paddy, '"Eagle-eye" might have been his nickname.' While Mayne was 'as tender-hearted as he could be quick-tempered', he missed nothing. Nothing escaped him. The long and short of his ruminations with Fraser et al. was this: A Squadron needed to be relieved. After so many weeks spent behind enemy lines, some of his men – very possibly, Fraser included – were showing clear signs of 'battle fatigue'.

As the stress and strain was cumulative, so it crept up on these warriors of the Morvan without their noticing. Mayne, being the newcomer, saw all. As the padre readily admitted, 'the strain of this peculiar type of warfare had left its mark . . . what told on us all was the necessity for constant vigilance. One could never wholly relax.' Their supposedly peaceful camp 'might be surrounded and attacked at any time . . . there was no safe area to which men could go for a rest. After two months of it, the strain was beginning to tell.' In twenty-four hours, Mayne had seen and noted all of this and his decision was made.

Explaining to Fraser that his men were 'overworked and needed a rest', Mayne announced that A Squadron would be replaced by C Squadron – commanded by Major Tony Marsh – just as soon as he could get the men and their jeeps spirited into the Morvan. In the interim, he had his own challenges to face. Some 250 kilometres to the north-west lay the Operation Gain base, at the Fôret de Fontainebleau – or at least, that had been its base of operations when last the commanders there had reported in. Despite the strictures constraining Mayne to 'coordinating actions and not to leading any missions', it was to Orléans that he intended to head, to discover what had befallen those who had gone missing.

One last matter needed addressing in the Morvan: the thorny issue of the wounded. Trooper Grady – shot in the arm during Wellsted's rail-sabotage mission – could more or less fend for himself by now, and Trooper Burgess could just about hobble about on his broken and splinted leg. Sergeant Chalky White's wounds were also mending well. But others were in a far worse condition. Lance Corporal Bromfield – shot in the leg during the Ouroux street brawl – was a stretcher case, while Corporal Adamson, who'd suffered his awful internal injuries in the jeep accident, barely looked as if he could survive any kind of a move. The answer was found to be a former top holiday resort for English tourists – the hotel Beau Rivage, at the nearby Lac des Settons.

Lying some fifteen kilometres to the south of the SAS camp, the lakeside hotel had a number of advantages. It was run by a former collaborator, who – sensing the way the war was going – was desperate to ingratiate himself with the Allies. With few tourists, the lakeside resort was empty, so the hotel had bags of room. The proprietor had fired all his staff, for obvious reasons, which meant that only he and his wife now lived there. The hotel itself was set well away from the main roads, and was unlikely to be hosting any visiting Germans any time soon. Warned to take great care of the wounded or else, that man and wife became the custodians of the SAS's makeshift hospital.

To an individual of 'lesser character', Mayne's proposed expedition to the Fôret de Fontainebleau may have seemed like 'a pilgrimage of death'. Such a man might have been frozen into inaction. Certainly, no SAS patrol had ever undertaken such a journey across France as the one Mayne envisaged, and especially since he and his fellows were heading into an area where their SAS brethren had suffered murderous predations at the hands of the enemy. The journey that lay before Mayne dwarfed any of those undertaken from the Morvan. But Mayne had promised. He had made his decision and 'action must follow'; it could not be gainsaid.

The following morning, 'at cockcrow', Mayne and his small party were gone, their lone jeep heading off into the dawn light that filtered through the trees.

Into the valley of death rode Mayne and his comrades, seeking to rescue the fortunes of a mission.

Chapter Eleven

LEAVE NO MAN BEHIND

It was on 9 August 1944 when Mayne, Sadler, Corps and Winterson began their daring mission. Amazingly, they would complete the entire journey within twenty-four hours, passing 'hundreds of miles over roads and lines ... patrolled by the enemy'. While it was innate and heartfelt chivalry and courage that had driven Major Fenwick – Operation Gain's commander – to his death, with Mayne and his three comrades it would be his sheer 'foxiness and sixth sense for danger' that would save their lives time and time again. That, plus Captain Sadler's incredible navigational skills and map-reading, plotting a route to avoid the enemy wherever he might lurk.

They reached the Fôret de Fontainebleau to learn the bitter truth: Fenwick had been killed in action, and all aboard his jeep were missing, presumed dead or captured. At first, blessed with Fenwick's drive and audacity – he could 'get anything done' – Operation Gain had prospered. Due to the daring sabotage operations of Fenwick's patrols, 'considerable material damage was done to rolling stock and railway lines,' noted one report. Since their early June deployment, Fenwick's raiders had hit a series of targets, including blowing up trains and petrol tankers, and cutting numerous railway lines. They'd also called in RAF airstrikes on key targets, one of which took out a million-gallon fuel dump in Orléans.

Indeed, an official assessment of Operation Gain would conclude that 'the German Army . . . was not safe from attack in the middle of villages from Dourdan to Orleans,' a patch of territory some 50 miles across. But then had come the 6 August assault by 600 enemy troops, and the warnings passed to Fenwick that nearly all of his men had been killed or captured. Driven into a rage by the news, Fenwick had sped off in his jeep, little knowing that his progress was being shadowed by a Fieseler Fi 156 Storch, a German spotter plane.

As he had raced towards Chambon-la-Fôret, Fenwick had been flagged down by an elderly woman, who was cycling furiously away from the village. The SS were up ahead, she warned, and they had been alerted to Fenwick's approach. They were preparing an ambush. And they had rounded up all the men and youths of the village, herding them into the church, with threats that either they revealed the whereabouts of the saboteurs, or all would be killed. Unbeknown to Fenwick, the vast majority of his men – Lieutenant Riding included – had slipped the enemy's trap and made good their getaway.

Undeterred by the elderly Frenchwoman's warnings, Fenwick had declared: 'Thank you, Madame, but I intend to attack them.' Fired up as he was, he was itching for a fight. But his actions were also driven by the realisation of the horrors the inhabitants of Chambon-la-Fôret were facing, unless someone intervened. Spurring the lone jeep forward at top speed, and with SAS Corporals William Duffy and Frank Dunkley manning the Vickers-K guns, Fenwick tore into the outskirts of the village 'all-guns-blazing'. With the jeep tearing ahead at sixty miles per hour, they took on the first machinegun nest, but the enemy proved to be in well-prepared ambush positions.

The enemy met fire with fire. When the speeding jeep was almost past the bulk of the enemy's guns, a 20mm cannon round struck Fenwick square in the forehead, and he was killed instantly. 'Major Fenwick fell across the wheel,' Corporal Duffy would report. 'I felt the blood, which I found later was his . . . just like water sprinkling on my face, and he flopped at the same moment . . . from then on I lost consciousness, I was hit.' Deprived of a driver, the jeep careered onwards, ploughing into a nearby patch of woodland. In the process, two Maquis who were riding in the vehicle were killed, and Corporals Duffy and Dunkley were injured, rendered senseless, and taken captive.

With Fenwick dead, leadership of Operation Gain had fallen to twenty-eight-year-old Lieutenant Jock Riding, who would go on to win a Military Cross for rallying the troops under such extreme circumstances. After the long weeks spent behind the lines, and having lost a man of Major Fenwick's stature, 'the morale of certain of the men cracked a trifle,' Captain Riding would report with masterly understatement. How welcome was it, then, when a lone jeep had sought them out in their Fôret de Fontainebleau base – Paddy Mayne and his cohorts riding to the rescue.

Jock Riding and his deputy, Lieutenant Jimmy Watson, briefed Mayne on all that had transpired. Many in that camp seemed shocked and dismayed by Fenwick's death, especially since SAS doctrine had it that 'you do not want to be caught, and you do not fight' unless you absolutely have to. Some went as far as arguing it had been a 'bloody stupid' waste of the life of 'a very gallant Englishman'. Of course, Fenwick had been misinformed, being led to believe that his squadron of fifty-eight men had been wiped out. In the circumstances, his seemingly suicidal charge into the teeth of the enemy was perhaps somewhat understandable.

In any case, similar lone-jeep shoot-'em-ups had scored startling successes already under Fenwick's command, so a precedent had been set. Not so long before, Lieutenant Jimmy Watson had driven into the nearby town of Dourdan, his jeep manned by two SAS on the Vickers-K guns, plus a local Maquisard serving as their guide. As they'd sped through the town, they'd been astonished to discover a long convoy of German Army trucks lined up in the town square. It seemed to be only lightly guarded, and Watson was amazed when he and his men sailed by without being challenged.

As they left the town, Watson ordered his driver to halt. Surely this was too great an opportunity to miss? The Vickers-K guns were readied, both the front and the rear pairs, before Watson told his driver to take them back in to do a 'speedy tour' of the square. As they entered it, both guns let rip, rounds tearing into the nearest trucks, causing havoc and carnage in the process, for the vehicles proved to be crammed full of enemy troops. Yet the response was swift. Machineguns sparked fire from those vehicles, targeting Watson's jeep as it was driven wildly around the square. The Frenchman riding in the rear was hit, and he tumbled out, though he would manage to crawl to safety.

Watson, meanwhile, yelled to his driver: 'Get us the hell out of here!' Which he did, speeding the SAS men to safety.

In a sense, Fenwick's lone jeep charge had been only mildly more suicidal than Lieutenant Watson's. The difference was, luck had been with Watson. Fenwick's death had deprived an SAS squadron of its iconic commander, and left two of their French comrades dead, plus two SAS men, Duffy and Dunkley, injured and held captive. Upon hearing the news, Mayne recognised that the fighting spirit of these men would need stiffening, and he was there both to raise morale and to get them back on track. At the new forest base which they'd moved to, one of Mayne's first actions was to promote Jock Riding to the rank of Captain, as he sought to steady the ship.

Then, acting as if the 'flap' was very much over, Mayne adopted the guise of a man taking a gentle afternoon stroll, as he played the homely Irish ballads on his wind-up gramophone. He ordered forty-eight hours of downtime, during which the men were to lie low, rest and recuperate as best they could. Mayne spent that time with Sadler, Riding and Watson, trying to ascertain what were the best options for Operation Gain. When the forty-eight hours were up, a strategy had been set. They would send out small groups, riding in jeeps wherever possible, to recce the nearby roads leading from Orléans north to Pithiviers and east to Montargis. If the enemy were still moving reinforcements towards the frontline, those routes would be busy. There would be targets still to hit. If not, then very possibly Operation Gain had run its course.

Mayne stressed the need for their vehicles to be camouflaged, to better resemble enemy transports. The jeep's 'lamp masks' – shields fitted to the headlamps to black out the lights – were to be removed. Instead, they should be draped in foliage, which was how the enemy achieved a similar effect. In fact, German vehicles on the move tended to resemble mobile bushes, so many branches and leaves did they attach to their upper sides. The SAS should do the same with their jeeps.

Gradually, a picture was assembled. Targets there were aplenty, it seemed. As many as 142 Tiger tanks were hidden in a nearby stretch of forest. Mayne radioed in the targets to London head-quarters, so RAF warplanes could swoop from the skies. 'Flap thought to be over,' Mayne informed headquarters, on 11 August. He added that they had identified an excellent DZ, 'that could take everything'. If reinforcements could be dropped in, they should come with vehicles. 'Can take 30 jeeps . . . All parties to bring MICHELIN maps and each jeep patrol should have 1 three inch mortar.'

While he was seeking to stiffen and strengthen the Operation

Gain offensive spirit, Mayne was also trying to kill two birds with one stone here. The thirty-strong jeep party he was suggesting be dropped into the Gain area was Tony Marsh's C Squadron. If they could parachute into the Fôret de Fontainebleau base, from there it was possible – as Mayne had shown – to flit across to the Morvan, to relieve the Operation Houndsworth party.

The local Resistance 'want arms, ammunition and medical supplies dropped', reported Mayne on 13 August. 'Code word ELLE A RETROUVE SON MARI.' The messages and the intel kept flowing, as Mayne's 'road watch' patrols – keeping eyes on the main routes of transport – continued to come up trumps. 'Reports 40 or 80 tanks going north ... Squadron road watch reported seeing 8 trucks and three ambulances travelling west on BELGARDE–CHATEAUNEUF road ... also 170 trucks and 96 horses travelling North East on ORLEANS–PITHIVIERS road ... Reports of German prisoners state that German transport using small roads in order to avoid R.A.F.'

The word back from SAS headquarters reflected how useful such intelligence was proving. 'Excellent. Please continue information especially of movements through gap. Best of luck to all.' Step by step, Operation Gain was getting back into the swing of things. But then, on 16 August, a brief five-word warning was dispatched to London: 'PACKMAN AND ION reported missing.' Earlier, two young troopers, Leslie Packman and John Ion, had left their forest base, with orders to check out the Orléans–Pithiviers road, which was throwing up some choice intel. Ion and Packman had left in fine spirits with a 'farewell nod from Paddy Mayne'. But as Riding reported shortly, they 'failed to return'.

After their last abortive attack on the Operation Gain base, the enemy were out there, quartering the Fôret de Fontainebleau, seeking the British saboteurs. Captured, Ion and Packman were spirited to the local Gestapo headquarters at the exquisite Château de Chamerolles, near the town of Chilleurs-aux-Bois. There, the two men were branded as being 'saboteurs' and 'terrorists', and their fates were sealed. Shortly, the chateau's caretaker would find two bodies in a semi-decomposed state, dumped not far from the moat. Each had been executed with a shot to the head.

Burying the corpses in the local cemetery, he first thought to remove anything that might help prove their identities. That evidence was passed over to the SAS. 'I recognise the rings and a pen they were wearing and carrying,' Jock Riding would report of the items the caretaker had retrieved from the bodies, 'and also such remains as had not been buried.' A tuft of blonde hair – Trooper Ion was sandy-haired – had also been retrieved from the killing ground.

Mayne had dispatched those two men into harm's way. He now had first-hand proof of the savage methods being employed by the enemy. He'd heard the rumours in Britain. He'd read the radio messages and the reports. And then he'd heard the eyewitness accounts from men returning from the field, like Captain John Tonkin. But here in the Fôret de Fontainebleau, he was experiencing what it all meant at first hand. As far as anyone could tell, *no* SAS captives seized in France were being extended the basic protections that should accrue to bona fide prisoners of war. Quite the reverse: it seemed that anyone taken prisoner would face only torture, deprivation, degradation, ridicule and murder.

As the padre had pointed out, Mayne was 'determined that he would never lose a single life if that could be avoided'. Here in the Fôret de Fontainebleau he was failing. He found it both heartrending and enraging. If he needed any further evidence of the unfolding horrors, shortly he was to get it. A patrol led by Lieutenant Leslie Bateman was ambushed by the enemy. While

Bateman managed a daring escape, his comrade, Corporal Wilson, was shot and captured. Tied to a tree, he was interrogated and beaten by the Gestapo. The men in black warned him that he was viewed as a 'terrorist' and that he was to be executed, on orders from on high. Some Maquisards had been captured alongside Wilson. He could hear the Frenchmen being marched away to be shot.

Having passed out, Wilson came to in some kind of medical facility. As luck would have it, he'd been taken to a hospital lying closer to the frontline. In the chaos of war, the Gestapo must have overlooked Wilson's presence and the threats they had made. Two days later the town in which Wilson was hospitalised was liberated by American forces. Wilson was set free, and he was able to report to Mayne exactly what had happened, in all its grisly detail. He'd escaped from a death sentence by the skin of his teeth.

So universal did this policy appear to be – this widespread extermination plan – it could not be happening by accident. No way could it be an ad hoc reaction of individual commanders on the ground. A guiding force was at work here, and in the totalitarian world of Nazism nothing ever happened unless sanctioned from the very highest level. In short, a picture had emerged that was stark in the extreme. Any SAS captives were being kept alive only for as long as they might yield useful intelligence, after which they were murdered.

The hunters were the Gestapo and the SS, and that meant that Mayne and his men now knew who their foremost enemies were. Increasingly, in this war with hate, the conflict was boiling down to a savage and brutal confrontation between those two parties – Gestapo and SS versus SAS.

By 17 August, barely a week after Mayne had arrived at the Operation Gain camp, he reported: 'AMERICANS getting very close and GERMANS trying to surrender . . . many enemy with-drawing towards MONTARGIS along ORLEANS canal, largely disorganised and mainly on foot or in carts. The FFI are dis-arming many but can't guard or feed them . . . enemy retreat continues East.' The 'FFI' were the *Forces françaises de l'intérieur*, the formal name for the united front of all French Resistance units. The enemy front was crumbling, as the harried armies of the Reich streamed eastwards towards Germany, with the inten-tion of setting up a new defensive line – for of course, the Allies had to be stopped from marching into the Fatherland.

The next message sent to SAS headquarters concerned Mayne, but wasn't from him. 'Reports he has reached LE MANS and requests position of the landing ground.' In forty-eight hours, Mayne had hit the road, flitted west 250-odd kilometres, moving from their Fôret de Fontainebleau base to the French city of Le Mans, which lay some 200 kilometres inland from the Normandy beaches, all the while moving across terrain that was crawling with enemy units, as their forces fell back from the frontline.

That same day – 19 August – Mayne was sent a 'demand' that he come up on air that evening, 'at 2200 hrs for urgent message'. Twenty-eight aircraft – Douglas C-47 Skytrain transports – were scheduled to land at Rennes, to the west of Le Mans, at an air-base recently taken from the enemy, each plane packed with SAS who had flown out from England. That entire force – Major Tony Marsh, with most of C Squadron, plus their jeeps – was ordered to rendezvous with Mayne 'at HOTEL CANTRALE at LE MANS'.

With Mayne at the heart of the battle, quartering hundreds of kilometres of hostile territory to stiffen fighting spirit and to bring in much-needed reinforcements, this wasn't quite as high command had envisaged things. The SAS commander had been permitted to deploy strictly to coordinate actions, as opposed to leading missions, and he had been cautioned to minimise risk. Quite the opposite was proving to be the case, as Mayne decided for himself just how his skills might best be utilised.

Repeated demands by radio were made for Mayne to check in, and increasingly, to return to Britain: 'come up on emergency frequency'; 'anxiously awaiting your call'; 'suggest you return immediately for urgent discussion . . . decisions needed concerning future policy . . . If you are unwilling to return . . .'

But Mayne had gone dark.

It would be days before he would finally break his silence. On 28 August Mayne dispatched a brief, three-line message: 'Sorry I have been out of touch . . . have no W/T. Have you anything for me? MELOT also here.' The claim to have no wireless with which to contact headquarters was a canny one. It had plausible deniability, for who could prove otherwise? In the interim, he'd been in the thick of the action, having linked up with one of his longest standing and closest comrades, the legendary Major Robert Emanuel Marie Melot. Known to all as 'Bob' and a decorated First World War veteran, Melot, a Belgian, was the grandfather of 1 SAS, being all of forty-nine years old by the summer '44.

Wounded in 1917 while flying as a pilot in the Belgian Air Force, two decades later and well into his late forties, Melot had volunteered his services when global hostilities broke out once more. Then living in Egypt, and with fluent Arabic and an intimate knowledge of North Africa, Melot was perfect for intelligence-gathering operations, if a little long-in-the-tooth for combat, or so those on high had presumed. He'd been recruited into the 'Inter-Service Liaison Department' (ISLD), a decidedly dull and boring name that served as cover for the British Secret Intelligence Service (SIS) in North Africa. Snapped up by the ISLD, Melot had spent months living among the Bedouin and the Senussi – the local Saharan tribes – somehow masquerading as one of their own.

In time, his desert sojourns with the ISLD had earned him an MC for 'sorties behind enemy lines', showing 'complete disregard for his own personal safety'. It had also brought him into contact with the SAS, and Melot – who secretly hungered to fight – had offered his services to David Stirling and his desert raiders. Immensely cultured, widely read, grandfatherly – he attempted to disguise his balding and somewhat avuncular appearance by adopting a shaven-headed look – Melot was particularly drawn to Mayne, and the two would become firm friends. In writing to the SAS commander, whom he addressed as 'Dear Paddy', Melot would caution him that there was 'no question for you to try and go to any operation without me!'

So it would prove, time and time again. Daring, courageous beyond measure, seemingly indestructible, Melot would next get hospitalised on the SAS's ill-fated September 1942 Benghazi raid, being all-but left for dead with multiple shrapnel wounds. In due course, he would check himself out of a Cairo hospital and return to raiding duties, seemingly unperturbed. Then, in Italy in 1943, Melot would get badly injured for a third time, during the siege of Termoli. He was only saved from capture or death by the heroic actions of one of his young comrades, Sergeant Ernest 'Buttercup Joe' Goldsmith, who evacuated Melot under heavy fire. 'Worshipped' by the men, an icon of 'patience and tolerance', they would go to superhuman efforts to 'not let him down', just as Goldsmith had done.

Melot had been shot through the chest, the bullet exiting through his back. But typically, two days later he was back on duty, refusing to step away from the battle, as Termoli was then under ferocious siege. Strictly speaking, he served as Mayne's intelligence officer, so he had every reason to avoid the cut and thrust of combat. But there was no keeping the old warrior down. The hunger for action drew Melot and Mayne to each other. But there was also another, deeper bond: both were outsiders. Mayne was an Irishman and an Ulsterman; Melot was Belgian by birth and international by upbringing. Neither hailed from the typical 'officer class' of the British military.

They were an equally dynamite combination at the hard end of war. As Mayne, Melot, Sadler and Corps buzzed across enemy-occupied France, even with Sadler's superlative navigational skills hostile forces simply could not be avoided. Travelling in one comparatively lightly armed jeep, they risked the same kind of confrontation as had proven fatal to Captain Roy Close and two of his men in the Morvan, when they had stumbled upon that convoy of German troops breakfasting by the roadside. When such a thing did happen – blundering into a far superior enemy force – only the kind of instant, instinctive decision-making that Mayne was renowned for would save the day.

Every day at this time Mayne 'took his life in his hands and walked the razor's edge' as did that small band of men riding with him. So much so, that when Mayne was awarded the second bar to his existing DSO for his actions in France, he would object that his comrades 'should have been similarly decorated'. One day in August '44, zipping along a dusty summer lane not far from where they believed the frontline to be, there was little to suggest danger might lurk anywhere thereabouts, apart from what Mayne's sixth sense detected and his 'lightning quick mind'.

Up ahead, they thought they heard the grunt of a powerful engine. Just as Corps was trying to spot a place to pull off the road or even to turn around – the narrow lane was hemmed in by hedgerows – a six-wheeled German armoured car came roaring around the corner, its 'gun pointing menacingly forwards'. Not a good situation at all. Summing matters up in the blink of an eye,

Mayne, who was acutely aware that none of their guns packed the kind of punch to penetrate the enemy's armour, yelled out an order to Corps.

'Pull up quickly!'

As Corps slammed the jeep to a standstill, he glanced around for Mayne, realising that the SAS commander was already gone. Leaping from the jeep even before it had stopped moving, Mayne had sprinted forward and taken cover in the hedgerow, at just the point where he figured the armoured car would come to a halt. Even as he'd made a dash for it, he'd had a grenade gripped in either hand. Sure enough, the enemy vehicle ground to a halt at exactly that spot, for it and the jeep barely had room enough to pass. The hatch was thrown back, as the enemy commander poked his head out to investigate. It was the last thing he would ever do.

First one and then a second grenade was tossed beneath the belly of the enemy vehicle. Moments later the blasts rang out and the entire armoured behemoth seemed to rise in the air with the force of the explosions, before smashing down again, as first the engine, and then the entire length of the vehicle was engulfed in a 'sheet of flame'. No one got out of the flaming pyre, and with the job well done Mayne returned to the jeep. Casual as anything he clambered back aboard, and signalled for Corps to get moving, as if what had just occurred was 'a mere bagatelle' – in other words, a trifle of little note.

Of course, and as Sadler would appreciate, those who believed that Mayne felt no fear were mistaken. Constantly on the move to ensure that his squadrons could fight and survive, constantly vigilant to avoid death or capture, Mayne was under enormous pressure in France. It was just that with most people he didn't ever let it show. His blithe confidence gave them great confidence in return, which was absolutely critical when nerves were so fraught. But with those few he was close to – Sadler and Melot first and foremost – he would let the truth bleed through.

At times Mayne 'admitted that he was frightened', Sadler would remark. But unlike many others, he was 'not so scared that he would fail to act'. Any fear he felt he kept absolutely 'under control'. Or as Derrick 'Happy' Harrison would observe, Mayne went from 'perception to action' in a flash. He headed right in and cleared the enemy out.

Right then, the enemy were being cleared out of north and central France in droves. While the SAS was 'operating in this twilight world', the massed ranks of the British, American, Free French, Commonwealth and other allied forces were steamrollering through. The bloody and attritional warfare of July had ground down the enemy's defences, and their eventual exhaustion had cleared the way for a series of August breakthroughs. British and Canadian forces were sweeping across the north of France, thrusting east towards the key Belgian port of Antwerp. By 4 September, it was to be in Allied hands.

Meanwhile, to the south of the Normandy front, the American First and Third Armies were driving towards Paris, along with their Free French comrades, with the aim of liberating the French capital. While Hitler had ordered Paris to be laid waste if the city threatened to fall to the Allies, the German commander there, General Dietrich von Choltitz, had refused to desecrate the City of Light as it is known. A jewel of civilisation, it should be spared the devastation of war, he believed. Von Choltitz would earn the moniker the 'Saviour of Paris' for his spirited defiance of the Führer, a man whom the German commander believed was by then quite insane.

Yet by late August 1944, Paris was still to fall. The German soldiery, despite being pushed back on all fronts, proved to have a remarkable tenacity and will to fight. There was much to be done.

*

As Tony Marsh would report, "'C' Squadron . . . equipped with 40 jeeps, left ENGLAND . . . Proceeded to ORLEANS, to RV with Col MAYNE on the 21st . . . The party left . . . on the 22nd, bound for KIPLING, which at that time was still behind enemy lines. The situation was extremely fluid – one column of Germans was encountered at LAMMERIE, one staff car being captured, and 3 Germans killed or wounded. The morning after this encounter, 11 German prisoners were taken, 3 being wounded before surrendering . . .' Shortly after reaching the Operation Kipling base in the Yonne – Captain Derrick 'Happy' Harrison's stalking ground – Marsh and his men would move south, into the Morvan, to relieve A Squadron, leaving the wannabe 'Colonel' Peter Davis to hold the fort in the Yonne, including his attempt to take the surrender of some 18,000 German troops.

Somehow, Mayne would seem to be everywhere all at once: ushering the Operation Gain force back to Allied lines, as that mission was now over; guiding Marsh's C Squadron east to the Yonne, and thereafter flitting southwards with them, headed for the Morvan for a second rendezvous with Bill Fraser and his battle-worn warriors. At every step, it wasn't only the enemy that Mayne and his raiders had to be watchful for – supposedly friendly forces were just as likely to mistake them for the enemy, when spying a column of armed vehicles moving deep inside hostile territory.

On 28 August, even as they probed a route towards friendly lines, Captain Jock Riding and some of his men had been 'captured' by US forces. The American frontline commanders simply refused to believe that Riding and his party were who they said they were. No matter that Riding tried to explain the jeeps had been parachuted deep behind enemy lines, and that they were simply returning to the Allied fold, his words seemed to cut little ice.

The American commanding officer studied Riding and his men with obvious disbelief, before taking them before General George S. Patton, so they could explain themselves.

Faced with 'Old Blood and Guts' Patton himself, the American general eyed the captives, balefully. 'If you're Brits, you'll be okay,' he growled. 'If not, you'll be shot – even if I have to shoot you myself.' Riding and his men were finally handed over to Patton's British liaison officer, who was persuaded of the veracity of their story. And in due course, Mayne himself would have his own altercation with the famously iron-arsed American general.

Upon the liberation of the city of Le Mans, Mayne, together with Mike Sadler, had driven through the streets firing off their Vickers-K guns in wild celebration. With the city's liberators being Americans, they suddenly found themselves being arrested and marched before General Patton. Mayne, unperturbed, had assessed the situation in an instant, throwing down a veiled challenge to the US commander: 'I hope we didn't frighten your men?' Making it quite clear that none of his men had been in the slightest bit scared, Patton had let them go with a dire warning ringing in their ears: there would be serious trouble should they contemplate any similar high jinks.

There would be another lighter moment at this juncture – a tale truly to lift the spirits of Mayne and his men. Corporal Duffy, one of the late Ian Fenwick's two gunners, would engineer a most remarkable escape. Injured as their jeep had executed its Charge of the Light Brigade moment at Chambon-la-Fôret, the last thing Duffy had remembered was the vehicle 'careering wildly in the direction of some woods'.

Duffy had come-to sometime later in a hospital run by the enemy. Being full of wounded German troops, he was to have 'a brush with some Huns', as he described it. They had mistaken the wounded British soldier for a Hawker Typhoon fighter pilot. 'They had had a slight "misadventure" with some Typhoon tank busters . . .' he would remark, 'and as they were the sole survivors of their former battery they were rather indignant.'

After the fisticuffs, Duffy was relocated to a separate ward, which he shared with 'eight Huns, one Russian'. No stranger to imprisonment and subsequent getaways – Duffy had escaped once before, after being captured in North Africa – he was alert to any opportunity for a breakout, despite his injuries. His chance was to come courtesy of one of the brave French staff, a young lady who worked as a cleaner on the ward. On 22 August she warned him that the Americans were closing in, and that the hospital was poised to be evacuated. He needed to try to escape now, or the moment would be gone. 'This was a chance so I jumped at it,' Duffy explained.

His means of escape was to be a German medical orderly's uniform. The courageous girl carried it into the ward hidden in her cleaning bucket, which she plonked down at Duffy's bedside. Then, while more of the French female staff got busy 'crowding around the Germans' and drawing their attention, Duffy pulled out the uniform and gave it a good looking over. It seemed to pass muster. But there was one problem – there were no shoes. He managed to attract the attention of one of the girls, motioning to the lack of suitable footwear. Later, a pair of shoes were delivered in the same fashion as the uniform.

Duffy waited for the enemy soldiers on the ward to fall asleep. Then, 'I did one of the fastest, if not the fastest, quick change acts in history.' Dressed in the uniform of an *oberartz* – a senior German medical officer – Duffy hobbled to the exit, for the shoes proved to be two sizes too small. Once there, he straightened his posture and strode across the courtyard, which was 'crowded with wounded and vehicles ready for the evacuation'.

As he reached the gate leading out of the hospital, Duffy spied the obligatory sentry. But as that man smartly drew himself to attention and saluted, Duffy 'naturally, out of courtesy' returned the gesture.

Salutes exchanged, he marched out of the hospital gate, 'rather painfully', for the shoes were pinching terribly. Dumping his footwear in a wood, Duffy hobbled towards the sound of the guns. He came across an old man leading a horse and cart. Once Duffy had explained his predicament – he was trying to escape barefoot – the kindly fellow helped him onto his horse. Like that, they ran into 'two Huns, on motor cycles' who asked for directions to their intended destination. Duffy didn't have 'the faintest idea where it was', but pointed confidently in one direction and made the right kind of noises to suggest that was the way. They thanked him and moved on.

A while later they came across the hulk of an enemy tank at the roadside. It had been knocked out by a group of Resistance fighters. Once they realised who exactly Duffy was, they took him to a safe house, where a doctor was called for. He bandaged Duffy's feet – he had 'twenty one blisters' on the left foot and 'twenty-eight' on the right. From there Duffy was taken to the Allied frontline and handed over into American custody. While recovering in one of their hospitals, he would receive 'the Order of the Purple Heart, an award given to all Americans wounded in action'.

For Mayne and his comrades, Duffy's incredible escape epitomised the very spirit of the SAS – with bluff, deception, improvisation and sheer grit to the fore, not to mention the burning desire to never, ever give up or give in. It also typified the SAS mindset – that one man could achieve the seemingly impossible, no matter his rank, birth or background. Duffy's raw confidence and chutzpah – the very cheek of the man – had seen him through situations where others of a less audacious and brazen mindset may well have baulked. But that was what the SAS ethos, training and esprit de corps inculcated in each and every one of these special warriors.

They would need all of that and more for what was coming – the bloody and bitter march on Berlin.

Chapter Twelve
GET PÉTAIN

Duffy had got himself ensconced in that American-run hospital by 28 August. The same day, a message was received at SAS headquarters: 'Mayne is at HOUNDSWORTH . . . As many jeeps as possible to go to QUARRE LES TOMBES and meet MAYNE there.' Quarré-les-Tombes lay deep in the Morvan, where Mayne was gathering his scattered forces. 'Colonel' Peter Davis would be called to that rendezvous, as would Johnny Wiseman from Dijon, and Captains Derrick Harrison and Roy Close from the Yonne. As for Bill Fraser and his men, they were poised to depart for Britain: 'Approx all ranks of "A" Squadron will leave here . . . in three or four days,' Mayne signalled.

During the time that Mayne had been away from the Morvan, Bill Fraser's raiders had been busy. The Autun synthetic fuel plant had taken a second pounding, as Muirhead – Bertie Wooster – had unleashed another blistering mortar barrage, and Wellsted – Captain Gremlin – had crawled into the facility's mine shaft itself, to lace it with plastic explosives. As a sequel to the first devastating assault it had proved wonderfully successful, as Muirhead's report made crystal clear.

As the mortar opened fire . . . Captain WELLSTED, covered by LT DUBREY, laid charges in the wheel-house.

Ten Milice bolted out of the area of the shaft, but as they made no attempt to interfere, LT DUBREY did not wish to disclose his position ... By this time mortar bombs were plumping most satisfactorily into the factory area at a range of 700 yards and dense clouds of steam were seen rising from broken pipes. The air raid siren was wailing and more bombs were whistling overhead. Then with a roar the seven Vickers Ks opened up at 200 yards, spraying the whole area with tracer and incendiary, each pouring two full pans into the rising storm.

Wellsted had gone on to blow up a rail terminal and points, plus a key bridge. At one point his jeep had got bogged down, only for an obliging French farmer to tow it free with a team of oxen. Then, late in August, Fraser received an urgent message from SOE agent Colonel Hutchison he of the plastic-surgery-altered features. Marshal Pétain – the puppet head of the puppet French Vichy state – was fleeing through the Morvan with a massive escort of German troops and Milice. The Maquis intended to seize him before he could make it through. Hutchison requested Fraser's SAS to join forces with the Maquis to get Pétain. But just as they had failed to get Rommel, so Pétain would slip through their clutches. They had to console themselves with capturing his chief of security, a raft of key documents and Pétain's personal camera, complete with undeveloped film.

Regarding the Rommel factor, Bill Fraser's war diary for late August 1944 noted: 'Five SAS jeeps with Capt. RAYMOND LEE, get through the lines to the camp.' Lee – Couraud – had just arrived in the Morvan, fresh out of Operation Gaff, his extraordinary mission to kill or capture Rommel. Barely two weeks earlier he had cycled into American lines disguised as a gendarme. After Rommel had been hit by the RAF, Couraud and his small band of raiders had spent their time and explosives wreaking havoc behind the lines. Now, Couraud had found his way to the Morvan seeking more of the same.

Felling trees to block the major highways running through the region, the SAS repeatedly ambushed retreating German convoys. Naturally, more railways were blown, as were the locomotives using them. In Bill Fraser's own last hurrah, on 3 September he and his men targeted a German staff car, cutting a final few heads off the Nazi snake: 'killed 7 Germans (officers) in an ambush at SOUZY, returned to Main Base.' That same day two of his men were reported to have killed 'General Deinherdt?' While they had captured a hoard of enemy papers, they weren't entirely certain of the spelling of the German commander's name, hence the question mark. A later reference in the SAS War Diary concluded of Operation Houndsworth: 'Enemy killed: 330 . . . This includes General Deinhardt.'

Just before pulling out of the Morvan, Peter Middleton – Wellsted's minder – had got shot through the buttocks. It was not the first time that he'd suffered such an embarrassing injury. As Wellsted noted, he emerged from a firefight 'clutching the seat of his pants. For the third time in this war, Middleton had been shot through the cheeks of his backside.' Or as the SAS War Diary would describe it, Middleton had been shot 'embarrassingly though not dangerously'. But mostly, the casualties suffered by Fraser's men in the Morvan were extraordinarily light.

With nine men killed and wounded, Operation Houndsworth had accounted for twenty-one railway lines blown, power and telephone lines brought down, a synthetic fuel plant being destroyed (twice), a gasogene plant 'demolished', rail turntables and goods yards blown up, trains derailed and wrecked, priceless intelligence being spirited to London, including details of enemy troop movements, plus 'flying bomb assembly and factory areas and ROMMEL's HQ sent as targets for RAF'. Some two to three thousand Maquisards had also been successfully armed. In short, Houndsworth could lay claim to being one of the SAS's most successful operations in France.

During his last days in the Morvan, Bill Fraser had been persuaded to give a farewell speech in a local village. Shy, retiring, tongue-tied in public, and especially so with his broken French, Fraser had dreaded being led onto the balcony of the Hôtel de Ville to address the crowd. But as matters transpired, he needn't have worried. Resplendent in his tartan kilt, which he'd asked to be parachuted into the Morvan, along with the rest of his Highland regalia, all he needed to do was step out dressed in his finery, for the crowd to break into wild, spontaneous applause. Considering how the locals had suffered due to the presence of the 'British parachutists', it was deeply moving.

As that sage observer Padre McLuskey would remark, their days in the Morvan would prove precious, irreplaceable. 'The circumstances that accounted for the degree of fellowship we all enjoyed were not likely to be repeated.' That fellowship had been initiated as they had climbed aboard the Stirlings to drop into enemy occupied France. It had received its 'baptism of fire' as they fought to retain their 'precarious foothold in the area, hunted out of our first few camps, going short of food together, being drenched to the skin together'. It had come to maturity in camps 'cut off from the life of the surrounding countryside' as they began to strike back hard against the enemy. It was cemented by 'casualties and disappointments' and 'adventure and success enriched it'. As McLuskey fully appreciated, 'it could not be repeated. The circumstances which moulded it had gone.'

For all who had served in the Morvan – French and British alike – they would never forget.

*

Fraser's men withdrew from the Morvan laden with their wounded, recently retrieved from their makeshift sick quarters at the Beau Rivage hotel, on Lac des Settons. Playing cat and mouse with the enemy forces that were streaming through the region, while nursing injured men all the way, their exfiltration would prove a risky undertaking, especially since many of their jeeps had given up the ghost. As they pulled out of their bases in the Morvan, their home for almost three months, Fraser's long convoy consisted of a hodgepodge of civilian cars, captured German trucks and halftracks, plus the odd surviving SAS jeep.

Just before A Squadron pulled out, Mayne had decided that a jeep trailer needed to be retrieved from the SAS's former Operation Kipling base in the Yonne. Asking for a volunteer to fetch it, Lieutenant Peter 'Monty' Goddard stepped forward, one of Tony Marsh's C Squadron men. A chartered accountant before the war, he was judged 'very popular, keen, good leadership, jumped well' at parachute school, where he'd been nicknamed Monty due to his close resemblance to the British Field Marshal. A former Royal Armoured Corps officer, Goddard had volunteered for the SAS in February 1942 but was yet to see combat with the unit.

Mayne glanced at Goddard, and then at Marsh. 'I think I'll go along for the ride,' he'd remarked, cryptically.

Marsh gave a wry smile. When Mayne said that, pretty much anything could happen.

With Mayne manning the twin Vickers in the passenger's seat, Goddard, at the wheel, set forth. The route ahead was deserted, save for the odd farmer's cart. But after a while, Mayne sensed danger. He signalled Goddard to stop. Up ahead they heard the throaty rumble of vehicles. Gesturing to pull the jeep into cover, he and Goddard waited, poised at their guns. But instead of an enemy force, it was a Maquis convoy that rounded the far bend.

The two parties stopped for a conflab. It turned out that the Maquis were preparing to ambush an enemy convoy that was heading out to attack their base. One glance proved them to be not overly well-endowed with arms. If the Maquis were to win through, they needed some proper firepower and back-up.

Telling Goddard to park the jeep ready for a rapid getaway, Mayne grabbed a Bren gun from the rear, plus a single Vickers and a quantity of ammunition. With Goddard taking the Vickers and Mayne hefting the Bren in his massive hands, they took up their ambush positions. Shortly, the enemy convoy hove into distant view. It was led by a Pak 36 mobile anti-tank gun, followed by a group of army trucks crammed with troops, plus a staff car bringing up the rear. Mayne signalled to Goddard to hold his fire until they were close. The Maquis shifted about nervously, wondering if they'd bitten off more than they could chew. They were armed with only an assortment of pistols, carbines and grenades.

Mayne gestured that he and Goddard were ready, so they should all hold their nerve. Glancing twice at the nearby jeep, he reassured himself it was good to go, whenever they needed to hightail it out of there. As the Maquis continued to vacillate, debating whether to stand and fight or take cover, Mayne strode among them and removed several hand grenades from their belts. Loaded up with those, he returned to his vantage point, which offered a fine view of the approaching convoy. As the lead vehicles came within fifty yards, Mayne rose from the under-growth with the Bren at his shoulder and opened fire, yelling for Goddard to do likewise. With the Vickers levelled at his hip, Goddard let rip.

The first salvoes tore into the leading vehicles, as the convoy ground to a juddering halt. Mayne and Goddard slotted in fresh magazines of ammo to keep up their lethal rate of fire on the enemy. But the Pak 36 was quickly in action, pumping out 37mm shells, as enemy troops spilled out of the trucks. Glancing around to check on the Maquis, Mayne realised they had simply vanished. For now at least, it was him and Goddard against several score of the enemy. Any thoughts of making a dash for the jeep were scuppered, when Goddard broke cover and advanced towards the Pak 36, the Vickers glued to his hip and belting out the fire. It was a suicidally brave move, even as his rounds ripped into the enemy gun.

Searching for a way to give cover, Mayne spied a vantage point – a high bank that would offer him a perfect view into the ditches within which the enemy had gone to ground. As Goddard's Vickers continued to spew out a barrage of fire, he made a dash for that slice of high ground. Below him, he could see the lone figure of Goddard zigzagging along the road as the Vickers continued to blaze defiance. One final burst, and Goddard had cut down the Pak 36's crew and silenced the weapon. As he went to advance, a new sound cut the air – some kind of cannon had begun firing from a truck towards the convoy's rear. As Goddard went to take it on, his lone figure was enveloped in a hail of fire.

Reacting on instinct, Mayne emptied a full Bren magazine into the enemy gun-truck, killing or wounding those manning it. Moments later it burst into flames, either the ammunition or the fuel catching fire. As the truck burned and more rounds cooked off in the heat, the cries of the dying and wounded were clearly audible, above the din of battle. A voice screamed at Mayne from somewhere near by. The Maquis were there in a patch of woodland, yelling at him to withdraw. A Spandau – the belt-fed MG34 machinegun – had begun to hammer in fire, targeting Mayne's position.

Seeing Goddard's body lying in a pool of blood, the Vickers beside him, Mayne swopped his Bren into his left hand, reached for a grenade and lobbed it into the nearest ditch. Firing left-handed with the Bren, he hurled more grenades, dropping down into cover whenever he needed to change a magazine. A Maquisard appeared at his side, trying urgently to drag Mayne backwards. While all below was carnage and chaos, the enemy were starting to regroup for a counter-attack. With a final burst from his Bren, Mayne allowed himself to be pulled away. There was no way that he could reach the jeep, let alone Goddard's body, which 'sadly . . . stained the road'.

Darting into cover, and with the Maquis acting as guides, Mayne managed to commandeer a civilian vehicle, and by that means he returned to the Morvan. When he arrived back at the SAS camp, Tony Marsh took one look at the SAS commander's face and knew the worst. Mayne was speechless with rage at having lost Goddard, though by his actions in going forward alone he had more or less signed his own death warrant. If the two of them had kept their position, they should have been able to give the convoy a good pasting, while at the same time being able to dash for their jeep and execute a getaway.

Mayne was consumed by sadness as well as anger at the loss of Goddard. He refused to talk about what had happened. It was left to his Maquis guide to describe the immense courage of both Goddard and Mayne. Later, when asked about it by Marsh in a quiet moment, Mayne would refer to the incident brusquely as 'just a scrap'. The official report on the action, penned by Marsh himself, lauded how 'Lt. GODDARD showed abnormal courage, knocking out the quick-firer with a Vickers-K fired from the hip.' There was no mention made of Mayne's role, which was doubtless just as he had wanted it.

At SAS headquarters there remained a strong sense that Mayne had all-but gone AWOL. He'd seized the initiative, and, like the grandmaster of special operations that he was, proceeded to orchestrate matters across the length and breadth of France, leading from the front as always. Earlier, when dealing with the fallout of Fenwick's death and Operation Gain's resulting malaise, Mayne had asked for the SAS's much-loved medic, Major Phil Gunn, to be parachuted into the field. It is understandable why Mayne would have felt the need for Gunn, a highly experienced frontline doctor whom he counted as a close friend. The request had been cleared, but it would come back to bite him now.

In early September a message was sent from their Morvan HQ: 'PADDY, MELOT and GUNN now arrived . . . OK for DZ tonight.' A parachutage was expected, Mayne, Bob Melot and Phil Gunn having just returned from one of their numerous jeep-borne sorties. The following morning, Brigadier Roderick McLeod, SAS Brigade commander, messaged back furiously: 'MAYNE from MCLEOD. You reported arrival of GUNN. When . . . asked whether GUNN could visit SAS first I agreed on specific conditions that visit was brief and that he did NOT visit HOUNDSWORTH. My orders were final and definitive on this point. Order GUNN to return to ENGLAND forthwith and provide necessary transport for him to reach an airfield from which he can get home. ACK.'

There was no record of any immediate 'ACK' – acknowledge-ment – from Mayne. Five days later McLeod messaged again: 'expedite Phil Gunn return.' The brigadier appeared to be like a dog with the proverbial bone. Mayne finally replied, laconically: 'have apprehended Gunn.' Even so, it wasn't until 22 September that the SAS medic would return to whatever duties McLeod felt he was so urgently required for at Brigade HQ.

As Mayne fully appreciated, many in A Squadron were all played out, just at the moment when they would need to be at their most alert if they were to weather the journey home. Hordes of enemy forces were retreating through the Morvan, and especially since the Allied landings in southern France, code-named Operation Dragoon, on 15 August. Some of the Morvan veterans would never recover the equanimity and nerve required for operations behind enemy lines. A number would simply not be capable of deploying for the remainder of the war. Mayne saw the state they were in, and it worried him. He knew he would need to shield such individuals – some of whom were among his most experienced men – from opprobrium, not to mention the shame they would doubtless feel.

Little wonder that he felt the need for Gunn to be with him, *especially* in the Morvan. To those who hadn't seen the horrors of the burned-out churches and the butchered French villagers, or experienced the sense that there-but-for-the-grace-of-God-go-I, it doubtless made no sense. To those who hadn't witnessed at first hand this war with hate, and how the SAS themselves were now being targeted directly, this doubtless did not compute. But to Mayne it did, and it was a powerful testament as to why he needed to be there with his men where they needed him most, sharing the impossible load.

Though McLeod had no previous experience of SAS operations before being appointed to his position, he wasn't a wholly bad brigade commander. In many ways his means of control had been suitably light touch. Later, he would openly admit that he'd only ever exerted minimal influence over 'these colourful and curiously dressed ruffians', for his previous experience had 'not prepared me for the problems of command over such an unorthodox unit as the S.A.S.'

Of Mayne he would remark, insightfully: 'Paddy Mayne and the 1st S.A.S. were straightforward. They said "Yes" to everything they were asked to do . . . they never bellyached, they were always cheerful and welcoming, and they regarded my H.Q. as an unnecessary evil who should be humoured providing it did not interfere with what the Regiment thought should be done.' That theme echoes again and again in McLeod's writings: 'I and my H.Q. were regarded . . . as an entirely unnecessary evil . . . eventually and rather reluctantly we became accepted as a necessary evil, but an evil we remained.'

For those like Mayne on the ground in France, the problem with McLeod was more that he simply didn't understand. Only by being there, with the men, in harm's way, and sharing in the stress and the trauma that so many had suffered, would a man like McLeod begin to comprehend, to know and appreciate the camaraderie and the brotherhood. Mayne got it. He knew it. It was in his blood.

A man like the padre knew it too, intimately and instinctively. So much so, that when Bill Fraser's A Squadron withdrew, McLuskey volunteered to remain behind to administer to the spiritual and morale needs of the inbound force, Tony Marsh's C Squadron. For this man of God, this parachuting padre, it was above and beyond. Likewise, Wellsted would be tempted to remain, to help bed in the new arrivals. But it was his wife Margot's statuette, her letters and the thought of her waiting patiently at home for him that swayed his mind and compelled him to leave.

On 6 September the main body of Bill Fraser's A Squadron crossed back over Allied lines. They had with them Hans, their German volunteer cook, medic and vehicle mechanic. A flight of B-24 Liberators was waiting to spirit them back to Britain, but for a night or two they lingered, for at Joigny, a town lying to the south-east of Paris and well within liberated France, the partying was about to begin. In a delicious irony, Hans and Sergeant Sturmey – 1 SAS's 'No. 1 Romeo' – went head-to-head to win the affections of a pretty French girl. Hans, the good German, won.

Revels over, Hans joined them on the flight back to Britain. According to Alec Borrie, Roy Close's driver, they would have a whip-round for the good German at war's end, sending him back to his home 'somewhere near Berlin', with a little something to help rebuild his shattered life in post-war Germany.

The veterans of the Morvan touched down at an RAF airbase and disgorged, aware at last of what 'extraordinary sights we were'. As Wellsted noted, 'Our clothes were old, torn and battle-stained. My pips were still those of makeshift parachute silk.' He'd lost his proper ones sometime during the weeks gone by. 'I still carried my trusty Schmeisser slung across my chest . . . an enormous, bedraggled blonde moustache crawled aimlessly across my upper lip.' Needless to say, Wellsted had won his moustache-growing competition with Johnny Wiseman hands down.

Back at home with his parents, Wellsted fell into a 'curiously emotional state. That night I went to bed tired, but strangely lonely and miserable.' Desperate to see Margot, he instead found himself lying awake, 'thinking back – living back – all those varied experiences of a most memorable summer'. His mind turned to the drip of rain on parachute silk, the drone of the wireless as they tuned in for a message, and to thinking about his brothers-in-arms, and oddly of how much he missed them. When Margot arrived the next day, it was to tell him that she was in love with someone else and wanted a divorce.

Margot had fallen for a former nightclub bouncer and American Military Policemen call Lew. Tortured by the rejection and the loss – Wellsted had carried the ivory statue of his wife and her letters all through his France operations – dark thoughts crowded his mind. He still had the 'vicious little automatic' that Alexis, the Red Russian, had seized from the wounded enemy officer in the Morvan. A .22 calibre pistol, it was the perfect assassin's weapon. Drinking heavily, picking fights for no good reason, Wellsted stalked the UK with that pistol, seeking to 'murder Lew undetected . . . I ought to have remained in the Morvan after all,' he reflected, bitterly.

Before they pulled out of the Morvan, Fraser and his men had heard a congratulatory message broadcast over the airwaves. Delivered by Lieutenant-General Frederick 'Boy' Browning, then Director of Airborne Forces, it included fulsome praise from none other than their old friend, Monty. On 1 September 1944, General Bernard Montgomery – the SAS's sometimes adversary, but increasingly one of their greatest supporters – had been promoted to Field Marshal. From the Morvan, Mayne had wirelessed: 'Give MONTY our congratulations.' That same day, 1 September, he'd received the reply: 'MONTY has been congratulated.' A day or so later, the new Field Marshal would send his personal thanks to Mayne, praising what he regarded as the 'splendid work you have all done' in France.

Boy Browning's broadcast got the message directly into the SAS camps.

I am speaking to you this evening in order to tell you what Field Marshal Montgomery and the commanders in the Field feel about your activities. The operations you have carried out have had more effect in hastening the disintegration of the German 7th and 15th Armies that any other single effort in the Army. Considering the numbers involved you have done a job of work which has had a most telling effect on the enemy and which, I fully believe, no other troops in the world could have done. I know that the strain has been great, because operating as you do entails the most constant vigilance and cunning . . . To say you have done your job well is to put it mildly. You have done magnificently . . . Good luck and Good Hunting!

Mayne replied to Browning – and Monty's – sentiments: 'General BROWNING'S [message] was terrific and greatly appreciated. Please thank him.' Indeed, Mayne himself was about to be singled out for high praise, as his third Distinguished Service Order (DSO and two Bars) was mooted. After detailing his drop to the Morvan, and his timely intervention in Operation Gain, the citation praised 'his penetrating the German lines in a jeep on four occasions in order to lead parties of reinforcements'. In other words, Mayne's idea of a 'low-risk' deployment had involved crossing the enemy lines *four times*, to usher men and machines to and from the theatre of war. 'It was entirely due to Lieutenant-Colonel Mayne's fine leadership and example and his utter disregard of danger that the unit was able to achieve such striking success,' the citation concluded.

Quite. Mayne's 'utter disregard for danger' had been absolutely to the fore, and it had delivered. Never mind that it ran contrary to his orders, when he had first won the right to deploy into France. This was vintage Mayne. He had always ploughed his own furrow, being impatient with pointless red tape and bureaucracy, and giving short shrift to pretence, humbug and hypocrisy. In 1938, when he'd volunteered for the Officer Training Corps at Queen's University, Belfast, where he was then studying law, he'd found the endless drill and mindless square bashing an abomination. The Queen's Training Officer had concluded that Mayne was 'unpromising material for a combat regiment, undisciplined, unruly and generally unreliable'. It had taken a unit like the SAS with its unique ethos to unearth his true warrior spirit.

Quartered in the Morvan with C Squadron, the war in France was winding down as the conflict shifted eastwards. Mayne gathered Tony Marsh and his C Squadron men – relatively fresh into the field – both to congratulate them and to warn them as to next steps. Shortly, the squadron was slated to head for Brussels – newly liberated by the Allies – to begin a new phase of SAS operations. Codenamed Operation Policeman, the unit was to hunt for SS, Gestapo and other Nazi war criminals. After learning of the fate of the Operation Bulbasket captives, plus those murdered on Operation Gain, and the gunning-down of the prisoners from Garstin's stick, this was something the SAS could truly embrace. 'Policeman very well liked here,' Mayne had signalled headquarters.

With the battle for France all but done, Mayne received warning that a group of staff officers were set to visit, to assess and report on SAS operations. Fittingly, their mission was code-named 'Good Time Charlie'. It was led by a Major Cliffe, a Brigade officer, together with three colleagues. After pootling around for a bit, Cliffe penned his report and recommendations. They included the suggestion that the SAS needed a mobile bath unit for ablutions. While the largely well-meaning Brigadier McLeod took most of Cliffe's suggestions at face value – he had neither the experience nor know-how to do otherwise – Mayne did not. In fact, he positively bridled at them. Cliffe's report had to be answered. Mayne's response pulled no punches, especially when leaping to the defence of his senior commander on the ground in the Morvan.

It would appear to me that Major Cliffe is taxing his ability overmuch in attempting to write an appreciation of an operational area on the strength of spending five hours there six weeks after the enemy have left . . . I also consider that his remark that the bases appear to be well sited is presumptuous . . . unless Major Cliffe believes that he is more experienced than Major Fraser, the officer who selected these sites . . . The statement that troops could have operated indefinitely unless their location was known to enemy, is like saying the Army could march to Berlin unless something stopped them . . . If, as Major Cliffe states, it is extremely difficult to maintain discipline and keep morale once parties have completed their tasks behind the lines, we may consider ourselves extremely fortunate. We have had, as far as my knowledge goes, no drunkenness, absence, desertion, looting or rape. A bath unit or laundry is unnecessary . . . I hope I haven't wasted as much paper as Major Cliffe.

Mayne's cutting response hit home. McLeod ordered no further action to be taken in response to Cliffe's report. But it also typified Mayne's attitude to those in command with whom he did not see eye to eye. He did not suffer fools. More than that, he told them as much, and very often, if not in writing, he did so to their face. Often, one withering look was enough to silence his detractors. Of course, the men he commanded loved him for his uncompromising attitude. But many of those who oversaw or supposedly commanded the SAS found it infuriating. Mayne, and the SAS, did their own thing their own way, regardless of the consequences.

It had gained him – and the Regiment – any number of enemies.

As the minds of those in the Morvan turned towards Brussels and Operation Policeman, Mayne briefed all on the route they should take, heading north to the Belgian capital. Newly liberated Paris was off-limits, he warned. It was the headquarters of American forces. In short, they were to rendezvous in Brussels in a few days' time for the next stage of operations. Of course, learning that Paris was 'out of bounds to British troops' was like a red rag to a bull. Even as Mayne had warned his men as much, there had been that familiar glint in his eye. As Captain Roy Close would observe, they settled upon a 'perceptive interpretation' of such orders, and all duly set a course for the City of Light. It looked like 'an opportunity not to be missed' and so it would prove.

As luck would have it, Close's French SAS man, Corporal Johnny Barongelle, had family in Paris. Having secreted their jeeps in a friend's lock-up garage, Close told his men they had 'twenty-four hours to enjoy Paris'. They paused at a café on one of the city's wide boulevards, and he warned them to be back there at mid-morning on the morrow. Anyone who got into trouble or was missing he threatened to 'personally shoot'. Barongelle led Close to his relative's place of residence, which was in a rundown part of the city. In a somewhat strained atmosphere, Barongelle's family claimed not to have enough food in the house to feed all, so they headed out to visit a 'restaurant'.

Shortly, Close found himself ushered into a room that didn't appear like an eatery at all. It was dimly lit, with sofas and armchairs scattered around the walls. 'The proprietor' returned with 'an attractive girl in a black lace kimono, which, although it hid little, she proceeded to discard to reveal all her considerable charms'. As Close was accompanied by Barongelle's family, in their starched Sunday best, the atmosphere 'could not have been more inhibiting'. Barongelle's cousin had assumed that after their long and celibate existence in rural France, they had a 'need more urgent than a good meal'. Regardless, the brothel was abandoned for a fine Paris restaurant and several bottles of wine.

Close's men, however, would have a somewhat different experience. Wild adventures awaited in the City of Light, no matter that they were not even supposed to be there. One of Close's troopers, J. 'Woody' Woodford – tall, balding and blessed with a large and protuberant nose – had already led a Free French victory parade, and all as the result of a case of mistaken identity. Quartered in what had been the Gestapo HQ in Dijon – 'plenty of evidence of the torture and killing of the local people and a large back garden full of graves' – Woodford had sallied forth seeking more salubrious surroundings. He'd ended up in the city's brothel. Which was all well and good, until he was reported missing.

Close's men had headed out by jeep to bring him in. Returning with Woodford perched in the rear, they had by accident found themselves at the head of a French band, leading the 'French troop's triumphant entry into Dijon. Woody, who bore some resemblance to General de Gaulle, being tall and having a long nose, was cheered all the way down the street, with flags waving and the band playing.' In Paris, Close's men were determined to go one better.

They were about to head on from the café, when a small dapper man had asked if they were British by any chance. He'd overheard their accents. Alec 'Boy' Borrie replied that they were. It turned out that the stranger and Borrie were fellow Londoners, both hailing from the city's East End. He asked Borrie if they had anywhere to stay for the night. As they didn't, their new acquaintance led them to a 'posh building' and ushered them inside.

In through the back door and up some stairs, they were lunched royally and given a tour of the Paris sights, before being brought back to the same building for an early supper. It was then a case of 'up a floor and through a pair of double doors to a large room, and much to our surprise, it was filled with about one hundred lovely young ladies in the nude . . .' Directed to choose one each for the night 'free of charge', they consented. As all would learn later, they were the guests of 'Fairyland', then the 'most well-known and upmarket brothel in France . . . so far the one and only time I enjoyed the spoils of victory,' as Borrie would remark.

As they were the first Englishmen to attend the august estab-
lishment since 1939, the proprietor of Fairyland had gone all out
to make them feel welcome. At one stage the 'ladies of the house'
had gathered together to give the assembled men a fine rendition
of God Save the King. When Roy Close was reunited with his
men, the following morning, he asked them what on earth they
had done when they were presented with the largely naked staff
of Fairyland singing the British national anthem.

'We saluted, of course, sir, at attention.'

With Bob Melot dispatched to Brussels to prepare the ground
for Operation Policeman, Mayne and Sadler had also headed for
Paris. Wild horses wouldn't keep them away. But Mayne – like
so many – seemed to find the bizarre transition to something
approaching peacetime troubling. Between them they had two
purloined vehicles, Sadler's being an iconic-looking Ford coupé,
while Mayne drove a luxury Delage, a classic make of French
sports car. Checking into the marvellous Hotel George V, in the
city centre, they were, by Sadler's own account, determined to
give themselves 'a holiday in Paris'.

At various venues there were 'charming ladies' to entertain
them 'with glasses of this and that'. Mayne tended to have a
somewhat puritanical streak when it came to the fairer sex.
Casual sex and brothels were not his thing. 'I don't think Paddy
enjoyed them as much as anyone else,' Sadler remarked. 'But he
was enjoying it.'

At one stage, dining at a club near the Champs-Élysées, Mayne
had bridled at the faux war stories being bandied about. He produced a grenade from his pocket, pulled the pin out and plonked
it on the middle of the table, where it started to smoke. Knowing
it had a seven second fuse, Sadler found it 'very disturbing'. Some
dived under the table, while others froze. Sadler had a split-
second decision to make. 'Was this a joke or had Paddy gone

mad? Should he stay in his seat or run like hell?' Sadler figured he 'knew Paddy well enough to think it was only a joke'. They sat and watched the fuse burn down.

It turned out that Mayne had removed the detonator from the grenade, so it was quite safe. 'It didn't go off, so we were able to laugh,' remarked Sadler. But there remained that cold-eyed wildness about Mayne, that raw edge, that in polite, peacetime company proved unnerving.

Paris won a special place in Mayne's heart. Again and again he would return to that magical city steeped in history. With Wellsted – Captain Gremlin – he would share a rare heart-to-heart there, Mayne being in a 'sad and sombre mood' the likes of which the junior officer had never witnessed. Wellsted had a 'tremendous admiration for Paddy', but he was not one of the SAS originals and while they'd shared a good few drinks at the bar, he was 'never one of his familiar companions'. Even so, during that Paris visit Mayne talked to Wellsted about 'all he had accomplished' in the war, recounting tales of daring operations as if he was 'thinking aloud' about what the future might hold. He seemed especially worried for the fate of such an unconventional military unit, with its 'novel means of subverting the enemy'.

There was another SAS veteran in Paris that September who'd found a strikingly 'novel means of subverting the enemy'. Corporal Charlie Hackney had been recruited into the SAS in North Africa, while imprisoned and facing a court martial. SAS Major Oswald Cary-Elwes had spirited him out of captivity, no questions asked, and David Stirling had shielded him, reckoning Hackney was worth 'more alive than dead . . . [and] told him to keep a low profile'. Deployed into France, Hackney had continued to plough his thoroughly unconventional furrow, purloining a red butcher's van, which he turned into a makeshift SAS gun-truck, jeeps then being in somewhat short supply.

Hackney and his comrades – 'a subdued bunch of cutthroats' – had been deployed on Operation Hardy, a 2 SAS mission with similar objectives to those of Mayne's raiders. Deployed north of Dijon, to the Plateau de Langres area, Hackney had discovered the red Renault van standing outside a butcher's shop. 'I am ashamed to say I did not ask the owner if I could take the vehicle,' Hackney would confess, 'but I have always hoped that he would have guessed that he was making a significant contribution to the Allied war effort.' A butcher's van proved 'certainly less conspicuous' than any jeep, and with a Bren mounted in the rear, 'one only had to open the doors to fire the weapon.' To the Bren was added a pair of three-inch mortars, and the DIY gun-truck was complete.

Hackney's 'little red van' had proceeded to sow havoc in and around the Plateau de Langres. The Operation Hardy force had targeted a convoy of tankers transporting 40,000 gallons of aviation fuel, and mortared the main German garrison headquarters, before ambushing a heavy enemy column sent out to exact 'reprisals' on the locals, among numerous other audacious operations. When French General Philippe Leclerc de Hauteclocque, then one of the foremost commanders of the Free French forces, had arrived in the region, he had congratulated the Hardy party on hitting the enemy exactly where it hurt. 'Bravo!' he had declared. 'Hit the enemy in the arse!'

Hackney's little red van never did 'arouse the suspicions of the Germans', and he had become 'quite attached to it'. So much so, he'd brought it to Paris. After a few days in which 'accumulated pay was spent letting hair down', Hackney would head to Britain for some 'well-earned leave'. Packing himself and a 'chum' into the redoubtable vehicle – Bren and mortars removed – they set off for Glasgow, his home turf. But on the outskirts of Birmingham the red van sadly gave up the ghost, the engine blowing up. The 'two heroes', as Hackney would describe himself and his chum, were obliged to abandon the smoking vehicle, and continue by train. The next day the national press reported that a mystery burned-out hulk had been found to the south of Birmingham, with foreign plates. The police were investigating just how on earth it had got there.

Fortunately, the burned-out van wasn't linked to Hackney or the SAS, or the news headlines might have got seriously interesting. But in Paris, Mayne was intent on ensuring that the regiment's finer exploits *would* hit the media. While supposedly enjoying his Parisian holiday, Mayne was impatient to return to war. As the City of Light was a long way from the frontline, he did the next best thing. Like so many of his men, he relived his recent war experiences. Earlier that year, Eisenhower had issued a decree that the press were to be viewed as valued members of the Allied war effort, for they played a key role in boosting morale. Accredited reporters were to be regarded as 'quasi staff officers', who needed to be given free rein 'in order to visualise and transmit to the public'.

Mayne had kept a copy of Eisenhower's order, and would use it to his best advantage. Believing that it was high time the SAS had its moment in the limelight – that it emerged from the shadows, to tell some of the tales of heroism and sacrifice – he would grant an interview to a reporter from *Reader's Digest* magazine. Having been awarded a Croix de Guerre by the French to add to his DSOs, Mayne was the archetypal hero figure, especially as he hailed from a daring, audacious and top-secret elite forces unit. The subsequent article, entitled 'Confusion Is Their Business', introduced to the world's public 'The story of Paddy Mayne's incredibles, who create havoc behind the German lines, here told for the first time.'

It lauded 'Britain's phantom army', who across North Africa, Italy and France had 'written one of military history's most fantastic chapters. In Africa their parachutists and jeep-borne commandos had struck at Nazi airfields 500 miles behind Rommel's front line, destroying more German planes on the ground than the RAF did in the air.' Moving on to talk about D-Day, the article spoke of how 'the designers of the invasion knew that its success depended in great measure on preventing the Germans from getting heavy reinforcements to the beach-heads ... The hardened, experienced, super-commandos of the Special Air Service ... were the only outfit for the job. They were brought up from Italy to tackle their toughest assignment.'

The article described how, 'in a desperate attempt to wipe out the invisible army,' the Germans 'unleashed the Gestapo and the so-called French Milice ... on a furious reign of terror ... people were rounded up by hundreds, tortured for information and shot.' It went on to chronicle some of the SAS's key battles, including the moment when Johnny Wiseman had tricked German troops and Milice into shooting each other up, at his Dijon camp. 'Four years of trial by fire have gone into SAS operations,' the article continued. It had all begun when a desperate British high command had listened to 'the crazy scheme' proposed by David Stirling, the SAS founder, that 'small groups of picked men, carefully trained, could live and wreak havoc far behind the enemy's lines.'

Describing Stirling's February 1943 capture by the enemy, and Mayne taking over command, the *Reader's Digest* article depicted him as 'this big, craggy faced Irishman ... with a gentle brogue and shy smile,' who is 'more than a commanding officer. He is a legend ... Montgomery, who thanked them officially in North Africa, thanked them again after the Battle of France even more enthusiastically. And they may in the future be thanked again.

For Paddy Mayne's incredibles are still going strong. Where and how is a story yet to be told.'

It was. All eyes were turning to the last big push, the thrust into Nazi Germany itself.

Chapter Thirteen
TO THE LAST MAN

Once back in Britain, and with the fellowship temporarily disbanded, several of Mayne's comrades were making headlines.
A raft of decorations followed the French operations, and with
those came newspaper coverage. Foremost among them was
Padre McLuskey, whose Morvan exploits would win him an MC
and make for fabulous news copy.

'Padre went in by parachute – to preach behind enemy,' ran
an autumn 1944 headline. 'Carrying a pack of hymn books in
place of weaponry and ammunition Padre J. McLuskey . . . stayed
with the men of the vaunted and hush-hush "SAS" . . . McLuskey
was the only non-combatant in this daredevil unit, the full and
almost unbelievable story of which cannot be told until after the
war . . . "The men were magnificent in the face of almost constant
peril," the padre told a reporter.'

That relatively small and 'hush-hush' British unit had also
caught the attention of the most senior American military leader.
General Eisenhower, Supreme Commander, Allied Expeditionary
Forces, wrote the following: 'I wish to send my congratulations
to all ranks of the Special Air Service Brigade on the contribution which they have made . . . The ruthlessness with which
the enemy have attacked Special Air Service troops has been an
indication of the injury which you were able to cause the German

armed forces both by your own efforts and by the information which you gave of German dispositions . . . To all of you I say "Well done, and good luck."' High praise indeed.

But the SAS's exploits had also come to the attention of less welcome parties. There was a flurry of top-secret memos and reports emanating from the forces of Nazi Germany concerning the mercurial raiders. One, originating from the 2nd Panzer Division – veterans of the 1939 seizure of Poland, the 1940 invasion of France, and most recently the 1944 Battle of Normandy – summed up the SAS with admirable aplomb: 'Their activities are extremely dangerous.' The report noted that there were several SAS regiments each some 500-strong, and all extensively trained for sabotage work. It also identified the key figures at SAS Brigade, including the overall commander, McLeod, plus the 'Commander of 1st S.A.S. Regiment . . . Colonel Kaine.' 'Kaine' was of course Mayne.

The 2nd Panzer Division report ended by warning that the 'presence of S.A.S. units is to be reported immediately to the divisions concerned'.

Another secret document, hailing from the office of the Wehrmacht's Chief of the General Staff, depicted the guerrilla-warfare-style prowess of these 'especially trained parachute troops . . . From captured . . . orders and papers it has been learned that the enemy intelligence service has tried to infiltrate single agents and teams and to build up Resistance groups in the rear of the present German front. In this work the S.A.S. troops will share the principal role with special espionage agents. By S.A.S. troops are meant specially trained parachute troops.'

The tactics and strategies of the SAS were chronicled in great depth, much of the detail coming from those men who had been captured before being subjected to horrific torture and interrogation. 'When the troops jump they are equipped with everything they need for this penetration. Besides the equipment and weapons which the paratrooper carries with him in his jump bag, containers are dropped holding the usual supplies of food, extra weapons, ammunition, explosives . . . The intention is the interruption of railway lines, the blowing up of bridges, traffic junctions and telephone communications . . . Single combat, characterised by ambush, deception, utilisation of all the weapons of hand-to-hand fighting . . .'

Each report ended with a similar warning. 'Units . . . will immediately report all observations pointing to the presence of such S.A.S. troops in the Army area.' And then, more chillingly, came orders that captured S.A.S. members were to be 'turned over' to those best qualified to interrogate and to deal with them – the Gestapo and the SS. Of course, the SAS's foremost Nazi adversaries had every means at their disposal to deal with any such captives. They had been given the ultimate sanction from on high, in what was to become known as Hitler's 'Commando Order'.

Three months after their return from France, SAS commanders would be handed absolute proof of who had decreed the murder of their comrades, and why. As so many had suspected, the horrors that had befallen the Bulbasket prisoners, the Gain captives, Captain Garstin's patrol and more had been dictated from the top. Four copies of a document entitled 'German Order to Kill Captured Allied Commandos and Parachutists' were delivered to SAS headquarters. Secured by the French intelligence services, this was the first ever copy of Hitler's Commando Order to fall into Allied hands. In perusing it, much that had happened over the summer of 1944 suddenly fell into place.

Issued by the Führer, it was allegedly his response to one of the earliest British cross-Channel raids. On 3 October 1942 a small, commando-style mission had been launched, codenamed

Operation Basalt. The Basalt raiders had sped across the water in a diminutive motor torpedo boat (MTB) known as the 'Little Pisser', or more formally MTB 344. Fast, relatively silent, and well-armed for her size, Little Pisser had delivered the party at midnight to the cliffs of the Channel Island of Sark. Scaling the rockface and stealing inland, the raiders had taken some of the occupying German garrison captive. But while trying to wrestle the prisoners down to the waiting boat, a number had broken free. In the ensuing melee some had been shot. Their hands had been tied when taken captive, and the discovery of their corpses led to banner headlines in the German press: 'British Attack and Bind German Troops in Sark. Immediate Reprisals for Disgraceful Episode.'

Upon learning of the incident, Hitler was apoplectic. Shortly after the Sark raid, his riposte was ready. On 18 October 1942 he'd issued his Commando Order in the greatest secrecy, for he was decreeing that war crimes were to be committed in his name. Efforts to conceal the order's existence from the Allies were exhaustive. Classified 'MOST SECRET', it was issued to the very highest-ranking officers only, after which it was to be committed to memory, and all printed copies destroyed. Such intense secrecy had worked. It took more than two years for a handwritten copy to fall into Allied hands.

This is what those at SAS headquarters read, as the Commando Order did the rounds:

In future, Germany will resort to the same methods in regards to these groups of British saboteurs and their accomplices . . . German troops will exterminate them without mercy wherever they find them. Henceforth all enemy troops encountered by German troops during so-called commando operations . . . though they appear to be soldiers in uniform or demolition groups, armed or unarmed, are to be exterminated to the last man ... If such men appear to be about to surrender, no quarter should be given to them.

The order ended with a spine-chilling warning to any German commander who might dare to oppose it. 'I will summon before the tribunal of war, all leaders and officers who fail to carry out these instructions – either by failure to inform their men or by their disobedience of this order . . .' Though the signature was barely legible, it had been signed off by Adolf Hitler himself. Following the Allied landings in Normandy, the Führer had issued a supplementary order to augment the October 1942 version. 'In spite of the Anglo-American landings in France, the Führer's order of 18 October 1942, regarding the destruction of saboteurs and terrorists, remains fully valid . . . All members of terrorist and saboteur bands, including . . . all parachutists encountered outside the immediate combat zone, are to be executed.'

Senior German commanders were ordered to: 'Report daily the numbers of saboteurs thus liquidated . . . The number of executions must appear in the daily communiqué of the Wehrmacht to serve as a warning to potential terrorists.' The already stringent measures regarding secrecy were stiffened. 'The copies going to Regiments and Gen Staff are to be destroyed by the latter when its contents have been noted. A certificate of destruction should be returned to this HQ.'

In Britain, the fallout from the revelations was heavy. Top secret communiqués zipped between SAS high command and the War Office. 'It will be appreciated that the whole policy regarding employment of SAS troops is affected by the treatment of any personnel captured,' read one. 'The enemy realizes this and obviously, as part of their propaganda to stop SAS activities, have issued orders that these parachutists are "saboteurs" and will be shot.' There was also the pressing issue of how much to tell the rank and file, the majority of whom were fresh out of the long months of waging war in France, and who were poised to be sent into Germany itself.

In a memo marked 'SECRET & CONFIDENTIAL', a decision of sorts seemed to have been reached. 'After consideration of this problem it has been decided not to inform the troops.' The reasons given were: '(a) They expect to be shot already. (b) It would only provide a good excuse for any delinquents that might wish to retire from the struggle.' In short, the SAS had earned a notoriety with the enemy, and once they returned to the field of battle they would be marked men. With the kill-order emanating from Hitler himself, it also meant the Führer was bang in their sights.

If the SAS could get Hitler, that would be fitting vengeance indeed.

That November, 1 SAS moved headquarters. The rolling hills of Darvel, Ayrshire, were swopped for the manicured, parklike terrain of Hylands House and its grand estate, in Essex. Dating back to 1730, the imposing, pillared, Romanesque façade of Hylands had before played host to British soldiers, when serving as a makeshift military hospital for 1,500 patients during the First World War. Now, in the winter of 1944, the estate's owner, the widowed Christine Hanbury, had every reason to again turn her beautiful property and its 574-acre grounds into a facility to aid the war effort.

Having lost her husband, John, in 1923, to illness, her only son, Charles 'Jock' Hanbury, had been one of the first RAF pilots to die in the war, tragically being killed in a flying accident. Widowed and childless, she would embrace Paddy Mayne and his raiders in no uncertain terms, epitomising the great British war spirit that such a herculean struggle called for. Ironically, the grounds of Hylands had been turned into a giant German POW camp. Into the midst of that descended the men of 1 SAS and their machines, as they sought the way and the means to head for the Fatherland to finish the job.

Regardless of the SAS's French experiences, and the emergence of Hitler's Commando Order, the German POWs were treated entirely properly. To accommodate the entire manpower of 1 SAS, there was much to be done at Hylands. The POWs provided a ready workforce. 'The German prisoners . . . preferred our camp work details,' as one of the SAS officers would remark. 'At least while in our camp they were fed the same rations as our troops and not treated as slaves' which was 'the fate of many' in Nazi-occupied Europe. At war's end they should 'go home with a reasonable impression of the British, although perhaps the ardent Nazi types wondered how they could possibly have been beaten by troops with our apparent casual discipline'.

Upon reaching Hylands after his leave, Johnny Cooper – The Kid – marvelled at the vast extent of the estate with its 'beautiful grazing lands and woodlands'. A back gate gave access to the charming village of Writtle, 'complete with green and duck pond'. Billeted in the grand house, the vast bedrooms were turned into dorms each housing ten officers. A cavernous banqueting hall was transformed into the 1 SAS mess. Mrs Hanbury was a regular guest, regaling the men with tales of her globe-trotting adventures, as she swirled her 'long string of pearls'. With SAS swarming over her house and grounds, she exhibited remarkable equanimity, regarding it all as 'doing her bit' towards dethroning 'that man Hitler'.

After all the trials and tribulations of France – the soaring highs and the crushing lows – Hylands took on something of a holiday atmosphere. If there was nothing pressing to do, the SAS tended not to 'mess you about', and especially after four years of back-to-back operations which had earned everyone a good chunk of downtime. At Hylands the 1 SAS family re-formed, if not quite the fellowship. Wellsted was there, wondering what did it really matter that Margot had dumped him? He had something better. Finer. 'Suddenly it dawned on me that, although my marriage was in a mess, I had the consolation of knowing that I had become an accepted member of the SAS fraternity.'

Alec 'Boy' Borrie was there, chuffed as nuts that he could sew his wings onto his left breast. 'This was an honour . . . it made you feel that you were really part of the Regiment, and not one of the newcomers.' Tommy Corps was there, regularly pilfering Mayne's car, loading it full of his mates, and heading off for a night on the tiles in London. Old friends were there, those who'd been absent in France for various reasons. Bill Deakins turned up, fresh from officer training, bearing his new lieutenant's pips. A Royal Engineer by trade, Sergeant Deakins had been Mayne's go-to person whenever he needed anything built, crafted or blown up.

As Mayne's raiders had sailed for Italy, in the summer of 1943, Deakins had carved a giant wooden 'Winged Dagger' complete with the SAS motto 'Who dares wins'. It was given to the captain of HMS *Ulster Monarch*, the vessel bearing them to battle, so that the warlike emblem could grace the ship's prow. Later, after they had taken the port of Augusta, Deakins' demolitions skills had been called for when Mayne and Corps had failed to blow up the town's safe using their own makeshift charges. Deakins, cobbling together an improvised explosive device, had made short work of it.

Upon their return to Britain, Mayne had urged Deakins to go for officer training. At first he had refused. If it meant leaving the SAS he wanted none of it. Finally, Mayne – he 'looks after his boys' – had persuaded Deakins that it would all work out for the best. A bizarre interview had followed, at which General Browning had asked Deakins – whose father ran a building firm – if he 'could afford to be an officer financially'. Tongue in cheek, Deakins had replied that his parents would subsidise him, though what 'money did to help one become a good soldier' Deakins couldn't quite get his head around.

Now, in the winter of 1944/45, Deakins was back. 'To me, most importantly, I was still with the 1st SAS,' Deakins remarked, as he thanked Mayne for all the support and encouragement he had provided. As with so many, Deakins had found it hard to be away. Away from the unit, but also from their unique way of waging war and the brotherhood. 'All very pleasant after the years on the move, although strangely, I found it very hard to adjust to social living . . . The war left scars on human lives in so many ways.' As with Wellsted, Deakins was overjoyed to be brought back into the fold, at Hylands.

As Deakins observed, from time to time German V-1s thundered down to earth in the near vicinity. It was a reminder that the Nazi enemy might be down, but were very much not out. Then came a far more worrying episode. 'One Saturday evening, with a few officers in the mess, there was this tremendous explosion,' Deakins observed. 'The whole building shook, the plate glass in the large lounge window smashed; thankfully the shutters had been closed for the night to maintain the blackout . . . The blast was a rocket [a V-2] which had fallen about one hundred yards away . . .' It had left a 'crater on the edge of a field, somewhere in the region of fifty feet across and thirty deep. The camp had been saved from extensive damage by a belt of trees . . .'

It was a powerful reminder of a job to be finished – the defeat of Hitler's Reich.

*

Sadly, there were absent faces too at Hylands, and not just the dead and injured. One of Mayne's stalwarts, a man he had written up for a Military Medal in Italy, was missing. His story was one of an intense personal tragedy. Joe Goldsmith was gone, and he would not be returning to the fight. In Italy, Goldsmith had rescued the injured Bob Melot under fire, before attacking the enemy with a Bren sited atop a massive petrol tank, little worrying that one stray bullet would set the entire thing ablaze. An inveterate songster and joker hailing from rural Sussex, his party piece had been to render his theme tune – the song which gained him his nickname – whenever the regiment was in a party mood.

> *Vor I can old a plow,*
> *And milk a cow.*
> *I can rip or mow,*
> *I'm as vresh as the daisies growing in the vield,*
> *And they call I butter cup Joe.*

Tragically, after the horrors of Termoli – it had 'a devastating effect on the whole Squadron' – Joe Goldsmith would be plagued by trauma and inner demons. Upon returning to Britain from Italy, he had married his sweetheart, Linda, in January 1944. But weeks later he was admitted to the Admiral Ballochmyle Military Hospital, in Ayrshire, suffering from 'psychoneurosis', which would today be termed Post Traumatic Stress Disorder (PTSD).

Discharged on 4 July, he overstayed his leave, was arrested by the military police for being AWOL, and faced disciplinary charges. At SAS headquarters, 'mindful of his achievements . . . and conscious of the fighting still to be done' they dropped the charges, on condition that Goldsmith rejoined his unit and

With France liberated, the SAS returned to Britain, where Brigadier James Mike Calvert (above left), a seasoned special forces operator, would assume overall command. But for some, the strain of operating deep behind enemy lines would take its toll. Suffering 'psychoneurosis' – or Post Traumatic Stress Disorder (PTSD) as it's now known – Sergeant Joe Goldsmith (below left, on jeep, directly behind fur-coated figure, and below right) would never again deploy to war. He was not alone.

With the forces of Nazi Germany retreating to the borders of the Reich, Hitler demanded the Allies be repelled from the Fatherland. Acting as the spearhead, the SAS took their jeeps into the teeth of enemy fire, facing elite paratroopers, armoured units, Hitler Youth diehards (right) and the *Volkssturm* – 'people's storm' – home guard, in hate-fuelled, bitter and bloody combat.

Channelled between the devastation of German towns, every ditch, wood and hillock teemed with *Panzerfaust*– 'armour-fist'–wielding fanatics (left), as the SAS's lightly-armoured jeeps tried to punch through (below), this one marked 'ZUTRITT VERBOTEN' – NO ENTRY. Running desperately short of ammo, vehicles and food, Mayne's raiders suffered increasing casualties, as the final push of April and May 1945 ground on.

With his trusted driver, Trooper Billy Hull (above left), plus his demolitions expert, Lieutenant Bill Deakins (above right), Mayne seized civilian vehicles to replace their ruined jeeps. Deakins stencilled 'winged dagger' badges onto all (below). The central figure beside the vehicle is Trooper Alec 'Boy' Borrie, recruited as a teenager by Mayne, who asked him how he'd feel about killing? 'I haven't done any yet,' Borrie replied, with disarming honesty. 'I think it'll be okay.'

Denkmal im Barackenlager der I. M.-G -in Schneeren.

At the German town of Schneeren (above) the SAS would suffer some of their worst casualties. Plagued by exhaustion, and harangued by the strain of these end-of-war missions, the jeeps increasingly fell victim to landmines (below). In one such blast, Alec Borrie was injured, and the vehicle commander, Sergeant Sandy Davidson, killed. As Mayne radioed to London: 'The battle is turning into a slogging match and ourselves into Mine Detectors.'

In the final horror, the SAS were the first into the Bergen-Belsen concentration camp – Josef Kramer (above left), 'The Beast of Belsen', in custody in a jeep. The photo above right shows Kramer, plus Irma Grese, 'The Hyena of Auschwitz', under guard. Victory in Europe (VE) day could not come quickly enough for Mayne and his battle-worn SAS warriors, as the free people of Europe garlanded their vehicles with flowers.

In a moment rich with symbolism, Churchill was photographed sitting on a chair from Hitler's Berlin bunker. Back in Britain, Mayne (second from right, below) had high hopes for the SAS's future, as did SAS founder, David Stirling. Yet by October 1945 the SAS had been disbanded and Mayne was forced to take the final march past.

READERS TELL THE REMARKABLE STORIES OF THEIR PRECIOUS KEEPSAKES

IS THIS THE GUN THAT SHOT HITLER?

NEXT WEEK—
● There are more remarkable stories to come in our keepsake competition. Next week, for example, there's an Edinburgh man's moving story of The Three Bears story book, the only link with his lost father. And the secret of an East Kilbride woman's 36-year-old bar of soap. Every story published is paid for and, at the end of the series, the best, in the Editor's opinion, will receive the top prize of an antique worth £1000.

The Speug Needed The Fire Brigade

THE keepsake of Charlie Hackney, 84 Holms Crescent, Erskine, Renfrewshire, is kept in a safe.

It may hold the key to one of the biggest mysteries of World War Two.

For Charlie is convinced the small revolver he keeps in that safe killed Adolf Hitler on April 30, 1945!

Charlie with the Walther .765.

VIC PINNOCK, a fireman in Brightlingsea, Essex, was called out with his crew to a fire under the eaves of a building at a railway siding.

Vic found a sparrow's nest with a lighted cigarette end smouldering in it!

He put things right, and checked the next hadn't suffered any serious damage.

The minute he climbed back down the ladder, the sparrow family flew back to their nest.

Had a Sparrow had picked up the cigarette end, thinking it was food, and taken it home for her brood—only to discover she'd set her home on fire.

So Vic had to write his strangest report ever!

Towards the end of the war, Charlie was a member of the S.A.S. in Germany.

On May 4, 1945 (five days after Hitler's death) Charlie and two others were on special operations in Lubeck, North Germany.

They overheard some refugees discussing the arrival in town of three high-ranking Nazis. They were said to be staying at a big house nearby.

Charlie and his colleagues cornered the men in the cellar.

The three were dressed in civilian clothes. Suddenly the tallest one reached into his pocket and pulled out a gun.

Charlie kicked it from him, picked it up and put it in his coat pocket.

The German began pleading with him. He said he had to have the gun back. It was the gun Hitler had used to shoot himself.

In the kerfuffle, one of the other prisoners made a run for it.

Charlie and a colleague chased after him as the third stood guard over the remaining two Nazis. But they couldn't catch him.

Later, Charlie says, he recognised the escaped German from pictures in the papers. He's convinced it was Martin Bormann, Hitler's deputy.

When he got back to the house, Charlie began interrogating the two Nazis. They refused to speak. They wouldn't even give their names.

NEXT day the main body of the British Army entered Lubeck. The two men were handed over.

Charlie never did find out who they were. All Army records of the event

were later destroyed.

After he was demobbed, it first lay for 12 years in a bank deposit box.

Later, he was given a special firearms certificate to keep it at home.

Four years ago, Charlie made a determined effort to check if it was really the gun that shot Hitler. He contacted the Ministry of Defence.

The gun is a self-loading Walther .765. Carved on the side is an eagle with a swastika between its feet —

the insignia of the Luftwaffe, the German Air Force.

The number on the butt is 142062.

The Defence Ministry, says Charlie, came to the conclusion the gun may have belonged to Hermann Goering, boss of the Luftwaffe.

But did Hitler use Goering's gun to kill himself?

The commonly accepted version of the Führer's death is that he was shot through the head by a Walther .765 just after biting a cyanide pellet.

But his body was seized by the Russians after they captured his Berlin bunker. They have never revealed full details.

So Charlie may never know for sure.

The clincher for him is that he believes the two Nazis who didn't escape that day were the S.S. men who wait Goebbels orderly and driver.

If it was ever proved, the gun would be the most valuable war trophy ever, worth hundreds of thousands of pounds.

BUT THE WHISKY STILL ISN'T

Post-war, Corporal Charlie Hackney (second from left, photo opposite) and Major Charles 'Pat' Riley (left of photo) reveal what they believed to be Hitler's suicide weapon, a Walther PP, captured during one of the SAS's final, unsanctioned, missions in Germany. Long before doing so, Colonel Blair Mayne, DSO (and three bars), Legion d'Honneur, Croix de Guerre, had died in a car accident, aged just forty years old. He is pictured left, as we may wish to remember him, in happier days with his mother in Northern Ireland.

deployed to France. In doing so they had not been overly mindful of Goldsmith's psychoneurosis (PTSD), of course.

On 14 August Goldsmith had parachuted in, as part of a mission codenamed Operation Haggard. Camped in the Fôret d'Ivoy, near the town of Nevers, their area of operations lay a hundred kilometres due west of Bill Fraser's Morvan base. A series of ferocious ambushes on German convoys and rail transports had followed. Then, on 26 August, they had joined forces with the Maquis to destroy two bridges heavily guarded by Waffen SS troops. In the ensuing firefight, one of Goldsmith's comrades was killed and another seriously wounded. Little daunted, two days later the raiders blew a railway line, which carried an armoured train that had been busy 'shooting up farms and killing peasants in the fields'.

Outwardly, there was little to suggest that Joe Goldsmith remained unwell. But by 9 October he was hospitalised in France, at an American-run facility lying on the outskirts of Paris. Though he was physically unharmed, letters his wife received at the time suggested that 'it would take him a long time to recover'. By 17 October Goldsmith was back in Britain, in a Southampton clinic. As we know today, PTSD accrues to those who've suffered intense incidents of trauma, often repeatedly, and is often coupled with 'survivor's guilt'. Goldsmith had seen one of his closest comrades killed and horrifically maimed, while walking away apparently scot-free.

Two events would have spurred Goldsmith's trauma. The first was the October 1943 Termoli truck bombing, in which a convoy of lorries packed with SAS had taken a direct hit from a shell, with dozens being killed and maimed. Goldsmith had escaped unscathed. He'd immediately volunteered to care for the terribly injured, despite having no formal medical training. More recently, the thirty-one captives who had been murdered on Operation Bulbasket included Goldsmith's best friend, Doug Eccles. This news had left him 'devastated', and may well have tipped him back into his psychosis, especially when coupled with the intense combat experienced on Operation Haggard.

As he'd written to his then fiancée, from Italy, Goldsmith valued the camaraderie and brotherhood of the SAS above all. 'I don't think I've ever told you about the boys with whom I work, they are the finest bunch of lads you could ever go into action with; we have been together now for nearly 18 months and we know one another off by heart and there's not one who would not lay his life down for his mate and they are all mates to each other.' It all begged the question as to whether Goldsmith should ever have been deployed on Operation Haggard in the first place. Either way, he would be declared 'unfit for further service', and 'would suffer badly with nerves' for the rest of his days.

Few were immune to such trauma, no matter their track record or apparent martial spirit. Sergeant Goldsmith was a four-year veteran of Commando and SAS operations, and an army boxer with a Military Medal to his name. Likewise, Lieutenant Johnny Wiseman, an SAS original, had been awarded an MC, plus a Croix de Guerre with Silver Star for his French operations. But after returning from commanding his daring and audacious Dijon mission, Wiseman too was suffering. As he would later admit, 'I'd reached the end of my tether.' But at the time, he was loath to face up to reality – that he was on the edge. It took Mayne to summon Wiseman for a frank chat, in which he told the veteran raider that he was 'no longer psychologically fit for front-line action'.

In his Second World War scrapbook, Joe Goldsmith would paste a news-clipping about Paddy Mayne, entitled, 'New facts about the most daring men of the war.' In his handwriting beside it he noted: 'Paddy Mayne was a founding member of the SAS.

He was immensely brave almost to the point of recklessness, always led from the front and was idolised by the men he commanded.' In part, Mayne was 'idolised' because of the care he took of them. Rightly, and in light of Goldsmith's plight, Mayne took the view that no one showing signs of 'crapping out', as they termed it, should deploy, no matter how much they might try to hide it or argue that they were perfectly fit.

Wiseman was offered a role in SAS headquarters, in Britain. For what was coming – the push into the Fatherland – he would play no active part. Yet in truth, Wiseman's plight was just the tip of the iceberg. Another SAS original, Sergeant Ernest 'Bob' Lilley was a similarly iconic figure to Wiseman. In North Africa, Lilley had been part of a small raiding patrol led by Mayne, attacking Berca airfield, in modern-day Libya. In the ensuing melee, Lilley had got isolated from the others at night. Come dawn he'd found himself in the midst of a vast enemy encampment. His solution was simply to emerge from hiding and saunter away, acting as if he had every right to be there. Dust covered, in khaki shorts and shirt, he would bluff it like the enemy.

He'd made it through the breakfasting camp, when, on the outskirts, a lone, but much younger, Italian soldier had challenged him. They'd 'got to wrestling', Lilley encircling his hands around the man's throat and strangling him. Leaving the Italian soldier 'sprawled out and looking up at the sun', he'd grabbed the dead man's distinctive cap and used that to better his disguise, and to spur his subsequent escape, for which he was awarded a Military Medal. But at Hylands, Mayne received a letter from Lilley's wife, Evelyn, revealing how much she believed her husband was on the verge of cracking up.

Bob Lilley had written to her, she disclosed, declaring the home was hers 'to do as I please with, and also he was not coming home on leave . . .' He'd also made 'hurtful remarks . . . I thought it was the thought of going out again and his "nerves going". All of this is just sending me to pieces and I cannot sleep ... so please do send him home – before anything more serious happens.' Others, Bill Fraser included – 'withdrawn, opaque ... something was crumbling within' – were drowning their trauma with alcohol. They were haunted by the 'internal demons' which just kept creeping closer. The fear of falling now, at the final hurdle, the push into Nazi Germany, seemed to hold a powerful grip on many.

From Brussels, where Operation Policeman had run into the sand – dogged by official inertia and red tape – Mayne received a lengthy letter penned by his long-serving and trusted deputy, Major Harry Poat. On one level, Poat, a former tomato farmer from Guernsey, with impeccable dress sense and a cut glass accent, could not have been more different to Mayne. But what united them was the keen battle nostril that each shared. Having enlisted in March 1940, and served with the SAS since the autumn of 1942, Poat, who'd won a Military Cross in Italy, was no fading violet or stranger to the harsh realities of war. Yet he was worried, and he sought to share his concerns with Mayne.

Those gathered in Brussels were hacked off at the lack of meaningful action. Any number were in urgent need of being sent home, one squadron being 'totally unfit bodily and mentally'. One senior commander even claimed that 'if he was asked to operate with them [B Squadron] he would be obliged to refuse.' That same commander described himself as being 'completely played out, and quite unsuitable for the job, and wishes to leave the unit'. That man, the chief of B Squadron, was Major Thomas 'Tommy' Langton, another long-serving veteran who had won a Military Cross for his epic desert escape in the autumn of 1942. As Poat pointed out, 'in his frame of mind he is not doing any good to the men under his command.'

In addition to those plagued by the demons in their minds, Mayne also had to deal with those bearing physical injuries. News reached him that Corporal Thomas 'Ginger' Jones, a real character of the regiment, was hospitalised. He and one other had escaped from the execution squad that had killed Captain Garstin and their comrades, back in August. Mayne encouraged his men to visit Jones, to see which of life's luxuries might cheer him up. All returned with the same verdict: only getting Jones out of there would lift his spirits. Despite all the calls on his time, Mayne went to see for himself. Clearly, both Jones's health and spirits were suffering. But when Mayne asked if the hospital might release him into the care they could provide at Hylands, his request was refused.

Mayne gathered his men. He briefed them on Jones's predicament. Warning those present that it called for 'delicate handling', he asked for volunteers to bust Jones free. Within twenty-four hours a small party had stolen into the hospital in the early hours, covertly removed Jones from his bed, and slipped away again just as inconspicuously. With the hospital staff none the wiser, Jones was quietly taken into the care of his brother warriors at Hylands, whereupon his spirits rallied and his health improved no end. But such physical wounds were so much the easier to heal.

As Padre McLuskey realised, after the Morvan he felt dislocated, like an alien in a hitherto familiar world. To be in normal, civilised society, he wrote, was like being 'a ghost in their solid houses and happy family life'. Describing a 'wraith-like existence', he spoke of how he 'lived between two worlds', and 'seemed hardly to live at all'. In his report on the Morvan, he noted the cumulative impact and strain of back-to-back missions. The inability to relax and the ever-present tension hit hard. Over time, the stress reached a 'danger point', and the effects could be seen in some of 'the best soldiers we have', causing 'carelessness, impatience, edginess and depression'.

One of the few who joked that he was immune to such tensions was a Corporal Thompson. In North Africa, he'd started to suffer from blackouts lasting for as much as thirty-six hours. Admitted to hospital, he was eventually told that his 'nerves were completely shattered' and that he'd be there for some time. There were all types of nationalities in the hospital and one evening Thompson had been listening to the BBC news. A Czech had come and retuned the radio. Thompson warned him he could do so at any time, but not during the BBC news broadcast. The Czech insisted, so Thompson persuaded him otherwise by 'depriving him of two teeth'. The Czech produced a cutthroat razor and went to slash Thompson's throat, but Thompson was quicker, hurling his locker at his assailant and scoring a direct hit on the man's head.

Thrown into a padded cell for his troubles, Thompson realised that he was in a 'lunatic asylum, and as a result of his conduct was considered a raving madman'. Reporting sick, he'd gone to see the medical officer and explained he was only there due to the blackouts he'd been suffering. It turned out that Thompson's records had got mixed up with a man of the same surname, who was suffering 'severe shell-shock and mental fatigue'. Not wanting ever to suffer a repeat performance, Thompson demanded he got a certificate asserting that 'he was sane'. As the SAS War Diary concluded, he 'proudly claims to be the only man in the Regiment able to prove his sanity!'

Corporal Thompson was the exception. Most men in the SAS could not prove their sanity. And as the winter of 1944/45 bit, any number were plagued by their inner demons and haunted by the loss of dear friends. Little wonder then that if an excuse arose they partied like there was no tomorrow, which, for them, there just mightn't be. All-night drinking sessions at Hylands were not uncommon, as were the high jinks that tended to accompany them.

Once, Mayne got his men to call up the Chelmsford fire brigade, claiming the SAS had a problem. Assuming it to be a fire at Hylands, they dispatched the fire chief and a full crew. They were met at the front of the grand house by the mess staff bearing trays of drinks. Getting right into the spirit of things, they soon had 'the entire Chelmsford force' sitting on the steps supping their ale. Thankfully there were 'no fires that evening', as Johnny Cooper remarked.

In perhaps the most infamous incident, several jeeps were somehow manhandled into the main hall of Hylands, before someone bet Mayne that he couldn't drive one up the main marble staircase leading to the floor above. Disregarding the fact that it had two right-angle bends, the SAS commander somehow navigated it up there, before driving it through the oak doors at the top and parking on the landing. Getting it down again the following day – sobered up and in the full glare of daylight – proved nigh-on impossible.

At the height of the uproar, Mrs Hanbury had appeared in her dressing gown. 'Now, Paddy, that is quite enough,' she had scolded him, in a decidedly motherly fashion. 'It's time you all got to bed.'

Suitably chastened, Mayne had escorted her back to her room, and bade all get some sleep, dismissing the boisterous, cheering crowd. In fact, Mrs Hanbury indulged Mayne in part because the iconic soldier reminded her in many ways of her son. And Mayne, it seemed, was equally fond of her.

Writing to his mother in Northern Ireland on 23 December 1944, Mayne described Hylands as 'a terrific mansion three times the size of Regent House,' which was the Newtownards grammar school where he was educated. Of the long-suffering Mrs Hanbury, he'd painted a picture of 'a very pleasant old woman . . . a wonderful talker, quite interesting but unending. I called to see her last night & she opened a bottle of champagne, then insisted I should stay for dinner when I had a very good venison cutlet, some excellent red wine, some good port and a fine cigar. What could be nicer?'

With Christmas 1944 approaching, Mayne had asked his mother to get him a job lot of turkeys, for the SAS's Hylands Christmas dinner. 'I had hoped to get over to collect them,' he wrote to her, 'but the fog was so bad I couldn't fly.' He wrote of bringing her some 'grapes back from Brussels' – he had been to Belgium for a fleeting visit. Fresh grapes in ration-starved Britain would have constituted a real treat. Mayne had hoped to give her the grapes when collecting the turkeys, but the fog had meant he couldn't fly. 'I am afraid I can't send them through the post,' he wrote, in his December 23 letter. 'A pity, because I know you would have liked them.'

Amid the Christmas wishes, he also wrote of tragic loss. 'Our doctor, Phil Gunn, has been killed in a car accident.' Mayne had attended the funeral, and stayed the night with Gunn's parents. 'I know they felt things very much, he was their second son to be killed but I did admire their courage.' In an obituary in *The Times*, Mayne would write of his friend Gunn: 'There are many patients who would wish to thank him for his work . . . In the Regiment his popularity, both amongst the men and officers, was founded not only on his cheerful and courageous conduct under all conditions but on the admiration which one could not but feel for his great talents both as a doctor and a soldier . . .'

The death of Gunn was made all the more difficult, in that Mayne had just lost another cherished brother-in-arms, and again to a senseless road accident. That September, he'd dispatched Major Bob Melot to Belgium, to prepare the way for SAS Operation Policeman. On 28 October, Melot was returning from checking out a shooting range – a potential SAS training ground – when his jeep had hit an especially wet and muddy stretch of road. On the narrow highway it lost traction, hit a culvert at the roadside, spun around and threw Melot free. He died from his head injuries.

'I find it impossible to tell you how sad I am about Bob's death,' Mayne had written to his widow. 'There is no officer in the unit who could have been spared less . . . Our Regiment suffered a very grievous loss . . . I myself have lost a very good friend and a person whose advice and counsel meant very much to me . . . Your husband was one of the finest persons I have ever known.' In the autumn of 1944, 1 SAS had lost the 'father' of the unit, and a man to whom Mayne was closest, of anyone, and just when they could least afford it. Heading into Germany, Mayne could have done with Melot's maturity and sage counsel. Melot had once told Brigadier McLeod that his selection for SAS bases in France was about as useful as throwing 'shit at a map'. In short, Melot was fearless, outspoken, indomitable, and Mayne had respected him hugely. Now he was gone.

Mayne signed off his 23 December letter to his mother, describing how he had 'been down to London several times lately, and been to a few very good plays'. Unfortunately, he was about to head for Holland – much of which had been liberated by the Allies – and that had scuppered all his plans. 'I had several arrangements made here; shooting today, partridges which should have been good fun and we had several parties arranged over Xmas, and on Boxing Day I was to have played rugby at Cambridge, but I am afraid we have to earn our living sometime.' The impression is of a man run ragged – his handwriting, previously so neat, shows signs of stress, with several words crossed out in haste. It is also of a commander trying his utmost to care for his men – collecting Christmas turkeys from Ireland – but with the weight of fate and circumstance seemingly set against him.

By contrast, Mrs Hanbury's letter to Mayne's mother – dated five days later – is faultlessly written and full of charm and warmth. 'I am writing to you to tell you how the people of Essex have taken your gallant son to their hearts. Personally it is a real joy to have him and his command in my house and park. They are a grand lot and devoted to their Colonel. It was pleasant to find he had mature friends.' As Mayne had just departed for Holland, she added, 'No one could have done more for me when he left. We had an amazing picnic meal . . .' Mrs Hanbury closed by inviting Mayne's mother to pay her the 'delightful courtesy of a visit . . . I should be delighted to see you and make your acquaintance.'

Throughout the early years of the war, Mayne – the sixth of seven siblings and an intensely family man – had been an extensive letter writer. His missives home were full of charm, playfulness, plus the offbeat humour that so typified him. Writing to his favourite niece, Margaret, he'd nicknamed her 'Funnyface' and warned her that if she got 'her Daddy' to read his letter, instead of doing so herself, 'I will tie your ears together when I come home.' He wrote of a whale coming through the porthole of a ship he'd been sailing on, and of life in the desert: 'We have fried sand for breakfast, grilled sand for lunch and cooked sand for dinner.' That kind of letter seemed to have stopped around the time that Mayne deployed to France.

Instead, he wrote to Molly, his eldest sister, from Belgium, in January 1945, describing how 'Xmas was amusing enough here, the food was good and we were able to find unlimited champagne.' Having thanked her for looking after 'the pup' – Mayne was an inveterate animal lover, and especially fond of dogs – he wrote of how 'everyone is very confident here & not at all frightened about the German counteroffensives, though it is terribly cold and wet and uncomfortable . . .' That December, the Germans had launched a surprise counter-attack in the Ardennes area, between Luxembourg and Belgium, but by January 1945 it was running out of steam. Mayne signed off his letter hoping 'to manage some leave, it would be pleasant to be home again', while also reminiscing about the war in the desert. He and his men were 'beginning to think that Libya was a very pleasant place'.

For Mayne, in the winter of 1944/45 the *joie de vivre* seemed to have gone. There is a nostalgic bent to his writing; a hankering after the free and easy ways of the desert; of a war without hate. As the 'unlimited champagne' remark reflects, Mayne – like so many – was drinking too much, and he was like a charge primed to blow. Mike Sadler, his long-standing comrade, noticed this pent-up, latent force. 'He was very good at containing himself most of the time,' he remarked of Mayne, 'but I always thought he was a bit of a volcano; and people were frightened of him because they felt that.' Recently, at a London cabaret, Mayne had glanced at Sadler and remarked: 'Why don't we both just break off a table leg and go around and see how many people we can get.'

It was a joke, but there was a lingering darkness that under-pinned it all. Or as Roy Close would put it, 'during any inactive period' such as this, Mayne would 'have a bit of a binge'. But once sobered up he would 'order a regimental parade', one that he would take 'perfectly. We all had to be properly dressed,' as was Mayne. Somehow, subliminally, all understood what this was about. Mayne was trying to show that while they'd all let their hair down, some more than others, control and discipline had to be re-established, especially bearing in mind what was coming.

*

The Belgian SAS operations had ground to a halt in the freezing winter snows. Alec Borrie wrote an account of a rare spot of action – a snatch mission. They'd headed across the River Maas, dashed thirty odd miles into Germany itself to an ancient castle, where they'd seized the owner. Imagining they'd captured a top Nazi war criminal, they were surprised when ordered to take him back again the next day. 'It turned out he was not wanted for any war crimes, but had valuable information he wanted to give in person to the British Army and no one else.' That was a rare spike of excitement. Mostly, the weather put a stop to all such activities.

'It snowed hard for several days to a depth of 4 or 5 feet, then froze solid and became so cold all the jeeps' radiators had to be drained every night, as the antifreeze we used couldn't cope. The war seemed to have come to a halt . . .' Borrie and his pals killed time running butchered pigs from the borders of the Maas to Belgium, to sell on the black market. Crossing to France with their ill-gotten loot, they'd load the jeep with fine champagne, to sell again in Brussels and 'make even more money'. While Borrie and friends spent the cash on the good life, one man saved every penny. He amassed 'two small suitcases full' of French francs, and had 'a lot of money when he finally arrived home after the war'.

With little proper work to do, C Squadron was dispatched back to Britain for twenty-eight days' leave. At the Belgian port of Antwerp, a boat was waiting to ship them home. Unfortunately, they drove into the port city just as the enemy decided 'to wipe out the docks at Antwerp through which most of the Allied supplies were being landed, with their long range V1 Flying Bombs and V2 Rockets,' as Borrie recalled. For four weeks the Squadron was trapped there, helping the Belgian civil defence forces recover dead and injured from wrecked buildings. They were shown where 'the Gestapo tortured and shot anyone they suspected of anti-German activities . . . the two posts the victims were tied to, and the rough pine coffins against the wall'.

It was a powerful reminder that the evil still needed to be fought and vanquished.

Chapter Fourteen

INTO THE FATHERLAND

With Allied forces massing on the western bank of the Rhine, the question vexing all was how exactly to use the SAS. As Charlie Hackney – he of the famous red butcher's van – remarked, 'proposals to drop the SAS deep into Germany were wisely cancelled.' Or as Wellsted – Captain Gremlin – put it, 'One idea was to parachute SAS troops into Germany to cause scares and tie down troops . . . But clearly this would have been suicidal.'

Such behind-the-lines guerrilla-style warfare needed one of two things: either vast open spaces devoid of human habitation in which to operate, as the SAS had enjoyed in the North African desert; or friendly populations within which to foster such operations, as they'd mostly had in France. Nazi Germany boasted neither. Which kept leading back to the question – how to use the SAS? Among many other bizarre ideas that were mooted was for 'plain clothes terrorism in Germany'. But even without Hitler's Commando Order, that would have amounted to a death sentence.

In Britain, Brigadier McLeod was replaced by Brigadier James 'Mad Mike' Calvert, DSO and Bar, fresh out of a long stint with General Orde Wingate's Chindits, an elite unit that waged war deep in the Burmese jungle. McLeod and Calvert could not have been more different, for the latter boasted a wartime career replete with daring feats behind the lines, most notably fighting the Japanese. He'd also run the Burma-based Bush Warfare School, training Chinese troops for guerrilla-style operations against the Japanese in China itself.

Upon his appointment, Calvert – unorthodox, driven, a rule-breaker through and through – addressed the men with a striking clarity and humility: 'I am glad and proud to take over such a fine command as that of all SAS Troops. I will try and do justice to this appointment. You are special troops and I expect you to do special things in the last heave against the Hun. There will be plenty of worthwhile jobs to do.' There would. There might. But what exact form would they take?

Though they didn't always get along, in many senses Calvert and Mayne were kindred spirits. United in a common cause, they were hungry for action, Calvert having been retired from Burma operations due to injury in September 1944. Both were determined that if a knockout punch were to be delivered to Nazi Germany, the SAS needed to be in the ring. Or as Mayne put it, he wanted his men 'in at the kill, to be there at the fall of Germany'. Finally, in the spring of 1945, plans for a series of missions began to take shape, predicated on exactly what kind of conditions Allied forces expected to face as they thrust into the heart of the Reich.

'The impression ... was that the enemy would fight a full-scale battle to the east of the Rhine in the initial bridgehead period,' read an SAS planning document. 'Thereafter the battle would become so fluid that the jeeps might be able to achieve penetration to a considerable depth.' With their bread-and-butter behind-the-lines operations off the cards, the SAS were to revert to a role they had played before, in Italy, serving as the spear-head to the Allied advance, cutting deep into enemy territory at strategic junctures. They'd execute probing patrols ahead of the

Allied frontline forces, identifying key pockets of resistance, and accepting the surrender of enemy units as they went.

This wasn't classic SAS-style warfare. It wasn't chiefly what they were trained to do, nor were they ideally equipped with their thin-skinned, largely unarmoured jeeps. But the keenness of those SAS troops chafing at the bit reflected the incredible esprit de corps that imbued their ranks. It demonstrated a flexibility of mindset that underpinned a burning desire to win. Orders were issued: '(a) to carry out short range reconnaissance with the airborne units in their bridgehead over the Rhine . . . (b) to achieve deeper penetration through the enemy lines as the real advance begins, attack enemy lines of communication and pass back information.' The die was cast.

With the SAS serving at the tip of the spear, very likely they would be among the first to reach the POW camps in Germany crammed with Allied prisoners. Orders were issued that 'jeep squadrons may be directed to POW camps to report on conditions and assist inmates.' The unit's POW-rescue mission was codenamed Vicarage, and plans were put in place for the names and identities of those liberated to be radioed back to Britain. As matters transpired, the SAS would end up being used in this way, and so would come their most shocking and hellish confrontation of the entire war.

But all of that lay some weeks in the future.

It was mid-March 1944 when Mayne's raiders were warned to prepare to deploy. They would be doing so in mixed units, 1 and 2 SAS working together to vanquish the last of the Nazi enemy. Montgomery, their old friend, paid a visit. He addressed the men. 'You are some of the original members of the glorious army, the Eighth Army. We've come a long way. We won the desert – brilliantly planned, brilliantly carried out. We went to

Sicily – brilliantly planned, brilliantly carried out . . . Now we are going to hit him [Hitler] where it hurts most, in the Fatherland.' Monty added that 'the only good German is a dead one.' That didn't go down so well. For those who'd soldiered with Hans, the good German, or even Rolph, the Hitler Youth captive who'd ended up as Padre McLuskey's medical assistant, they knew differently.

Germans were the victims of this war, just as much as their adversaries.

At Hylands, Mayne readied his men for their mission, code-named Operation Howard, but more informally known as 'Paddy Force'. Fittingly, among the berets, rucksacks, sleeping bags, coats, Thermos flasks, gloves, windproof suits, torches and batteries, M1 Carbines, Vickers-K guns, plus '10 windscreens bullet proof' sought for the deployment, Paddy Force also ordered up '50,000 cigarettes, 3 cases Whiskey'. 'Whiskey' spelled the Irish way, of course.

They were busy readying their jeeps, adding armoured plating to protect the driver and front gunner, bullet proof half-moon windshields, copious rear armour, plus a large rack bolted to the backend, to carry rucksacks, kit and additional weaponry. The radiators were also encased in armour, long range self-sealing fuel tanks were added, the machineguns were fitted with spotlights, to aid night-fighting, and many of the jeeps were kitted out with a radio. To add to the Vickers-K firepower, every third jeep was fitted with a Browning M2 .50-calibre heavy machinegun bolted to the rear. To accommodate all the extra weight, the vehicles' springs had to be specially strengthened.

The final touches made to their steeds added a hint of panache and élan, each jeep taking on 'the rakish individuality' which so typified the SAS. Wellsted's looked suitably suicidal, for he'd vowed that after losing Margot only death or glory awaited.

With its massive Browning M2 crouched in the rear like some long-necked beast, and with its rounded radiator armour jutting out in front, it had the name 'RHINO' scrawled across it in bold lettering. Another jeep had a purloined police helmet bolted to the bonnet. A third was christened 'JUST MARRIED', having a 'bridal veil and baby's dummy' dangling out front. A jeep baptised 'THE GRIMBLE PIG' was named after its driver, Lance Corporal Pringle Gibb, the man who'd provided blistering covering fire when Reg Seekings had been shot in the neck, back in the Morvan. As for 'THE RAMBLING WRECK', the name spoke for itself.

Another had the German word 'WEHRWOLF' daubed across the armoured shield that graced its rear Vickers-K guns. This was an archaic spelling of *Werewolf*, the name given to one of Hitler's key military headquarters. But it was also the codename for the forces of the Nazi resistance, which were supposed to rise up should the Allies dare to enter the Fatherland. Either way, it signalled that the crew of Wehrwolf intended to go all the way.

Amid the frenetic activity at Hylands, there was a weird, wired undercurrent. Peace was so close. Many had fought for five long years, and at last the end was in sight. Excitement was mingled with the 'chill of trepidation' for what lay ahead. Any number of the men were only recently back from Brussels and supposedly on leave, when they had the call at home to deploy. Captain Roy Close – one of those recalled from leave – felt as if his break had 'scarcely begun' when he was summoned back to war.

The forty-eight hours he had to prepare were marred by a tension – and a later tragedy – that would haunt Close for the rest of his days. One of his men, Sergeant Alexander 'Sandy' Davidson, was late in. A long-standing veteran of both No. 11 Commando and then the SAS, he'd soldiered in the North African desert and across Italy with Paddy Mayne's raiders. This was quite out of character. While Close stalled reporting him as being AWOL – for a court martial would likely follow – at the eleventh hour Davidson pitched up. Massively relieved that he was there, Close wondered what could have kept him, causing them all so much worry. He asked as much.

'I don't fancy this one, sir,' Davidson told him, simply. 'I don't want to go.'

Close, shocked, gave the only reply he could. 'I'm sorry, but I can't do anything about that.'

'I know,' Davidson replied, fatalistically.

Davidson had got married in June 1944, to Elsie Williams, a widowed WAAF, the 'sweetest girl in the world'. With a baby daughter not yet a year old, Davidson's reticence to deploy was understandable, especially since the coming mission promised to be the bitterest yet – 'the killer thrust against an enemy determined to defend the soil of the Fatherland,' as Close would describe it. Alec 'Boy' Borrie had likewise received the knock at the door and the telegram. He'd lingered for 'one more home cooked dinner', and to 'say cheerio to my friends', before heading north to Hylands. To Borrie it was 'obvious that it would be a different type of war. Germany was now fighting on its own soil and everybody was the enemy.'

Derrick 'Happy' Harrison was there, pulled in by a telegram which he'd expected to announce a welcome extension to his leave. Instead, it had ordered him to 'report back at once'. He'd bade farewell to his wife, reached Hylands long after dusk, and worked late into the night 'by the lights of the jeeps, fixing the guns and filling the magazines'. All anyone knew was that Paddy Force was heading for Germany. Orders and fuller details would be revealed once they were deep in the field. For now, it was a case of hurry up and get moving.

It was 7 April 1945 when Mayne led a massive column of heavily laden jeeps south towards Dagenham Dock, on the Thames – embarkation point for the Belgian port of Ostend. Some three hundred troops and their vehicles were loaded aboard ship, for a crossing on a bright spring day. Having docked at Ostend, the men lay about in the sun while the ship unloaded, the sandy shoreline stretching away to one side. Lieutenant Deakins recalled reminiscing 'of similar beach days some years before . . . of how, with comparatively few survivors, I had left a beach some way down the coast . . . Now, hopefully, the Allied armies were moving up . . . to release my earlier friends who had been captured at that time . . .'

Unloading done, the jeeps formed up in convoy. At the lead, Mayne had a fresh driver, Trooper Billy Hull, a fellow Ulsterman, at the wheel, plus his new signals corporal, David Danger, manning the radio. Fittingly, for Paddy's Force, he had a rudimentary public address (PA) system bolted to the jeep, courtesy of Danger's technical expertise, and his gramophone strapped to the rear. Mixed in with the Percy French songs which he intended to play all through this madcap deployment, Mayne would broadcast 'rude words' to the enemy via the PA system. Or, as Danger would recall, he would harangue the enemy through his loud speaker, calling on them to surrender.

The way ahead switchbacked this way and that, as blown bridges had to be avoided, and canal and river crossings negotiated. Many of the houses had bed sheets draped from the windows as makeshift white flags. Mostly, the streets were deserted, as residents feared another German counter-attack, 'the rout of 1940 still in many memories'. Passing through Nijmegen and Arnhem, there was evidence on all sides of the ferocious fighting to capture those crossing points over the Rhine. Pressing on to Apeldoorn, Deventer and Almelo, in the eastern Netherlands, they found towns reduced to 'heaps of rubble. Bulldozers had pushed aside the debris' just enough for vehicles to pass. Some parts of the north of the country were still held by the enemy.

They were close now.

During the war, British troops had taken to singing the popular song by Flanagan and Allen, 'We're Going to Hang out the Washing on the Siegfried Line', by Irish songwriter Jimmy Kennedy. The Siegfried Line was a series of defensive fortifications running along Germany's western border, boasting some 18,000 bunkers, tunnels and tank traps. The opening verse went:

We're going to hang out the washing on the Siegfried Line.
Have you any dirty washing, mother dear?
We're gonna hang out the washing on the Siegfried Line.
'Cause the washing day is here.

The jeeps reached a dense forest. There was a poster in its midst, declaring 'Siegfried Line'. Near by, someone had erected a sign announcing: 'This is the washing.' Next to it was a line of laundered underwear. Passing those two markers, and with little other fanfare, Paddy Force entered into 'the Reich of Adolf Hitler'. It was the afternoon of 9 April as the convoy roared into Meppen, a town in the Lower Saxony region of today's Germany, in the northwest of the country. With the Channel crossing included, they'd just completed a 500-mile drive pretty much non-stop, in their heavily laden vehicles.

Pulling into some woodland on the town's outskirts, Mayne gathered his officers for a briefing. They squatted on the forest floor, maps on their knees, in a semi-circle around their leader.

'We're just outside of Meppen,' Mayne began. 'The Canadians took the bridge there this morning. Tomorrow the Canadian 4th Armoured Division is going to push on to Oldenburg – that's about sixty miles away. We are to operate on its left flank. Once we reach Oldenburg, we will push up north to the Wilhelmshaven area and make a nuisance of ourselves. Now, is that clear?'

There were nods all around. It was a given that they *would* reach Oldenburg, as far as Mayne was concerned, though their objective lay over one hundred kilometres north-east, across terrain thick with a desperate and diehard enemy.

Mayne outlined the mission plan. They would divide their force; Tony Marsh would lead one column, while a relatively new recruit, Major Dick Bond, would command the other. The two columns would continually link up with each other, before pushing on ahead again. As they probed forwards, the foremost vehicle would keep being changed, for 'leading the advance in open jeeps for very long . . . was a bit of a strain'. The spearhead vehicle was bound to serve as the bullet-magnet. Mayne would play a roving role, flitting between the columns as the need arose.

The going was unlikely to be easy. The terrain was nightmarish, being 'crossed and recrossed by dykes and canals, making it extremely difficult for jeeps to operate with any degree of freedom'. It was impossible to head off road, and there were 'very few places in which vehicles could reverse and turn around'. The fields were boggy, and the bridges and culverts were rigged with charges, and primed to blow. To add to their worries, the enemy up ahead were no slouches. They consisted of German paratroopers, who had 'fought well and even fanatically at times'. Their ranks were stiffened by the 'wild eyed kids' of the Hitler Youth and the *Volkssturm* or 'People's Storm' – Nazi Germany's home guard – all determined to defend the Nazi homeland, or die trying.

Before heading into action, there was one last cautionary measure everyone needed to take. In response to Hitler's Commando Order, all men were to sanitise themselves. Anything that might hint at an SAS pedigree was to be discarded. The men had to remove their distinctive SAS berets, replacing them with the more sombre black beret of the Tank Corps. All references to the SAS were to be struck from pay books and related documents, while on the radio those three letters were never to be used. Instead, they were to refer to themselves as 'The Little Ones'. As for their commander, orders had been issued for 'security silence personal movements MAYNE', for they knew he was a marked man. In light of Nazi Germany's predations, Mayne had become the ghost commander of a ghost regiment, one that dare not speak its name.

Thus forewarned, in the 'misty morning light' of 10 April the long convoy of jeeps stole out of its woodland encampment. Canadian tankmen, woken from their sleep by all the racket, stared incredulously as the diminutive vehicles roared past their heavy M4 Sherman tanks, the Willys jeeps dwarfed by the armour. One of the tankies cracked a joke about Brits in their 'little mechanised mess tins'. The name stuck. From then on, the SAS became 'Our little friends in their mechanised mess tins!'

The convoy of mechanised mess tins approached the first bridge that crossed the Dortmund–Ems Canal, a major shipping lane in the north of Germany. It was blown. Fire erupted from the far side, and a jeep returned it with interest, before racing back to report. It was no use. The bridge was down. They'd have to try to find another way.

Repeatedly the lead vehicles probed for a crossing point, but each time they reached the near bank of the canal only to find the crossing blown, and the enemy ready and waiting on the far side. Roy Close slipped into pole position, nosed ahead and found a track leading to another possible crossing point. He halted the column, left his jeep in cover and belly-crawled ahead 'in approved training schools style' to spy out the land. Pulling out his binoculars, he scanned the opposite bank and the hoped-for crossing.

A voice interrupted his thoughts. 'Can you see anything down there, Roy?'

Glancing up, Close saw 'a pair of brown boots, battledress trousers and a tunic . . . I saw Paddy standing there.' Somehow, Mayne had silently joined Close and was gently mocking him in his unmistakable Ulster brogue.

'You get a better view from up here,' Mayne added, quietly.

Feeling a tad foolish, Close got to his feet.

'Well, they're not defending this one, but we still can't cross,' Mayne remarked.

There were no enemy troops on the far bank, but the bridge had been well and truly trashed. Close tried the same thing a few more times, but with the sinking feeling that they were getting nowhere. Each bridge was down. Then a radio message buzzed around the vehicles. Their sister column, commanded by Major Dick Bond, had found a crossing point. Even now they were preparing to move over. All vehicles were to head to that one point, to link up and proceed as one united force.

It had to be beginner's luck that Bond had found a way through. Major Charles Frederick Gordon Bond – known to all as Dick – was the Harrow-educated scion of a military and farming family. His father had been killed in action in the First World War, and young Dick had been commissioned into his old regiment in 1932. In 1937, he'd changed profession from soldier to farmer, running the family farm near Cullompton, in Devon. But in 1939 he'd rejoined the forces, seeing fierce action in the June 1940 defeat in France, being twice Mentioned in Despatches for gallant service. After France, he'd served in the highly secretive Auxiliaries, otherwise known as the British Resistance Organisation (BRO), formed to wage guerrilla warfare should the Nazis invade Britain.

When that didn't happen, Bond, like so many BRO members,

had volunteered for the SAS. In January 1945 he'd stepped forward to replace Major Tommy Langton, whom Poat had warned was burned out – 'completely played out, and quite unsuitable for the job'. Poat had proposed that, with Bond seeming in fine fettle, 'the answer appears to be Bond replace Langton'. Mayne had given his blessing and so it had come to pass. Despite Bond being a relative newcomer, key figures in 1 SAS spoke 'very highly of him', and Mayne himself was fond of Bond, viewing him as a brave and committed commander.

There were many in Paddy Force who were anxious about these final chapters of the war. The fear of being killed now, when victory was so close, spurred an irrational foreboding. There was no argument why action now, in the spring of 1945, should be any more dangerous to life and limb than action with the SAS upon its formation, back in the summer of 1941. But still the dread bit deep. Equally, there were those who remained unblooded within the SAS, and who sought to prove themselves in what might be the last actions of the war. Perhaps Bond was one of those. Alec Borrie certainly seemed to think so, for Bond 'only came . . . to get first-hand knowledge of what it was really like'. Whatever the case, as the ghost regiment crawled across the bridge over the Dortmund–Ems Canal, Major Bond and his section were in the lead.

Back at Meppen, Mayne and his senior officers had been briefed by the Canadian 4th Armoured Division's commanders. There had been one thing that had struck the Canadians as being odd. Why were men of Mayne's rank and his immediate deputies – Majors Tony Marsh and Dick Bond – so determined to lead from the front? By their rank and experience alone, they'd earned the right to keep a step or two back, and especially during the kind of high-risk missions that the SAS specialised in. But the stalled

Canadian advance needed kickstarting, and that would only be possible with daring action and decisive leadership.

In any case, it was the SAS way.

Bond's jeep crawled across the bridge over the Dortmund–Ems Canal, and 'blasting away at road blocks' the advance got under way. Ahead lay the villages of Börger and Lorup, as the vehicles 'tore into the heart of German territory ... across quickly improvised bridges, along ... narrow lanes'. The terrain on all sides – part of the Hümmling wilderness – was a patchwork of dense beech and birch forests, interspersed with waterlogged moor and peatland, and narrow-cut waterways. Signs of an ancient culture – megalithic tombs – reared from the undergrowth, as testament to the deep roots of human habitation here. For five millennia the people of the Hümmling had made their homes here; raised their families here; buried their dead here. Over the centuries, Germany's royalty had ridden here, the Hümmling being their favoured hunting ground. But now the people of the Hümmling were facing an invasion, and staring the seemingly impossible in the face – the defeat of Nazi Germany and the fall of Hitler's Reich.

At the wheel of his vehicle Bond had a German-Czech Jew, known to all as 'Trooper Mike Lewis'. That was his cover name, for if his real identity – Max Levinsohn – became known to the enemy, he didn't stand the slightest chance if captured. Levinsohn had escaped the Nazis and fled to Britain at the outbreak of war. His parents, Ludwig and Fanny, had died in the concentration camps, along with Levinsohn's sister. He had every reason to hunger to fight. In April 1944 he'd volunteered for the SAS, being rated as 'good, quiet but reliable' during parachute training. Two months later he'd married Lotte Jelinek, a Czech WAAF. He'd gone on to deploy into France, serving alongside Joe

Goldsmith on Operation Haggard, causing 'considerable damage to the retreating Germans'.

The third figure riding in Bond's jeep was Sergeant Joe Schofield, an experienced operator who'd left school at age fourteen, but at the onset of war was still too young to fight. Frustrated, as soon as he was old enough Schofield had volunteered for Special Service, joining No. 8 Commando, the same unit in which David Stirling had served. Long before signing up to the SAS, Schofield had been wounded in a 'short and bloody' action in North Africa, gone back to rescue a fallen comrade 'under continuous fire', before undertaking an undercover mission into neutral Turkey. On his first jump during SAS training, the parachutes of the three men ahead of him had 'roman candled'. The dispatcher had just managed to grab Schofield and stop him from leaping to his death. A born soldier, with hard, unyielding features, Schofield was a man who wouldn't back down from a fight. Serving as Bond's rear gunner, he had bags of experience.

Bond and his men were approaching the village of Lorup, some sixty kilometres into German territory, when they first hit trouble. They had just negotiated a crossroads, turning north towards the village, when they were targeted by a massive barrage of fire. From a cluster of farm buildings to left and right, a torrent of incoming rounds tore into Bond's jeep, plus the three others that formed the spearhead section, as they were hit by 'machineguns, panzerfausts, sniper rifles and small arms'. The *Panzerfaust* – 'armour fist' – was a single-shot man-portable anti-tank weapon, somewhat similar to a modern-day Rocket Propelled Grenade (RPG), and the first of its kind. Up ahead, dense woodland flanked the road, and beneath the shadowed boughs the air sparked with fire, as more and more enemy fighters joined in the turkey shoot.

Having blundered into a well-prepared ambush launched

from 'strongly held positions', the jeeps and their occupants were trapped on a narrow road, unable to retreat and assailed by the enemy on all sides. Turning their Vicker's-K guns and the big Brownings – which could punch bullets through walls – onto the enemy, Bond's men traded savage fire with fire. From some of the farm windows white sheets emerged, as a German family tried to surrender to the SAS column. But still the storm of deadly accurate rounds raked the vehicles. As Bond's jeep was assailed by *Panzerfaust* blasts, Sergeant Schofield found himself pierced by shrapnel in one leg, and 'pinned to the bodywork of the vehicle'. Dragging himself free in an effort to return fire, Schofield was hit in the other leg by what he presumed to be a sniper. By then his situation was desperate, as he was 'bleeding profusely' from his wounds.

The rear gunner of the third jeep in line was also hit. Only one option seemed open to the besieged men: taking cover in the deep ditch that flanked the left-hand side of the road. Grabbing their Tommy guns and M1 carbines, figures leapt from the vehicles, which were the proverbial bullet-magnets. Lieutenant Philip Schlee was one of Bond's deputies. The ditch in which he landed was deep and filled with water, but even there he found himself targeted by heavy machinegun fire. Schlee was in the most exposed stretch, at the very head of the stalled column, and where the most seriously wounded had been dragged into cover. They were trapped and going nowhere.

Sensing the desperation of the situation, Bond tried to edge forward. A short section of concrete drainpipe lay between his stretch of ditch and that to the front, sheltering Schlee and the worst of the wounded. It was too narrow to crawl through, so Bond tried to skirt around it. Right behind him was his driver, Levinsohn, determined to stay on his commander's shoulder. Bond paused at the pipe, and made a decision that while brave, would prove fatal. Momentarily, he popped up over the lip of the pipe, to try to get sight of the enemy's fire positions. Instantly, a German sniper round struck Bond in the head. As Levinsohn went to try to drag him back into cover, he too was hit. Both men had been shot in the forehead, and death was all but instant.

As *Panzerfaust* blasts hammered into the ditch where the wounded were trapped, word reached Schlee that Bond and Levinsohn were dead. They hugged the sodden depths of the gulley, heads well down, as the battle raged. Schlee ordered Corporal Edward Ralphs to crawl back, to get word to Mayne of what had transpired. A veteran of the SAS's Italy raiding operations, Ralphs' courageous work with a Bren at the siege of Termoli had saved many lives, for which he'd been awarded a Military Medal. With typical courage, he wormed his way back through the ditch under murderous fire, to deliver the message.

A radio report was dispatched to Mayne. He received the awful news in a silent, white-faced rage. As the official report on Operation Howard would put it, the 'situation became critical and immediately Col. Mayne personally directed operations'. In fact, he would do far more than simply 'direct operations' driven on by a cold fury.

With the column stalled, William 'Billy' Hull, Mayne's driver, had been busy brewing tea at the roadside, as David Danger, the signaller, manned the radio. In the short time they'd served together, Hull and Mayne had grown close and their friendship would endure long after the war. Hailing from Belfast's Donegal Road, Hull, twenty-two years old by then, was seven years Mayne's junior. He had lied about his age to join up, and while he'd heard all about the legendary exploits of the SAS commander, it wasn't until the spring of 1944 that he'd got to join the SAS and to serve alongside him.

Tall, muscled, with classic rugged Irish good looks, Hull, like

Mayne, was an accomplished boxer. In summer 1944 he'd been scheduled to deploy as part of Captain Garstin's ill-fated mission. At the eleventh hour Mayne had stood him down, instead dispatching Hull and one other deep into France, charged to blow up a train packed with German troops and war materiel. During that epic two-man assignment, Hull had more than proven his worth, at one stage resorting to eating his own carrier pigeon, so starving hungry was he. It had 'met its end gracefully', Hull reported, being roasted over an open fire.

Though hunted remorselessly by the enemy, the intrepid duo had made it to the tunnel where they intended to attack the train. Guarded by a sentry, it had fallen to Hull to silently dispatch him with his dagger. The train, once blown, was rendered into a 'terrible mess', Hull reported. It wasn't what they had expected at all. Rather than carrying soldiers to the front, it was laden with the enemy's wounded.

When Mayne had heard about Hull's pigeon-roasting story, he'd declared: 'So Hull's the man who eats pigeons.' In recent days, as they'd crossed Europe heading towards Germany, Mayne had asked: 'Eaten any pigeons lately, Hull?'

'Only when the army provides them, sir,' was Hull's reply.

It had become their catchphrase.

But now, upon learning of Bond's death, all such levity was gone.

In an instant Mayne grabbed Hull, as he prepared to move out. As Hull fully appreciated, the SAS commander was in one of his 'silent rages'. Compelled by a 'white hot fury' he was determined to wreak havoc on the enemy troops who had taken the life of his friend.

Kicking Danger out of the vehicle – they needed to move light and fast – Mayne told Hull to make like the devil for the front of the column. As Hull gunned the jeep and drove 'like mad' along the road, an ashen-faced Mayne just kept repeating, 'Poor Dick. Poor Dick.' They careered towards the heart of the action, Mayne knowing that he'd lost Major Fenwick in France, and now Major Bond, another of his senior commanders, in Germany. Bond and Mayne had become 'firm friends', yet Mayne had failed to protect him. And right now he had wounded men 'trapped, helpless, alongside their pinned down comrades'.

Reaching the crossroads, Mayne's jeep juddered to a halt. Though much was chaos and confusion, one man stepped forward to brief Mayne. Lieutenant John Scott revealed how Bond had been killed, and how Levinsohn, a small, slender fellow, had tried to slip past the same chokepoint, but still the sniper had got him. As Scott had been one of those urging Levinsohn on, he was consumed by guilt that by his own actions he'd caused the death of the twenty-three-year-old Operation Haggard veteran. 'He was a very brave man,' Scott reflected of Levinsohn, ruing that he had ordered him forward to his doom.

That past September, the then Sergeant Scott had been congratulated by Mayne on being awarded a Military Cross for a truly incredible series of escapes. Having broken out of a POW camp in Italy, Scott had ambushed a German convoy while en route back to Allied lines. He'd then volunteered to return to enemy territory, sailing for Termoli, with the aim of helping more Allied POWs escape. Inserting behind the lines, he'd linked up with a badly injured 'Captain Lee' – the French-American SAS supremo, Raymond Couraud, and the future Rommel assassin – helping him to safety.

A month after Scott was awarded the MC, Mayne had recommended him for an immediate commission 'for gallantry and ability as an officer'. Scott had joined 1 SAS as a lieutenant. Promoted from the ranks, driven, fearless but with a strong moral compass, Scott was Mayne's kind of an officer. A veteran of the Morvan operations, Scott was, as Mayne knew, 'most capable and conscientious', a man who 'takes great pains to ensure that any job he commences is properly finished'. He would certainly prove that today, and his account of Bond's death galvanised Mayne into action in no uncertain terms.

Moving off alone, Mayne flitted across to the nearest building, the house to the right of the crossroads from which the German family had appeared, bearing their white 'flags' of surrender. In short order, he established that the enemy had either been killed or cleared out of that building. As he hurried back to the jeeps, a plan of attack was coalescing in his mind. Grabbing his trusty Bren and a handful of spare magazines, Mayne outlined to Billy Hull exactly what he had in mind. As the din of battle rang out from up ahead, he needed Hull to head for that house, to provide covering fire from the top floor while Mayne himself edged forwards.

Together they doubled back to the building, whereupon Hull crept upstairs and readied himself at a window overlooking the enemy's positions set to the north. Meanwhile Mayne crept to the far corner of the house, Bren at the shoulder as he prepared for Hull's first salvo. From the upstairs window Hull broke cover and opened fire with his Tommy gun. Just as Mayne had hoped, Hull's very visible defiance drew the enemy out. Within seconds all hell had let loose, as Hull's room was filled with thick and choking smoke, incoming tracer fire ricocheting off the walls and ceiling.

Mayne spied a sniper taking aim at his friend. In that instant he emerged from cover and cut down the enemy marksman with a shot from his Bren, a highly-accurate weapon. Single-handedly, Mayne cleared the next building ahead of them – a large barn packed with the enemy – 'firing burst after burst from the shoulder, killing or wounding all', and even though he was 'in full view of the enemy and under heavy fire'. A further barn lay past it, and from there, and the woodland beyond, the enemy were still hammering in the fire. Eyeing the terrain, there was little Mayne could do from his present position, for the woods were simply too dense to winkle out the enemy. Likewise, trying to move past the woods was impossible due to the terrible nature of the surrounding terrain.

Only one option remained, as far as the SAS commander saw things.

It would have to be a do-or-die suicide-run, directly onto the enemy's guns.

Chapter Fifteen

MURDER RUN

Mayne signalled for a jeep to come forward, so it could cover the ground that he and Hull had just won. It was now that he 'decided to take a seemingly suicidal risk in a bid to save the trapped men', as one of the officers then present would describe it. Yelling out for Hull to remain in position, and to give further covering fire, Mayne went to mount up his own vehicle. For what he had in mind – a desperate rescue mission – he had need of a rear gunner, and he called for a volunteer.

'Who wants to have a go?' he demanded.

Several figures stepped forwards. Not surprisingly, it was Lieutenant Scott who Mayne selected to slip behind the twin Vickers-K guns in the jeep's rear. Scott had little idea what he had let himself in for, and even less exactly what Mayne had in mind. Only audacious action might save the day, that much was clear, and Scott didn't doubt that was what Mayne intended. As he would note of Mayne, there was 'a coldness' about the SAS commander when in the heat of action, a coldness that enabled him to 'sum things up quickly'.

Scott described what happened next. Completely disregarding his own safety, Mayne proceeded to drive north up the road, past the exact spot where Bond had been killed, issuing 'precise fire orders', and even as the enemy concentrated all their attentions on that lone jeep. With Mayne seemingly oblivious to the storm of incoming fire, Scott braced his legs in the vehicle's rear, and ramped the Vickers this way and that, pummelling the woodlands and lacing the shadows with long bursts of fiery tracer.

'The woods – fire at the woods,' Mayne kept urging, realising that was now the apex of the enemy resistance.

The jeep drew level with the ditch where Sergeant Joe Schofield and the other wounded were lying, 'still held down by enemy fire'. Mayne slowed, and yelling above the din of battle he cried out: 'I will pick you up on the way back!'

With that, he gunned the engine, and 'with his guns blazing at the positions in the woods . . . continued for a couple of hundred yards,' all the while getting raked by enemy fire. Somehow, miraculously, Scott, Mayne and the vehicle weathered that first hell-storm. Still under fierce attack, Mayne went to turn the jeep around. Meanwhile, from his position in the upstairs window of the house, Hull was trying to give them what support he could. Witnessing Mayne's suicide run, and believing that 'the guv'nor's copped it this time,' he sensed the precariousness of his own fate. The enemy poured incendiary rounds into the roof above him, setting it aflame. With one hand wielding his Tommy gun, Hull had to use the other to 'try to keep the sparks from going down his neck', as above him the roof crackled and burned.

With the jeep facing southwards, Mayne retraced their steps, all the while Scott 'with guns still blazing . . . killing or wounding many of the Germans who were defending the woods'. To the onlookers – the main body of the squadron – it appeared inconceivable that Mayne and Scott could brave such a suicide run twice, and emerge unscathed. 'There can be only one explanation why Colonel Mayne was not killed by what had already proven deadly and concentrated fire: the sheer audacity and daring he showed . . . momentarily bewildered the enemy,' as one observer put it. Even so, by the time Mayne and Scott had made it back to the main body of the men, the road was still awash with 'accurate fire'. It made it appear 'impossible to extricate the survivors', as Scott described it.

Seemingly unfazed, Mayne executed an about-turn, warning Scott they were going back in, and this time they *would* retrieve the wounded. One glance at Billy Hull's redoubt showed it to be etched with angry flame. If Hull had even survived, there was little hope of any covering fire from that direction. Arranging his men to give what cover they could, Mayne set forth once more, driving into the heart of the valley of death for a third time, and with Scott hunched over the guns. As Scott recalled it, the 'Germans must have been more surprised than us', as their vehicle roared north for yet another murder run. Reaching the abandoned jeeps, Mayne pulled to a halt and jumped out, making for the ditch.

Scott followed suit, before realising that covering fire was desperately needed. Mayne was already dragging the wounded out of the ditch, when Scott jumped onto the nearest vehicle and got its Vickers-Ks into action. Spying a German soldier with a terrible stomach wound, Scott cut him down with a burst of fire. He would later regret it, for the man no longer posed a threat, but his nerves had been 'frayed'. Braving the fire, Mayne 'lifted the wounded one by one into the jeep', before executing an about-turn and thundering back again to the main body of the squadron.

As the badly wounded Sergeant Schofield would later remark: 'Mayne . . . personally rescued me and others under fire.' Or as Sergeant Albert Youngman, another of the men trapped in that ditch, would comment: 'It was such a brazen thing to do . . . they were throwing everything back at him. God knows how they didn't hit him . . . Finest act of bravery I have ever seen in my life.' Or as Captain David Surrey-Dane, a veteran of Operation Bulbasket and another of Mayne's officers who had witnessed the rescue mission, would conclude: 'Mayne . . . dominated the scene . . . Many brave deeds are done in the heat of battle, but throughout this whole episode Colonel Mayne was cool and calculating.'

The last word on the incident should perhaps go to John Scott, who had shared those four suicide runs, in which 'Colonel Mayne, fully realising the risk' had continued to 'run the gauntlet'. Regardless of Mayne's unsurpassed bravery – plus that of Hull and Scott – Major Bond was dead, as was Levinsohn, and there were several injured. Retrieving the bodies – the enemy resistance had by now been well and truly broken – the column pulled back a mile or so, and there they paused to bury the fallen at the roadside. Sergeant Schofield, the most seriously wounded, was evacuated to hospital.

Later, both Hull and Scott would ask Mayne just what had gone through his mind that fateful day. To Hull, Mayne argued that he'd made the 'right calculation at the right time'. Scott asked what he'd thought their chances were of survival. After a brief pause, Mayne had replied that they'd been about fifty-fifty. 'People think I'm a big mad Irishman, but I'm not. I calculate the risks for and against, then have a go.'

As Youngman put it, while the SAS commander could be wild when on the drink, when on operations he 'had only two things on his mind: the job we had to do and the safety and welfare of his men . . . He was terrific, because A. you knew he'd never tell you to do anything he couldn't do himself; B. he always led from the front; and C. he'd never leave anyone behind. He was really special. A born warrior.'

After Bond's death, some were deeply unsettled. They blamed him for his own demise. Or, as one of the unit's most experienced

NCOs, Bob Lowson, recalled, Bond had hit trouble because 'he didn't realise if you hit the bloody ditch and stay there you're done for. You've got to get your weapons into action. You had to seize the initiative.' Whatever the truth of it, Bond was gone and Mayne needed to galvanise Paddy Force back into action, knowing they would face more of the same.

As the men paused to reflect, standing beside those two hastily dug graves, few doubted this was a dark moment in their fortunes. On their first day thrusting into the Fatherland, they'd lost a senior commander of Bond's stature, plus a popular and capable trooper, with more wounded. It was now that Mayne's special magic really came into play. Somehow, he had this unique ability to imbue confidence even in the intense heat of bloody combat. His ability to convince those trapped in the tightest spots that 'all would be well' was second to none. As his men averred, regardless of how bad things looked, 'once Paddy appeared it was *magic*.'

When Mayne had burst into action to save the men trapped in that ditch, for many of the newer recruits it had been a total revelation. To David Surrey-Dane it constituted a 'wonderful demonstration' of exactly how the SAS should behave when in a desperate spot. Or as Alec 'Boy' Borrie would express it, when facing 'a spot of bother' as they just had, Mayne would only have to 'turn up and you'd think: "It's alright now because he's here and we'll be okay."' Mayne was 'an officer we would follow one hundred per cent. No doubt about that. One hundred per cent.'

As the official report on Operation Howard concluded, enemy resistance was far stiffer than anyone had feared. Worryingly, there were also 'no apparent signs of the Canadian armour following closely on the heels of the SAS', as they had expected. Regardless, the column formed up again and moved off, heading back through the scene of the epic battle just gone and into the village beyond. There, every house seemed to have white sheets hung from its windows. Following a short, sharp battle in a further village, Mayne's raiders found themselves taking the surrender of enemy fighters in their droves. But with the boggy terrain restricting the jeeps to the highways, this made for perfect ambush territory. It was all too easy for the 'fanatical Hitler Youth to conceal in copses and ditches to cause us trouble', as Roy Close noted.

Mayne split the column, in an effort to divide the enemy's attentions. The jeeps pressed ahead. 'It was progress, but slow progress.' And while they could hear the sound of fighting echoing from far behind, still there was no sign of the big Canadian Shermans. Roy Close's patrol took point, as they headed for a straight, open stretch of highway. All of a sudden, a group of Hitler Youth erupted from a ditch in screaming defiance, unleashing *Panzerfäuste* at close range. Massively outgunned, within moments two or three of them lay dead, while others had fled. One, limping, tried to surrender. Hands raised, he had a wound in his lower back and was unable to walk far.

Already, Paddy Force was burdened with more POWs than they could easily manage. They'd taken to disarming the enemy and sending them on foot towards the Canadian lines. But this young lad was unable to go anywhere under his own steam. A farmer's cottage lay near by. Close and his men took the wounded boy to it. Two middle-aged women were there. The lad showed them his injuries, while jabbering away in German. All of a sudden, in halting English, the younger of the two women began to berate Close and his men for being 'cowards' and for shooting a young boy in the back. As Close tried to explain the truth of the matter, the older woman grabbed a saucepan and began wielding it about, at which point Close and his men left them to it.

War with hate was really coming home.

A warplane swooped from the skies. It was friendly – American – but still the jeep convoy halted and laid out their distinctive recognition flags on the ground. Better to be safe than sorry. The fighter aircraft buzzed the convoy, then came around for what all presumed was a closer look. Instead, its wing-mounted cannons blazed fire. Fortunately, the pilot missed. But as he rolled in for a second strafing run, 'we opened up with 40 Vickers-K guns, and he went off trailing black smoke,' as Alec Borrie noted. Even their friends couldn't be trusted, when pushing this deep into the enemy's heartland. Even their allies seemed to be the enemy.

They drew into a laager – a defensive circle, formed by the jeeps – in a dense patch of woodland. There they would lie up for the night, surrounded as they were by hostile forces and with hostile locals on all sides. Still there was no sign of the Canadian armour, apart from the distant sound of the guns.

By the afternoon of 11 April – their third day in Germany – Paddy Force was advancing on the town of Friesoythe. It lay just twenty-five kilometres north-east of Lorup, reflecting how painfully slow their progress was proving. Crawling across a patch of flooded woodland, they came to the outskirts of the town, hemmed in on a narrow road. Perfect ambush territory. Out of nowhere, mortar bombs began to rain down on the lead vehicles. While some managed to swing the jeeps around and withdraw, two were hit, the occupants diving into flooded ditches by the roadside.

Tony Marsh was one of those who ended up soaking wet, hunkered down and sheltering from the fire. Derrick 'Happy' Harrison's patrol tried to race to their aid, advancing from a different direction. Attacking from the flank, and within easy sight of the town, Harrison and Close's men began to lay down a barrage of supporting fire. Their column of jeeps was perched on a raised roadway with zero room for manoeuvre. Unbeknown to them, they faced no *Volkssturm* or Hitler Youth unit here at Friesoythe. Up ahead were the battle-hardened troops of the 7th German Parachute Division.

A squad of SAS dismounted, as mortar rounds started to hammer into Harrison and Close's jeeps. Undeterred, Lieutenant Gordon Davidson led his seven-man patrol on foot, threading a path through the marshy fields to try to get behind the enemy positions. They'd not gone far when a German motorised column roared to a halt, not a hundred yards away. As Davidson and his men went to ground, so the enemy paratroopers disgorged from their transports. Shortly, the SAS patrol found itself surrounded. Davidson was trapped in a ditch, with only a 'Schmeisser before and behind me'. His entire patrol was taken captive.

The eight men were forced to perch atop an ammunition truck, as the German column began to withdraw. They had been put there as human shields, to deter the SAS from launching an attack. Suddenly, a jeep emerged from the woods with the familiar figure of Mayne behind the Vickers-K guns. 'That's Paddy, and we're in the shit,' one of the captives thought. Sure enough Mayne opened fire. To their immense relief he missed the ammo truck. They emerged from the fracas alive, but still as prisoners of the enemy.

Friesoythe had proved a costly battle for Paddy Force. They'd lost six jeeps, and eight men had been captured. As Borrie would remark, grimly, they were 'suffering casualties, so replacing jeeps was not so much of a problem'. They simply took over the vehicles of the dead and of those who had been captured. Borrie and his comrades ended up with a jeep mounted with a .50 calibre Browning, 'a brute of a weapon that could penetrate brick walls and kill anyone hiding inside.' Shortly after the battle of

Friesoythe, they were cooking breakfast by the roadside, when a shot from a nearby house 'hit the frying pan and sent it flying'. Enraged, Borrie and his cohorts 'put a burst from the Browning into the front of the house', after which 'we cooked some more food and ate in peace.' They were 'more annoyed' at having their 'breakfast ruined than being shot at'.

As all appreciated, the outcome of the battle for Friesoythe could have been far worse. With scores of jeeps pinned down under heavy mortar and machinegun fire, in truth they'd got off very lightly. Which was more than could be said for Lieutenant Davidson and his seven men. Ominously, the eight SAS captives had been driven to a nearby SS base. Taken to a farmhouse, the interrogations began, as a 'mini-Himmler' fired questions at Davidson and his fellows. 'Small . . . sallow faced, with sharp malevolent eyes lurking behind rimless steel frames, he exuded menace.'

After being beaten, the captives were thrown into a pigsty for the night. There, the 'mini-Himmler' informed them they were to be shot come morning. Overnight, their SS captors were ordered to move west, to plug a gap in the German lines. The SAS captives were handed over to the *Volkssturm*, who clearly hadn't been briefed about the dawn executions. According to one of the captives, Corporal Peter Payne, their lives were saved by 'a good German'. A senior paratroop officer had intervened. He'd found a pair of Afrika Korps binoculars in one of their captured jeeps, and he told the captives he knew exactly which unit they hailed from. In the spirit of the brotherhood of airborne warriors, he was determined that they would not be murdered.

Instead, the *Volkssturm* were ordered to march the prisoners east, as they kept pace with their bicycles and stood guard. At villages along the way Lieutenant Davidson and his men were beaten, insulted and spat at, as furious inhabitants vented their spleen on those who had dared to invade Hitler's Reich. Those eight captives were living within the war with hate now, their lives hanging by a delicate thread.

A message winged its way to London, addressed to 'Mrs Payne, 16 Kenauld Cottages, Currie, Mid-Lothian', alerting her to the fact that her husband had been 'posted as "Missing" . . . in Western Europe on 11th April 1945 . . . The report that he is missing does not necessarily mean that he has been killed . . .' Corporal Payne was a veteran of Mayne's Italy operations. During the battle for Termoli his patrol had been surrounded and most had been captured or killed, but not Payne. He'd managed to crawl into a patch of thick scrub. He'd stayed there, lying 'doggo' for hours, even as the enemy yelled out warnings and sprayed the bushes with fire. Payne had remained hidden and got away. In fact, he was a serial escapee . . . and not always from the enemy.

After a difficult childhood he'd signed up at sixteen, being sent to Dorset for training with the Royal Artillery, at Bovington Camp. Bored, he'd 'borrowed' an officer's car, gone AWOL, was eventually caught, absconded from custody, was tracked down in London, arrested again, and finally sentenced to six months in prison 'without hard labour'. Discharged from the military 'with ignominy', he'd re-enlisted, having listened to Churchill's 'we shall fight them on the beaches' speech to the nation. 'In the circumstances the Army were prepared to have him back!'

Volunteering for special service, Payne had joined No. 11 Commando, and began jumping off Scottish piers at night and in full kit, as part of the rigorous training process. Unable to kick the AWOL habit completely, 'and getting into bother for it', he'd absconded numerous further times, mostly to visit his sweetheart, whom he'd eventually married. Now, in April 1945, as the *Volkssturm* and the German villagers hounded Payne and his fellow captives eastwards, escape was once again foremost on his mind.

The grinding advance of Paddy Force took its toll on both men and machines. Another message winged its way to London. 'Send me elephants.' 'Elephants' was code for jeeps. 'Salvaged armour from brewed up jeeps cannot be used again as not bullet proof.' The response from headquarters was less than encouraging: 'Regret elephants with SAS modifications in short supply.' The SAS raiders would have to make do and mend with whatever vehicles they could patch up, or with any they might beg, borrow or steal.

Hull and Mayne came across a large German farmhouse. There was an affluent, privileged feel to the place. The family who lived there had servants, and evidently had been among the favoured of the Reich. While Mayne questioned them intensively, he ordered Hull to search the outbuildings. Having bagged a few chickens for the journey, one bird darted away and disappeared into a large haystack. Hull went after it, for the vanishing trick just didn't make sense. Hidden beneath the screen of hay he discovered a vehicle propped up on bricks.

The hay was removed to reveal a large, well-maintained Mercedes saloon car, with curving, graceful lines. It was maroon, and shone with a luxurious gloss once the last of the hay had been dusted off. Back inside the house, Hull informed Mayne. The family tried to claim they had hidden the vehicle to stop the German military from commandeering it as a staff car. Having discovered where the wheels were, Mayne ordered Hull to get the vehicle going, for they were in need of the extra carriage. Sending for Lieutenant Bill Deakins, Mayne led him to the barn, to reveal, magician-like, the 'marvellous maroon Mercedes car'.

As it was now in his service, Mayne explained that he wanted an SAS winged dagger etched onto each wing.

'I was no sign writer, but who was I to argue,' Deakins mused. He pointed out that he had no paint or brushes, but that was no excuse as far as Mayne was concerned. Deakins had served in the Royal Engineers, and as everyone knew, a Royal Engineer could 'do just everything'. Deakins went and sought out the woman of the house. With a piece of chalk, he sketched a design on the vehicle, and by gestures explained what he needed. 'I had no German and the woman no English.' Understanding finally dawning, she retrieved 'various odds and ends of paint, but no brushes'. Deakins finally cobbled together a brush of sorts, using tiny filaments of wood, 'tying up the ends with cotton carried in my sewing kit'. The final paint job on the Mercedes just about passed muster.

As the fight for Germany became ever more bitter and bloody, the SAS found itself facing the Nazi diehards and those most easily brainwashed. But children were still children, despite being *Hitlerjugend*, and the horror of shooting kids hit hard. Here and there bodies had been hung from trees. Reg Seekings – long recovered from being shot in the neck in the Morvan – came across a group of elderly men and women strung up and left where they were hanging. Why or by whom was unfathomable.

Mired in the guts of this war with hate, Mayne's men needed his guidance, especially the newer recruits. One of those was Lieutenant John Randall. With an opera singer mother and with his father being a coffee farmer in Kenya, Randall had enjoyed a privileged, international upbringing, full of wanderlust. When sent to a British boarding school he'd hated it, proving to be something of an academic lightweight, yet a sports heavyweight, excelling at boxing, rugby and football. Volunteering for the military, he'd joined the Royal Artillery and had met Winston

Churchill when still only nineteen years old. He moved in those kinds of circles.

In March 1944 Randall had been seconded to 1 SAS from the Phantoms, more formally known as GHQ Liaison Regiment, a specialist communications and reconnaissance outfit. Arriving at Darvel around the same time as Padre McLuskey, he'd come to appreciate the quiet, firm command of Mayne. 'He expected people to work hard at being good soldiers and expected them to behave like gentlemen because he was one himself . . . With a leader like that you had the basis for a fantastic regiment and that's what we were.'

Randall had discovered a young German soldier hiding in a dugout. The bodies of the dead were scattered everywhere and the place was 'like a wasteland', he recalled. They brought the captive before Mayne, assuming he was the 'only German left alive' in the area. The prisoner seemed terrified, as they walked him closer to the SAS commander's jeep. They asked Mayne what they should do with him. Momentarily, his hand went to his Colt .45, before he reholstered it. He glanced around at the scene of carnage, before telling Randall that the German should be made to bury his dead comrades.

A short while later Seekings was edging through some woodland, when he felt the uncanny sensation that he was being watched. Moments later, a young lad of around fourteen emerged from the undergrowth, with a long-handled 'potato masher' stick grenade clutched in each hand. Seekings had his weapon trained on the youngster, as the boy fingered his grenades. Time seemed to freeze, the old soldier and the boy staring at each other in knife-edge silence. Finally, the youngster lowered his grenades. Later, Seekings learned that he'd been under close observation by a group of German paratroopers. If he'd shot the boy, they would have gunned him down.

As Johnny Cooper recalled, 'some of the poor little blighters were only 13 or 14 years old. They were crawling out of holes everywhere. The Germans put schoolboys in uniforms and forced them to fight.' Often, those adolescent recruits displayed a blind arrogance and haughtiness that had largely been eliminated from the regular German soldiery as they faced a crushing defeat. Recently, Alex Muirhead – Bertie Wooster – and his patrol had surrounded two score of Germans stationed on a ridge. Forcing their surrender, they turned out to be young cadets attached to an SS unit. Some had been injured, and Muirhead's men gave 'each a shot of morphine' to dull the pain.

Armed with 'three Spandaus on bicycles, three Schmeissers, fifteen Panzerfaust, ten rifles and three pistols', they seemed extremely arrogant, even though they had been on the losing end of the battle. As an SAS Operational Report recorded of the incident, 'they were very cheeky – one asked us to light his cigarette, another for chocolate and another for a comb. He had his hair parted with a .45.' The report remained unclear as to whether the bullet had been fired just over the young man's head or he had been shot dead.

Tempers were fraying. Again and again, the SAS received warnings of German troops – especially the SS – dressing in 'British and French uniforms'. At one point they searched a former SS headquarters located in a farmhouse. There they found items of British uniform, including 'new issue' shirts and leather jerkins. Increasingly, it was proving difficult sorting friend from foe. But Mayne had his objective – Oldenburg – and the grinding advance had to continue.

Fuelled by brew stops along the way, the drive east was bloody and relentless. Snipers seemed everywhere, perched on vantage points in the thick woodland. At one point Sergeant Bob

Lilley – still on operations, despite his wife Evelyn's worries of his 'nerves going' – dispatched three men to search for a missing SAS trooper. Nosing down a forest track, their jeep was spotted by an enemy sniper. Within seconds one man had been shot in the head and killed outright, a second in the thigh and a third in the leg. Forced to leap clear of the jeep, the two injured men went to ground and had to be rescued by their comrades.

On the long road to the city of Oldenburg, Mayne split his force into ever smaller patrols, to try to counter the ambush threat. During a rest break, Hull was brewing up a billycan of tea when all of a sudden Mayne appeared.

'Hurry up, boys!' he announced. 'Get into the jeep. We have work to do.'

Anxious to get under way, Mayne slid himself behind the wheel, while Hull and one other manned the guns. At breakneck speed they roared down the main road, before Mayne turned off onto a narrow lane lined with trees. In the distance lay a patch of woodland, beyond which was a major highway. Without a word of explanation, Mayne got Hull to train his weapons on the road.

'Hold your fire,' he hissed, 'until I open up.'

A convoy of German halftracks hove into view, each packed with around a dozen German troops. Mayne let the leading vehicle trundle past before opening fire, with Hull and their other companion following suit. Within seconds the convoy had been raked with armour-piercing and incendiary bullets, the hidden jeep letting rip. As screams rose from the besieged convoy, first one vehicle and then more blazed into flame. With the dead scattered around the burning pyres, Mayne tried to radio for reinforcements, but there was no joy. As the enemy gathered for a counter-attack, the only option was to execute a crazed drive back the way they had come.

For fifty yards Mayne gunned the jeep in reverse, before he

finally found a patch of wider road where he could turn around, although it proved a tricky manoeuvre, for the enemy continued to unleash wild bursts of fire. Having pushed some eighty kilometres into Germany by now, they were still around fifty klicks short of their objective, Oldenburg. Supplies of all kinds were running short. In a sense, Paddy Force were the victims of their own sheer grit and audacious determination. Having thrust this far into the Fatherland, they'd amassed some 300 POWs. Food, petrol and ammunition were running low, and while they'd tried to set up a series of DZs as they advanced, the drops kept getting delayed.

That mass of POWs was becoming a burden. Captain Roy Close had only recently survived a sniper bullet colliding with 'the semi-circle of bullet proof glass' in front of his face – his jeep's windscreen. He was also painfully aware that those 300 POWs 'outnumbered' the SAS party, their captors. Being dragged along in Paddy Force's wake, as the SAS fought, killed or captured yet more of their comrades, wasn't their idea of fun. But Mayne figured they needed to keep a good number of the prisoners as an 'insurance policy'. He selected the 'best-looking' ninety, sending the rest on foot plodding back towards the Canadians somewhere to their rear.

They passed Cloppenburg, forty kilometres short of their objective, and made for a wide patch of woodland to hole up for the night hours. Unbeknown to Mayne and his men, the enemy had realised by now that this jeep convoy didn't constitute the Allied frontline forces. Instead, it was a distinct, isolated group of raiders set well to its vanguard, with no tanks or heavy weapons in support. As the enemy knew full well, the SAS in their 'little mechanised mess tins' were outnumbered and outgunned. They were ripe for being surrounded and captured, or better still wiped out.

In that forest on the outskirts of Cloppenburg, the German forces set their trap.

Chapter Sixteen
MECHANISED MESS TINS

That night, the SAS formed their laager – jeeps as the cordon, sheltered beneath the trees, sentries on guard on the perimeter, with the ninety-odd POWs huddled in the centre. While the closely packed pine forest provided great cover, it hampered the ability to see and to engage with the enemy, plus the escape routes out of there were limited. As the darkness thickened, their position received sporadic machinegun bursts and sniper shots. At first, no one was overly worried. This felt like harassing fire, designed mostly to deprive the men of sleep and to add to their growing burden of exhaustion.

The prisoners seemed more concerned than anyone. Eventually, a spokesperson came and found Mayne, demanding proper 'protection under the Geneva Convention'. After all the SAS commander had seen, and witnessed and knew, the request provoked 'a short but explicit reply from Paddy'. As the fire intensified, Mayne sent out the odd probing patrol, with the aim of discovering the enemy's positions and strengths. One such two-man party headed back to the laager, but sadly lost their way. With all the pine forest looking pretty much alike, they'd returned by a mistaken route. Even though they'd been issued with passwords, they were fired upon by their own side. One of the two, Captain Tim Iredale, was severely wounded in the thigh.

Despite every precaution, suffering casualties to 'friendly fire' was one of the harsh realities of war, especially when operating behind the lines. Iredale's leg injury was serious and there was no way he could be treated in that SAS encampment. As Mayne quickly realised, it was a case of keep him there and he would die, or hand him over to the uncertain mercies of the enemy. An officer volunteered to drive the wounded man to the nearest enemy positions, in a jeep bearing a white flag. It was now that Mayne's insurance policy came into play. A German prisoner was obliged to accompany them, with instructions for the German commander: if Iredale wasn't properly cared for, 'eighty-nine German prisoners' would pay the price. The POW was given an added warning: he was not to divulge the position of the SAS laager.

Just as the jeep had departed with the wounded man, 'the white flag flying', Roy Close came in with his patrol. He'd been out probing the enemy's positions, and had reached the dire conclusion that there was no way to 'penetrate the encirclement'. There were tanks and 88mm Flak anti-tank guns out there, meaning the SAS was surrounded and massively outgunned. As Close delivered the news, so the jeep bearing the white flag returned. While Iredale had been handed over to a seemingly sympathetic enemy commander, there was every sign that the German POW had given their position away. He'd been spied consulting a map, and he seemed to be indicating their exact whereabouts. It was then that Mayne made one of those life-saving decisions, 'a fine example of his quick, tactical brain'.

The SAS commander mounted his jeep and ordered all to do the same, while grabbing as many POWs as they could carry. As the long column of vehicles snaked out of the laager, Close found he was the last in line. They'd made maybe a hundred yards, when the first of the mortar rounds landed exactly where they had been parked up, with heavy shelling soon following. 'Again, Paddy's quick thinking saved lives.' Even so, the situation was desperate. Petrol was low, 'many of the jeeps had been hit and were on tow', and the forest was cloaked in darkness.

Pushing deeper into the woods, Mayne chose a spot for a second laager, and the POWs were herded into the centre once more, under Bren gun cover. Now to spend 'an uneasy night waiting for the dawn'. All through the dark hours the forest resounded to the 'thunder of guns and the whine and crash' of artillery and tanks shells. The enemy were pounding the forest with fire, before sending in their troops. 'How long before they found us?' wondered Derrick Harrison.

As first light filtered through the trees, Mayne sent out a patrol to try to make contact with the Canadians. Shortly after they had gone, a round snarled in and pinged off a mess tin. The shot had the distinctive sharp crack of a sniper's rifle. As figures dived for cover, the by now all-too-familiar game began of searching the wall of trees for signs of the hidden gunman, as he continued to unleash carefully aimed shots. Bullets thumped into the far side of the tree trunks behind which Mayne and his men had taken cover.

After a while, the SAS commander seemed to have had quite enough. By now they'd realised that jeeps were practically useless against a lone sniper hidden in a forest. Silently, and without a word to his men, Mayne drew his Colt and slipped away, weaving this way and that, as he darted from tree to tree. Mayne was stalking the sniper, and shortly he disappeared from view completely. A series of shots rang out through the trees. Then silence. A while later Mayne was back, again without a word to his men. But the sniper fire had ended, that much was for sure. Mayne's actions had resembled a 'shootout in a Western', as one of his officers would observe of the incident.

The sniper was gone, but the enemy had located the SAS laager. A cry of alarm went up from a perimeter sentry, followed by bursts of fire, as rounds 'whipped through the trees and whined angrily across the clearing'. The attack was coming from a side of the woods where Peter Davis – he who'd masqueraded as a colonel to take the surrender of 18,000 German troops in the Yonne – was positioned. Immediately, Davis's jeep-mounted machineguns spat fire, 'blazing away into the woods at the unseen enemy'. On the opposite side of the laager, Derrick Harrison and others were unable to fire from their vehicles for fear of hitting their own side.

A group of figures dismounted and with Brens levelled at the hip advanced into the woods, guns spitting defiance. With them went Paddy Mayne. But the enemy lay thick among the trees and in good cover. Knowing the location of the SAS encampment, they had every advantage. Step by step the Bren gunners were driven backwards. Alec Borrie, in the thick of the firefight, sensed how dire things were getting. 'We were trapped. Things began to get a bit naughty and we lost quite a few.' As bursts of fire and grenade blasts echoed through the trees, Mayne's men were taking casualties from ricochets and flying shrapnel.

With the knowledge of Hitler's Commando Order, there could be no thought of surrender or capitulation. This was a do-or-die last stand. The German POWs were caught in the open and in the midst of the hell-storm. The senior German officer came to speak with Mayne. Might they be permitted to withdraw to the low ground behind the laager, and to take cover there, he asked. On his assurance that none would try to escape, Mayne gave permission that they could do so.

Worming their way backwards, on hands and knees the POWs began to dig shallow shell scrapes and foxholes. With that modicum of cover, they settled down to ride out the storm, as burning lances of tracer laced a latticework through the dawn shadows. One POW grabbed a book to read. Momentarily, he glanced upwards, before yelling out a warning. On Harrison's right flank a shadowy armoured behemoth was crashing through undergrowth. As it crept through the trees, its long snout of a muzzle vomited massive gouts of orange fire.

They had a flame-thrower incoming.

Inching slowly up the track towards the SAS laager, that fire-spurting tank was the real threat now. Fortunately, Mayne had positioned an anti-armour team concealed in the brush, just in case of such an eventuality. When the fire-breathing monster drew within range, there was a gout of flame and smoke as a US-made bazooka wielded by Mayne's raiders let rip. The round flew true, blowing 'one of the tracks off the tank which spun sideways, revealing . . . Canadian Army markings. Luckily, the crew of the tank were not hurt, only their tempers,' as Alec Borrie noted.

The enemy fire petered out. The cavalry had arrived just in the nick of time. With the tank had come Canadian infantry carriers, while out in the open, a squadron of Shermans advanced in line abreast, driving the enemy backwards. Mayne took this opportunity to hand the German POWs into the Canadian's care. Then he formed up a ragged line of battle-worn jeeps, many of which were out of service and on tow. With 'casualties in men' as well as vehicles, Paddy Force set off back the way they had come – for without a resupply, refit and replacement of vehicles, they were spent as an effective fighting force.

As Canadian Major-General G. Volkes, their senior commander on the road to Oldenburg, would write of Mayne's exploits: 'I learned then that his force had had some severe fighting, were out of ammo and food and at one time had over 400 prisoners of assorted shapes and sizes. They had disarmed the lot and held about 100 of the toughest type, mostly paratroops, and had chased the others back in the general direction of our advance. This had been slowed somewhat by determined enemy resistance . . .'

Pulling back to positions near Meppen – their starting point – Paddy Force paused for a brief rest and refit, and to offload the wounded. There they would learn that Captain Iredale, the most serious of their injured, had lived. Taken to the headquarters of the German forces then besieging the SAS laager, Iredale had had his leg amputated on a school desk, in an effort to save his life. After the operation, the stump had been bound up with the only 'bandages' that came to hand – fresh loo paper. From there, he was taken to a German military hospital and he would survive the war.

Short of able-bodied fighters, Mayne was understandably reluctant to lose anyone. A blistering message came through from headquarters, from a Major Esmond Baring. Two Royal Electrical and Mechanical Engineers (REME) specialists had been attached to Mayne's unit, but Baring claimed that this was 'against direct, direct orders. Return both at once . . .' Those REME types were providing crucial vehicle maintenance support, plus they were a vital link in the SAS's long and difficult supply chain. As he'd done with McLeod, Mayne deflected Baring's ire first by silence, and then by clever prevarication. The two men were 'volunteers', Mayne replied, and thus he was keeping them on a fourteen-day 'approbation' – basically, a trial period to see how they fared.

Baring fired back a spiky riposte: those REME chaps weren't free to volunteer, as they had only been lent to Paddy Force to ready their jeeps. 'High powered rockets already plentiful,' Baring added. In other words, he was causing Mayne trouble at the top. 'They must return earliest.' Mayne sent a reply that was a masterpiece in turning the army's own rules against the worst of their chairborne bureaucrats. It also revealed the canny lawyer that lurked within the buccaneering raider-commander, for Mayne, who'd taken law at university, had been working as a solicitor before the war. If Baring had read the relevant Army Council Instruction (ACI), he'd realise that 'men cannot be prevented from volunteering and joining us,' he argued.

Still Baring steamed and fumed: 'Not REME such as these,' he shot back, demanding again the men be returned. Unperturbed, Mayne would retain those two highly valued volunteers for several weeks more, until the fighting was basically over.

Rearmed and resupplied, Paddy Force got back on the road, returning to the fight. Motoring past Oldenburg, which had been taken by the Canadians, they spurred towards the vanguard. But still they were 'losing jeeps and men more often than in France', as the enemy fought with a fanaticism that belied the hopelessness of their cause. At the town of Celle, which lies a good way east of Oldenburg, the real darkness was about to descend. Due to the terrain and a series of partially blown bridges, only the SAS with their jeeps could make it through Celle's quaint-seeming narrow streets, lined with the timber-framed houses that made up this ancient settlement.

Lying on the banks of the Aller, itself a tributary of the Weser, Celle was a key hub in this part of the country, yet it had remained remarkably untouched by Allied bombing attacks. On 8 April an air raid had hit the town, but only a fraction – some 2.2 per cent – of the place had been destroyed. By a dark twist of fate, some of the bombs had fallen upon a train crammed with some four thousand concentration camp inmates, which was steaming away from the Allied advance. Hundreds had been killed, but many more had escaped. That had in turn spawned the *Celler Hasenjagd* – the 'Celle hare hunt' – in which the townsfolk had combined with the SS to hunt down the escapees in the thick woodlands that lay thereabouts.

To the south of Paddy Force, a second SAS contingent had also been in the thick of the action, pushing into Germany, forming a joint spearhead. Codenamed Operation Archway, it was led by Lieutenant-Colonel Brian Morton Franks, an officer of long experience who'd taken over command of 2 SAS when Bill Stirling had resigned, with SAS stalwart Major Harry Poat serving as his second-in-command. As with Mayne's raiders, they had suffered high casualties during bitter and bloody fighting. As the jeep-borne raiders pushed some 300 kilometres from the German border into the heart of the Reich, individual squadrons were split into smaller and smaller patrols, the better to fox the enemy.

All would be drawn to Celle, as the very worst of Nazi Germany's horror revealed itself. The city was teeming with 'sinister persons', as an SAS message dispatched to headquarters warned. Amid the odd short skirmish and firefight, the men busied themselves rounding up the 'leading Nazi party and SS officials', plus 'the Kripo, as well as certain prominent Nazis'. Kripo was short for the *Kriminalpolizei*, Nazi Germany's criminal investigations division, which worked closely with the Gestapo. Scores of Allied POWs were also freed, including American servicemen who'd been held captive in and around the town.

It was in Celle that Captain Joe Patterson, an SAS medic and a veteran of Dunkirk, was approached by a concerned citizen. Patterson spoke decent German, and the local explained there were some patients in need of urgent medical attention. They were being held in a *Konzentrationslager* – a concentration camp. To Patterson, as to all then present, those words had no special significance. Not yet, anyway.

Patterson was well aware of the extent of extremism still gripping Germany, and of the degree to which the German people had been brainwashed by Nazism. A few days earlier a young boy, 'a nipper of 3', had given Patterson the Nazi salute, and with a yell of '"Heil Hitler" ran off as fast as his legs would carry him.' The German populace had been warned that the British would 'carry away their women to slavery in England'. As the SAS had discovered, the roads were clogged with escaped 'slaves . . . there are more slaves than Germans, all nationalities, but mostly Poles and Russians, with some French and Dutch'. They'd been brought to Germany as captives and forced to work on farms and in factories.

Unsurprisingly perhaps, the warnings of the British being poised to do the same thing had struck home with the German people. At one stage Patterson had been asked by a distraught female when they would be 'deported to work in England'. She wanted to know when they would have to start to learn English, and if the 'British Secret Service was the same as the Gestapo'. None could believe that in Britain you could speak freely, and they were 'amazed to hear that anyone who wanted to criticise the government could do so'. The extent of Nazi propaganda and indoctrination was shocking.

But still Patterson could never have conceived of the depths of the depravity and horror that Nazism had spawned, here in Celle. He was guided to an enclosure, where a barrier of matting attached to a perimeter fence prevented him from seeing inside. A German soldier was standing guard. Patterson ordered him to open up, which he did 'pretty smartly'. As he stepped through Patterson all-but gagged. Already 'the stench was overpowering'. Three days earlier, a salvo of mortars had fallen all around him, one landing on a roof a few feet away. It had detonated as it hit the tiles, fragments of which were blasted out in a cone of death. Miraculously, the explosion had left Patterson, at ground level, shaken but unscathed.

Yet the shock of all that paled into insignificance beside his Celle discovery. Lying before Patterson was a first hut, and inside that was a scattering of filthy straw, and in among that, 'half buried in the manure', Patterson discovered scores of 'creatures with life in them, not much, but a little. The staring eyes gleaming out of the slate skeletons . . . made an impression it is impossible to describe . . . We were absolutely horrified . . . It was difficult to imagine that these had once been men.'

As Patterson discovered, these were the survivors of the *Celler Hasenjagd* – the 'Celle hare hunt'. Several thousand prisoners had been loaded onto that train, and told they were to be 'taken away to be gassed and shot'. These were the few score that had survived. Having triaged the worst of the wounded and the dying, Patterson loaded the most desperate cases aboard an ambulance, and rushed them to the Celle hospital. 'I was so raging I brought out the first doctors I could find . . . more or less by brute force, and stormed and raged at them in French, German and English.' Patterson ordered the medical staff to make ready for an influx of cases, and he warned they were to be treated as well as any German patient, or else. By his eloquence and his righteous rage, he reduced many of the medics to tears.

As there were too many sick and wounded for the ambulance to ferry across, Patterson organised stretcher-bearer parties made up of local Celle citizens, 'including some parsons. We made them go into the stinking cabins and bring out the prisoners. Some of them were genuinely horrified at what they saw . . .' At one stage Patterson was informed about the German 'Kapos' – criminal types, whose role it was to 'spy on and beat up the prisoners'. The more able bodied inmates rounded up the Kapos, and begged that Patterson shoot them. The French inmates pleaded with him to 'grant them this one small favour', and to let them watch.

At first Patterson demurred. Then a massive, lumbering

figure appeared and the inmates yelled out that he was the worst Kapo of all. Seeming oblivious and arrogant all at once, the Kapo demanded: *'Keine Deutschen hier?'* Are there no Germans here? Noting how 'well-fed' he seemed, something in Patterson just seemed to crack. *'No! Kein Deutschen hier,'* he snarled. Moments later Patterson had whipped out his pistol and was 'on the point of shooting him out of hand'. It was then that he noticed a senior Allied officer coming through the gate, so he stayed his hand.

A warning message winged its way to SAS headquarters, encapsulating the shock and the horror. 'Tell England that Nazi concentration camp to be seen to be believed. 200 French Maquisards dead or dying from starvation, beatings etc.' As Patterson was horrified to learn, this small prison enclosure was but a substation of a much larger concentration camp – places wherein the enemies of the Reich were gathered together to suffer and to die.

At a nearby farmhouse, Patterson discovered yet more nightmares. The body of a dead German soldier had been dragged into a barn. The skull had been cracked open and a pig was busy feeding on the dead man's brains. The farmer had felt that the corpse of the German trooper was best suited as pig's feed. Patterson gazed at the pig, 'up to its eyebrows in gore', in speechless horror. Staring defeat in the face, Nazi Germany was descending into hellish anarchy and chaos.

Reg Seekings witnessed the SS forcing women and children to walk out of a building bearing white flags, only so that they could be used as human shields. The 'surrendering' civilians were supposed to lure their adversaries into a false sense of security, whereupon the SS could open fire. In order to force their own people to act in such a way, the SS had wiped out an entire family; 'killed their own people because young kids wouldn't take rifles and fire. These nine or ten year old kids weren't even big enough to hold a rifle.'

Tempers were at boiling point. A group of SS were discovered, sleeping in a barn. Handed shovels, they were ordered by some of the SAS troopers to dig a large hole. A mass grave. Their own grave. A senior SAS officer appeared. Having discovered what his men intended, he forbade the executions. With a burst of Vickers fire unleashed over the captives' heads, they were ordered instead to bury their own dead, before being marched into captivity, to face justice, Allied style.

Five days after making his nightmarish discovery in Celle, Patterson was wounded in the hand by a gunshot. One finger was 'badly smashed' and he risked losing it. Evacuated to Brussels, he was warned the injury would mean his return to Britain for treatment. 'I hope to avoid that,' he noted at the time. 'If the finger just goes ahead alright I shall try to slip back soon.' Despite the horrors he had encountered, he was determined to rejoin his brothers-in-arms.

At his new laager, Mayne received news from Harry Poat, his long-standing deputy on so many previous operations. The former Jersey tomato farmer had found time to pen a detailed report, which he wanted forwarded 'to Paddy . . . he is off in battle, but have no definitive news of him . . . would like it very much.' Poat chronicled all that Operation Archway had achieved, plus its trials and tribulations. While the men were in good spirits, 'the fighting is very hard and we have mixed it many times with the Hun . . . they are all S.S., the real thing and no doubt about it . . . they are fighting cleverly in a guerrilla role . . . We have suffered casualties, but on each occasion the chaps have fought magnificently and killed many S.S. and captured a large number.' The first action that Poat highlighted was the 'rather sticky one' that Captain Wellsted's troops had run into on 8 April. Around the German village of Schneeren, and facing the rump of the 12th SS Panzer Division *Hitlerjugend* (Hitler Youth), they'd suffered the most bloody confrontation of the Archway mission, the enemy fighting 'like devils'. As Poat reported, Wellsted had been shot in both legs as he 'tried to advance through a hail of bullets to a wounded man'. In trying to rescue Wellsted, Swag Jemson had executed yet another daredevil offensive with his Bren gun, just as he had back in France, when single-handedly taking on the enemy at the canal bridge crossing.

Under the cover of Jemson's fire, Wellsted had been dragged back to the relative safety of the main body of the jeeps. Rushed to the nearest field hospital, Poat reported him to be 'very cheerful and think will be OK'. His spirits had been bolstered by the men sending him off with four bottles of 'Château Blotto', a potent local brew. Despite his injuries, Wellsted was apparently desperate to get back to the fight and to be 'in at the kill'. In that same Schneeren firefight, Trooper Owens MM had been shot in both arms and Trooper Blackhouse had been wounded, both men being hospitalised. Sergeant Jeff Du Vivier – who'd led the bicycle patrol in the Morvan, blowing the forty-wagon ammunition train at Entrains-sur-Nohain – had also been wounded.

Du Vivier had been shot in the leg, but as Poat reported; 'not very serious, was able to walk about, drove jeep back, now in hospital.' Far worse was the toll of the dead. Four men had been killed or were missing in action. Trooper John 'Taffy' Glyde – veteran of Johnny Wiseman's Dijon operations – had died in the initial ambush. Three others – Troopers Dougie Ferguson, Roy Davies and Jim Blakeney were also feared dead. Davies and Blakeney had been captured during the SAS's first ever mission, the ill-fated Operation Squatter, in North Africa in November 1941. More recently, they'd managed to escape from an Italian

POW camp, making it back to Allied lines. Rejoining the SAS, they were viewed as iconic figures within the unit. Mayne had personally intervened to ensure that Blakeney could be brought back into the SAS fold.

Among other news that Blakeney had brought the SAS commander at the time, was final confirmation of how one of Mayne's closest friends had come to lose his life. Lieutenant Eoin McGonigal was a southern Irish Catholic, and one of Mayne's dearest pals before the war. A talented rugby player, the two had met at Queen's University, and they'd bonded upon the sports fields and in the bars of Belfast. They'd volunteered for No. 11 Commando together and gone on to join the SAS together, as founders under David Stirling.

McGonigal had led one of the Operation Squatter patrols, while Mayne commanded another. Dropped by parachute into the teeth of a seething desert storm, barely a third of the sixty-odd men had returned at the end of the mission. None of the enemy airbases had been hit, as far as anyone could tell. And McGonigal, like so many, seemed to have been swallowed without trace into the desert storm. Blakeney had served in McGonigal's patrol and, as he was able to reveal to Mayne in the autumn of 1944, McGonigal had been injured during that hellish parachute drop, later dying of his wounds. For Mayne, a chapter had been closed.

But right now, in mid-April 1945, it constituted a real blow to learn of Blakeney and Davies's loss. 'If Bill Fraser is back with you, give him all our regards,' Poat continued. 'Kick the wee man up the pants, what news of him, please write.' In one of Archway's earliest skirmishes, Fraser had led a jeep charge against an enemy position, outflanking their defences, but in the process he'd been shot in the hand and evacuated to hospital. Ever since he'd been sending radio messages, demanding to rejoin his men, and refusing to be repatriated to Britain. 'Let me have further details of your wounded and missing please,' Poat requested of Mayne.

He'd found the time to write, Poat explained, for his men were at that moment resting, 'as the country ahead is very wooded and not our cup of tea at all'. Having listed out their achievements – 'we have killed approx 189, captured 233, and taken much equipment – approx 37 Panzerfausts, 42 machineguns, 1 88mm, 1 searchlight and many more light weapons' – Poat added, 'Please have this letter typed . . . and a copy sent to Paddy.' Among other signal achievements, the Archway force had captured an enemy train packed with V-2 rockets, plus a German chemical factory, and escaped unscathed when several jeeps had been crushed under enemy Tiger tanks

They'd also endured a ferocious ambush at the German town of Oestrich-Winkel – a massive firefight; a bedlam of close-quarter fighting and wounded; a charnel house, with piles of enemy dead. At one point in their fortunes, Padre McLuskey had grabbed a rare moment of quiet to hold an Easter communion. Gathered in a farmhouse with Wellsted, Johnny Cooper, Poat and a handful of others, the padre had repeated the time-honoured rituals of the Morvan: he'd covered the farmer's table with his maroon altar cloth, embroidered with the Winged Dagger badge, and lit a candle. Then, to the 'thundering accompaniment of the distant guns . . . the dim light shining on our war-worn faces, we sang those well-remembered . . . hymns'.

As he ministered to the scattered SAS forces in Germany, McLuskey had with him his trusted bodyguard-cum-driver, Harry Wilson, know to all as 'the Padre's Private Army'. After their operations in France, and on leave with his wife, Irene, McLuskey had felt oddly 'impatient to get back to the Regiment', experiencing an 'overt anxiety to "drive to the sound of the guns"'. But here in Germany, his ministry had grown 'correspondingly difficult' as the fighting had ground on. 'Harry and I needed all of our skills as we tried to disentangle ourselves from the endless convoys and keep the jeep intact.'

Mayne dispatched a radio message in response to Poat's detailed letter. 'Very sorry to hear of your casualties. Congratulations on your successes. Go easy on the payroll. All well here. Regards to everyone with you from everyone with me.' That phrase – go easy on the payroll – meant for Poat not to drive his men too intensively. Mayne also asked for the full names and numbers of the Schneeren fallen – Glyde, Blakeney, Ferguson and Davies – so he could write to the families.

Paddy Force pushed on, 'driving a wedge all the time'. From the skies above came the scream-howl of Hitler's new vengeance weapon, the graceful, sleek lines of the Messerschmitt Me 262 *Sturmvogel* – storm bird – pouncing from the skies. The world's first ever operational jet-powered warplane, a fighter-bomber with a top speed of 900 kph, there was nothing the Allies had that could catch it. Pushing on towards the Elbe River, Charlie Hackney – no longer riding in his red butcher's van – felt horribly exposed. This series of bitter, last-ditch battles were 'all the more frightening' with the 'debut' of the *Sturmvogel*, which seemed even more terrifying than the Stuka dive bombers that had hounded him and his comrades during the retreat to Dunkirk.

To Hackney, there seemed little 'glory to be had' in this final chapter of the war. As the *Sturmvogels* unleashed air-burst bombs – devastating munitions that emitted a 'shower of red hot shrapnel' – he saw the jeep directly in front of him grind to a halt. As he drew level with it, the bloodied form of the driver was slumped over the wheel, dead. Repeatedly, Hackney and his comrades came across groups of SS soldiers at the roadside who seemed 'quite happy to fight and die . . . We never took prisoners on those occasions.'

By 15 April, Mayne's deep frustrations with the terrain, the grinding attrition and the unsuitability of how the SAS was being used – they were basically serving as bullet-magnets – began to bleed through. 'Can you send PADRE to us . . .' he messaged to Poat. 'Intend coming down to see you shortly. This country absolutely bloody to work in. The battle is turning into a slogging match and ourselves into Mine Detectors.' Several of the Paddy Force jeeps had hit mines, and the result was more men lost to death and injury.

What Mayne hungered for most – apart from a spiritual and morale boost for his men, from the padre – was a proper SAS-style mission to get his teeth into. In a sense, out of the blue, it was coming – though it would blindside all concerned.

The SAS was about to set foot into hell.

Chapter Seventeen

FIRST INTO HELL

On 15 April – the same day that Mayne has asked Poat to dispatch the padre to join Paddy Force – the SAS landed a new mission. The first inkling was a seemingly innocuous message received from headquarters. It reported that main Allied forces were having a 'sticky time' on the approach to the region of Bergen, which lies just to the north of Celle. In light of this, the SAS was given orders to 'carry out small task in conc camp' – so in a concentration camp lying just outside of the village of Belsen.

That April morning had all the appearances of being a fairly ordinary spring day at war. Lieutenant John Randall – the twenty-four-year-old Phantom officer, with the coffee farmer father and opera singer mother – was riding in a jeep at the vanguard of those charged with that 'small task' in the concentration camp. Back in the summer of 1944, Randall had served in Mayne's 1 SAS headquarters, as his signaller. Having seen little action in the war, he hungered to be tested, and he'd grown more and more anxious as his comrades had been dispatched to France.

One day he'd asked of Mayne: 'Sir, when are you sending me?'

'You're not going,' Mayne had countered. 'You're a signals officer. I need you here.'

'Colonel, I didn't join the regiment to stay at home.'

Mayne had paid due note. He could appreciate the man's angst. He was longing to deploy himself.

Two days later Randall had drifted down into rural France beneath his 'chute, with Mayne's blessing, as part of Operation Haft, a satellite mission to the ill-fated Operation Gain. Shortly, he'd been in the thick of it, as the Haft party had called in air-strikes on enemy targets, Randall being the radio operator who had to ensure that he got all of that just right. He'd gained a reputation for steely courage, being Mentioned in Despatches for 'organising and transmitting information . . . irrespective of personal safety or of proximity of enemy concentrations', and being praised for his 'invaluable assistance and devotion to duty'.

Today, on this morning of 15 April 1945, Lieutenant Randall's jeep was in the lead as they rumbled along a narrow rural lane. The spring sun felt warm. Groves of silver birch and pine lined the roadway. At the wheel of Randall's vehicle was a Corporal Brown, and behind them trundled a few more jeeps and a truck. With Brown's eyes glued to the route ahead, it was Randall who spied them first – a pair of odd-seeming gates to one side of the road, standing wide open. High, they were made of intricate wrought iron. Randall ordered Brown to take a right turn, for at the end of the track leading through those gates lay their destination.

As a subsequent report would make mention, the 'little village of BELSEN . . . had less than 100 inhabitants', and it lay in 'one of the prettiest wooded areas of the LUNEBERGER HEIDE', which 'afforded ample seclusion for a concentration camp'. Despite the picturesque scene, Randall detected there was something in the air – some tension; a spine-tingling animal malevolence – that put him distinctly on edge. The first concrete manifestations of it were a group of SS in their field-grey uniform and death's head caps, watching the jeeps, warily.

Confrontations with the SS, the reviled adversaries of the SAS, generally ended with one side or the other dead. As Randall's vehicle nosed ahead at a crawl, he fingered his Colt, imagining how many bullets were in the magazine versus how many SS guards he could see. Already, there were far more than in his eight-round magazine. He wondered about reaching for the big Browning machinegun and swinging it around, but the odd thing was that none of the SS showed the slightest hint of having any fight in them.

Randall glanced further about. The SS were clearly guarding some kind of a facility. The fences, rows of barbed wire and the guard towers proved as much. But not a man among those guards seemed inclined to raise a weapon. Randall had come across prisoners of war, of course, for the SAS had captured hundreds here in Germany. He knew the glazed look of defeat in a man's eyes. But these men seemed different. They appeared reasonably fit and well and they looked to be very much in charge still. It was just that the fight seemed to have drained out of them, or perhaps they had nothing left to fight for.

It was bizarre. The jeep made another thirty or forty yards, before they came to a fortified gatehouse. Beyond that and to either side lay serried ranks of barrack-like huts. Low-lying, made of rough wooden planking, ugly. As Brown edged the jeep towards the gatehouse, Randall became aware of an odd smell. At first it struck him as being sickly-sweet. Cloying. Not a nice sweet. A sweet that made you want to gag. As the jeep neared the wire, the smell became overpowering, until suddenly it struck Randall exactly what it was. This was death. Death incarnate. The smell of putrid decay and of death lay heavy on the air.

They eased through the gates. Brown hit the brakes and brought the jeep to a juddering halt. Ghostly figures began to emerge, as Randall and Brown sat glued to their seats, the engine idling.

A crowd gathered. Randall could not bring himself to look, but even so the hair on his 'scalp was crawling'. A tide of wretched humanity washed around their jeep – the desperate and the damned. Some were dressed in striped pyjama-like uniforms, all a deathly grey. Others were clothed in rags. Yet more wore nothing – men, women and children seemingly utterly uncon-cerned at their nakedness. They resembled walking skeletons. Their eyes were sunken pits, their cheeks hollow and cadaverous, their skin bleached yellow and looking as fragile as tissue paper.

Hands reached out for Randall and Brown, as they did for those riding in the jeeps behind. Voices cried out in all the languages of Europe – asking for food, for water, for help, for medicines. The smell that assailed Randall's nostrils was like nothing he had ever imagined; something that he could not put into words. In fact, there were no words for what he was experiencing right then. It was almost impossible to process. He had to remind himself that these were human beings, and that here he had stumbled upon some devilish manifestation of Hitler's Reich, the likes of which the world had not even begun to imagine.

The camp seemed to roll on and on, as far as the eye could see. How many of these living dead were there? Hundreds? Thousands? Tens of thousands? How great – how immeasurable; how inconceivable – was their need? Shaking himself out of the numbness that gripped him, Randall roused himself to action. Trying to hide the shock and distress he was experiencing, he rose to his feet in the jeep and began to address the crowd. He was a British soldier, he announced, and there were more behind. In fact, thousands upon thousands were coming. They would bring help – food, medicines and freedom for all.

Having no idea how much of that had hit home, Randall told Brown to move on. Gunning the engine and blasting the horn, they forced a passage through. They neared what Randall at first thought to be a potato field. White objects jutted out of the earth. Then he realised they were human limbs. Heaps of them, arms, heads and legs locked in a sickening embrace of death. Figures moved zombie-like across the heap, scavenging. Plucking an item of striped uniform here, a cap there, a pair of clogs from the feet of the dead. Speechless, struck dumb, with a silent gesture Randall motioned Brown on. Further scenes from Dante's Inferno – mass graves, piled with heaps of putrid corpses – met their gaze, as they drove ahead in a daze.

While it felt like a lifetime, it could only have been minutes before a second jeep rolled up beside them. At the wheel was Reg Seekings, and if looks could kill, those he threw at the SS guards would have scythed all of them down. In the passenger seat sat John Tonkin, the Operation Bulbasket commander, a man of equally long experience at the sharp end of war. Seekings and Tonkin epitomised the bravery and courage evidenced by the SAS. But it took a different kind of fortitude and a more formidable kind of willpower to get down from the jeeps and to confront what was here.

The men dismounted. They had their weapons gripped tightly. Ahead, a group of German soldiers were approaching. At their centre was a striking, stocky individual, his eyes sunken yet glittering, his face scarred and pockmarked, yet unshaven, his eyebrows thick and bristling, his black hair dragged backwards over his scalp, like an oily slick. At his side was an equally bizarre looking figure; the contrast between the two of them was glaring. The Gretel to his Hansel, she had her long blonde hair pulled back from her forehead and braided into pigtails, wore a smart checked woollen skirt, which was pulled far too high up her waist, so it seemed to be fastened across her stomach, above knee-length polished black boots. Smaller, younger, her blue eyes and thin lips seemed to be fixed into a permanent sneer.

The man was the first to speak. 'I am Josef Kramer,' he began. 'Welcome to KL Bergen-Belsen.'

The SAS was face to face with the man known to the prisoners as 'The Beast of Belsen', plus Irma Grese, his newest sidekick, who was herself dubbed 'The Hyena of Auschwitz', for she had until recently worked at that camp as well.

More SAS began to arrive. Johnny Cooper was there, aghast at what he was witnessing. 'We simply could not comprehend how it was possible for human beings to treat their fellows in such a brutal and heinous way.' The more of the horror Cooper and the others saw, the 'more we found it difficult to keep control of ourselves'. Seekings, in particular, was gripped by an 'utter rage', Cooper observed. 'I could see that he was on the verge of pulling out his pistol and shooting the first German guard he came across.'

Padre McLuskey was there, and this day of all days was when he would gladly have taken up arms and gunned down the enemy. All the misgiving he'd shared with Seekings, back in the Morvan, about a man of God bearing weapons, were gone. Doubly so, when he bore witness to the first incident of casual, savage brutality. Seemingly oblivious to the fact that a new sheriff was in town, the guards were intent on maintaining their murderous rule. A female prisoner tried to reach under the wire to grab a stray turnip. A guard stepped up, drew his weapon and simply shot her dead. The padre was standing only a few feet away. As Cooper glanced at his face, he realised McLuskey 'would have shot the first German he could get his hands on'.

Oddly, Kramer seemed only too keen to offer the new arrivals a tour of his charnel house. While insisting that he was not responsible for the state of those held there, Kramer led the visitors to a nearby hut. Randall found himself 'overpowered by the stench' as 'emaciated figures peered out at us in fear and surprise'. On the bunks the dead mingled with the living, and often it was hard to tell the one from the other. Reeling, Randall, Cooper, Seekings and Tonkin stumbled back into the light. Once outside, another sickening sight met their eyes. A camp guard was beating a prisoner with the butt of his rifle.

Seekings – 'a very tough man', as Randall recalled him – was beside himself now; shaken to the core. He glanced at Tonkin and asked for permission to intervene; 'to teach the guard a lesson'. It was granted. The British Army boxing champion came to the fore now. Seekings marched up to the SS thug and unleashed a powerful punch, the rage within him ensuring that he did not hold back. One blow to the head floored the guard. He tried getting up again only to get more of the same. This time, wisely, he stayed down. Taking a grip on the shock and revulsion he was feeling, Tonkin ordered Kramer and Grese to be arrested and locked in the camp guardroom.

'We are now in charge,' Tonkin announced, to all within earshot, 'not you, and any guard who attempts to treat a prisoner with brutality will be punished.' To drive the message home, he gathered all the SS officers, lined them up, and warned: 'Unless the shooting stops immediately, you are all going to die very horribly.' The shooting did stop. Right then, that kind of rough and ready justice was the only way to deal with this. With time, a greater justice – a proper reckoning – would follow.

The SAS had been warned that one of their own, a Trooper Jenkinson, was incarcerated in this place of hell. This was the chief reason they had come – to check for Allied prisoners. Amid the chaos of a collapsing Nazi Germany, POWs from all directions had been shipped to the interior of the Reich, to avoid the Allied forces closing in from all sides. As a result, the population of Bergen-Belsen had swollen to some six times what it was designed to hold, so some 60,000 prisoners. They were dying in their thousands – from starvation, abuse and disease.

As law and order broke down across Germany, anyone could have ended up here, including SAS captives. Sure enough, one of the SAS officers then present 'found a soldier of his unit who was a prisoner in Camp 1'. Trooper Jenkinson had been discovered, and he was brought out alive. That done, the men in the jeeps began to hand out whatever rations they could muster.

At the same time, Sergeant Duncan Ridler, one of Mayne's intelligence officers, who spoke decent German and French, tried explaining that the camp had been liberated, and that all were free. A long-serving SAS veteran, in Termoli Ridler had been shot twice through his beret, the bullets missing him by millimetres, while single-handedly fighting off a far superior enemy force, and winning a Military Medal for his courageous actions. Yet nothing could have prepared him for Bergen-Belsen.

As with all the SAS then present, Ridler had imagined a 'concentration camp' to be something similar to an army barracks. He was struck most by how little his words and sentiments seemed to matter to his audience. 'Their faces were dull, exhausted, emotionless, not capable of expressing joy and excitement . . . We had never seen people looking like this.'

One of the SAS officers kept a diary. Of entering the camp, he wrote: 'The worst thing by far was Belsen. We were the first there. It was a dreadful sight. People were starving, scratching about for food. We were giving them our own food, but they weren't used to it, it was too rich. There were people in the villages around who said they didn't know it was happening. And the Commandant, Kramer, you should have seen him with his polished boots. He thought he was doing a good job.'

Shortly, the SAS force was relieved at Belsen by the advancing Allied troops. It fell to Ridler to translate for Kramer, as he formally surrendered the camp to Lieutenant Colonel Taylor of the 63rd Anti-Tank Regiment, 11th Armoured Division. Once Taylor had made careful note of Kramer's full identity, he warned the Beast of Belsen that if any further camp inmates came to any harm, Kramer would be held 'personally responsible . . . for every internee that was killed, 1 S.S. man would be shot.'

After a final check that there were no known British POWs remaining in the camp, Ridler was stood down. Along with the other SAS then gathered, he filed through a delousing centre that the incoming troops had established, having a 'white powder puffed inside our collars'. As the SAS jeeps pulled away from the gates of Bergen-Belsen, Johnny Cooper – just twenty-one years old at the time – knew that those scenes would 'stay with me for ever'. He, like so many, would be haunted by them. What made it all the worse were the blanket denials that Cooper and others would encounter in the surrounding countryside. Locals insisted that something such as Belsen simply could not exist. It was dismissed as British propaganda. This added insult to injury. 'As long as I live,' Cooper would write, 'I will never forget the Germans who perpetrated such acts.' He, like Randall, and so many more, would be haunted by the memories of Belsen for the rest of his days.

The day after the SAS liberated Belsen, Richard Dimbleby of the BBC made it there, along with some other reporters. By then, Lieutenant Colonel Taylor had set Kramer and his SS guards to work 'carting corpses from the camp to the big pit – the women joined them later . . . They were given the same rations as the internees had had prior to our entry. During the first night 1 committed suicide and 2 more attempted but failed to do so. The next day 2 tried to run away, but were immediately shot.' In the first twenty-four hours after the camp's liberation, the death rate was between '500 and 1000', Lieutenant Colonel Taylor noted.

Dimbleby's broadcast would galvanise the British and wider publics, as they listened in revulsion and disbelief:

I have just returned from the Belsen concentration camp . . . I find it hard to describe the horrible things I have seen and heard. But here, unadulterated, are the facts. There are 40,000 men, women and children in the camp . . . Of this total 4,250 are already ill or dying of virulent disease . . . 25,600, three-quarters of them women, are either ill through lack of food or dying of starvation . . . I wish with all my heart that everyone fighting in this war, and above all those whose duty it is to direct the war from Britain and America, could have come with me through the barbed wire fence . . . Beyond the barrier was a whirling cloud of dust – the dust of thousands of slowly moving people, laden with the deadly typhus germs. And with the dust was a smell, sickly and thick – the smell of death and decay, of corruption and filth. I passed through the barrier and found myself in the world of a nightmare . . . Dead bodies, some of them in decay, lay strewn about the road . . .

Patrick Gordon Walker, of the BBC's European Service, would report of Belsen that the former SS guards were forced to dig the mass graves to bury the dead. Some fell exhausted into those pits, to be jeered at and spat on by those camp inmates still with the strength to do so. Some guards committed suicide. One female guard was shot while trying to escape. Walker ended his broadcast with the following sentiments: 'To you at home, this is one camp. There are many more. This is what you are fighting. None of this is propaganda. This is the plain and simple truth.'

*

Belsen did not mark a pause for the SAS. The struggle continued. Those serving at the tip of the spear were dispatched in search of high-ranking SS officers, the architects of so much of the evil. One SAS figure, who had shot off a roll of film while in Belsen, paused at a chemist to have it developed. Instead of getting his photos back, he was paid a visit by the British Military Police. The German chemist had reported what the photos showed, concerned about the horrors they revealed. When he was told that his fellow countrymen were responsible, and that this was KL Bergen-Belsen, he refused to believe it. 'No German could be guilty of such barbarity,' he insisted.

It was hugely enraging, and that rage fuelled much of what was to come.

Chapter Eighteen
GET HITLER

On 19 April a report was sent from the SAS to headquarters: 'Good shoot had by all . . . brewed up staff car. Several killed and many PW.' In light of their Belsen experiences, 'brewing up' – shooting up and setting aflame – a German staff car must have proved doubly satisfying. By way of return, London messaged back with surprising news: 'David Stirling reported released.' The SAS founder had indeed been freed from a liberated Colditz Castle, more formally known as Oflag IV-C (officer prison camp 4C). A day later Stirling was reported as being 'in great heart and sends many messages and congratulations to all, and hopes to come out and visit you soon'.

In response, Lieutenant-Colonel Franks – the commander of the Operation Archway force – messaged back: 'Delighted at news of STIRLING's safe return. All ranks presume he will reassume command after a period of leave.' Mayne's response was somewhat more measured. 'Pleased to hear of DAVID's rescue. Hope he has long leave and rest he deserves.' Since Sterling's capture in February 1943, the SAS had soldiered across Italy, France and now Germany, and their operations bore very little resemblance to the kind of fast-moving, hit-and-run warfare that Stirling and Mayne had pioneered in the desert. Much that Stirling might be 'impatient . . . to get back to the SAS', the suggestion that he might be ready and suited to resuming overall command during the grinding, embittered and nightmarish advance into Germany was somewhat naïve.

Paddy Force was bolstered by the arrival of the Belgian SAS squadron, under the command of Lieutenant Edouard 'Eddy' Blondeel. As Mike Calvert messaged Mayne from SAS headquarters, he had been assigned the Belgian contingent 'to increase your command and effectiveness and to give them the benefit of your leadership'. But as Mayne was quick to point out, and Blondeel concurred, 'Operations unlikely for few days . . . Country on our entire axis bog, marsh and canals.'

They were billeted in a clutch of deserted farm buildings, and it was raining heavily. One morning, Sergeant Sandy Davidson's sleeping bag proved to be covered with chicken droppings. Worse still, he'd managed to smear the mess all over 'his arms and face'. Davidson, one of Roy Close's deputies, had been late returning to Hylands, confessing to his fears about deploying into Germany. As he was the only one in the barn so affected, 'everyone fell about laughing and holding their noses' in best British squaddie tradition. Davidson appeared far 'more upset by this than he should have been'.

Shortly, Close's patrol got under way, his jeep taking point for that morning's advance. The handbrake on one of the jeeps jammed solid and started to smoke. Alec Borrie did his best to release it – 'chopping it free' – but while he was busy doing so Davidson started complaining. It was 'wrong to expect married men to take part in the actual fighting' this late in the war, he argued. Under way again, Close, having led the column for a good hour or more, handed over the pole position to another vehicle. In short order, that jeep was put out of action as it drove over a buried mine. As it was only a 'small one' no one was badly injured, but the vehicle was finished.

It was then that Close made a fateful decision. He signalled for Davidson's vehicle, with Borrie at the wheel and Trooper Freddy Caldwell serving as the rear gunner, to take the lead. They were to make a right turn, to avoid any further mines that might be planted on the road ahead. The chosen route was a gravel track, leading to a distant farmhouse. Borrie was charged to drive there and seek assurances that the road continued beyond. If it did, that was the route the entire column would take.

They set off. Halfway to the farmhouse, Davidson made the sensible suggestion that they should follow the tracks left by previous vehicles. Borrie did as instructed, sticking to the tyre imprints where possible. But shortly 'there was a mighty flash and the jeep rose into the air, and the next things I knew I was sitting in the field at the side of the road in perfect peace and quiet, not realising that the blast had made me deaf,' as Borrie recalled it. Close had watched in horror, the blast lifting the jeep 'high into the air', with Davidson being thrown in one direction, Borrie and Caldwell the other.

A large, blackened crater lay in the centre of the road, and the jeep was a twisted, smoking heap of wreckage. Yelling at the vehicles behind to give covering fire – this might well be the trigger for an ambush – Close dashed forward to where Davidson lay. Badly injured, he was the most in need of care. Having injected him with morphine and bandaged the worst of his wounds, Close got the injured man loaded aboard another jeep. Borrie and Caldwell would also need evacuating. While the former was bleeding from head wounds, the latter was badly burned on his forearms.

The medevac jeep hurried the three wounded men back towards Allied lines. En route, they ran into a field ambulance with a Canadian crew. The injured men were loaded aboard. The Canadians applied schnapps – a local fruit brandy – to their wounds, as a temporary antiseptic, 'one dab on the cuts for us, and one swig from the bottle for themselves'. By the time they reached the nearest field hospital, Davidson would be taken to one side and covered with a blanket. He had died, most probably from the shock of the blast. They'd been taken to a hospital captured off the enemy the previous day. There, Borrie had his face stitched back together by a German surgeon, while Caldwell's burns were treated.

There was a mix of German, Canadian and British troops in the facility. All were treated the same, regardless of nationality. The need for medical care was so acute that shortly all 'walking wounded' were asked to vacate the wards, to make way for fresh arrivals. Borrie volunteered to go. Flown back to Britain in a C-47, he was admitted to Crumpsall Hospital, in Manchester (today's North Manchester General). Placed on a military ward, Borrie soon realised that the matron, who was known as 'Adolf Hitler' by all, was a harridan. 'It was worse than being in prison.' He vowed to escape as soon as he could, to rejoin his SAS brethren.

A message was sent from London headquarters: 'Sergeant Davidson now reported died of wounds.' Upon learning of his death, Close was haunted by the loss, and especially by the man's dark premonition that Germany would prove the death of him.

Discontent with the way the SAS was being used deepened. As Mayne averred, and Mike Calvert agreed, 'owing to tightness of front, mines and canals, cannot operate efficiently without heavy casualties . . .' Finally, the SAS's vulnerable jeeps – the 'little mechanised mess tins' – were abandoned. Instead, the men took to riding on the Canadian Shermans, and to soldiering pretty much like regular infantry. This was not what they had trained for, nor specialised in with such spectacular success throughout the war.

As Mayne reported to headquarters: 'Now formed into Infantry platoons. Advanced 1 mile today . . . Men remarkably cheerful considering all their disappointments in role and country chosen for them.' But later that evening he'd send a message to Harry Poat, expressed in far starker terms. They were 'plodding along through bog and rain on their feet. Trooper Kent killed by mine. Nobody very happy.' Soldiering in their dismounted role, Trooper Thomas Kent had trodden on a mine. A March 1944 volunteer for the SAS, with a long record of operations as a paratrooper, Kent was a highly experienced airborne warrior. That had done little to safeguard him in fighting such as this.

Achieving a one-mile daily advance for such losses made for agonising progress. So bad was the terrain, Calvert offered a radical solution: 'Have available EIGHT MAN RANGER inflatable boats which can be dropped . . . Do you want some sent out.' In other words, did Paddy Force fancy trying to take to the canals and rivers to try to better their chances. Mayne's reply was short and to the point: 'No thanks.' The intense, slogging, up-close combat such as they were engaged in needed to be led by armour – there was no other way.

On 25 April there was a rare snippet of good news. Details emerged of the eight-man patrol commanded by Lieutenant Gordon Davidson and captured at Friesoythe. Incarcerated at Stalag X-B at Sandbostel, around a hundred kilometres to the east of where they had been captured, two men had managed to break out. Held separately from the other ranks, Lieutenant Davidson and his deputy, Sergeant Albert Youngman – the man Mayne had rescued from the ditch at Lorup – had been threatened repeatedly with execution by the Gestapo. If they were going to be killed, they'd reasoned, 'we might as well be killed trying to escape.'

Smuggled out of the camp by French prisoners making up a

labour party, the pair had moved only at night, sticking to the woods and remote heathland. In this way they'd made it on foot back to Allied lines. They came bringing horror stories all of their own. Stalag XB was known to those held there as 'Little Belsen'. Men like Corporal Payne – the serial escapee – were aghast at what they witnessed: 'enormous numbers of badly dressed, half-starving poor souls, half out of their minds, crammed in behind high wire fences.'

At first built as a POW camp, in 1943 Stalag XB had morphed into a concentration camp too. In 1944 things had worsened markedly, when the SS had seized control. The Allied POWs were held in basic conditions, but the Soviet prisoners were far worse off, while the 8,000-odd concentration camp inmates were kept in an 'utterly horrifying' state: 'everywhere the dead and dying sprawled amid the slime of human excrement.'

On 30 April 1945, less than a week after they had escaped, Davidson and Youngman would return to Little Belsen, along with a force of Canadian armour. They were there to rescue their brethren, releasing the 'remainder of the men who were captured with them', as the SAS War Diary noted. While the camp was being liberated, Payne and his comrades witnessed inmates turn on their guards, beheading one and proceeding to play football with the decapitated head, which was 'kicked around like a football'. While it was revolting, so too had been the savage behaviour of those guards.

Another figure then present in Germany was equally revolted at what he had witnessed. Charlie Hackney, he of the red butcher van fame, was quartered in a Lüneburg farmhouse along with the rest of his men. They'd pressed so far ahead of the Allied frontline, they had been ordered 'to halt and lay-up for a while'. In that deserted farmhouse, and with little fighting to be done,

Hackney reflected upon the present state of the war and its dark horrors and madness. 'We knew that somewhere in the Reich Chancellery, Adolf Hitler was trying to convince his general staff that all was not lost, that the tide would indeed turn in their favour!' It was that which gave Hackney his big idea.

If someone from Allied forces could make it through to Berlin, could they somehow convince Hitler of the sense of making peace with the British and Americans, rather than letting the Russians take Berlin? To Hackney, it seemed just the sort of mission that the SAS ought to embrace. He put the idea to the men billeted in that farmhouse. Two stepped forward to volunteer. One was Jack Maybury, the other a young soldier known to Hackney only as 'Jack'. He never learned the man's surname. So began their 'last desperate mission of the war', one that hearkened back to the earliest roots of the SAS.

Taking a German car that had been commandeered by their troop commander, Lord John Manners, the three intrepid adventurers set forth. They'd managed to secure some civilian clothes, so they would 'not be shot at by any desperate Nazis' they might encounter along the way. With their uniforms bundled into the boot, and their weapons hidden, they began the 300-kilometre journey east to Berlin. It was the very early hours of 3 May when the trio hit the road. They made for the nearest autobahn, banking on a four-to-five-hour journey, if the motorway proved to be clear.

On the outskirts of a major conurbation the car suffered an electrical fault. They pulled over to the side of the road and attempted to fix it. By now it was starting to get light, and coming along the road was a stream of refugees. All were intent on 'getting away from the Russians' who were advancing from the east. They pushed ahead of them their sad belongings, loaded in carts, prams and wheelbarrows. Worried the refugees might see through their disguises, Hackney told Maybury, the only one of them who could speak decent German, to 'keep on his toes', in case they were challenged.

Some of the refugees paused to talk. Curiosity had got the better of them. Either Maybury's German didn't pass muster, or they must have noticed some item of uniform the three had forgotten to conceal. Either way, the refugees began to talk excitedly about a group of senior Nazis they knew to be hiding in a nearby building. The refugees had been sheltering there, for the house was deserted, but the Nazis had come and kicked them out, hence they were on the road. With the car now fixed, Hackney was 'all for pushing on to Berlin', but the others were keen to investigate the mystery house. As Hackney was outvoted, he fell into line. After all, who knew what or who might be in there?

Gathering their weapons and rucksacks they set off on foot, reconnoitring the house, while making sure not to be spotted. It was a large old building with an extensive garden to the rear. With the other two watching the exits, Hackney stole in through the front door, checking the rooms that gave off to either side of the hallway. Moving silently, he started to climb the stairs, as the ground floor seemed to be deserted. It was then that he heard it – an odd creaking sound coming from one of the rooms he'd just checked. Moving swiftly, he slipped in there, only to see a trapdoor set in the floor closing. Grabbing it before it was completely shut, Hackney yanked it open and fired a couple of shots down into the blackness below.

Shouting for his comrades to join him, Hackney yelled into the darkness for whoever was there to show themselves or 'suffer the consequences'. After a few seconds – 'which seemed like an eternity' – three figures came clambering up the steps, their hands in the air. All were dressed in civilian clothes, with leather jackets or greatcoats to ward off the chill of the cellar. The leader of the trio was a thickset, swarthy, bullnecked fellow. Leaving the three under the guard of his comrades, Hackney searched the cellar. It was empty apart from some old wine bottles. Hackney then explained to their prisoners just who they were. Surprisingly the captives responded by saying they knew all about the SAS, who were 'held in awe' by the German military.

Hackney said the men would have to be searched. As he began to do so, the tallest of the trio reached inside his coat and pulled out a pistol. 'Like a flash I knocked it from his hand,' Hackney remarked, while Maybury retrieved it from the floor. As Hackney slipped the weapon inside his battledress blouse, so the tall fellow seemed utterly distraught. Speaking in broken English, he explained that was the weapon that 'Adolf Hitler was shot with'. It seemed Hitler had committed suicide and here was the weapon that had fired the magic bullet. The tall fellow kept pleading to have it back, as some kind of memento of the Führer. Well, they were POWs now, Hackney explained, so no longer allowed to carry weapons of any sort.

As these extraordinary revelations were being made, the stocky fellow had been 'inching his way along the wall towards the passage'. With the SAS men's attentions riveted by the tall fellow's claims, he suddenly made a break for it. Maybury and Ralphs went after him, saw him leap the back garden wall and slip into some outbuildings. But search as they might they could find no trace of him. The two prisoners who remained were taken to an upstairs room and interrogated under close guard. At first they refused to talk, not even to give their names, but after Hackney had threatened to shoot them, the taller of the two relented a little.

He had been present when Hitler had killed himself, he explained. He was a physician, and he had attended to the Führer's body after the shot was fired. That was how he had come by the precious pistol. As Hackney remained keen to head for

Berlin to check out this seemingly incredible story, they decided to take the captives with them. But once they'd explained what they intended, the tall fellow objected in no uncertain terms. He had no desire to return to Berlin, and he 'protested strongly about being used' by his captors. As the argument went back and forth, the growl of engines was heard from outside. A pair of army jeeps had arrived, bearing the unmistakable forms of the Military Police (MPs).

Hackney sent Maybury to receive the visitors – a Provost Marshal (an MP commander) plus two of his men. But once Hackney had explained who they were and what they were doing there, the MP commander made it quite clear that he did not believe a word. British soldiers did not sully forth this far in advance of the frontline, especially dressed as civilians. They were 'under close arrest', he declared. Taken to a central command building, Hackney and his men were separated from the German prisoners, who they never saw again. The following day, Lieutenant-Colonel Franks arrived, for contact had been made with SAS headquarters to check on the captives' bona fides.

Once Franks had vouchsafed for his men, they were released into his care. Driven back to the nearest SAS base, and still under close arrest, Hackney, as the commander of their rogue mission, was threatened with court martial. But once he had given a full account of his 'mad scheme', and Franks had been given time to appreciate its initiative, flare and dash, he ordered the trio to be released from custody, and for the means of Hitler's supposed suicide to be reported up the chain of command. Hackney had made sure to keep the alleged suicide pistol hidden, always wondering if it was 'indeed the pistol which brought about Hitler's death'.

He could only imagine the tall fellow was Hitler's personal surgeon, but as to the other two, it remained a mystery. In time, Hackney reflected that the stocky man who had broken free seemed familiar. Finally, he figured it had been Martin Bormann, head of the Nazi Chancellery and Hitler's private secretary. And if the tall figure was Hitler's physician, it had to be Ludwig Stumpfegger. Or so he assumed. But all evidence suggests that Bormann and Stumpfegger were killed while trying to flee Berlin, shortly after Hitler's suicide, so Hackney was very likely mistaken.

Nevertheless, with the help of the SAS Regimental Association (SASRA) post-war, significant efforts were made to establish whether the pistol that Hackney had seized – a Walther PP 7.65 mm – was indeed Hitler's suicide weapon. Carved into the side of it was an eagle grasping in its talons a swastika, above the serial number 142062. Handed over to the SASRA post-war, as custodians, it remains a striking and tantalising memento.

As the war ground to a close, Paddy Force found itself nearing Lüneburg, some 350 kilometres from where they had first crossed the German border at Meppen. A 3 May 'Sitrep' – situation report – radioed to headquarters read: 'SAS entered LUBECK ... continuing to Kiel ...' Mayne, of course, had witnessed the unspeakable inhumanity of the camps, and was 'sickened to the marrow'. Enemy soldiers in combat were one thing – something he understood, and from whom he asked no quarter, nor expected to be shown any. But to prisoners and captives – those then at his mercy – he was typically compassionate. The Nazis' factories of mass murder and for the extermination of the defenceless – they sickened him to the core, as did those ultimately responsible.

Cooper and Seekings reached the outskirts of Lüneburg. There, they were charged to seize senior Gestapo and SS officers, who were known to be changing into civilian clothing in an effort to slip away. Issued with detailed maps of the suspects' whereabouts, the snatch missions were to take place in the dead of night. Pressing on into Lüneburg centre at 3.00 a.m., the Canadian Shermans began rooting out the last defenders of the Reich – Hitler Youth fighters. As Cooper realised, many were not even big enough to heft their *Panzerfäuste* properly – 'the poor little blighters were only thirteen or fourteen years old.'

With the youth of Lüneburg 'crawling out of holes everywhere and surrendering', it seemed to Cooper and Seekings to be such a 'disgrace . . . that the Germans put schoolboys into uniform and forced them to fight', especially since their chances of survival were so minimal. Taking pity on those young kids, the role of the SAS had become one of coaxing schoolboys into surrendering before they could be killed. But the snatch operations that followed were a roaring success, as they rounded up a 'motley crew of SS and Gestapo' who were handed over into Allied custody.

Knowing an armistice was in the offing, Cooper and Seekings decided to head for the Baltic port of Kiel, 150 kilometres to the north. They'd been on the road for a quarter of an hour when their jeep was forced to a halt. A pair of German generals were blocking the road. They gestured towards a field, which was packed with their fellow officers keen to surrender. Parking the jeep in the centre of the field, Cooper and Seekings proceeded to take the capitulation of some 500 German officers, the generals coming forward first, and then the others by order of seniority. Each placed his revolver on the bonnet of the jeep, before giving a traditional military salute.

Not one 'attempted a Heil Hitler'.

Leaving the 'prisoners' to await the rest of the Allied troops, Seekings and Cooper motored onwards towards Kiel. Unbeknown to them, the armistice had just been signed, which set a demarcation line to the south of Kiel; Allied troops were not supposed to cross it. Blissfully unaware, they sped into the city, made for the mayor's office, and took the conurbation's surrender, after which they decided to have a 'rare old time tearing down numerous pictures of Hitler'. It was then that a message finally made it through: 'Cooper of 1 Troop, get out. Get back to your original positions. You are well over the Armistice line . . .' Leaping back into their jeep, they retraced their steps, waving 'cheerily' to the 500 German officers whose surrender they had taken earlier.

In the dying days of the war in Europe, Captain Peter Davis – the self-proclaimed 'Colonel', who'd tried to take the surrender of 18,000 German troops in France – was shot while trying to take on an enemy sniper. Hit in the shoulder, he was medically evacuated, but would recover well. As Paddy Force laagered for one of their last nights at war, Mayne made a sudden jeep charge, his 'point five thumping away' – the .50-calibre Browning letting rip. Spotting movement in a ditch some two hundred yards away, Mayne went 'bald-headed for the German lurking there'. It was a group of enemy armed with *Panzerfäuste*. Two were killed, two escaped and the rest were taken prisoner.

And so the sun went down on the SAS's war in Germany. Pillars of smoke rose on all sides, where buildings burned. All the houses thereabouts seemed to be draped in the white flags of surrender, sheets hung from windows and trees. Orders were issued for the SAS to pull back: 'For FRANKS and MAYNE. All British SAS being withdrawn . . . Will reach concentration area for embarkation with vehicles and stores.' A response winged its way back to London: 'Location BORSTEL. I always expected we would end up here.'

Borstel is a small settlement to the south of Kiel. Of course, the message was a pun on 'borstal', the informal name for detention centres in which juvenile delinquents were incarcerated, supposedly for 'corrective training'. Today, they're termed 'young offender institutions'.

Though a fittingly humorous sign-off, the borstal reference would prove sadly prescient.

Chapter Nineteen

BORSTAL BOYS

Victory in Europe Day was celebrated on 8 May. Churchill sent a glowing message to Montgomery. 'At last the goal is reached. The terrible enemy has unconditionally surrendered.' He congratulated the British Field Marshal on 'gathering as captive . . . upward of 2 millions of the once renowned German Army'. In that the SAS had played a key role, of course. Fittingly, the men of Paddy Force would spend VE Day in a wild, crazed Château Blotto extravaganza.

In London, Churchill delivered a speech to ecstatic crowds:

My dear friends, this is your hour. This is not victory of a party or a class. It's a victory of the great British nation as a whole. We . . . were left alone against the most tremendous military power that has been seen. We were alone for a whole year . . . So we came back after long months from the jaws of death, out of the mouth of hell. I say that in the long years to come not only will the people of this island but the world . . . look back at what we have done and they will say, 'do not despair, do not yield to violence and tyranny, march straightforward and die if need be – unconquered.'

The SAS listened to Churchill's broadcast, but then they turned their minds to the matter at hand – celebrating in style. On his first day released from hospital, Wellsted – Captain Gremlin – zipped about in Poperinge, a city in western Belgium, organising a Château Blotto party to remember. En route to Poperinge, long columns of jeeps crawled across the countryside. Or, more accurately, long lines of vehicles including the odd jeep, plus scores of requisitioned civilian saloon cars, and any number of captured Germany military transports. In fact, SAS headquarters had had to issue formal clearance for those German halftracks and trucks to enter Britain: 'Allow all captured enemy transport to cross . . . This particularly vital as many jeeps broken down . . .'

Passing near Ypres, one of the jeeps picked up a hitchhiking RAF officer. There was room, and there was Château Blotto enough to share. A little further on they came across a glass-sided horse-drawn hearse parked at the roadside. Someone suggested it should be taken in tow. A jeep was reversed into the shafts, which seemed to fit perfectly, and off they went, even as the irate owner dashed across his fields. Towing the empty hearse seemed far too tame, so the RAF officer, with the help of an extra generous dose of Château Blotto, was persuaded to clamber inside, 'stretching out as a corpse'.

All was well for a good while, but then the RAF man – 'our somewhat macabre passenger' – became mightily distressed. He made it clear he wanted out. The convoy was halted, the hearse opened and the corpse-lookalike was helped free. He refused the offer of any further lifts, being 'not at all happy over his encounter with the SAS', and doubtless having 'nightmares for the rest of his life'. The progress of the VE Day convoy continued. In Ypres a victory parade was in full swing. The SAS convoy joined it, hearse and all. At the town square a rostrum had been set up, ready for the speeches. The SAS unhitched the hearse and left it in front of the speechifying platform, as a comment on events so far.

They retired to a side street and a café-cum-wine bar. After a good dose of quaffing, the men decided there was just too tempting a target to hand. A few salvoes of Vickers-K fire were unleashed 'to cut the telephone wires . . . the noise itself echoing between buildings . . . the flashes of the tracer and phosphor bullets adding to the uproar . . .' By now the speeches were in full swing, and the SAS decided it was time to encircle the square. With engines racing, the smoke cannisters fitted to the jeeps were let off, 'the fumes absolutely filling the streets'. As the SAS officers and men present were displaying racks of high valour medals, no action was taken towards such 'outrageous behaviour', even though there was a contingent of military police in town.

Unable or unwilling to travel much further, a Château Blotto party ensued. At the town hall dancing and drinking were soon in full swing. Each SAS man seemed to magically acquire a young Belgian lady as a chaperone, perhaps in an effort to keep a lid on the worst of their excesses. There were the odd 'murmurings of suggested court martials' from the immaculately dressed and decidedly stuffy rear echelon army officers who were also in attendance, but all seemed to come to naught. Carousing done, the SAS column got back on the road, for the onward journey to Poperinge and Ostend beyond.

As any number of jeeps were in tow, it had seemed nonsense to retain the engines. Instead, they had been removed, the engine compartments being been stuffed full of a variety of loot – mostly crates of fine wine and champagne, 'taken from the German camps where some of the elite could still live off the best'. Mayne's maroon Mercedes was there. An adopted dog was there. A German shepherd guard dog had been discovered, chained and abused terribly. Over time it had been tamed by

Trooper Gill. The dog was loaded aboard a jeep, just the tip of his nose showing beneath a pile of blankets. 'It stayed absolutely quiet for the whole trip.'

Huge swastika flags fluttered from several of the jeeps, as the SAS reclaimed that ancient symbol for what it originally signified – a symbol of peace, prosperity and goodwill (the word 'swastika' originates from the Sanskrit *svastika*, meaning 'conducive to well-being'). 'Homer' the jeep was there, one of those vehicles captured during the bloody battle for Schneeren, and then reclaimed by the SAS. The *Chronik* of Schneeren town was there, a massive leather-bound tome that was Hitler's gift to his favourite townsfolk, but which had been claimed by the SAS as their own.

Thick gothic lettering adorned the cover, while on the spine were engraved the symbols dear to Nazi Germany: the first, an eagle with outstretched wings grasping a swastika; next, a dagger over an oak branch; the third, Thor's hammer adorned with an oak leaf; finally, an odal rune, an ancient Anglo-Saxon symbol co-opted by the Nazis, plus a plough tilling the German soil. All *Gemeinde* – councils – in Nazi Germany had been ordered to maintain such a chronicle, 'in the spirit of our Führer and Chancellor', in which to record the area's history 'from its beginnings up to the World War'. Each *Chronik* documented local life, cultural traditions, the seasons and political rallies – the essence of what had welded the nation together under Nazism.

In time, the best of the *Chroniken* were to be amalgamated into *The Book of The Germans*, but before that could happen the tide of the war had turned. Instead, the Schneeren *Chronik* had been loaded aboard one of the SAS jeeps and spirited away. As the convoys neared Ostend, the roads were lined with 'triumphant arches of green boughs, entwined with flowers'. Locals in bright costumes were 'dancing in the streets', everyone was cheering, and whenever the jeeps were forced to a halt, the men were 'showered with kisses'.

In such fine manner the SAS made it back to Britain.

One man had failed to make the Château Blotto celebrations. Instead, Alec Borrie had managed to break out of his 'prison ward' hospital. Slipping the matron Adolf Hitler's clutches, and still recovering from his injuries, he hit a 'local pub and got very drunk'. At one stage he grew extremely angry with some rude individual who refused to get out of his way – 'then he discovered it was a mirror.' He'd been arguing with his own reflection. Upon returning to the hospital ward he was reported for being AWOL and put on a charge. When Mayne returned, he ripped the charge to shreds, of course.

After docking at Dagenham, all the pubs proved to be drunk dry. But there was a store of beer at Hylands, so the partying continued. The next day it came to an abrupt end. The SAS was told to prepare to deploy to the Far East, for Japan had yet to be defeated. This was an idea that Stirling had been working on during his time in Colditz. He'd christened it the 'Chunking Project', after the Chinese city of the same name (todays Chongqing). After his release, Stirling put flesh on the bones of the idea, with Mike Calvert's help. The two of them had lunched with Winston Churchill, to win his backing. In many ways, they proposed a classic SAS mission. The jeeps would deploy to China's vast Gobi Desert to try to sever the Japanese supply lines running overland.

With Churchill's blessing, Calvert would ask for volunteers to fight the Japanese. At the time, 1 SAS's strength ran to some 490 officers and other ranks, while 2 SAS boasted some 587. Field Marshal William 'Bill' Slim, commander of the 14th Army – those forces fighting the Burma campaign – would write to

334

Calvert, promising to explore the issue of the deployment of the SAS to his area of operations. Before he could do so, the Americans would drop the first of the atomic bombs on Japan, and that nation would be forced to sue for peace. The SAS, meanwhile, had been deployed to Norway, to disarm the 300,000 German troops stationed there.

That August, the SAS sailed back from Norway to Britain. Their Norway deployment had proved largely uneventful, compared to all that had gone before, and more of a much needed holiday. In the interim, during June 1945, citations had been drafted for Paddy Mayne to be awarded the Victoria Cross, Britain's highest award for valour, for his actions at Lorup, where he, with Hull and Scott's help, had rescued the injured men trapped in the roadside ditch.

In his write-up for the VC recommendation, Scott praised Mayne thus: 'Throughout the entire action Colonel Mayne showed a personal courage that it has never before been my privilege to witness.' Captain Surrey-Dane concluded of Mayne's actions that, 'His cheerfulness, resolution and unsurpassed courage were an inspiration to us all which we will never forget.' Canadian Major-General Volkes added his voice, declaring that 'Lt. Col Mayne's leadership and dash were a most important contribution to the success of the operations . . . In my opinion this officer is worthy of the highest award for gallantry and leadership.'

The official account of the Lorup action submitted to support the VC award concluded:

Any attempt at rescuing these men under these conditions appeared virtually suicidal owing to the highly concentrated and accurate fire of the Germans . . . by superlative determination and by displaying gallantry of the very highest degree and in the face of intense enemy machinegun fire he lifted the wounded one by one into the jeep ... From the time of the arrival of Lt. Col. Mayne his cool and determined action ... together with his unsurpassed gallantry, inspired all ranks. Not only did he save the lives of the wounded, but also completely defeated and destroyed the enemy.

It was signed off by Brigadier Mike Calvert, and by none other than Field Marshal Montgomery himself, commander in chief of British forces in Germany.

In short, Mayne's VC citation included the endorsements of the two officers who were eyewitnesses to the actions on the ground, the overall commander of the unit that Paddy Force were embedded with at the time, the commander of the SAS Brigade, *and* the supreme commander of British forces in Germany. Inexplicably, the recommendation for that award of the 'V.C.' was subsequently crossed out by hand, a single line striking through it. In its place were scrawled the words '3rd Bar to DSO' followed by the illegible signature of whoever had made that decision.

Behind the scenes, skulduggery was afoot. An objection was apparently raised that as Mayne's actions at Lorup were not a 'single act of heroism', the VC was not appropriate. Of course, Lieutenant Scott had accompanied Mayne during much, but not all, of that day's heroic actions. Yet nowhere in the 1856 Royal Warrant for the VC does it ever stipulate such a stricture. On the contrary, it only defines a 'signal act of bravery' as being the criteria for granting the award. *Signal not single.* Perhaps the naysayers had trouble reading the Royal Warrant properly. Disturbed, King George VI himself asked Churchill to intervene in the decision to downgrade, but by then it was a fait accompli.

On 28 August 1945, Major General Robert 'Bob' Laycock,

Britain's Chief of Combined Operations, would write to Mayne, expressing 'the deep honour of being able to address, as my friend, an officer who has succeeded in accomplishing the practically unprecedented task of collecting not less than four D.S.O.s . . . You deserve all and more, and, in my opinion, the appropriate authorities do not really know their job. If they did they would have given you a V.C. as well.' Laycock signed off the letter stressing his 'deep sense of honour in having, at one time, been associated with you'.

Earl Jellicoe, a former SAS comrade of Mayne's, and latterly the commander of the Special Boat Service (SBS), the sister regiment of waterborne raiders to the SAS, would add his voice, concurring with Laycock's judgement. Mayne should have been awarded the VC, Jellicoe averred, and especially for his actions in Germany, 'controlling operations with his customary skill and courage in the very forefront of the battle'. Or as Albert Youngman would put it, 'I saw Paddy carry out many brave actions but Oldenburg overshadowed everything. I genuinely thought I wasn't going to make it. He was an unbelievable man and I owe him my life.'

Tellingly, David Stirling himself would declare that the downgrading of the VC was a 'monstrous injustice . . . faceless men . . . didn't want Mayne and the SAS to be given the distinction.' Even so, on 1 October 1945, Montgomery would sign off on the official documentation: 'Robert Blair Mayne DSO and 2 Bars' would receive a 'Third Bar to DSO'.

A while later, Mayne would visit Buckingham Palace to receive his award. At the investiture, a perplexed King George VI inquired of Mayne how the VC had 'so strangely eluded him'. Even the British head of state was flummoxed by the decision. 'I served to my best, my Lord, my King and Queen,' Mayne replied, 'and none can take that honour away from me.' With characteristic modesty, he would always maintain the VC wasn't important to him.

He wasn't in it for the gongs or accolades.

Even as the SAS had slogged their way into Germany, serving in a way in which the founders had never intended, so a debate was under way regarding what to do with these men post-war. In a sense, all had hinged around the Far East and the war with Japan. With many believing there was scope for 'guerrilla warfare going on in China for a period of two to three years', deploying the SAS to that theatre would give the unit a concrete post-war role. And that would very likely spell their survival. It would help convince the War Office that the so-called 'private armies' of the SAS could have a purpose outside of that they had carved out so successfully in the Second World War. Otherwise, the fear was that their 'role will finish with the European war'.

After his release from Colditz, David Stirling had argued force-fully for an expansion of the SAS, and for the formation of a new 'SAS battalion from ex-PW' – former prisoners of war – 'to fight against the Japanese'. During his time in captivity Stirling had collated 'the names of individual officers for key positions' in the new outfit, provisionally called 'SAS-PW', to recognise its unique genesis. 'It would be a great example for future generations,' Stirling had argued, 'and be a great morale tonic to all prisoners.' Stirling had further proposed that 60 per cent of recruits would be formers POWs, while the remainder should be long-standing SAS veterans, 'in order to get personnel with recent operational experience'.

The French and Belgian SAS regiments were also 'keen to fight anywhere', and were eminently suitable for the war against Japan, the French SAS having done 'extremely well in the Ardennes operations during the German offensive'. The Belgians likewise were hungry for 'another go', and right then fighting the Japanese was the only game in town. Of course, the dropping of the atomic bombs had put an end to all of that. In the vacuum so formed, arguments were put forward as to why the SAS still should have a peacetime role. At the vanguard was Major General Sir Richard Nelson 'Windy' Gale, Commander 1 British Airborne Corps, the unit under which the SAS then sat.

Gale, a decorated First World War veteran, had bags of airborne and irregular warfare experience. He appreciated wholeheartedly what the SAS had to offer, and he proved a sterling champion. Citing the Normandy campaign as the SAS's greatest wartime success, Gale argued that 'Figures of enemy casualties and enemy communications cut, dumps and trains blown up, bombing targets passed to the Allied Air Forces etc., convey only a small part of the total effect which these many small operations contributed towards the German defeat in France . . . The results were so outstanding that the Supreme Commander has circulated certain reports to all U.S. Theatres of War.' In other words, even the Americans – Eisenhower – had taken good note.

As Gale stressed, 'the dividends paid by introducing small parties of well trained and thoroughly disciplined . . . troops to operate effectively behind the enemy lines can be out of all proportion to the numbers involved.' Gale added that 'the SAS idea is as yet only in its infancy,' and a peacetime role was essential. 'There is little doubt . . . that if a small SAS nucleus could be kept in being it would prove very valuable in the many varied and urgent situations which so commonly arise in British spheres of influence . . . we shall want SAS Troops from the very start of the next war.' With the unit's international flavour, and its 'great individualism', this would be a regiment of thinking men's soldiers, those drawn to 'the hope of being able to exercise individual initiative, however hazardous the situation'.

Sadly, Gale's words, and the endorsements of others, were destined to fall upon deaf ears.

In late September 1945, Paddy Mayne, Bill Fraser and David Stirling would each be awarded the Légion d'honneur, France's highest order of merit. Brigadier Calvert and Major Franks would be similarly honoured. Yet even at that juncture, their unit was on the verge of being disbanded. With Winston Churchill voted out of power in a shock election, that July, their chief champion was no more. On 4 October 1945 the axe fell. A War Office 'urgent memorandum' declared: 'It has been decided to disband the Special Air Service Regiment . . . Disbandment will commence on 5 October '45 and will be completed by 16 November '45 . . . Completion of disbandment will be reported to the War Office.'

In recent days, Paddy Mayne had been invited to the sergeant's mess at Hylands House for a surprise function. He had entered the room, to triumphant chants of, 'DSO, DSO, DSO, DSO', for a reception was being held in his honour. But now, the news that the SAS Regiments were 'deemed to have served their purpose . . . was received with great sadness'. As Wellsted remarked, the surprise decision reflected 'the antipathy held towards "private armies" by those of more conventional thinking'. True, the SAS had very often been referred to in that way, or by those less politic as 'raiders of the thug variety'.

As Mrs Hanbury made clear, she would be sad to see them all go, and especially since they were being done away with as a unit. Or as Alec Borrie would put it, 'They couldn't get shot of us quick enough. We'd never been popular. We did things our own way. Didn't pay much attention to what they told us on high . . . Didn't have powerful friends. So they did away with us just as soon as they could.' Or as Albert Youngman, one of those Mayne had rescued from the ditch at Lorup, would explain: 'The war was over. We had a good war, we were still alive and we had a good time. And then the next day a parade and you're not wanted any more. You're all split up . . . Thank you very much, goodbye. And that was so demoralising it wasn't true. Unbelievable thing to do and I think Paddy took it to heart.'

Or, as Reg Seekings would lament, 'It was like the bottom dropping out of the world. You were lost.' Or, as John Randall, the first man into Belsen, would write, 'There would be no more "Lili Marlene" around an old piano now; no Padre McLuskey at the keyboard; no James McDiarmid doing his "Puddle Dance"' (a riotous variation of the Scottish sword dance, with lots of booze, muddy puddles and getting soaked to the skin thrown in). Or, as Mayne would write to his mother at the time, it was 'all rather despondent. Saying goodbye is never a pleasant thing.'

The French and Belgian SAS were the first to go, although in the ultimate irony their governments had not the slightest intention of disbanding their SAS regiments. They would return to their home countries, where they would be rightly cherished, continuing to soldier under the winged dagger emblem and motto, even as the British regiments – the founders of the SAS concept; those who had blazed the trail – were given the chop. Men like Captain Roy Close found it doubly galling, in light of the French and Belgian foresight, that the top brass still somehow 'disapproved of the somewhat "irregular" methods of the SAS, and thus would have them culled'.

It was all so short sighted and vindictive. More to the point, Close wondered with trepidation just how men such as these were supposed to adapt, as all they had held dear fell apart before their eyes. Trouble was coming, of that he felt certain. 'There were unpleasant memories to be suppressed, frightening dreams to be exorcised, and the war's legacies were everywhere to be seen and felt.' Civilised living was not something they had 'thought about for years. It was not an easy transition to make. It took time to get used to, to feel part of the civilisation we had fought to protect. Some never did.'

Though few could believe it, a series of final parades were organised: a general 'march past of farewell to the Colonel and for him to give his return salute to "his boys"', as Bill Deakins would describe it. They'd already offered the 'almost casual handshakes to friends, despite the inner concealed sadness of knowing that this period of comradeship was over, rough seas, hot suns, shortage of water, reduced rations, heavy rains, little or no mail, hilarity, sadness – we had shared them all'.

On 17 October 1945 there was a last farewell dance at Hylands. Typically, this was a day after the War Office deadline for disbandment – the SAS defiant to the last. Printed invitations had been circulated. 'Lt Col. R. B. Mayne D.S.O. and the officers of the 1st Special Air Service Regiment, request the pleasure of the company of . . . at a FAREWELL DANCE . . . Evening dress or uniform.'

Then the final parade.

A tall, proud figure stood to take the march past, his entire persona standing out, as much due to the beige beret – the colour of desert sand – which he still stubbornly wore, despite orders otherwise, as for his martial bearing. Though none could know it – Mayne had kept it hidden from his men for the entire duration of the war – he was nursing a painful injury. He'd damaged a vertebra during operations in the desert. Parachute drops into France had further exacerbated it. But while he was aware that he needed medical treatment, he'd kept it a closely guarded secret, in case it might have taken him away from his men. 'His boys'.

Mayne addressed them now. His shy, softly spoken tones seemed almost choked with emotion. He spoke to warriors, with many of whom he'd spent five years waging war deep behind enemy lines. Together, they had braved countless near-suicidal missions, as the war had turned from one without hate, to one that had been defined by hatred and unimaginable, inconceivable horrors.

Still, they had endured.

They'd witnessed their brother warriors and their closest friends wounded, captured, maimed and killed, losing so many of them in the process. They'd been the first into Bergen-Belsen, at a time when few even realised what terrible nightmares the concentration camps might harbour. In spite of all of that, the fellowship was being broken up. As decreed from on high, their proud regiment – one that had acquired a legendary repute, pioneering elite forces soldiering – was to be consigned to the graveyard. Ashes to ashes, dust to dust.

Most of those parading before their commander faced two bleak choices: either to return to their parent unit, or be released onto civvie street. For the majority of the war, Mayne had been forced to wage a battle on two fronts. The first, and what all had volunteered for – the fight against Nazi tyranny. The second, as unwanted as it was unnecessary – a fight against those who wished to do away with the maverick, free-spirited SAS and its ranks. Mayne had triumphed in the former battle. But today, as he paraded his men for the last and final time, he was forced to accept that the latter had been lost.

He finished off his speech by quoting from 'The Boys of Killyran', an Irish folk song:

> *Some they went for glory,*
> *Some they went for pillage,*
> *Pillage was the motto,*
> *Of the boys of Killyran.*

He followed up, as if in afterthought, with a few final, self-deprecating words, which were replete with a wry and bittersweet humour so typical of the man. The sentiments embodied what would then have seemed to be the epitaph of the SAS: 'We came for the pillage, but maybe we got a wee bit of the glory as well.' The RSM called the men to attention, to offer the final salute. Four hundred and ninety hands snapped crisply to their berets.

And then the men of 1 SAS turned sharply in unison, marching out of history into the fire and heat of legend.

Afterword

Mayne and a core of stalwarts were unwilling to let the history of this proud unit die with its dissolution. Instead, they took the *Chronik* of Schneeren town, unscrewed the brass bolts that held its spine together, removed the original pages – which would be carefully preserved for posterity – and within those massive leather covers they bound together the history of a unit. They included mission reports, diary entries, signals logs, newspaper clipping, photographs, humorous stories, cartoons, character sketches, maps, diagrams and more. Once complete, what became known as the 'Paddy Mayne Diary' was secreted in the Mayne family home, at Mount Pleasant, in Newtownards, in Northern Ireland – the secret history of a secret unit that had ceased to exist.

In the 1950s the SAS was formally re-founded, as a response to the irregular conflicts and small wars that Britain was then involved in – first in Malaysia, and then further afield. In the interim, the regiment had been kept alive by dint of a top-secret and deniable operation. At war's end, the SAS had dispatched to Germany a small unit formally known as the SAS War Crimes Investigation Team. Their remit was to hunt down the Nazi war criminals responsible for their comrades' murder, though in time they would achieve so much more. With the SAS's disbandment, what then became known as 'The Secret Hunters' carried on their work, using a black budget massaged out of the War Office, and nursing their battered jeeps across liberated Europe as they hunted evil. Their full extraordinary story is told in my book, *SAS Nazi Hunters*.

The Secret Hunters kept the SAS's spirit and soul alive, for they openly wore the SAS uniform, beret and cap badge, hiding in plain sight and acting as if they had every right to be there, through to 1948. Re-formed as a territorial unit under the Artists Rifles, as 21 SAS Regiment (V), in 1949, the regular unit, 22 SAS, was re-formed in 1952. In time the Paddy Mayne Diary was able to come out of the shadows. Long after Mayne's tragic early death in a 1955 car accident, it was offered to the SAS Regimental Association by his younger brother, Douglas, in 1997. In that way, and renamed the 'SAS War Diary', the precious founding history of this legendary unit was preserved for posterity.

In a 1947 newsletter of the SAS Regimental Association – of which Churchill, Stirling and Mayne were key figureheads – the editorial of issue No. 6 stressed the value of 'COMRADESHIP', something that 'incorporates the wellbeing . . . of each individual member'. As the editorial stressed, 'it is a thing that is so well known it becomes so easy to forget and we of the Association must not allow that to happen.' It spoke of how Comradeship was what had glued the men together, welding them into unbreakable units, during long periods of fraught and deadly work deep behind the lines. It underlined the value of Comradeship then, in 1947, 'a greater asset during the critical days of peace . . . let everyone of us remember this, and not just think of ourselves as individuals . . .' It urged members to 'regain this spirit of COMRADESHIP', in all their best interests.

In truth, many of those SAS veterans were troubled. Today, we would recognise their post-war trials and tribulations as being the typical behaviour and symptoms experienced by those suffering from Post Traumatic Stress Disorder (PTSD) – the kind of malaise that had prevented Johnny Wiseman from deploying, after his French exploits, or which had led to Joe Goldsmith's hospitalisation post-Italy, and his then diagnosis with 'psychoneurosis'. It accounted for the heavy drinking and signs of 'battle fatigue' that Padre McLuskey had noticed in the Morvan, where the stress and trauma of this type of warfare left deep scars. It accounted for Bob Lilley's wife, Evelyn, and her fear for her husband's 'nerves going'. Or for Harry Poat's January 1945 warning to Mayne that an entire squadron were 'totally unfit bodily and mentally' for war.

This book, *SAS Daggers Drawn*, is in a sense the third in a trilogy telling the story of Lieutenant-Colonel Blair 'Paddy' Mayne and his raiders, from the earliest days of the war until the very end (the first two volumes are *SAS Brothers in Arms* and *SAS Forged in Hell*). I have had each volume read by Ros Townsend, an acclaimed expert in Post Traumatic Stress Disorder, who works with the charity PTSD Resolution, and her conclusions are telling. The cumulative effect of the drip, drip, drip of tension and trauma over five years of such operations was immense, and especially for a figure like Mayne.

As Townsend pointed out, Mayne could flip in an instant from poetry to killing, 'from offering succour to mass destruction so rapidly and so effectively'. Those moments of instant action sent Mayne into a 'trance state' – just as any intensely focussed state of attention is akin to a trance. Innumerable factors contributed to that trance: duty, service, doing what was right, the training, the need to safeguard his men, plus the driving imperative of survival – for him and more for those under his command. Once the trance was broken, the wider ramifications of the action would crowd in.

Mayne was a deep thinker; someone drawn to music, verse and writing. He did not choose to 'skim across the surface of life'. Rather, he would delve into his thoughts, his emotions, and the impacts of his actions, both from his own worldview and 'through the eyes of others, too'. The sheer 'enormity of what . . . he [Mayne] had done and the losses suffered, would . . . have increased with time', and especially as Mayne 'stepped away from the immediacy of the "trance" . . .' Over time, the ghosts would have drawn closer.

The one way to banish those ghosts – at least, temporarily – was through the oblivion of drink. But of course, that way only desolation lies. This was particularly true of Mayne, who abhorred losing – failing to protect – a single one of the men he commanded. As Padre McLuskey would remark, with sagacity, of Mayne, 'he had a natural sensitivity . . . with the men he commanded. If they were in trouble . . . if they suffered from a raid, he would suffer with them . . . More than that, he was both loved and trusted by them in a unique degree.'

After Mayne's premature death in a road accident in 1955, several attempts were made to have the Victoria Cross awarded retrospectively, the one he was arguably denied in 1945. These included petitions to the then Queen at the time of her Golden Jubilee (2002), and several early day motions in the House of Commons. The most recent, in 2005, was signed by 105 MPs and it declared: 'This house recognises the grave injustice meted out to Lt Col. Paddy Mayne' in not awarding the VC.

In November 2009 *The Times* published an article entitled: 'Fight for justice for Paddy Mayne, hero of rugby and battlefield, gathers pace'. It argued that the individual who downgraded Mayne's VC appeared to be General Sir Henry Colville Barclay Wemyss (pronounced *weems*), assistant to the Secretary of State for War, who sat on the Grant of Honours committee, the body that oversees the granting of military decorations and civil honours. In 1941, Churchill had replaced Wemyss with Field Marshal Sir John Dill, serving as head of the British military mission to Washington. That decision had seemingly rankled, leaving Wemyss 'deeply unhappy'; a man with an axe to grind.

When Mayne's VC recommendation passed across Wemyss' desk, he decreed it should be downgraded, despite Winston Churchill's private backing for the award; by then, Churchill had been voted out of power in that month's general election. According to *The Times*, Wemyss' decision was laid out in a July 1945 letter arguing that as Mayne's actions at Lorup were not a 'single act of heroism', the VC was not appropriate. That argument, of course, was flawed.

At the time of the 2005 early day motion, the Labour MP Ian Gibson complained that 'We have had no satisfactory answers why he cannot be awarded the VC. It is small-mindedness.' Don Touhig, then Veterans Minister, claimed it would be wrong to reverse commanders' decisions of sixty years ago – a stunningly ill-informed position to take, one that disregarded the fact that *all* commanders with any direct bearing on the issue had universally endorsed the VC recommendation at the time. All such subsequent efforts have been defeated by a supposed blanket policy of government not to make gallantry awards retrospectively.

It is not good enough. It is, as the Commons early day motion declared, 'a grave injustice'. The refusal to right this wrong is, as Ian Gibson said, 'small-mindedness'. Or, as the author and founder of the Victoria Cross Society, Brian Best, wrote in his seminal work *Unrewarded Courage, Acts of Valour that were denied the Victoria Cross*, 'Of all the unrewarded Victoria Cross recipients, the most worthy must be Blair "Paddy" Mayne.'

After the War

Note: Some of the names below were covered in the two previous books of the Second World War Blair 'Paddy' Mayne trilogy, and their details are also included herein. Where present-day status is unknown I have left that section blank.

Bob Bennet: Bennet went on to join 21 SAS post-war, serving as its Regimental Sergeant Major, and then 22 SAS in 1950, so as to serve in the Malaya campaign (Malaysia), as one of the unit's Squadron Sergeant Majors. He went on to be awarded the British Empire Medal (BEM) in 1963, as a result of twenty-one years of exemplary service, at which point he was serving as the RSM of 22 SAS. He emigrated to Canada and died in 2000 aged eighty-six.

Douglas Berneville-Claye: Berneville-Claye was the British officer and serial fantasist and fraudster who served for a short period with the SAS in North Africa, before his capture. Under German captivity he was turned, became a traitor, and ended up serving in the Waffen SS and subsequently the British Free Corps (the Waffen SS unit comprised of British renegades and Nazi sympathisers). After the war Berneville-Claye was tried for treason, dismissed from the military and sentenced to just six months in prison. A philanderer and bigamist, he married four times, sired ten children, rubbed along with criminals and finally emigrated to Australia. How he only ever served those six months in prison, and wasn't executed for treachery, remains a complete mystery. In short, for his multiple wartime betrayals Berneville-Claye got off scot-free.

Alec Borrie: Borrie post-war joined a training regiment, as an instructor, but he tired of that and left the army in 1947. When he tried to enlist as a territorial, he was refused on medical grounds – getting blown up by the mine had damaged his hearing. He returned to the only trade he knew well in peacetime – carpentry and joinery. He met Jean Spurgen and they married in 1952. He spent the rest of his life working in his chosen trade and raising a family. He died in 2023 aged ninety-eight.

Mike Calvert: Calvert's Brigadier rank at war's end had been only temporary – he was just thirty-three years old at the time. After the war he continued to serve in the military, but his career came to an abrupt and controversial end when he was accused of 'gross indecency', court-martialled and dismissed from the military. He moved to Australia, but his life was plagued by alcoholism, and he was at times a vagrant. Returning to the UK he published three books about his wartime career, and was made a research fellow at Manchester University. Calvert died in 1998 aged eighty-five.

Johnny Cooper: Cooper joined the family wool business post-war, but found it hard to settle. In 1951 he rejoined the re-formed SAS, being awarded an MBE for his actions during the Malaya Emergency, and going on to soldier with the unit across Oman and North Yemen. He retired in 1966 with the rank of lieutenant colonel and moved to Portugal. He died in 2002 at the age of eighty.

Raymond Couraud (aka Jack William Raymond Lee): After soldiering in the Morvan, Couraud served under Major Roy Farran in 2 SAS. In December 1944 he left the SAS and after the war joined the French Army. Earlier in the war he had been known as 'Killer', due to his apparent murdering of the English language. For his wartime service Couraud had been awarded a Military Cross by the British and a Croix de Guerre by the French. He died in 1977 in the UK, aged fifty-seven.

David Danger: Danger worked for a printing firm after the war, but finding he missed the military life he re-enlisted in 1949, serving in Germany, Hong Kong and Cyprus. Awarded an MBE in 1964, he retired as a lieutenant colonel in the 1970s. He died in 2009 aged eighty-five.

Gordon Davidson: Davidson left the army and became a businessman, while keeping in close contact with his SAS comrades. He died in 1990.

Peter Davis: Davis emigrated to South Africa post-war and moved into business. He died in suspicious circumstances during a 1994 robbery at his Durban home, and was believed to have been murdered. He was aged seventy-two.

Bill Deakins: Deakins married his sweetheart, Josephine, whom he'd met during the war and who was also in the military. They left the services and moved to the west country, where Deakins worked in the building trade. They started a family, but as with so many, Deakins struggled with the return to civilian life, haunted by 'the remembrance of the loss of so many friends'. He found it hard to 'begin new lives after the cessation of hostilities, into a civilian life . . .' Even so his family life was happy and his business prospered. Eventually, the back injury he had suffered during the early stages of the war was properly diagnosed and he received a disability pension. In 2001 he wrote a biography of his wartime experiences, entitled, with typical Deakins humour, *The Lame One – 'Sod this for a game of soldiers.'* It was written largely at the behest of his family, who believed his story and that of his comrades needed to be told. He died aged eighty-six in 2004.

Jeff Du Vivier: Du Vivier went back to his pre-war career in the catering industry, becoming the restaurant manager at the Prestwick Airport Hotel for many years. He died aged ninety-four in 2010.

Brian Franks: Franks returned to working at the Hyde Park Hotel (today's Mandarin Oriental), in London, from where he also oversaw the secret work of the SAS War Crimes Investigation Team/The Secret Hunters. He was appointed the honorary colonel of 21 SAS and served in that role for many years, becoming the Colonel Commandant of the SAS Regiment. He died in 1982 aged seventy.

Bill Fraser: Fraser had never expected to survive the war. He led a troubled life. With the rank of major and holding a Military Cross with Bar and a Croix de Guerre with palm, he had been wounded in action three times. In 1946 he was court-martialled and demoted in rank for being drunk in charge of a company of Gordon Highlanders. He left the army shortly after. In 1954, a year before his own death, Mayne would write to a former comrade that 'poor old Bill Fraser has collected a three year prison sentence for breaking into some thirty odd houses.' He battled alcoholism and penury for life, going on to work in a bakery and then as a clerk in a Midlands engineering company. He died in 1975 aged fifty-eight.

Joe Goldsmith: Goldsmith was invalided out of the services in August 1945. Due to his 'psychoneurosis' diagnosis, he was granted a 40 per cent pension, and in 1947 was awarded a King's Badge 'for members of the Armed Services . . . who are disabled as a result of war service'. Plagued by what we would now recognise as PTSD, in 1952 he was discharged from all further military service, 'leaving to fulfil Army Medical requirements'. In 1986 his pension was reaffirmed in a letter citing 'degree of disablement 40 per cent arising from PSYCHONEUROSIS'. Haunted by PTSD for life, Goldsmith nevertheless remained married and raised a family in Sussex, nurturing a love of the countryside and of fishing. His stoic humour remained undimmed until the end. He died aged seventy-five in 1989.

Charlie Hackney: Hackney worked for William Collins & Sons, the Glasgow printer and publisher, and then trained as a carpenter. With his wife Madge they had three sons, Charlie moving on from building jobs to work with Rolls-Royce, and then the Yarrow Admiralty Research Department (YARD), at the Yarrow shipyard on the Clyde. He rejoined 21 SAS, the territorial outfit, and in later life he was a Chelsea Pensioner. In the 1980s he tried to prove whether the Walther pistol he had retrieved in Germany was really Hitler's suicide weapon, including getting stories published in the press. It was inconclusive. He died in 2008 aged eighty-one.

Derrick Harrison: Harrison became a news reporter post-war. He married and raised a family. In 1988 he published his excellent wartime biography, *These Men Are Dangerous*. He died in 2003 aged eighty-six.

Billy Hull: Hull married Elizabeth Caddell in 1944, raising three boys, Billy Jnr, Victor and Gary. After the war he moved to Newtownards, in Northern Ireland, to a prefab hut. He worked as a labourer and tiler, joining the Royal Ulster Rifles Territorials.

He was an enthusiastic and active member of Newtownards Royal British Legion for many years. When Blair called upon him, Billy often went out with his former commander on the odd epic 'bender', reliving old times. He worked in the nylon factory in Bangor until he retired, and was also the local Royal British Legion doorman. He passed away in July 1987 aged 65, and was buried in Movilla Cemetery, Newtownards, diagonally across from his former commander, Blair Mayne.

Tim Iredale: Iredale survived the injuries he suffered during that final push by Paddy Force into Germany. Liberated by Allied forces, he was repatriated to the UK for hospitalisation and recovery. Iredale would always speak well of the German military surgeon who had amputated his leg in order to save his life. He never experienced pain or numbness in his stump. Iredale's catch phrase when setting forth in an SAS jeep had always been, 'We're off to see the wizard . . .' Despite the loss of his leg, he retained his jovial demeanour for the remainder of his life.

Bob Lilley: Lilley rejoined the SAS after its re-formation, becoming the Regimental Sergeant Major of 21 SAS. Later he was the landlord of a Folkestone pub. He died in 1981 aged sixty-seven.

Tony Marsh: Marsh remained in the military, serving through the 1950s, after which he worked for the Trade Development Board in Bermuda. He played a very active role in the Bermuda Yacht Club. He died in 1984 aged sixty-four.

Paddy Mayne: After the war Mayne joined John Tonkin and Mike Sadler – two of his closest comrades and friends – on a British Antarctic Expedition survey, supposedly to spend a year or two working in Antarctica. On the voyage south, Mayne wrote to Billy Hull, helping him and his wife find a house to live in, and wishing all the best to the 'chaps'. His mood sounded upbeat. Antarctica promised the time to think, to decompress and to write. And to spend a year or two dry – to kick the booze. Sailing ahead of Tonkin and Sadler, he set up parties for them en route, complete with drink and with female company. In Antarctica he'd kept a detailed journal, which ominously perhaps made almost no reference to the war years, except for noting: 'A lot of water under the bridge since then.' Antarctica could have been the therapy that Mayne needed. While there he planned to write a book about the SAS, entitled *Growth of a Unit*. He was to have neither the time nor the space to do so. During the long journey to Antarctica, his back injuries would get the better of him, and he was forced to return to Northern Ireland to seek treatment. This condition also prevented him from resuming his fine sporting career. Instead, he would be appointed the Secretary of the Law Society of Northern Ireland. In March 1946, a diary entry made by his niece, Margaret – 'Funnyface' – described the dashing SAS commander, her uncle, visiting her at school to take her for lunch, and how all the other girls were jealous. Mayne remained plagued by his wartime memories – the ghosts growing closer – and he struggled with bouts of heavy drinking. While some of his men thought of Mayne as being more or less happy, others felt he was unfulfilled and depressed. All sensed the deep longing for 'those grand days' they'd shared at war. One of Mayne's greatest salves during these years was tending to his rose garden at the family's Mount Pleasant home. In 1955 he was out on the town, drinking with friends, and driving his beloved red Riley Roadster sports car. On the way home he collided with a parked truck, the Riley coming to rest wedged between a house and telegraph pole. The impact broke the pole in two, brought down the wires and killed Mayne almost instantly. He died from a fractured skull. He was forty. He is buried at the family grave in Movilla Cemetery, Newtownards. In 1997 a statue of Mayne was unveiled in Newtownards, his hometown. Notably, he holds in his right hand not a gun, but a book – a reference to his habit of carrying the poetry anthology *Other Men's Flowers*, by A. P. Wavell, into war. Among the thousands of mourners, there were a dozen SAS veterans at the funeral, at which the band played 'Lili Marlene'. Fittingly, Mayne's good friend and comrade, Padre Fraser McLuskey, gave the eulogy. In 1980, Lieutenant Colonel Keith Farnes of SASRA wrote to the Mayne family, stating, 'To me, and all those of my generation and the younger ones who are now the soldiers, Paddy is still the mythical man of the SAS . . . "That's where it began. They were the masters" . . . Blair remains the epitome of the SAS leader.'

James McDiarmid: McDiarmid emigrated to Australia at war's end, and became a cadet instructor at the Armidale School, a New South Wales public school. He died in 2009.

Fraser McLuskey: In the closing stages of the Second World War, McLuskey visited the German city of Wuppertal, and the family home of his German wife, Irene Calaminus. Tragically, he discovered that both of her parents, plus several other Calaminus family members had been killed during one of the last air raids of the war. Post-war he opted to travel the length and breadth of the UK, informing the families of the SAS fallen of how their sons or husbands had died during the conflict. He went on to help establish the Royal Army Chaplain's Training Centre, before going back to his Scottish roots, serving as Chaplain to the University of Glasgow, as a Church of Scotland Minister, as a Moderator of the General Assembly of the Church of Scotland, before making the move to England, where he spent twenty-six years as Minister of St Columba's Church of Scotland, in Pont Street, London. Well known as a religious broadcaster, he was referred to by SAS founder David Stirling as 'an honorary, if unofficial, chaplain to the SAS'. He would retire to Edinburgh, and a series of locums included an interim chaplaincy in the independent Loretto School, set just outside of Edinburgh. He died in 2005 aged ninety.

Peter Middleton: Middleton went for teacher training in 1947, at Brincliffe Emergency Training College, Sheffield. In September 1946, Paddy Mayne had written to Middleton, urging him 'not to be too hard on your pupils', after Middleton had asked for his former commander to act as a reference, to which Mayne had agreed. 'You may certainly use my name, if it is of any use to you, and I'm willing to give a testimonial on your behalf.' Middleton was assessed as being 'an earnest but rather nervous student' who showed 'a friendly manner with children', and whose 'blackboard work gradually improved'. He married and became a teacher, first in Africa and thereafter in the UK, teaching at the Rowena School for Girls in Kent. He died in 1980 aged fifty-nine.

Tom Moore: Moore, the Operation Gaff veteran, went on to soldier in India post-war, and to be arrested on treason charges raised by the Indian state. He had been serving as an officer in the Nizam of Hyderabad's State Forces, against which the Government of India's forces marched in 1948. Moore was captured 'while laying mines before the Indian troops reached Secunderabad'. Referred to as a 'British ex-commando', he was to be tried for treason in India, but was finally repatriated to the UK on the 'first available ship'. After the war Moore worked for Rootes Motors Ltd in Coventry as a machinist/toolmaker. He was a very good rugby player, captaining his works team (Rootes) and the local Coventry team, Trinity Guild RFC. In 1951 he was invited to rejoin the re-formed SAS: 'as a result of your experience during the war . . . you have been provisionally selected for service with the Special Air Service Regiment.' He served with the unit through to 1954. He kept a press cutting for the rest of his life entitled 'War hero killed in car accident', regarding the untimely death of his former commander, Blair 'Paddy' Mayne. He also kept cuttings concerning the wartime discovery of the concentration camps. He passed away in 1987 aged sixty-five.

Alex Muirhead: After the war Muirhead trained as a medical doctor, becoming a GP, before going on to work for many years as the BBC's chief medical officer. He died in 1999.

John Noble: Noble joined the Metropolitan Police, but by the early 1950s he had emigrated to British Columbia, where he signed up with the Canadian Army. After eighteen years' service, and then retirement, he died in 2009 aged eighty-seven.

Peter Payne: Payne married and raised a family, having a daughter and a son, and grandchildren. He was diagnosed in the 1990s, when in his seventies, as suffering from PTSD due to his war experiences, and he was granted an army pension as a result. He was largely hale and healthy right up until the end, still doing sit-ups and push-ups every day. 'Some habits die hard.' He passed away in 2005 aged eighty-six. Upon his death, Lieutenant Colonel Keith Edlin, the then Secretary of the SASRA, wrote to his family that Payne had 'helped establish the high standards in the Regiment that have stood as an example to those who have followed'.

Sid Payne: Payne went back to working for the engineering firm that he'd been working for before the war. He remained with them until retirement.

Malcolm Pleydell: after his time in the SAS, Pleydell worked in a Malta hospital, until hospitalised himself, with what would today be diagnosed as PTSD. While a patient, Pleydell wrote his sublime account of the SAS's war in North Africa, which would be published under the title *Born of the Desert*. 'I felt an alien, totally out of place in this new environment,' he wrote of his homecoming to the UK. 'I still found myself avoiding social gatherings years after that because of my traumatic experiences.' Of Paddy Mayne he would say, 'This is what Mayne laboured for and helped to make practicable: a unit that was founded on comradeship and high endeavour.' Pleydell married and raised a family, and his life's work became dedicated to the National Health Service, to which he was devoted. He died in 2001 aged eighty-six.

John Randall: Randall was twenty-five when the war ended and met Jane shortly after. They married and raised three children. Randall ran a successful business consultancy, in the field of sales and management training. Later in life he became a senior lecturer at the Institute of Marketing college. He published his wartime memoir *The Last Gentleman of the SAS* in 2014.

Duncan Ridler: Ridler studied at the London School of Economics post-war, before working as an economist for the United Nations. He died in 2005 aged eighty-five.

Pat Riley: Riley joined the Cambridge police after the war, but finding policing too mundane, he volunteered for the re-formed SAS in 1950. Serving in Malaya (Malaysia) as a major, Riley turned forty in SAS service, before deciding to retire from the army. Leaving in 1955, he became the landlord of the Dolphin Hotel hostelry in Colchester, Essex, before going on to join Securicor, the security company, where he held various management positions. Already married in 1940, he and his wife had the one son. He was a stalwart at organising SAS reunions. He died in 1999 aged eighty-three.

Mike Sadler: Sadler joined the same Antarctica expedition as Mayne and Tonkin, after which he worked for the Foreign Office, remaining a very active member of the SAS Regimental Association. He died in 2024, aged 103.

Joe Schofield: Schofield spent ten months in plaster after being shot and wounded in the ditch at Lorup, and rescued by Mayne and Scott. Once recovered, he became a staff instructor with 21 SAS, before serving with 22 SAS in Malaya (Malaysia). In 1965 he was commissioned into 22 SAS as a captain and served through to 1979. In 1969 he was appointed MBE. He died in 2012 aged ninety.

Theodore Schurch: Schurch, under the alias John Richards, had served as a 'stool pigeon' for the Germans and Italians, having served as a British soldier during the early years of the war. A Fascist spy, he did much to penetrate and frustrate SAS operations in North Africa, his traitorous actions leading to the death and capture of SAS men. Arrested in Rome in March 1945, he was tried in London and found guilty on nine counts of treason and one count of desertion with the aim of joining the enemy. Sentenced to death, Schurch was hanged in January 1946. He was twenty-seven years old. He was the only British soldier to be executed for treachery committed during the Second World War.

Reg Seekings: Seekings ran the Rifleman's Arms in Ely, Cambridgeshire, post-war, together with his wife, Monica. After nine years they emigrated to Rhodesia (today's Zimbabwe), where he became a tobacco farmer. He also helped train that nation's law enforcement units. In front of friends and family Seekings never appeared to suffer any PTSD or similar symptoms. Even when asked about Termoli, he would simply reply: 'Termoli was terrible.' He did keep a folded photograph in his wallet of the Belsen atrocities, to show to people if they ever tried to deny such things had happened. After returning to the UK, he died in 1999 aged seventy-eight.

Bill Stirling: Stirling became a successful businessman after the war. He eventually retired to run the family estate, as the laird of Kerr. He died in 1983 aged seventy-one.

David Stirling: Made an OBE in 1946, Stirling moved to Rhodesia (today's Zimbabwe) and founded the Capricorn Africa Society, an organisation that strove to further community relations devoid of racial or social bias. Returning to the UK in the 1960s he set himself up in the private security business, running Watchguard (International) Ltd, which trained security outfits for Arab and African leaders. In 1984 the SAS headquarters in Hereford was named after him as Stirling Lines. Knighted in 1990, he died that year aged seventy-four.

John Tonkin: Tonkin was part of the Antarctica expedition, along with Sadler and Mayne, during which he fell into a crevasse. This called for a long and taxing rescue operation, throughout which he retained his signature good humour. Travelling the world thereafter, he eventually settled in Australia, where he became a mining engineer and businessman. Tonkin would remark that he lost his faith in God during the war, after he was forced to stuff back in the stomach contents of a fellow soldier who had been hit by shell fragments. His 'perception of life had changed for ever'. He died in 1995 aged seventy-four.

Peter Weaver: After the war Weaver ran an Essex chicken farm, while playing cricket for his local club into his fifties. He died in 1991 aged seventy-seven.

Ian Wellsted: Wellsted divorced Margot immediately post-war; 'I never saw her again.' Undaunted, he went on to marry again, in 1947. With his new wife, Diana, he was happily married, and he remained in the army until 1967. At that point they emigrated to New Zealand, where they ran a holiday camp. He died in 2002 aged eighty-three.

Fred Chalky White: White was discharged from the military in November 1945, returning to his pre-war career as a footballer with West Bromwich Albion. But, as the club noted, injuries he had suffered while in the services prevented him from playing regularly. Eventually, he was forced to retire from top-class football. He lived in Great Barr, West Midlands, with a wife and daughter. He died in 1982 aged sixty-six.

Johnny Wiseman: Wiseman went to work for the family business making spectacles post-war, and ended up as the company director. He died in 2005 aged eighty-seven.

Albert Youngman: Youngman left the UK after the war, working first in Nigeria, before running a lucrative import-export business in Hong Kong.

Acknowledgements

First and foremost, thank you to my esteemed readers. You go out and buy my books, in the hope that each will deliver an enjoyable and illuminating read, bringing a moment from history to life. I hope I have managed to deliver that kind of reading experience in this book. Without you, there could be no author such as myself. You enable individuals like me to make a living from writing. You deserve the very first mention.

The second massive thank you is extended to Fiona Ferguson (née Mayne) and her husband, Norman, for inviting me into your family home repeatedly, so that I might delve into Lt Col Robert Blair Mayne's war chest and the plethora of other wartime memorabilia you offered so generously, and to discuss with you his wartime and post-war story. I have gained invaluable insight in the process. Your unconditional welcome and your openness is hugely appreciated, as is the correspondence we have shared over the years. I am most grateful.

I owe another debt of gratitude to Peter Forbes and his wife, Sally, and their children, who hosted me in their home in Northern Ireland and who, in Peter's case, first alerted me to the wealth of private family archives held by Lt Col Mayne's family. Peter, you are in your own right an expert and an authority on the life and soldiering of this great war hero, and I have been privileged to have been given access to your unnerving wisdom and advice. You have been enormously generous with your hospitality, not to mention your time and expertise.

I extend my enormous thanks to John O'Neill, great-nephew of Lt Col Mayne and author of *Legendary Warrior of the SAS*, for entrusting me with me your extraordinary private family archive concerning your great uncle's war years, and also for offering personal insight into your great-uncle's wider character. John, you remind me so much of your great-uncle – physically, of course, but also in your soft-spoken tones, your off-beat humour and your laughing eyes. Huge thanks for all your help and support.

Enormous thanks to Doug Goldsmith and his wife, Annie for inviting me into your wonderful Devon home and for allowing me to peruse your late father, Joe Goldsmith's, war records, memorabilia, letters and the like. Again, this proved hugely insightful, and our discussions thereafter illuminating.

A huge thank you to brothers Andrew and Kenneth McLuskey, for generously allowing me to quote from your father's books, *Parachute Padre* and *The Cloud and the Fire*, and for the photos you were able to share with me of your father. I am most grateful.

Huge thanks to Roger Deakins, for the correspondence we shared over your father Bill Deakins' wartime service, for permitting me to quote from sections of his book *The Lame One* and for permission to use the photos that I have. I am most grateful.

Enormous thanks to Nabil Lawrence Jamal, the grandson of Derrick Harrison, and to the wider Harrison family, for inviting me into your London home, for corresponding with me as you have, for reading and commenting on the manuscript for this book, and for the kind permission to use those quotes from Derrick Harrison's excellent book, *These Men Are Dangerous*, and also for the photos I have used. I am in your debt.

Huge thanks to Gary Hull, the son of SAS operator Billy Hull, for inviting me into your Belfast home and for sharing with me your stories and recollections about both your father's wartime exploits, and those of his commander and close friend, Lt Col Robert Blair Mayne. Thank you also for giving me access to your father's wartime letters, records, photos, memorabilia and other materials, which proved so useful.

Thank you to Scott Hackney, for sharing with me the private family archive of your father, Charlie Hackney, including his unpublished and detailed account of the war years, and a plethora of associated materials from the Hackney family archives, and for all of our correspondence over the same. I am enormously grateful.

Thank you to Catherine Cary-Elwes and family, for inviting me into your Oxford home and for sharing with me the wartime story of your father, Oswald Cary-Elwes, and also for allowing me access to the Cary-Elwes family archive. Our long correspondence and numerous meetings during the gestation of this book were extremely useful, as were the materials and records you kindly sent me. I am most grateful.

Thank you to Christine Gordon, the daughter of British and Irish rugby international George Ernest Cromey, for your insight into the rugby years. Thanks to David Robson, for sharing with me the stories of how Lt Col Mayne helped guide him as a young man in his life choices. Thanks also to Barbara Coffey, whose father, Dr Cole, was a close friend of Lt Col Mayne's, and who shared with me stories of childhood memories. Thanks to Harold Hetherington for sharing with me the stories of how Mayne was in the habit of rounding him and his brothers up as young and somewhat wayward boys, and ensuring they did attend the local school.

Thanks once again to Amy Barkworth, the daughter of Major Eric 'Bill' Barkworth, for sharing with me his wartime reports concerning Hitler's 'Commando Order' and related materials.

Thank you to Stephen Evans, the grandson of Tom Moore, for our meetings and discussions on your grandfather's fascinating wartime story, and particularly on Operation Gaff. Thanks also for allowing me to use the photos and documents that I have in this book.

Thank you to Ian Thomson, the grandson of Peter Payne, and his uncle, also Peter Payne, for the long and detailed correspondence we have exchanged to and from Australia concerning SAS veteran Peter Payne's wartime service and especially his capture by the Germans and subsequent liberation, in spring 1945, and for the use of the photos.

Thank you, as ever, to my long-standing friend and reader of early manuscripts, and commentator thereon – LRDG, SAS and SBS veteran, Jack Mann. As you knew Lt Col Robert Blair Mayne personally, your comments and remarks on an early draft of this book are immensely treasured, as always.

Thank you also to the late, great Alec Borrie, SAS veteran, who served alongside Lt Col Mayne and many others portrayed in this book, for speaking with me about your wartime experiences and memories, and for inviting me into your London home. Again, such contributions from one who was there have been invaluable and I am hugely privileged and grateful for all your help and insight. Thanks also to Ed Borrie, Alec's son, for the many ways in which you have assisted in the research for this book, not least for the use of the photos herein. I'm hugely grateful.

Thanks to Michael Watson, for sharing with me documents, recollections and photos regarding your grandfather Lieutenant Jimmy Watson's wartime service. I am most grateful.

Thank you to Eric Lecomte and Arnaud Blond, for all the correspondence, help and generous assistance you were able to furnish concerning my research into the operations of the Free

French SAS, and also for your kind invitations to France to look into more of the same. This was invaluable and I am grateful.

Thank you to Ros Townsend, a specialist working with the fantastic charity PTSD Resolution, for reading an early draft of this book, and for sharing with me your expert perspective on the history of diagnosis and recognition of PTSD and your personal feedback and observations on the trauma suffered by Second World War veterans, and especially those serving behind the lines. This was invaluable, and I have leant on your analysis heavily. Thank you also to Colonel A. de P. Gauvain (Retired) FHGI, Chairman and CEO of PTSD Resolution, for all the help, support and advice you kindly extended to me in connection with the writing of this book. It was so good to meet you both,

Thank you to Joshua Levin, for sharing with me a pre-publication copy of your excellent work, *SAS An Illustrated History of the SAS*, which includes a trove of previously unpublished photographs of the unit in action in the Second World War.

Enormous thanks to Henrik Beermann, who was born and raised in Schneeren, in Germany, for your kind and generous time, correspondence and conversations about the Schneeren episode of this story, and all things concerning the *Chroniks* and their purpose and intent. This proved hugely enlightening.

Thanks also to Mark Johnston, for sharing with me your dissertation on Lt Col Blair Mayne, '"The Bravest Man Never to Have Been Awarded the V.C.": A Re-examination', and for the correspondence we shared, and to your partner, Eimear, for reaching out to me in the first place about this.

Thanks to Jon Baker and all at Paradata, Duxford (The Airborne Assault Museum, IWM), for sharing with me your excellent archive. So glad we got to meet and thanks again for all of that invaluable insight.

*

Thanks are also extended to the following individuals, who are all experts in their own right on various aspects of Second World War history, and helped me in my research: Jonathan Woodhead, Michael Caldwell, Tom Hunter, Thomas Harder, Jimmy Russell, Will Ward, Norman and Andrew Glenfield. Thank you Scilla Tappenden, for sharing with me your personal insights into SAS founder David Stirling. Thank you to David, of the FFLSAS, for your insights into Operation Gaff. Thank you to fellow author Tony Rushmer, for your insights into Reg Seekings. Thank you to Rob Barnes for sharing with me the SAS signals logs. Thank you to the late, great, P. J. Cabut, for all your insights into the French side of operations during 1944. Thank you to Dr Bob Sherwood, for your insights and correspondence regarding Bergen-Belsen, and the SAS remit and role there. Thank you to Stewart McDermott, for sharing with me the details of Doug Nash's wartime exploits and also the photos, some of which I have used in this book. Thank you to Alan Griffiths for the correspondence and photos regarding George Eric Sharrocks. Thank you to Dirk G for the correspondence and photos regarding the Belgian SAS in the Second World War. Thank you to Jeff Hetherington, for the correspondence and insight into Joe Goldsmith. Thank you to Thomas Liaudet, of the AFPSAS, for your expert guidance over the French SAS. Thank you to Ross Stewart, for sharing the ordbat of the SAS in 1944. Thank you to Euan Goodman for sharing with me the citations for Lieutenant-Colonel Mayne's decorations. Thanks to podcast host Dodge Woodall, for introducing me to the family of SAS veteran Tom Moore. Thank you to Colin Hayes, for our long correspondence over Stanley Hayes, and the Morvan operations. Thank you to Mike Watson, for our correspondence over Jim Watson and his Morvan operations. Thank you to David Neagle for sharing with me the unpublished diary of an SAS officer who was among the first into Belsen. Thank you to Perry Smith, for helping in the many ways that you have – much appreciated.

Thanks as ever to Julie Davies, ace researcher and translator, for sharing with me the journey of discovery embodied in this book, and for your astute and pertinent observations, assessment and guidance; but most of all for your heartfelt enthusiasm that the full story of Lieutenant Colonel Blair Mayne's wartime story, and that of his comrades, should be told. With this book it is complete.

I also extend my warm thanks to my early readers: Paul and Anne Sherratt, as always, at the top of the list of 'thank yous'. Long may you keep providing me with such pertinent and telling feedback and comment. Sandy and Erica Moriarty, as our wonderful neighbours just across the track – again, your detailed remarks, and your enthusiasm for this story, proved invaluable.

Thank you again to Nina Staehle for your excellent research in Germany concerning this story and for your translations from German to English. As ever, with remarkable tenacity you unearthed some true gems concerning this story, and for that I am hugely grateful.

Huge thanks as always to Simon Fowler, my researcher in the UK – your hard work and insight was invaluable. Your work winkling out the files from where they were hardest to find, as always, was remarkable. Bravo!

Thanks also to Paul Hazzard, long-standing reader and friend, for perusing an early draft and for your deeply perceptive comments. Thanks to John R. McKay, a fellow author and Second World War historian of great talent, for reading an early iteration of this book and for all your invaluable comments. It was great to have that support, as ever.

Thanks especially to SAS veteran Des Powell (with whom I co-authored *SAS Bravo Three Zero*). It was immensely refreshing to have the thoughts and feedback of a more modern-generation 'pilgrim' – an SAS veteran – on the SAS in its founding years. Well done, my friend, and massively appreciated. The legacy lives on in individuals such as yourself.

Thank you also to the Winston Churchill Fellowship, for backing me with a Fellowship many years ago, which ignited the spark in a young man to be curious about all things Winston Churchill, and especially the legacy of this extraordinary wartime leader.

I have benefited greatly in the research for this book from the resources that the British, German and other governments, and related institutions, have invested into preserving for posterity the archives from the Second World War era. The preservation and cataloguing of a mountain of papers – official reports, personal correspondence, telegrams, etc. – plus photographic, film and sound archives is vital to authors such as myself, without which books of this nature could not be written. Devoting resources to the preservation of this historical record, and to making it accessible to the public, is something for which these governments and other institutions deserve high praise.

All at my publishers deserve the very best of praise for their committed, enthusiastic and visionary support of this project from the get-go. In the UK, Richard Milner, my long-standing editor and good friend, provided seminal guidance and feedback, as always. The wider Quercus team also deserve the highest praise, and especially Dave Murphy and Jon Butler.

My gratitude is extended to my literary agent at DHA, Andrew Gordon. Thank you also to Sophie Ransom, of Ransom PR, for your huge enthusiasm for this story from the very outset, and for working your special magic, as always.

Finally, I need to extend my deep thanks and heartfelt gratitude to my family – Eva, David, Damien Jr and Sianna – who once again had to put up with 'Pappa' spending far too long locked in his study trying to do justice to this story. That I have – if I have – I owe to you all; to your forbearance, your love and support and kindness, and for putting up with me through it all.

This, of course, is a very special story for the Lewis family, if for no other reason than because of our deep links to Ireland, and because my wife, Eva, has played a very hands-on role in the research, archiving, and the revisions of this book, not to mention overseeing the business side of things. This book has been a labour of love, and you stayed the course over the long years that it has taken to come to fruition, for which I am hugely grateful.

Acknowledgements on Sources

I am indebted to the following authors, who have covered some of the aspects of the story I have dealt with in *SAS Daggers Drawn* in their own writing. For those readers whose interest has been piqued by this book, these authors and their titles would reward further reading.

Alec Borrie, whose book *Autobiography of Alexander Campbell Borrie* – sadly, not in print – presents a deeply personal account of his life and war years, from the post D-Day deployment to France through to the push into Nazi Germany.

Roy Close, whose book, *In Action With the SAS*, offers a detailed and compelling account of the author's wartime experiences, from France in 1944 through to the push into Nazi Germany.

Johnny Cooper, *One of the Originals*, which constitutes Cooper's dramatic account of his wartime service in the SAS, and his ongoing service thereafter.

Peter Davis, *SAS Men in The Making*, whose wartime account provides the gripping story of the SAS at war in Italy and France.

W. A. Deakins, whose book, *The Lame One* – sadly long out of print – is an autobiography of the author's wartime service, including his time spent with the SAS in North Africa, and Italy and Europe thereafter, based upon his detailed wartime diaries.

Martin Dillon and Roy Bradford, *Rogue Warrior of the SAS*, whose book is a comprehensive biography of Blair 'Paddy' Mayne.

Roy Farran, *Winged Dagger*, whose book is a gripping account of his wartime service in Italy, France and elsewhere.

Derrick Harrison, whose book, *These Men Are Dangerous* – sadly long out of print – is a compelling account of the author's war years, and especially of his time serving with the SAS both in Italy, and thereafter in France, in the battle to liberate Nazi-occupied Europe.

Sir James Hutchison, *That Drug Danger* – again, regrettably long out of print – which constitutes his wartime story of derring-do with the SOE.

Patrick Marrinan, *Colonel Paddy*, whose book is a gripping biography of the life and times of Lieutenant-Colonel Blair 'Paddy' Mayne.

Fraser McLuskey, whose book, *Parachute Padre* – sadly long out of print – is a wonderful account of the padre's time with the SAS during 1944–45.

John O'Neill, the great nephew of Lt Col Robert Blair Mayne DSO, and the author of *Legendary Warrior of the SAS*, whose biography of his great-uncle relied upon access to the O'Neill (Mayne) family archive, and is rich in biographical detail.

John Randall and M. J. Trow, whose book *The Last Gentleman of the SAS*, recounts the wartime story of John Randall, including the gripping tale of those who were first into Belsen.

Hamish Ross, *Paddy Mayne*, whose book constitutes a comprehensive biography of the life of Lieutenant-Colonel Blair 'Paddy' Mayne.

Ian Wellsted, whose two books, *SAS With The Maquis* and *With The SAS Across The Rhine* offer a fabulous account of the 1944 French missions of the SAS and their subsequent push into Germany.

Ex-Lance Corporal X QGM, *The SAS & LRDG Roll of Honour 1941–47*, whose three-volume work – now out of print – is a comprehensive guide to those from the LRDG and SAS who made the ultimate sacrifice in the Second World War.

I am grateful to the following publishers, authors and estates for granting me permission to quote from their works (full details in Bibliography):

Alec Borrie, *Autobiography of Alexander Campbell Borrie*, 2015 – all rights reserved.

Roy Close, *In Action With the SAS*, 2005 – all rights reserved.

Peter Davis, *SAS Men In The Making*, 2015 – all rights reserved.

W. A. Deakins, *The Lame One*, 2018 – all rights reserved.

Roy Farran, *Winged Dagger*, 1986 – all rights reserved.

Charles Hackney, *A Soldier's Life For Me*, unpublished – all rights reserved.

Derrick Harrison, *These Men are Dangerous*, 1988 – all rights reserved.

Fraser McLuskey, *Parachute Padre*, 1951, and *The Cloud and the Fire*, 1993 – all rights reserved.

Ian Wellsted, *SAS With the Maquis*, 2016 – all rights reserved.

Ian Wellsted, *With the SAS: Across the Rhine: Into the Heart of Hitler's Third Reich*, 2020 – all rights reserved.

Reference to Sources

Material quoted from the UK archive files listed below is courtesy of the British National Archives. This book contains public-sector information licensed under the Open Government Licence v3.0.

Imperial War Museum

Documents
Private Papers of Captain M L Pleydell MC, IWM Documents 337

Private Papers of Mrs. A M Street, IWM Documents 6433

BBC The Archive Hour SAS Originals, IWM Catalogue Number 29806

Private Papers of J. H. Patterson, IWM Documents 13225

Audio Archives
Bob Bennet interview, IWM Sound Archive 18145

Earl George Jellicoe interview, IWM Sound Archive 13039

Reg Seekings DCM MM, IWM Sound Archive 18177

Wiseman, John Martin, oral history, IWM Sound Archive 20337

Liddell Hart Centre for Military Archives

Street, Major-General Vivian Wakefield (1912–1970), GB 0099
   KCLMA Street
Major B G Barnett papers (1912–1988), KCLMA Barnett B G

Churchill Archives Centre, Churchill College, Cambridge

CHAR 1/369/3–4
CHAR 20/65/106–145
CHAR 20/205/49
CHAR 20/65/146–148

The National Archives, Kew

AIR 20/8937 – Op Gain
PREM 3/330/9 – Combined Ops
PRO WO 218/193 – Special Service War Diaries
WO 201/727 & WO 373/46 – Middle East Forces
PRO WO 373/53 – Recommendations for Honours and Awards
WO 331/7 – Hitler's Kommando Order
WO 222/1568 – Locations of British General Hospitals during
   WWII
WO 373/26 – Pleydell's MC Citation
WO 373/185/19 – French Awards Stirling/Jellicoe
WO 373/185 – French and American awards for Stirling etc
WO 218/222 – SAS WCIT Missing Parachutists
WO 218/160 – Middle East Commando A Squadron

WO 372/185 – CdeG citations

WO 201/765 – Raiding Forces: signals in

WO 218/119 – HQ SAS Troops Norway

WO 373/46/23 – Raiding Forces

WO 218/119 – Operation Archway

WO 218/91 – War Diary 1 SAS 1943

WO 218/119 – Op HOWARD

WO 218/191 – Op Gaff

HS 9/1647 – Courand

WO 309/659 – More Statements

KV 2/626-1 – Douglas Webster St. Aubyn Berneville-Claye

KV 2/626-2 – Douglas Webster St. Aubyn Berneville-Claye

KV 2/627-1 – Douglas Webster St. Aubyn Berneville-Claye

KV 2/627-2 – Douglas Webster St. Aubyn Berneville-Claye

KV 2/77-1 – Theodore John William SCHURCH: deserted to the Italians and collaborated with them and . . .

KV 2/77-2 – Theodore John William SCHURCH: deserted to the Italians and collaborated with them and . . .

Other Published Sources

Max Arthur, 'Obituary: Reg Seekings', *The Independent*, 3 May 1999

Ron Gittings, 'Tarnished Hero of the SAS', *Medal News*, April 2007

Jack Loudan, 'Braves bullets to save his wounded men', *TV Post*, 27 September 1962

Jack Loudan, 'The Man Who Dared', *TV Post*, 23 August 1962

Alastair McQueen, 'How the spirit of bravest SAS hero will live on', *The Express*, 1 March 1997

Margaret Metcalf, 'My father the war traitor', BBC News, 29 March 2002: http://news.bbc.co.uk/1/hi/uk/1898942.stm

Mark Souster, 'Fight for justice for Paddy Mayne', *The Times*, 9 November 2009

The SAS, WarAndPeaceShow.com, undated

'Padre Dropped with Paratroops', *Scottish Daily Express*, 13 December 1944

Obituaries, John Elliot Tonkin, Kevin Walton, Published online by Cambridge University Press, 27 October 2009

General Roderick McLeod, 'On Taking Command', *Mars & Minerva*, Vol. 1 No. 9, June 1963

'Confusion is Their Business', *Readers Digest*, February 1945

Phil Gunn obituary, *The Times*, 16 January 1945

Major Joe Schofield obituary, *The Telegraph*, 12 February 2012

Lt. John Randall obituary, The Telegraph, 10 April 2005

Duncan Ridler, 'On a Spring Evening in 1945', *Mars & Minerva*

Richard Dimbleby, 'Belsen Eyewitness', BBC Broadcast, April 1945

Patrick Gordon Walker, 'Belsen Facts and Thoughts', European Service of the BBC, 27 May 1945

Clifford Barnard, 'Two Weeks in May 1945', Quaker Home Service, 1999

'VE Day 8 May 1945', International Churchill Society

Unpublished Sources & Miscellaneous

Amicale Belgian SAS Vriendenkring vzw, 'A Short History of the Belgian SAS in WWII', translated from the Flemish by Geert, G., 2020

Anon., 'Major William (Bill) Fraser MC, 1917–1975', undated paper

Anon., 'Blair "Paddy" Mayne', World Rugby Museum, 2013, Mayne family collection, undated

Anon., 'Unveiling of the Memorial to Lt Col Robert Blair Mayne DSO', Ards Borough Council, 2 May 1997, Mayne family collection, undated

Anon., *Robert Blair Mayne of Newtownards: A Commemorative Booklet*, Rotary Club of Newtownards, undated, Mayne family collection, undated

Anon., 'Olympians Sports Gossip – Some Stories of Blair Mayne', *Johannesburg Star* draft article, 26 February 1942, O'Neill family collection

Anon., 'The Second World War: All RAF aircrew were volunteers', Royal Airforce Museum, undated

Messages sent to and received from Operation Archway, SAS Signals Logs, courtesy Rob Barnes private collection

Major Eric 'Bill' Barkworth, 'Report on the Commando Orders of 18.10.42 and 25.6.44 with reference to Certain of the War Crimes caused by them', Barkworth family collection, undated

Michael Beattie, *In the Footsteps of Blair Mayne*, documentary transcript

Author interview with Alec Borrie, 2023

Letter from Lt Col Keith Farnes, 21 SAS, to Douglas Mayne, 25 June 1992, Mayne family collection

Doug Goldsmith, *Joe Goldsmith's War Diary*, Goldsmith family collection, undated

Joe Goldsmith's WWII Scrapbook, Goldsmith family collection, undated

Charles Hackney, *A Soldier's Life for Me*, unpublished memoir and notes, Hackney family collection, undated

Messages sent to and received from R. B. Mayne DSO and Bar, Gary Hull private family archive

Operation Houndsworth War Diary, Gary Hull private family archive

Author interview with Gary Hull, 2024

'Churchill's Government defeats a No Confidence motion in the House', International Churchill Society, 12 March 2015

Mark Johnston, '"The Bravest Man Never to Have Been Awarded the VC": A Re-examination', LM Dissertation, MA Military History DL, undated

Letter from Mayne to his mother, 23 December 1944, and various other family correspondence, Mayne family private archive

Letter from Brigadier Rod McLeod ref. SAS fight to retain wings, Paradata Duxford Archive

Rev. J. Fraser McLuskey, 'Between You And Me', eulogy for Lt Col R. B. Mayne, Mayne family collection, undated

A Squadron 1 SAS Song Sheets, Middleton family archive

Letters home and other wartime documents, Middleton family archive

Unpublished SAS diary, on Belsen entry, courtesy of the David Neagle private collection

'Lili Marlene' (SAS version), John O'Neill family archive

Formation of SAS Regiment from PW, 25 February 1945, courtesy of Paradata Duxford

SAS SACSEA, 1 March 1945, courtesy of Paradata Duxford

Future of SAS Troops, R. N. Gale, 21 March 1945, courtesy of Paradata Duxford

Letter from Major Harry Poat to Mayne, 21 January 1945, and other miscellaneous wartime correspondence, Mayne family private archive

'Report for Term Ending 18th December 1925', Newtonards Academy, John Rodgers, B.A., Principal, Mayne family collection, undated

SASRA newsletter 1947, Stephen Evans private collection

A. J. Schofield, 'Special Raiding Squadron Sicily & Italy 1943', 1999

Quotes from Schneeren *Chronik*, translated into English, courtesy of the Mayne family collection

Personal Correspondence between the author and Tony Rushmer, 2024

Author correspondence with Ian Thomson, and the Thomson family archives

Ros Townsend, PTSD Resolution, various emails to author, 2022–24

Author correspondence, with Mike Watson, ref. Jim Watson, SAS

Selected Bibliography

Anon., *The SAS War Diary*, London: Extraordinary Editions, 2011

Lorna Almonds-Windmill, *Gentleman Jim*, Barnsley: Pen & Sword, 2011

Michael Ashcroft, *Special Ops Heroes*, London: Headline, 2014

Michael Asher, *Get Rommel*, London: Weidenfeld & Nicolson, 2004

———, *The Regiment*, London: Viking, 2007

Brian Best, *Unrewarded Courage*, Barnsley: Frontline Books, 2020

Roy Bradford and Martin Dillon, *Rogue Warrior of the SAS*, Edinburgh: Mainstream Publishing, 2012

Chelsea Pensioners, *Before They Fade*, Skipton: Dales Large Print Books, 2002

Roy Close, *In Action With the SAS*, Barnsley: Pen & Sword, 2005

Johnny Cooper, *One of the Originals*, London: Pan Books, 1991

Virginia Cowles, *The Phantom Major*, Barnsley: Pen & Sword, 2010

Peter Davis MC, *SAS Men in The Making*, Barnsley: Pen & Sword, 2015

W. A. Deakins, *The Lame One*, Ilfracombe: Arthur H. Stockwell Ltd., 2001

Roy Farran, *Winged Dagger*, London: Arms & Armour Press, 1986

Roger Ford, *Fire from the Forest*, London: Cassell, 2003

Raymond Forgeat, *Remember: Les Parachutistes de la France Libre*, Vincennes: Service Historique de l'Armée de Terre, 1990

Derrick Harrison, *These Men are Dangerous*, Poole, Dorset: Blanford Press, 1988

Robin Hunter, *True Stories of the SAS*, London: Weidenfeld & Nicolson, 1986

Sir James Hutchison, *That Drug Danger*, Montrose: Standard Press, 1977

Malcolm James, *Born of the Desert*, Barnsley: Frontline Books, 2015

Nicholas Jellicoe, *George Jellicoe*, Barnsley: Pen & Sword, 2021

Joshua Levine, *SAS: The Illustrated History of the SAS*, London: William Collins, 2023

Damien Lewis, *Churchill's Secret Warriors*, London: Quercus, 2014

——, *SAS Ghost Patrol*, London: Quercus, 2018

——, *SAS Band of Brothers*, London: Quercus, 2020

——, *SAS Great Escapes*, London: Quercus, 2020

——, *SAS Brothers in Arms*, London: Quercus, 2022

——, *SAS Forged in Hell*, London: Quercus, 2023

B. H. Liddell Hart, *The Rommel Papers*, New York: Harcourt Brace & Company, 1953

David Lloyd-Owen, *The Desert My Dwelling Place*, London: Arms & Armour Press, 1986

Ben Macintyre, *SAS Rogue Heroes*, London: Viking, 2016

Jan Maingard, *Agent S.O.E. Ils l'appelaient SAMUEL*, Imprimerie et Papeterie Commercial Ltée, 2018

Patrick Marrinan, *Colonel Paddy*, Belfast: Ulster Press, 1983

Eoin McGonigal, *Special Forces Brothers in Arms*, Barnsley: Pen & Sword, 2022

J. Frazer McLuskey, *Parachute Padre*, Spa Books, 1985

Gavin Mortimer, *David Stirling*, London: Constable, 2022

———, *The SAS in World War Two*, Oxford: Osprey, 2011

Robin Neillands, *The Raiders: Army Commandos 1940–46*, London: Fontana, 1989

John O'Neill, *Legendary Warrior of the SAS*, Eastbourne: Menin House, 2015

John Randall and M. J. Trow, *The Last Gentleman of the SAS*, Edinburgh: Mainstream Publishing, 2014

Hamish Ross, *Paddy Mayne*, Stroud: Sutton Publishing, 2003

Ben Shephard, *After Dark: The Liberation of Belsen 1945*, London: Jonathan Cape, 2005

Gordon Stevens, *SAS in Their Own Words*, London: Ebury Press, 2005

Dan Stone, *The Liberation of the Camps*, New Haven: Yale University Press, 2015

A. P. Wavell, *Other Men's Flowers*, London: Jonathan Cape, 1978

Adrian Weale, *Renegades: Hitler's Englishmen*, London: Pimlico, 2002

Ian Wellsted, *SAS With the Maquis*, Barnsley: Frontline Books, 2016

———, *With the SAS Across the Rhine*, Barnsley: Frontline Books, 2020

Charles Whiting, *Death on a Distant Frontier*, Barnsley: Leo Cooper, 1996

Ex-Lance Corporal X QGM, *The SAS and LRDG Roll of Honour*, 2016, SAS-LRDG-RoH

Index

Adamson, Eric, 133, 184
Afrika Korps, 57–8
Aillant-sur-Tholon, France, 2–4, 16
'Airborne Folding Paratrooper Bicycles',
    144–5, 151
'Alexis' (Russian soldier), 84–5, 125,
    216
Antwerp, Belgium, 100, 250
Armistice, 327–8
Army Air Corps, 179
Augusta, Sicily, 5, 174, 236
Auschwitz concentration camp, 310
Autun, France, 114–17, 205–6
Avenue Foch Gestapo HQ, Paris, 172

Ball, Ooly, 144–5, 151
Baring, Esmond, 293–4
Barongelle, Johnny, 39–40, 221
Bateman, Leslie, 192–3
Battle of the Java Sea (1942), 141
BBC (British Broadcasting Corporation),
    99–100, 244
Beau Rivage hotel, Lac des Settons, 184,
    209
Belgium, 250
Belsen, Germany, 305–6
Bennett, Bob, 57–8, 350
Berca airfield, Libya, 241
Bergen-Belsen concentration camp,
    305–15
Berlin, Germany, 322, 325–6
Berneville-Claye, Douglas, 350–51
Best, Brian, 349
Blackhouse, Trooper, 300
Blakeney, Jim, 300–301, 303
Blondeel, Edouard 'Eddy', 317

Bond, Charles Frederick Gordon 'Dick',
    260, 262–9, 275–6
Bonin, France, 100
Book of The Germans, The, 333
Bormann, Martin, 326
Borrie, Alec 'Boy', 28–30, 33–4, 36, 41–2,
    44, 216, 257, 263, 291, 340, 351
    at Friesoythe, 279–80
    at Hylands, 236
    injured by mine, 317–19, 334
    Mayne and, 276
    in Paris, 222
    'snatch mission', 250
Borstel, Germany, 328
Bouerat, Libya, 80
'Boys of Killyran, The', (folk song), 343
Bradford, Laurence Roy, 60, 67, 144–7,
    150–55, 160, 182
Brearton, Tony, 8, 12, 15
British Resistance Organisation (BRO),
    262
British Secret Intelligence Service (SIS),
    195
Bromfield, Lance Corporal, 156–8, 184
Brown, Corporal, 306–8
Browning, Frederick 'Boy', 217–18, 237
Browning machineguns, 255–6, 266, 279
Brussels, Belgium, 219–20, 223, 242
Bryce, Tom, 24–6, 47
Burgess, Trooper, 86, 97, 132–3, 184

Cairns, Les, 60, 71–2
Calaminus, Irene, 62
Caldwell, Freddy, 318–19
Calvert, James 'Mad Mike', 252–3, 317,
    319–20, 334–5, 336, 340, 351

Canadian Army, 292
    4th Armoured Division, 259, 261,
        263–4
Canal du Nivernais, France, 149
Capo Murro di Porco, Italy, 79, 91
Cary-Elwes, Oswald, 139, 224
Celle, Germany, 294–9
    'Celle hare hunt', 294–5, 297
Chaleaux, France, 74
Chambon-la-Fôret, France, 187, 201
Champlatreux, France, 42
Château de Chamerolles, France, 192
Château de La Roche-Guyon, France,
    135–8, 140–41
Château de Rosny-sur-Seine, France, 135
Château de Vermot, France, 87–90, 92–3,
    95, 97, 101, 132
Châteauroux, France, 169
Châtillon-en-Bazois, France, 32–3, 40, 42
    Chateau, 41–2
Cherbourg, France, 61
Chilleurs-aux-Bois, France, 192
China, 334, 338
Chindits, 252
Chronik of Schneeren, xvii, 333, 345
'Chunking Project', 334
Churchill, Winston, 281, 283–4, 330–31,
    334, 336, 340, 348–9
Claudette (French Resistance), 131
Cliffe, Major, 219–20
Cloppenburg, Germany, 287
Close, Roy, 23–4, 30–33, 205, 277, 279,
    287, 289, 341
    Davidson and, 256–7, 317–19
    German convoy ambush, 33–7, 197
    German military HQ raid, 43
    Marquis de Pracontol and, 38–43
    Mayne and, 24–8, 249, 261–2
    Paris and, 221–3
Colditz Castle, Germany, 316
'Commando Order', 231–4, 260–61, 291
comradeship, 346
concentration camps, 297–8
    Auschwitz, 310
    Bergen-Belsen, 305–15
    Pisticci, Italy, 139
Connor, Corporal, 51–2
Cooper, Johnny, 78, 80, 87, 112, 115, 117,

166, 235, 245, 285, 302, 310–11,
    313, 326–8, 351
Corps, Tommy 'Geordie', 174–5, 186,
    197–8, 236
Couraud, Raymond, 138–41, 206–7, 269,
    352
Craig, Joe, 38

D-Day landings, 20, 22, 178–9
Danger, David, 258, 267, 352
Darvel, Ayrshire, 4, 26, 63, 72, 234
Davidson, Alexander 'Sandy', 256–7,
    317–19
Davidson, Gordon, 279–80, 320–21, 352
Davies, Roy, 300–301, 303
Davis, Peter, 45–54, 200, 205, 291, 328,
    352
Deakins, Bill, 236–7, 258, 282–3, 342,
    352–3
Devine, William 'Andy', 145–7, 150, 154
Dijon, France, 113, 156, 158, 164–5, 167,
    222
Dill, John, 348
Dimbleby, Richard, 313–14
Donzy, France, 51
Dortmund–Ems Canal, Germany, 261–4
Douglas C-47 Skytrain, 132
Dourdan, France, 189
Du Vivier, Jeff, 144–5, 151–4, 300, 353
Dubrey, Lieutenant, 205–6
Duffy, William, 187–9 , 201–5
Dun-les-Places, France, 98–103, 105, 155
Dunkley, Frank, 187–9

Eccles, Doug, 240
Eisenhower, Dwight D., 130, 226,
    229–30, 339
Elbe river, 303
Elizabeth II, Queen of the United
    Kingdom, 348
Elster, Botho, 53
Entrains-sur-Nohain, France, 151

'Fairyland' brothel, Paris, 222–3
Fauchois, Marcel see Friedmann, Marcel
Fedossof (Russian SAS operative), 139
Fenwick, Ian, 173, 186–9, 201
Ferguson, Dougie, 166, 300, 303

Ferguson, Fiona, xvii–xviii
Ferguson, Norman, xvii
Flynn, Micky, 68–9, 110, 159
Forces françaises de l'intérieur (FFI), 194
Fôret d'Ivoy, France, 239
Fôret d'Orléans, France, 173
Forêt de Donzy, France, 49, 51
Fôret de Fontainebleau, France, 172,
    183–4, 186, 188, 191–2
Fôret de Merry-Vaux Base, France, 4, 15,
    32, 54
Fôret des Dames, France, 144–51, 153
France, 1–17, 20–23, 30–31, 55–6, 142–4,
    168, 199
  Free French, 130
  French Resistance, 7, 18, 40, 130–31,
      194
  Nazi occupation, 41–2
  see also Operation Houndsworth
Franks, Brian Morton, 295, 316, 325,
    340, 353
Fraser, Bill, 69–70, 72, 90, 130, 136–7,
    200, 208, 353
  Légion d'honneur, 340
  Maquis and, 74, 163
  Mayne and, 181–3
  mental health, 183, 242
  Operation Archway, 301
  Operation Houndsworth, 93–7,
      99–103, 106–7, 115, 117, 127–9,
      131–3, 137–8, 144, 152–6, 162–4,
      175–6, 205–9
French, Percy, 175, 181, 258
Friedmann, Marcel, 6–8, 14–17
Friesoythe, Germany, 278–80, 320
Frythe, The, Welwyn Garden City,
    Hertfordshire, 153

Gale, Richard Nelson 'Windy', 339–40
'Gammon Bomb' (No. 82 Grenade), 78,
    81
Garstin, Patrick, 171–2, 231, 243
gasogene, 168
Geneva Convention, 18
George VI, King of the United Kingdom,
    179–80, 336–7
German Army
  German cadets, 285

7th German Parachute Division,
    279
12th SS Panzer Division, 300
Germany
  forced labour, 7, 296
  German POWs, 287, 288–9, 291–2
  missions in, 252–71, 272–87, 288–315,
      316–28
  reprisals, 86–7, 97–9, 105–6, 155
  war crimes, 169–72, 192–3, 219,
      231–2, 250–51, 298, 345
Gestapo, 193, 222, 296
GHQ Liaison Regiment, 284
Gibb, 'Pringle', 93, 256
Gibson, Ian, 349
Gill, Trooper, 333
Glyde, Emlyn, 166
Glyde, John 'Taffy', 166, 300, 303
Gobi Desert, 334
Goddard, Peter 'Monty', 209–12
Gold, Mary Jane, 139
Goldsmith, Ernest 'Buttercup Joe', 196,
    238–40, 264–5, 347, 353–4
Gordon Highlanders, 70, 136
Grady, Trooper, 118–26, 133, 184
Great Sand Sea raids, 22, 91
'Green Eyed Yellow Idol, The' (song),
    79–80
Grese, Irma, 310–11
'Grey Russian' troops, 76, 88, 156
Grierson, Trooper, 47–8
Gunn, Phil, 59–60, 213–14, 246

Hackney, Charlie, 224–6, 252, 303,
    321–6, 354
Hall, Jimmy 'Curly', 5–6, 8, 11–16, 18
Hanbury, Charles 'Jock', 234
Hanbury, Christine, 234–5, 245–6, 248,
    340
Hans (German prisoner), 158–61,
    215–16, 255
Harrison, Derrick 'Happy', 2–17, 20–22,
    32, 44, 47, 199–200, 205, 257,
    278–9, 290–92, 354
Hitler, Adolf, 118, 133, 141, 155, 172, 199,
    231–4, 322, 324–6, 333
  'Commando Order', 231–4, 260–61,
      291

Hitler Youth (*Hitlerjugend*), 260, 277, 283, 327, 300
Home Guard, 65–6
Hotel George V, Paris, 223
Hull, William 'Billy', 258, 267–8, 270, 272–3, 275, 282, 335, 354–5
Hümmling, Germany, 264
Hutchison, James, 89–90, 130–37, 206
Hylands House, Essex, 234–8, 243, 245, 248, 255–6, 334, 340, 342

Inter-Service Liaison Department (ISLD), 195–6
Ion, John, 191–2
Iredale, Tim, 288–9, 293, 355
Italy, 168, 238

Japan, 334–5, 338–9
Jean-Paul (Maquis guide), 118–25
Jelinek, Lotte, 264
Jellicoe, Earl, 337
Jemson, 'Swag', 118–27, 300
Jenkinson, Trooper, 311–12
Joigny, France, 215
Jones, Thomas 'Ginger', 243

Kapos, 297–8
Keevil Aerodrome, Wiltshire, 175
Kent, Thomas, 320
Kiel, Germany, 327–8
Koenig, Marie-Pierre, 130
Kramer, Josef, 310–13
Kriminalpolizei (Kripo), 295

La Charité-sur-Loire, France, 52–3
La Nièvre Libre (newspaper), 44–6
Lac des Settons, France, 184
Langridge, Bob 'Lofty', 156–8
Langton, Thomas 'Tommy', 59, 242, 263
Laycock, Robert 'Bob', 336–7
Le Mans, France, 194, 201
Le Vieux Dun, France, 101
Lebaudy, Jean 'Johnny', 131–2, 135–7
Leclerc de Hauteclocque, Philippe, 225
Lee, Jack William Raymond, *see* Couraud, Raymond
Les Ormes, France, 4, 6–16
Levinsohn, Max, 264–7, 269, 275

Lewes bombs, 120
Lewes, John Steel 'Jock', 120
'Lili Marlene' (song), 57–9, 72
Lilley, Ernest 'Bob', 241–2, 285–6, 347, 355
Lilley, Evelyn, 241, 347
Long Range Desert Group (LRDG), 170, 178
Lorup, Germany, 265, 335–6
Lowson, Bob, 276
Lucy-sur-Yonne, France, 145, 154, 160–61
Lüneburg, Germany, 326–7

M1 carbine submachine guns, 12
machineguns
    M1 carbine submachine guns, 12
    MG34 'Spandaus' machineguns, 35–6
    MP40 'Schmeissers' submachine guns, 12
    Thompson 'Tommy guns' submachine guns, 12
    Vickers-K machinegun, 9, 34
Macon, Robert C., 53
Mâlain, France, 168
Manners, John, 322
Maquis (guerrilla fighters), 7–8, 69, 73–4, 77–8, 83–5, 87–9, 98, 103, 112, 130–31, 165, 206, 209–12
Marigny l'Église, France, 129
Mark, Sergeant, 139–40
Marsh, John 'Tony', 21–3, 28–32, 44, 47, 60, 183, 191, 194, 200, 209, 212, 218, 260, 263, 278, 355
Marshmallow airstrip (near Saulieu), 133–6
Maybury, Jack, 322–5
Mayne, Blair 'Paddy', xvii–xviii, 2, 44–7, 58–9, 64, 71–2, 168–9, 176–8, 197, 253, 258, 355–7
    alcohol and, 26–7, 91, 249, 275, 348
    David Stirling and, 316–17
    death, 346, 348
    in France, 176–91, 194–201, 205, 209–15, 217–20
    Hylands and, 243–9, 340
    injury, 342
    leadership, 22–3, 30, 106–7, 177–8, 218, 237, 240–41, 276

Mayne, Blair (*cont.*)
  Légion d'honneur, 340
  letter writing, 142–3, 247–9
  McLuskey and, 60–61, 177
  mental health, 347–8
  Operation Houndsworth, 106–7,
    127–8, 161
  Operation Howard, 255, 257–71,
    272–80, 282–7, 288–92, 303–4,
    317–20, 328
  operations report and, 219–20
  'Paddy Mayne Diary', xvii, 345–6
  parachute drop into France, 172–6
  in Paris, 223–4, 226
  prisoners of war and, 19, 161, 172,
    192–3, 284, 288, 326
  Reader's Digest article and, 226–8
  SAS beret and, 179, 342
  SAS final parade and, 342–4
  SAS recruitment, 3, 25–9
  temperament, 10, 91, 180–81, 183,
    249, 268, 272, 347
  Victoria Cross, 335–8, 348–9
Mayne, Douglas, 346
Mayne, Molly, 248–9
Mazignien, France, 97, 103, 128, 133,
  135, 163–4, 180
McDiarmid, James 'Jock', 17–19, 341, 357
McGinn, Cornelius 'Maggie', 145–50
McGonigal, Eoin, 301
McLeod, Roderick, 180, 213–15, 219–20,
  247, 252–3, 230
McLuskey, Irene, 302
McLuskey, Rev. J. Fraser, 56–69, 73–6,
    93, 103–5, 128–9, 133–4, 150–51,
    165–6, 208, 215, 229, 357–8
  mental health and, 243–4
  Bergen-Belsen and, 310
  Mayne and, 176–7, 348
  Operation Archway and, 302–3
  Parachute Padre (McLuskey), 176
McReady, Mike, 103, 133
Melot, Robert Emanuel Marie 'Bob',
    195–7, 199, 213, 223, 238, 247
mental health, 238–42, 244–5
Meppen, Germany, 259, 263, 293
Messerschmitt Me 262 *Sturmvogel*, 303
methanol, 100

MG34 'Spandaus' machineguns, 35–6
Middleton, Desmond Peter, 78–80, 82,
  118, 126, 156–8, 207, 358
Milice, 165, 167
Montgomery, Bernard, 217, 227, 254–5,
  330, 336–7
Montsauche-les-Settons, France, 76, 81,
  83, 86, 155
Moore, Jack, 141
Moore, Tom Triplett, 139, 141, 358–9
Morvan region, France, 44, 56, 77, 87,
  92, 97, 103, 114, 127, 145, 154, 156,
  161, 181–2, 205, 214
  see also Operation Houndsworth
Morvillier, Jaques, 145, 147–50
Mount Pleasant, Newtownards, 345
MP40 'Schmeissers' submachine guns, 12
Muirhead, Alex, 76–8, 81–3, 99–100, 103,
  182, 285, 359
  Autun fuel facility raids, 114–17,
    205–6
Mycock, Ed, 24–6
Mycock, Mike, 54

Nannay, France, 47, 49–50, 54
Nazi propaganda, 296
Nazi war crimes, 169–72, 192–3, 219,
  231–2, 250–51, 298, 345
Nazism, 24, 62, 295–6, 333
Netherlands, 258–9
Nevers, France, 37, 53, 239
Noble, John 'Nobby', 78–9, 83, 85, 144,
  155–8, 359
Normandy, France, 95–6, 99, 141, 155,
  169
  see also Operation Overlord
North Africa, 5, 18, 195–6, 241
Norway, 335

Oestrich-Winkel, Germany, 302
Oflag IV-C (Colditz), 316
Oldenburg, Germany, 260, 286–7, 294,
  337
Operation Archway, 295, 299–303, 316
Operation Basalt, 232
Operation Bulbasket, 169–72, 175–6,
  180, 219, 231, 240
Operation Chariot, 139

Operation Dragoon, 214
Operation Gaff, 138–41, 206
Operation Gain, 169–70, 172–6, 180,
    186–93, 200, 218–19, 231, 306
Operation Haft, 306
Operation Haggard, 239–40, 265
Operation Hardy, 225
Operation Houndsworth, 73–88, 95–129,
    137–40, 144–68, 191, 207–8
  Mayne and, 106–7, 127–8, 161
  War Diary, 99, 107, 113, 116, 137, 144,
    155, 162–3
Operation Howard, 255–71, 272–87,
    288–94, 303–4, 317–20, 326–8
  German POWs, 287, 288–9, 291–2
  Mayne and, 255, 257–71, 272–80,
    282–7, 288–92, 303–4, 317–20, 328
  Mayne's rescue mission, 268–76
Operation Husky, 5
Operation Kipling, 20, 47, 200, 209
Operation Lüttich, 169
Operation Overlord, see D-Day landings
Operation Policeman, 219–20, 223, 242,
    247
Operation Squatter, 300–301
Operation Torch, 80
Operation Vicarage, 254
Ordnance ML 3-inch (81mm) mortars,
    49
Ordnance Quick Firing 6-pounder gun,
    161, 163–4
Orléans, France, 31, 169, 175, 183, 186
Ostend, Belgium, 258, 333
Ouroux-en-Morvan, France, 86, 155–9
Owen, David Lloyd, 177–8
Owens, Trooper, 300

Packman, Leslie, 191–2
Paddy Force see Operation Howard
Pagan, Trooper, 47–8
Panzer divisions, 114
Panzerfaust anti-tank weapon, 265–7,
    277
parachute drops, 12–13, 55–7, 59–61
  bicycles, 144
  jeeps, 107–8
  mail, 109–10
Parachute Padre (McLuskey), 176

Paray–Digoin railway line, 119–24
Paris, France, 199, 220–25
Patterson, Joe, 295–9
Patton, George S., 201
Payne, Peter, 280–82, 321, 359
Payne, Sid, 359
Pétain, Philippe, 206
pigeons, 72
Pisticci concentration camp, Italy, 139
Planchez, France, 87
Plateau de Langres, France, 225
Pleydell, Malcolm, 27–7, 359–60
Poat, Harry, 242, 263, 295, 299–304, 320,
    347
Poole, Puddle, 70–71
Poperinge, Belgium, 331–2
Post-Traumatic Stress Disorder (PTSD),
    238–40, 347
Pracontol, Marquis de, 39–42
prisoners of war (POWs), 18–19, 84
  Allied POWs, 295, 321
  'Commando Order', 231–4
  German, 161–2, 235
  Maquis and, 155, 159–60
  POW camps, 254
  SAS, 155, 170–72, 192–3, 338
  see also Nazi war crimes

Quarré-les-Tombes, France, 205

RAF (Royal Air Force), 113
  RAF Fairford, 56–8, 173
Ralphs, Edward, 267
Randall, John, 283–4, 305–11, 313, 341,
    360
Reader's Digest magazine, 226–8
Rhine river, 252–4
Richards, J., 175
Richardson, Stewart, 4, 8, 15–16
Riding, Cecil 'Jock', 143, 169, 172–3,
    187–90, 192, 200–201
Ridler, Duncan, 312–13, 360
Riley, Charles George Gibson 'Pat', 92,
    360
'Roger' (Maquis mechanic), 156
Rolle, France, 164–5
Rolph (German medical assistant), 134,
    255

Rommel, Erwin, 16, 22, 70, 80, 141–2, 206
  kidnap plot, 135–40
Rose, Graham 'Johnny', 109
Royal Electrical and Mechanical Engineers (REME), 293–4

S-phone, 127–8
Sadler, Mike, 80, 173–6, 186, 190, 197–9, 201, 223–4, 249, 361
Sahara desert, 22
Saint-Valery-en-Caux, France, 70
Sark (Channel Island), 232
SAS, 22–3, 25–6, 52–3, 55–6, 229–31, 338–40
  1 SAS, 26, 57, 64–6, 214–15, 234–6
  2 SAS, 179, 225
  2nd Panzer Division report, 230
  4 (French) SAS Regiment, 6
  21 SAS Regiment (V), 346
  22 SAS, 346
  A Squadron, 44, 47, 76, 127, 175, 183, 200, 205, 209, 213
  B Squadron, 242
  Belgian regiments, 338–9, 341
  berets, 8–9, 111, 179, 260–61
  C Squadron, 44, 53, 183, 191, 194, 200, 218, 250
  'Château Blotto', 300, 330–32
  D-Day landings and, 178–9
  desert operations, 18
  disbandment, 340–44
  ethos, 203–4
  final parade, 342–4
  French regiments, 338, 341
  fuel facility raids, 114–17, 168, 205, 225
  German speakers, 30–31
  Hitler's 'Commando Order', 231–4
  in North Africa, 18, 57, 87, 168, 227, 300
  jeeps, 1, 22, 190, 255–6, 161, 282, 319
  'Lili Marlene' (song), 57–9, 72
  medical evacuation, 132–4
  motto, 57, 236
  operations report, 219–20
  parachute drops, 12–13, 55–7, 59–61, 107–10, 144, 161, 181

railway line raids, 117–27, 126, 167–8, 186, 268
rations, 33, 110–11
regimental HQ, Darvel, 26, 64–5, 72
SABU call signs, 99–100
'SAS-PW', 338
SAS Regimental Association (SASRA), 326, 346
SAS War Diary, xvii, 94, 178, 207, 244, 321, 346
selection process, 25–30
training, 72
uniforms, 8–9, 111–12, 179–80
War Crimes Investigation Team, 345
'winged dagger' badge, 8–9, 236
SAS Brothers in Arms (Lewis), 346
SAS Forged in Hell (Lewis), 346
SAS Nazi Hunters (Lewis), 346
Saulieu, France, 86, 132
Scheldt river, 138
Schlee, Philip, 266–7
Schneeren, Germany, xvii, 300, 333
Schofield, Joe, 265–6, 273–5, 361
Schurch, Theodore, 361
Scott, John, 269–70, 272–5, 335–6
'Secret Hunters', 345–6
Seekings, Albert Reginald 'Reg', 90–93, 114–15, 283–4, 298, 326–8, 341, 361–2
  Bergen-Belsen and, 309–11
  injuries, 92–3, 97, 103–5, 114–15, 166, 256
Service du travail obligatoire (STO), 7
Sicily, Italy, 5, 77
Sidi Haneish airfield raid, 5
Siegfried Line, 259
Slim, William 'Bill', 334–5
Soviet POWs, 321
Special Boat Service (SBS), 337
Special Operations Executive (SOE), 89, 127, 130–32, 139
  Experimental Station IX, 153
SS (Schutzstaffel), 10, 193, 280, 298–9, 307
St-Nazaire, France, 139
St-Yan airfield, France, 117–19
Stalag X-B, Sandbostel, 320–21
Stephens, Tomos, 170

Stewart, Ian, 96
Stirling, Bill, 179, 295, 362
Stirling, David, 80, 91, 174, 177–8, 196,
    227, 265, 316–17, 334, 337–8, 340,
    362
Stumpfegger, Ludwig, 326
Sturmey, Sergeant, 144, 215
Supreme Headquarters Allied
    Expeditionary Force (SHAEF),
    114, 138
'Sur le Pont d'Avignon' (nursery rhyme),
    99, 125
Surrey-Dane, David, 275–6, 335
swastika symbol, 333
Sylvester, F. 'Sylvo', 78, 81–5
synfuel, 114–17

Taylor, Lt. Col. Richard, 312–13
Termoli, Ital, 4, 17, 22, 87y, 170, 238–9
Terry, Jack, 92–3, 113, 166
Thompson, Corporal, 244
Thompson 'Tommy guns' submachine
    guns, 12
Tilling, Chris, 33
Times, The, 246, 348–9
Tonkin, John Elliot, 170–72, 192, 309,
    311, 362
Touhig, Don, 349
Toulon-sur-Arroux, France, 118
Townsend, Ros, 347
Trower, Tony, 113
Tyrebuster mines, 153

Ulster Monarch, HMS, 236
Unrewarded Courage, Acts of Valour
    that were denied the Victoria Cross
    (Best), 349
US forces, 200–201

V-1 flying bombs, 118, 250
V-2 Rockets, 250
Vermot, France, 93–4, 97–8, 105–6, 155
Vichy France, 206
Vickers-K machinegun, 9, 34
Victory in Europe (VE) Day, 330–33

Volesvres airfield, France, 117–19
Volkes, G., 292, 335
Volkssturm (German home guard), 260,
    280–82
Volkswagen Schwimmwagen, 156
von Choltitz, Dietrich, 199

Walker, Patrick Gordon, 314
Watson, Jimmy, 188–90
Weaver, Peter, 170, 362
Wellsted, Ian 'Captain Gremlin', 69–86,
    99–103, 112, 114, 117, 158–9, 182,
    206–7, 252, 331, 363
    Autun fuel facility raids, 205–6
    at Hylands, 236, 237
    Mayne and, 224
    mental health, 216–17, 255
    Operation Archway and, 300, 302
    Operation Howard and, 255–6
    Paray–Digoin railway raid, 117–27
    relationship with Margot (wife),
        109–10, 215–16, 236
Wellsted, Margot, 71, 109–10, 215–16
Wemyss, Henry Colville Barclay, 348–9
Westland Lysander warplane, 131–2
Weyland, Otto P., 53
White, Fred 'Chalky', 87–8, 101, 145–50,
    184, 363
Williams, Elsie, 257
Wilson, Corporal, 193
Wilson, Harry, 302
Wingate, Orde, 252
Winterson, Lieutenant, 175, 186
Wiseman, Johnny, 90–93, 96, 113, 164–8,
    205, 216, 227, 240–41, 347, 363
Woodford, J. 'Woody', 221–2

Yonne river, France, 3, 17, 20, 32, 44–5,
    53–4, 149, 200
Youngman, Albert, 274–5, 320–21, 337,
    340, 363
Ypres, Belgium, 331–2

Zellic, Sergeant, 78–9
'Zoubinettes', 131, 135, 137

Counselling Forces' Veterans & Reservists
registered charity no. 1133188

PTSD Resolution, Charity No. 1133188, provides therapy for the mental welfare of Forces' Veterans, Reservists and their families. Treatment is free, effective and delivered promptly and locally through a network of 200 therapists nationwide. Contact www. PTSDresolution.org.

Founded in 2009, and with over 3,500 referrals to date, the charity delivers therapy in an average of six sessions, with 78% of cases seeing an improvement in reported symptoms to where the client and therapist agree that no further therapy is required.

The charity is one of the only organisations to provide therapy to veterans suffering with addiction issues or who are in prison – as well as to family members, including partners and children, who may experience the symptoms of trauma from living with a traumatised veteran.

PTSD Resolution has a unique 'lean' operation, with no salaried staff or assets – funds are used to deliver therapy and for essential research and public information.

Key features of PTSD Resolution's service:

- Free, local, prompt and effective help for Veterans, Reservists and families suffering from mental health issues
- Confidential, no GP referral is needed
- Local help through a UK network of 200 therapists

- Fast treatment, issues usually resolved in an average of six sessions
- Easy to access – first session booked often in days
- Compassionate: clients do not have to talk about events in their past
- Cost-effective, £750 per programme – free to the people we help
- Transparent, results are monitored and reported
- No one is turned away: including HM prisoners and those with addiction issues
- Cobseo members, working with other Forces' charities. (Cobseo, the Confederation of Service Charities, provides a single point of contact for interaction with Government, the Private Sector; and with other members of the Armed Forces Community)
- 'Lean' charity management: we own no assets, have no salaried staff: donations are used for essential treatment, research and communications